Assessment in Emergent Literacy

Emergent and Early Literacy Series

Laura M. Justice, Series Editor

Assessment in Emergent Literacy

A Volume in the Emergent and Early Literacy Series

Edited by Khara L. Pence, Ph.D.

PLURAL
PUBLISHING
INC.
SAN DIEGO
OXFORD
BRISBANE

PLURAL PUBLISHING
INC.

5521 Ruffin Road
San Diego, CA 92123

e-mail: info@pluralpublishing.com
Web site: http://www.pluralpublishing.com

49 Bath Street
Abingdon, Oxfordshire OX14 1EA
United Kingdom

Typeset in 11/13 Garamond by Flanagan's Publishing Services, Inc.
Printed in the United States of America by Bang Printing

Library of Congress Cataloging-in-Publication Data

Pence, Khara L.
    Assessment in emergent and early literacy / Khara L. Pence.
        p. cm. — (Emergent and early literacy series)
    Includes bibliographical references and index.
    ISBN-13: 978-1-59756-097-9 (softcover)
    ISBN-10: 1-59756-097-9 (softcover)
    1. Reading (Early childhood)—Evaluation. I. Title.
    LB1139.5.R43P46 2006
    372.48—dc22

                                                    2006032656

Contents

Series Foreword

The purpose of Plural Publishing's *Series on Emergent and Early Literacy* is to provide clinical and educational professionals with usable, practical, and evidence-based resources for enhancing their ability to include literacy as an integral part of their services to toddlers, preschoolers, and school-age children. The books in this series provide professionals with a portfolio of contemporary resources that keep them up to date in theories, scientific findings, and practices relevant to emergent and early literacy.

As the editor of this series, I select topics that represent the pressing needs and interests of clinical and educational professionals and then select authors who can provide an accessible yet expert perspective on these topics. The topics and authors represent the diverse interdisciplinary fields sharing an interest in emergent and early literacy, including education, psychology, speech-language pathology, audiology, and health sciences, to name but a few.

My particular interest as the editor of this series is to provide professionals with timely guidance on theoretically sound and empirically based tools and techniques they can readily use and incorporate into their everyday practice to promote the literacy development of the children and adults with whom they work. For instance, professionals who work with preschoolers exhibiting underdeveloped emergent literacy skills need up-to-date information about effective storybook reading techniques that they can use to accelerate literacy learning. Likewise, professionals who work with school-age children with reading challenges need to know about different assessment tools they can use to evaluate the literacy-learning environment of classrooms in which they teach or consult so that they can enhance these environments systematically. And, professionals who work with adults with limited literacy or those who have lost literacy skills due to illness or injury need to know about effective techniques for remediation. In short, professionals need access to up-to-date information on theoretically sound and empirically based techniques concerning how best to improve the literacy achievements of individuals across the lifespan. Responding to professionals' needs for timely and practical information that is both theoretically sound and empirically based is my foremost goal as the editor of this series, which will take on timely issues of practical import and disseminate these in a reader-friendly manner for the busy professional.

This book, *Assessment in Emergent Literacy*, edited by Khara Pence, provides an excellent resource on a topic of considerable importance to speech-language pathologists and other professionals who work with young children. Presently, there is a clear consensus that emergent and early literacy difficulties can be mitigated for many young children if these difficulties are identified early and then systematically addressed through evidence-based interventions. Central to such efforts is access to assessment tools that allow professionals to identify children requiring such interventions. This book provides a seminal resource to these professionals, with its comprehensive and accessible discussion of approaches to and tools for emergent and early literacy assessment. Professionals in a variety of disciplines—including speech-language pathology, early childhood education, and special education—will find this text one of their most importance sources of information as they seek to promote children's earliest successes in literacy.

Laura M. Justice, Ph.D.
Series Editor

About the Editor

 Khara L. Pence, Ph.D., is a Research Assistant Professor at the University of Virginia in the Curry School of Education and the Center for Advanced Study of Teaching and Learning, with an appointment in the Preschool Language & Literacy Lab. Dr. Pence's interests are in language and literacy development, particularly for children who are at risk for language and literacy difficulties.

Contributors

Angela R. Beckman, M.S., CCC-SLP
Assistant Professor
Communication Disorders and Sciences
Eastern Illinois University
Chapter 10

Katrin L. Blamey, M.A.
Graduate Research Assistant
School of Education
University of Delaware
Chapter 4

Kathryn E. Bojczyk, Ph.D.
Assistant Professor
Family and Child Sciences
Florida State University
Chapters 5 and 9

Sonia Q. Cabell, M.Ed.
Graduate Research Assistant
Curry School of Education
University of Virginia
Chapter 7

Stephanie M. Curenton, Ph.D.
Assistant Professor
Family and Child Sciences
Florida State University
Chapters 5 and 8

Marcia R. Davidson, Ph.D.
Assistant Professor
College of Education and Human Development
University of Maine
Chapter 2

Sarah A. F. Friel, M.Sc, CCC-SLP
Research Faculty
Curry School of Education
University of Virginia
Chapter 1

Staci L. Grant, M.Ed.
Doctoral Student in Special Education
Curry School of Education
University of Virginia
Chapter 3

Laura M. Justice, Ph.D., CCC-SLP
Associate Professor
Curry School of Education
University of Virginia
Chapter 7

Joan N. Kaderavek, Ph.D., CCC-SLP
Professor
Early Childhood, Physical, and Special Education
University of Toledo
Chapter 10

Tamika D. Lucas, M.Ed., CCC-SLP
Doctoral Student in Special Education
Curry School of Education
University of Virginia
Chapter 8

Kelly A. Marshall, M.Ed.
Special Education Teacher
Drew Model Elementary School
Arlington, VA
Chapter 1

Anita S. McGinty, M.A., CCC-SLP
Predoctoral Fellow
Risk and Prevention in Education Sciences
Curry School of Education
University of Virginia
Chapter 7

Erin M. McTigue, Ph.D.
Assistant Professor
Department of Teaching, Learning, and Culture
Texas A&M University
Chapter 10

Paula F. Moore, Ed.D.
K-12 Literacy Consultant
Brewer School Department
Brewer, Maine
Chapter 2

Prema K. S. Rao, Ph.D.
Reader in Language Pathology
Department of Speech Language Sciences
All India Institute of Speech and Hearing
Mysore, India
Chapter 6

C. Melanie Schuele, Ph.D., CCC-SLP
Assistant Professor
Department of Hearing and Speech Sciences
Vanderbilt University
Chapter 6

Lori E. Skibbe, Ph.D.
Postdoctoral Fellow
Department of Psychology
University of Michigan
Chapter 6

Amy E. Sofka, M.Ed.
Research Faculty
Curry School of Education
University of Virginia
Chapter 5

Margaret M. Sutton, M.Ed.
Research Faculty
Curry School of Education
University of Virginia
Chapter 5

Sharon Walpole, Ph.D.
Assistant Professor
School of Education
University of Delaware
Chapter 4

Alice K. Wiggins, M.Ed.
Research Faculty
Curry School of Education
University of Virginia
Chapter 1

Rihana S. Williams, Ph.D.
Postdoctoral Fellow
Florida Center for Reading
   Research
Florida State University
Chapter 9

Tricia A. Zucker, M.Ed.
Graduate Research Assistant
Curry School of Education
University of Virginia
Chapter 3

Introduction

Measuring Contexts of Learning and Development and Children's Emergent Literacy Abilities and Growth

Khara L. Pence

The Importance of Measuring Contexts for Learning and Development and Children's Emergent Literacy Abilities and Growth

Similar to other developmental accomplishments, literacy (the ability to read and write) is not an all-or-nothing skill that children acquire once they enter the academic milieu. Rather, research over the past few decades supports the notion that the acquisition of literacy begins early in childhood through exposure to and participation in literacy activities in social contexts. This perspective, termed *emergent literacy*, has received an abundance of empirical support. Research relating children's emergent literacy competencies and experiences to their later reading outcomes is compelling, but beyond the scope of this chapter (for overviews, see Dickinson & Neuman, 2006; National Early Literacy Panel, 2005; Neuman & Dickinson, 2003; Teale & Sulzby, 1986).

As an emergent literacy professional or someone who is interested in emergent literacy, you likely want to know as much as possible about how to successfully promote young children's literacy development. *Assessment*, or the process of collecting data to measure the abilities, performance, or progress of an individual, group, or program, is one important component in this effort, and is the focus of this book. We envision that emergent literacy professionals will use this book to understand both how and why various aspects of children's emergent literacy should be assessed and, Lfurther, to construct and implement a battery of valid and reliable assessments that meets the purposes of their community or program.

Section I of this book explores assessments of contexts for learning and development. From a social-interactionist perspective, children will not acquire literacy unless those around them arrange activities and the environment to support such development. Fostering emergent literacy from a social-interactionist perspective emphasizes both authentic modeling of literacy activities by parents and caregivers, as well as literacy materials that are appropriate for and interesting to children (e.g., cardboard books for infants and toddlers, picture books with few words for children who are not yet able to follow a story, books with pictures and text for children who are just beginning to read, and books with pure text for experienced readers [Rogoff, 1990]). The idea that children's emergent literacy develops in collaborative interactions with others and in supportive environments with appropriate materials does not preclude its measurement. In fact, it is crucial that contexts for children's learning and development be operationalized and measured, to the extent possible, in the same way children's demonstrable emergent literacy competencies are measured. In this book we discuss five important contributions to children's contexts for emergent literacy learning and development and assessments to measure each of these areas: (1) the language and literacy richness of early childhood classroom environments, (2) professionals' content knowledge and pedagogical knowledge, (3) the home literacy environment, (4) the use of language and literacy curricula in classroom settings, and (5) the shared storybook reading experience.

Section II of this book describes assessments of children's emergent literacy abilities and growth. Assessments in this area might be more familiar to emergent literacy professionals in that they measure children's demonstrable competencies rather than social and environmental contributions to those competencies. We have elected to focus on five emergent literacy areas that are predictive of children's later reading success, including: (1) phonological awareness, (2) print knowledge (including alphabet knowledge), (3) narrative abilities, (4) vocabulary knowledge, and (5) literacy motivation.

Specific Purposes for Measuring Contexts for Learning and Development and Children's Emergent Literacy Abilities and Growth

The National Education Goals Panel in 1998 submitted principles and recommendations for early childhood assessments in accordance with their panel's charge, which was to "create clear guidelines regarding the nature, functions, and uses of early childhood assessments, including assessment formats that are appropriate for use in culturally and linguistically diverse communities, based on model elements of school readiness" (Shepard, Kagan, & Wurtz, 1998, p. 3). Specific purposes for early childhood assessments as proposed by the National Education Goals Panel include assessments designed to support children's learning and development, identify children who may require special services or interventions, and monitor children's progress or a program or intervention's progress toward specific goals.[1]

Assessments to Support Children's Learning and Development

Assessments with the goal of supporting children's learning and development might take one of a few forms. Such assessments might consist of *observational protocols* in which an examiner observes the nature of classroom instructional practices, teacher-child interactions, parent-child interactions, or aspects of the caregiving environment itself. Assessments with the goal of support-

---

[1] The National Education Goals Panel report also describes how assessments can be used for high-stakes accountability purposes; however, the panel recommends that standardized achievement measures are not sufficiently accurate to be used for high-stakes purposes before age 8 and that such assessments should be delayed until (preferably) the fourth grade.

ing children's learning and development might also be conducted in an *interview* format or in a *paper-and-pencil* format to target the aforementioned areas. To assess children's abilities directly to support their learning and development, emergent literacy professionals might make *observational notes* as children work or play or they might devise *structured* or *semi-structured tasks* to elicit evidence regarding children's emergent literacy abilities that can be informative to structuring classroom activities to that end.

Assessments to Identify Children Who Require Intervention or Special Services

Assessments with the goal of identifying children who may require intervention or special services are generally conducted in two parts. The first step is to implement a *screening* measure. Screening measures typically are brief and easy to administer. They are designed to provide a global measure of children's emergent literacy skills and abilities and may provide a "snapshot" of children's performance in a particular skill area (Lonigan, 2006).

The second step in identifying children who may require intervention or special services is to conduct a *diagnostic assessment* (or battery of diagnostic assessments). Diagnostic assessments measure specific areas of language and emergent literacy in a thorough fashion. Often, diagnostic assessments include items or subscales that tap specific dimensions. For example, an oral language diagnostic assessment might include subscales that measure syntax, semantics, phonology, and pragmatics. Diagnostic assessments are *standardized* and require that specific administration procedures be followed in order to interpret a child's results in comparison to the *norming sample* (which usually includes children from a variety of racial, ethnic, and socioeconomic backgrounds). Diagnostic measures should be administered and interpreted only by persons with formal training, such as speech-language pathologists, educational psychologists, diagnosticians, and others with appropriate experience with standardized assessments.

Diagnostic assessments may provide a host of scores in addition to a raw score, including scaled scores, percentile ranks, stanines, normal curve equivalents, and grade-equivalent scores. *Scaled scores* are configured differently for each assessment and provide information about the degree to which a student's score deviates from the average score on that assessment. A *percentile rank* indicates a student's performance on an assessment relative to other students in the norming sample. To obtain a score corresponding to the 50th percentile means that a student scored as well as or better than half of the children in the norming sample. Some persons confuse percentile scores with *percent correct*, which describes the proportion of items a student answered correctly. *Stanines* provide information about a student's performance in comparison to the norming sample using a 9-point scale. Although there is no exact mean, a stanine of 5 encompasses the mean as well as the middle 20% of the distribution of scores. A *normal curve equivalent* (NCE) is a standardized score that has a mean of 50 and is divided into 99 equal intervals. Unlike percentile ranks, NCEs can be used to ascertain how far above or below grade level a student is. Finally, a *grade-equivalent score* is based on grade levels and months. A grade-equivalent score of 1–2 means that a child's score is the same as the median score for first graders in the second month of school. Many persons misinterpret grade-equivalent scores to mean that a child has mastered concepts relative to what would be expected for a student at the grade level equivalent, and for this reason grade equivalent scores are not commonly used.

Assessments to Monitor Progress

Progress monitoring assessments might be used to measure students' progress or a program's progress. When measuring a student's progress over time, generally three or more assessments should be conducted to chart his or her growth. Progress monitoring assessments need not be lengthy or intensive. In fact, quick screening-type assessments administered repeatedly over the course of a year can serve to monitor progress. Progress monitoring assessments might also take the form of a developmental checklist administered by an emergent literacy professional at various intervals, or they might utilize *parallel forms* of a standardized assessment (forms that have been co-normed and that measure the same construct using different items to prevent learning due to repeated exposures to the stimulus items).

Progress monitoring assessments can also be used to measure progress made by a program or intervention in what is called a *program evaluation*. This type of progress monitoring assessment is usually conducted with a sample of children who are participating in a particular program or intervention, and for this reason it does not provide information on how to improve instruction for specific children, rather it allows the program evaluator to make judgments about the effectiveness of the program in order to develop and refine implementation goals.

It is recommended that emergent literacy professionals use measures for the specific purposes for which they were designed. For example, it would be inappropriate to use a screening measure as a diagnostic assessment and likewise it would be unnecessary to administer a full diagnostic battery to all children in a classroom as a screening measure.

Selecting Valid and Reliable Measures

In addition to selecting measures for specific purposes, emergent literacy professionals should know how to look for emergent literacy measures that are reliable and valid and should select these measures when they are available. Not all assessments have been subjected to a complete psychometric review. When measures have been analyzed in this way, there is usually an accompanying technical report that presents information concerning the instrument's validity and reliability.

Construct Validity

Construct validity describes the extent to which the operationalization of a construct accurately reflects the construct. For example, if the technical manual for a particular vocabulary measure claims high construct validity for that measure, this means that items on the instrument have been examined and that they do indeed measure the construct of vocabulary. A brief summary of six types of construct validity is provided in the following chart.

Type of Validity	Description
Face validity	Relies on subjective judgment to determine whether *on its face* the operationalization of a construct accurately reflects the construct
Content validity	Uses a detailed description of the content domain (e.g., in a checklist format) and determines whether all criteria for that content domain are met in the operationalization of the construct
Predictive validity	Uses a correlation to determine the extent to which a measure can predict something it should theoretically be able to predict
Concurrent validity	Determines the extent to which a measure can distinguish between two groups it should theoretically be able to distinguish between
Convergent validity	Examines the extent to which a measure is similar to other theoretically similar measures
Discriminant validity	Examines the extent to which a measure is different from theoretically different measures

Source: Compiled from *The Research Methods Knowledge Base* (2nd ed.), by W. Trochim, 2000. Atomic Dog Publishing, Cincinnati, OH.

Reliability

Reliability estimates the amount of consistency in a measure and in the administration of a measure. Reliability estimates can range from 0 to 1, with scores closer to 1 representing greater consistency or repeatability. As with construct validity, there are multiple ways to estimate a measure's reliability. A summary of four types of reliability is presented in the following chart.

Type of Reliability	Description
Inter-rater (inter-observer) reliability	Assesses the degree to which independent raters provide consistent ratings on the same measure Uses either percentage agreement or correlations between both persons' ratings
Test-retest reliability	Assesses the consistency of a measure from one administration to the next Uses correlations between scores on two separate administrations
Parallel forms reliability	Assesses the consistency of two versions of an instrument that were designed to measure the same content domain Uses split-half reliability
Internal-consistency reliability	Assesses the degree of consistency across items within a measure May use average inter-item correlation, average item-total correlation, split-half reliability, or Cronbach's alpha

Source: Compiled from *The Research Methods Knowledge Base* (2nd ed.), by W. Trochim, 2000. Atomic Dog Publishing, Cincinnati, OH.

Although the information provided in this chapter concerning construct validity and reliability is by no means comprehensive, it should at the very least alert emergent literacy professionals to some key terms that they may encounter as they search for adequate measures of emergent literacy. In summary, emergent literacy professionals have an important responsibility to assess children's contexts for learning and development and their abilities in emergent literacy that are predictive of their later reading success. When selecting the assessments that best address the purposes and goals of a program, it is important to adopt valid and reliable measures when they exist.

References

Dickinson, D. K., & Neuman, S. B. (Eds.). (2006). *Handbook of early literacy research* (Vol. 2). New York: The Guilford Press.

Lonigan, C. J. (2006). Development, assessment, and promotion of preliteracy skills. *Early Education and Development, 17*, 91–114.

National Early Literacy Panel. (2005). *Report on a synthesis of early predictors of reading.* Louisville, KY: Author.

Neuman, S. B., & Dickinson, D. K. (Eds.). (2003). *Handbook of early literacy research* (Vol. 1). New York: The Guilford Press.

Rogoff, B (1990). Structuring situations and transferring responsibility. *Apprenticeship in thinking: Cognitive development in social context* (pp. 86–109). New York: Oxford University Press.

Shepard, L., Kagan, S. L., & Wurtz, E. (Eds.). (1998). *Principles and recommendations for early childhood assessments. Report to the National Education Goals Panel.* Washington, DC: National Education Goals Panel.

Teale, W. H., & Sulzby, E. (Eds.). (1986). *Emergent literacy: Writing and reading.* Norwood, NJ: Ablex.

Trochim, W. (2000). *The research methods knowledge base* (2nd ed.). Cincinnati, OH: Atomic Dog.

Whitehurst, G. J., & Lonigan, C. J. (1998). Child development and emergent literacy. *Child Development, 69*, 848–872.

Section I

Assessing Contexts of Learning and Development

Chapter One

Assessing Classroom Language and Literacy Richness

Alice K. Wiggins
Kelly A. Marshall
Sarah A. F. Friel

The Importance of Classroom Language and Literacy Richness to Emergent Literacy

In the fields of ecological psychology and eco-behaviorism, the influences of environment on perception, meaning, and action or behavior have been well documented (Heft, 2001). In 1968, Roger Barker published a seminal work that pioneered the theory of "behavior settings." Barker viewed the environment as "much more than a source of random inputs to its inhabitants" (p. 205); rather, he described the inputs of the environment as controlled both by the environment itself and by the attributes of the persons within the environment. In this chapter, we explore how the language and literacy environment influences meaning for and behavior of students, and how the inputs of this environment are influenced by its physical components as well as the actions and attributes of adults in the environment.

We begin by describing nine characteristics of language- and literacy-rich preschool classrooms and their importance to children's language and literacy development. Then we describe two constructs typically assessed by measures of the language- and literacy-richness of classrooms. The chapter concludes with an exploration of special considerations for assessing the language- and literacy-richness of preschool classrooms and a discussion of how to interpret the results of these assessments.

As early childhood educators, our interest in the relationship between language- and literacy-rich preschool environments and emergent literacy is fueled by the current educational policy climate of quality and accountability. Federal legislation such as the "No Child Left Behind" Act recognizes the importance of quality preschool programs; however, agreement as to what constitutes classroom or teacher quality is still debated in the literature. Different approaches to the measurement of quality can be distinguished (Perlman, Zellman, & Le, 2004). First, some measures assess global quality of the classroom taking into consideration the structural, procedural, and administrative elements of the setting (e.g., the materials available, the instructional formats used by the teachers, and the means by which professional development is conducted). A second approach focuses on the quality of specific process indicators such as adult-child interactions. A third and very common (but by far the least satisfactory) means of measuring program quality is by *distal* quality indicators such as teacher credentials, class size, or direct child assessment (Pianta, 2003). Such measures are less helpful in identifying strengths and weaknesses in the classroom because they are disconnected from what actually happens on a daily basis and they are by no means strongly related to observed quality. Most importantly, in the case of direct child assessment, the competencies measured are typically unstable in young children and situationally dependent (La Paro & Pianta 2000).

Regardless of the measures used, without a reliable understanding of quality, teachers, administrators, and policy makers are poorly equipped to set accountability standards for the classroom. Our goal in this chapter is to describe in detail one aspect of classroom quality, namely language and literacy richness, and to illustrate how this might be measured using an array of contemporary assessments. In doing so, we will highlight the benefits and pitfalls of measuring quality and, hopefully, assist readers in their interpretation of data collected using these measures.

Nine characteristics of language and literacy rich classrooms include (1) the presence of an abundance of high-quality literacy materials; (2) a physical arrangement that encourages reading and writing; (3) the occurrence of daily literacy routines including read-alouds, independent reading, writing, and sharing; (4) the use of a culturally sensitive and integrated curriculum; (5) the use of assessment to guide instruction; (6) the use of a variety of instructional methods; (7) implementation of a variety of grouping patterns for classroom activities and instruction; (8) the presence of high-quality, deliberate, and recurrent verbal input; and (9) high levels of adult responsiveness (Justice, 2004; McGee & Richgels, 2004). In defining each of these characteristics of a language- and literacy-rich classroom, we will illustrate research that supports the influence of these characteristics on children's language and literacy outcomes.

An abundance of high-quality literacy materials refers not only to the quantity and quality of individual literacy materials, but also the variety among the available materials. Children independently choose to read more often in classroom environments that provide availability and accessibility to many high-quality books (Morrow & Weinstein, 1982). One often cited guideline is that there should be 5 to 10 books accessible for every child in the classroom (Fractor, Woodruff, Martinez, & Teale, 1993; Morrow, 2005; Neuman, 1999). Characteristics of high-quality children's literature include presentation style suitable to audience age; use of visually appealing illustrations, integration of text and illustrations; clear character definition and development; accuracy, organization, and clarity of factual information; and captivation and motivation of readers. The selection of books in a high-quality collection should include a variety of genres, interests, representation of diverse cultural groups, and difficulty levels. Table 1–1 includes a list and definitions for the broad categories, or genres, of books available at the preschool level.

The influence of writing on literacy growth has also been supported by much research (Dickinson, 2003; Dickinson & DiGisi, 1998; Snow, Burns, & Griffin, 1998). During the preschool years, children's writing skills develop and may include writing forms such as marking, scribbling, copying, and letter writing. Children's writing ability is influenced by perceptual-motor skills that are not fully developed in all preschool children (Laszlo, 1986, in Dunsmuir & Blatchford, 2004). Progress in writing skills is associated with regular opportunities to write for a variety of purposes (Snow, Barnes, Chandler, Goodman, & Hemphill, 1991). Just as variety is

Table 1-1. Book Genres

Genre	Definition
Alphabet Books	Are organized based on the sequence of the alphabet.
Biographies	Are stories about the lives of real people.
Fables	Are characterized by use of animal characters to share a lesson or moral.
Fantasy	Include characters and settings that are exaggerated in nature.
Folktales	Often include magic, and are characterized by good, evil, and tricky characters. Folktales typically have a happy ending with good triumphing over evil.
Historical Fiction	Are fictional stories with correct historical time, place, and or settings.
Informational/ Nonfiction	Provide realistic, accurate, and authentic information.
Myths	Explain natural occurrences of phenomenon.
Picture Books	Use illustrations to tell a story.
Poetry	Is literature written in meter; verse, often containing rhyme and or alliteration.
Predictable/ Repetitive Books	Are characterized by repetition of dialog or events.
Traditional Narrative	Includes traditional stories from various cultures, typically passed down through oral storytelling.

important in stocking the classroom library, the classroom writing center should also exhibit variety in materials that are available to children. An assortment of writing utensils (e.g., fat markers, thick pencils, rubber stamps) can support the varying levels of motor development exhibited by the children.

In addition to the distinct reading and writing centers of the classroom, evidence suggests the benefits of provisioning other areas of the classroom with literacy-related tools and artifacts. A literacy enriched play environment provides a setting that supports the development of language and literacy skills and provides opportunities to build connections between oral and written expression (Roskos & Christie, 2001). In play environments that have been enriched with literacy materials (e.g., magazines, phone books, recipe books, note pads, calendars, writing instruments, etc.), children use more language and literacy acts ("reading," writing, printing) than in play environments that have not been enhanced with such props (Morrow, 1990; Neuman & Roskos, 1989, 1990, 1992; Vukelich, 1991). In particular, children's language use in dramatic play centers is shown to be more syntactically complete and complex than language used by children engaged in other types of play (Vedeler, 1997).

Elements of the physical arrangement of the classroom should encourage both reading and writing. Making physical design changes to the classroom library center to make it more accessible and inviting increases children's use of literacy during free play (Morrow & Weinstein, 1982). Research studies support the notion that children make literacy gains in classrooms where teachers have been trained to display books in an appealing and accessible manner (McGill-Franzen Allington, Yokoi, & Brooks, 1999). Books should be arranged on low shelves with the covers facing out. If open-faced shelving is not available, some books can be displayed with their covers facing out on table tops, windowsills, and shelf tops.

The occurrence of daily literacy routines is a characteristic of language- and literacy-rich classrooms that support children's language and literacy growth. The most common example of such a literacy routine is *story time* or *read-aloud* time. Research supports the importance of this time, particularly when children are actively involved in the story process (Lonigan & Whitehurst, 1998). Teacher training that promotes interactions involving literacy supports children's literacy development (McGill-Franzen et al., 1996). Morrow and Weinstein (1982) described the types of activities that define the occurrence of daily literacy routines. Such routines include implementing daily read-alouds, making the read-aloud book available in the library center, discussing the story before and after reading, using creative storytelling techniques (e.g., puppets, felt boards), making books with the class, and integrating books into content area lessons (McGill-Franzen et al., 1999; Morrow & Weinstein, 1982; Neuman, 1996).

Developmentally appropriate practice is the basis for the remaining characteristics of language- and literacy-rich classrooms. Developmentally appropriate practice is an instructional method supported by the International Reading Association (IRA), the National Association for the Education of Young Children (NAEYC), and the American Speech-Language-Hearing Association (ASHA) for language and literacy instruction (IRA & NAEYC, 1998). Instruction is developmentally appropriate when it is suitable for the age of the children within the group and is implemented with attention to the differing needs and developmental levels of each student.

Cultural sensitivity and curriculum integration is an important characteristic of language- and literacy-rich classrooms. Unless practices are sensitive to cultural and linguistic diversity, they cannot be developmentally appropriate (IRA & NAEYC, 1998). Integrated curricula are supported "so that children's learning in all traditional subject areas occurs primarily through projects and learning centers that teachers plan and that reflect children's interests and suggestions" (Bredekamp, 1987, p. 67). Through this integration of content and concepts, and through opportunities to engage in in-depth study, children see connections across disciplines and attain deeper conceptual development (IRA & NAEYC, 1998). Additionally, this integration provides rich opportunities for intentional repetition that supports language development.

The *use of assessment to guide instruction* is another characteristic of language- and literacy-rich classrooms. In addition to the integration of instructional content across subject areas, developmentally appropriate practice advocates the integration of assessment and curriculum. The use of assessment to guide instruction is essential to maximizing the vast opportunities presented in early childhood education classrooms to support language and literacy development. However, for teachers to capitalize on each opportunity, they need to know and understand each child's present level of development, and possess strategies for advancing student learning and development (Johnston & Rogers, 2002; McGee & Richgels, 2003). This book presents a variety of strategies for assessing children's early and emergent language and literacy skills as well as provides descriptions of related language and literacy measures. These measures focus on phonological awareness (Chapter 6) and print knowledge (Chapter 7), among others. The use of assessment to guide specific areas of language and literacy instruction is covered in detail in the remaining chapters of this book; here, we provide an overview on how to use assessment to guide instruction.

Assessment is used in this chapter "to refer to the broad repertoire of [teacher] behaviors involved in noticing, documenting, recording, and interpreting children's behaviors and performances" (Johnston & Rogers, 2002, p. 377). It is important to note that testing is a subset of assessment, a commonly practiced assessment method that measures children's behaviors and performance within controlled, standardized conditions. Effective assessment practices, however, include a combination of observations of children's behaviors and performance during naturally occurring classroom events (e.g., dramatic play, one-on-one storybook reading), as well as the use of specially devised assessment tasks (McGee & Richgels, 2003). Johnston and Rogers (2002) define two principles with regard to assessment practice. First, the interpretation of assessment data is influenced by teachers' values, beliefs, and language. Second, teacher interpretations produce implications for future language and literacy instruction and, therefore, for the language and literacy skills each student develops. Although the purpose of assessment is commonly thought to be strictly for identifying children's strengths and needs, the principal purpose is to plan instruction and identify appropriate instructional supports necessary to foster development in individuals and small groups (NAEYC, 1991).

To select an appropriate assessment for designing instruction based on student needs, teachers need to be knowledgeable about the different assessments available, their functions, and what each purports to measure (Walpole & McKenna, 2004). Recall from the introduction to this book that there are three general categories of assessments: screening, diagnostic, and progress-monitoring. Screening assessments take relatively little time to administer, but provide extremely useful information by alerting teachers to the presence of problems children may be having pertaining to the development of specific language and literacy skills. Diagnostic assessments are administered only after a problem has been identified, and provide in-depth information regarding the specific instructional needs of individual students. Once specialized, targeted instruction has been provided, progress-monitoring assessments can be used periodically to quickly and efficiently determine if instruction is having the desired effect of accelerating student growth in a particular area (Walpole & McKenna, 2004). Assessment will be most useful in designing and delivering effective instruction if each tool is used purposefully and in combination with additional assessment information. Assessments conducted alone do not serve as a reliable measure of a child's understandings or performance, especially when paired with teachers' unconfirmed conclusions about a child's ability (McGee & Richgels, 2003). Tentative conclusions drawn by teachers can only be formalized by follow-up assessments, which help refine conclusions and clear up possible misinterpretations. Together, the information gathered from screening, diagnostic, and progress-monitoring assessments is then subsequently analyzed and used to design instruction; this works to ensure that instruction targets children's specific needs (Christie, Enz, & Vukelich, 2003; Walpole & McKenna, 2004).

One of the principles supporting developmentally appropriate practice is that "children demonstrate different modes of knowing and learning and different ways of representing what they know" (IRA & NAEYC, 1998, p. 9). This principle implies that teachers should provide opportunities for individual children both to use their preferred learning mode and to exercise alternative modes of learning. Pianta, La Paro, and Hamre (2005) use the term *instructional learning formats* to define how teachers engage students in and facilitate activities so that learning opportunities are maximized. These instructional learning formats include both teacher processes (what teachers do) and teaching materials (what teachers use) during instruction. Adequately addressing students' diverse needs requires that teachers use a variety of instructional learning formats.

Meeting children's individual needs and learning styles also implies that teachers use a variety of *grouping patterns* for activities and instruction. Morrow and Smith (1990) found that children who were read stories in small-group settings had better comprehension of the stories than children who were read the same stories in one-on-one or whole group settings. Additionally, children in both the small-group and one-on-one readings elicited more interaction from the children.

Weitzman and Greenberg (2002) describe a number of classroom grouping patterns that encourage and maintain interactions between teachers and children. They suggest that a classroom should have well-defined play areas that create intimate and private spaces for quiet activities such as reading. Areas should be large enough for children to play comfortably, but large open spaces should be avoided as they encourage boisterous play and require regular directions to set limits and thus divert the teacher's attention away from instructional time. Areas that encourage noisy play, such as the block area, should be positioned well away from quiet areas; conversely, complementary areas such as block play and the dramatic play area should be adjacent to one another to encourage materials to be shared between them.

To encourage interaction between peers, Weitzman and Greenberg (2002) also suggest that the classroom should be arranged to encourage different kinds of groupings, depending on the language level and social competencies of individual children. For example, setting up some activities for pairs of children will be more supportive for preschoolers with a language or cognitive impairment. Positioning children opposite each other, rather than adjacent, permits greater eye contact and imitation of play, and in these circumstances teachers can pair children appropriately to provide a child with a language impairment with a typically developing peer model.

More casual groupings, where children can come and go as they wish, (e.g., at the sensory table), also can be less demanding for children who struggle with communication. In these contexts, the teacher can provide materials at a variety of developmental levels to encourage socially isolated children to participate in parallel play amid peers.

Finally, more sophisticated cooperative groups can be encouraged in the dramatic play area or block area. Such areas tend to be more demanding and attract children with more competent language and imaginative play skills. Teachers can offer supports to children who need assistance by providing materials that offer a particular role to play (e.g., a tool kit for a handyman to visit the home corner) or by placing less demanding toys in the block area to encourage parallel play (e.g., placing cars in the block area).

High quality input is another characteristic of language- and literacy-rich classrooms. Adult input that is diverse in the three main components of oral language— *content, form,* and *use* (Justice, 2004)— can be described as "high quality." As Justice describes, language content refers to the meaning of language, including the words we use and the meanings they convey; language form is how words, sentences, and sounds are organized and arranged (e.g., grammatical structures) to convey meaning; and language use is how we draw upon language functionally to meet personal and social needs (i.e., how we use language in different contexts such as formal versus informal settings). Preschoolers need to have a varied language content experience. This includes a full range of word types (nouns, verbs, adjectives, etc.), a hierarchy of vocabulary groups (mommy, parent, family), and the conceptual organization of words (e.g., colors, animals, foods). Accurate and varied models of *language forms* are also important for preschoolers. Examples of language forms one might use in the preschool classroom include simple versus elaborated noun phrases (e.g., "a dog," "a big spotted dog"), regular and irregular tense forms ("he kicked the ball," "he hit the ball") and simple versus complex sentence forms (e.g., "the boy sang and the girl danced," "the girl is dancing because the boy is singing a song"). Finally, preschoolers need to understand that people use language in different ways according to the context (e.g., talking to friends and family as compared to talking to teachers or strangers) and that successful interactions depend on initiating a topic well, maintaining that topic, and then closing the conversation appropriately. Research has demonstrated that children's success in these three areas of language is a reflection of their language environment (Hart & Risley, 1995), and, as such, they should be an intentional focus in the preschool classroom environment.

High quality input also is *deliberate,* referring to the level of intentionality teachers use to choose the most stimulating yet supportive language when talking to children. Research has demonstrated that children who engage in extended conversations with adults have more advanced language and literacy skills (Barnett, 1995; Howes, Phillipsen, & Peisner-Feinberg, 2000). An important feature of these extended conversations is the intentional variation in the level of abstraction that teachers encourage, from labeling and describing to hypothesizing and predicting. In order to maintain conversations with children, teachers need to keep their questions and comments just within the child's zone of proximal development (Vygotsky, 1978); in this way, the child's contributions are scaffolded appropriately.

A final important element of a language-rich preschool environment is the *recurrence* or repetition of key words and specific linguistic concepts throughout the curriculum (Justice, 2004). This means that new vocabulary needs to be introduced consistently in different classroom activities (e.g., circle time, storybook reading, dramatic play). Additionally, meaningful repetition should be fostered as an integral part of the class routine so that children have multiple opportunities to hear and practice new words or concepts.

High levels of adult responsiveness refers to the adult's (in this case, the teacher's) ability to support interactions with children in a way that provides reassurance and encouragement at a developmentally appropriate level. Research has shown that, when early childhood educators provide feedback to children using scaffolding and support the children to maintain their engagement in activities for extended periods, this in turn provides the potential for increased learning (Girolametto & Weitzman, 2002). Furthermore, teachers who display responsive behavior toward children tend to be more in tune with the academic needs of their pupils (Helmke & Schrader, 1988). Other teacher qualities such as warmth, which is a feature of responsiveness, have been shown not only to correlate positively with children's development, but also to produce gains in classroom performance (Matsumura, Patthey-Chavez, Valdez, & Garnier, 2002).

One prevailing instructional perspective utilizes a social-interactive model, whereby children acquire language optimally in environments that are *highly responsive* to their communicative attempts (Conti-Ramsden, 1990). In such an environment, adults take an interest in, and comment on, children's actions. They use conversational devices to promote interaction, such as asking open questions, linking comments to questions, and keeping test questions to a minimum. Additionally, adults who are socially interactive respond to preschoolers by using utterances that expand or extend the child's utterance, thereby increasing its semantic and syntactic content (Girolametto & Weitzman, 2002).

The mechanism by which these strategies enhance children's language is as yet unclear; also unclear is the threshold level that these strategies should occur in the classroom in order to produce any benefit (Girolametto & Weitzman, 2002). However, it would appear that such modifications to adult-child conversations create opportunities for joint attention, thus facilitating the child's connections between words and their meanings (Girolametto & Weitzman, 2002). Moreover, if communication between child and adult is easy, the child's attention and motivation level will be enhanced and thus greater cognitive resources can be deployed in language processing (Girolametto & Weitzman, 2002). Finally, if the adult is a responsive communicative partner, his or her language input will be simplified to match the child's zone of proximal development (Vygotsky, 1978), thereby scaffolding the conversation to greater levels of syntactic and semantic complexity.

It is important to remember that conversational responsiveness works in a reciprocal fashion. Teachers' responsiveness encourages preschoolers to communicate, and children who actively participate in conversations elicit from teachers better quality and greater quantities of language input. Simply put, competent or skilled language learners create for themselves better opportunities to hone their communication skills with adults (Bohannon & Bonvillian in Gleason, 1997). Conversely, children with language difficulties (e.g., those with cognitive delays, specific language impairment, second language learners, children from low socioeconomic backgrounds) engage in linguistically simple interchanges because their utterances are brief and/or simple, and these in turn are less likely to be expanded or extended by teachers. For this reason it is vital that teachers of prekindergarten children with weak language skills *intentionally* provide them with high-quality, responsive conversational opportunities.

Evidence from research regarding the nature of teacher-child interactions in preschool environments has presented a rather bleak picture of the quality and frequency of supportive interchanges. Teachers and children engage in relatively few extended conversations that encourage decontextualized exchanges containing novel or complex information (Tizzard & Hughes, 1984). This disappointing trend has shown little sign of improvement in the last decade, especially for children with language impairments who are integrated into preschool environments (Girolametto, Hoaken, Weitzman, & van Lieshout, 2000). However, more recent research by Girolametto & Weitzman (2003) has demonstrated that staff members who receive specific training on language facilitation techniques are more likely to be socially responsive and less directive in their interactions with children.

When considering the influence of language- and literacy-rich classrooms on young children, research has shown that young children's experiences in the classroom have a strong bearing on their future school success. Characteristics of teacher responsiveness such as feedback and warmth can have consistent and measurable effects on children's academic and social achievement (Barnett, 1995; Howes et al., 2000). After all, the interactions between teachers and children are the primary mechanism by which preschoolers experience their introduction to learning and literacy; therefore, any deficits in the quality of these interactions are likely to have lasting effects.

Measures for Assessing Classroom Language and Literacy Richness

Each of the characteristics described in the previous section is included in the more broadly defined domains of the *structural* aspects of the environment and the *procedural* aspects, or *instructional processes,* within the environment. Presence of an abundance of high-quality literacy materials and arrangement of the classroom to encourage reading and writing both fall within the structural domain. Instructional processes within the environment include high-quality verbal input, adult responsiveness, the occurrence of daily literacy activities, use of a culturally sensitive and integrated curriculum, use of assessment to guide instruction, use of a variety of instructional means, and the use of a variety of instructional grouping patterns. Table 1–2 summarizes the characteristics that comprise the structural and procedural aspects of classroom language and literacy richness.

The following sections describe both commercial and noncommercial measures that can be used to assess the structural and procedural constructs. For each measure, we provide available information regarding time required to administer, how the measure is administered (e.g., checklist, work sample, observation), the names of the subtests for each measure, possible score types (e.g.,

Table 1–2. Constructs Illustrating Language and Literacy Richness in the Classroom

---

Structural Aspects of the Language and Literacy Environment

Availability of high-quality literacy materials

Arrangement of classroom to support reading and writing

Instructional Processes/Procedural Aspects of the Language and Literacy Environment

---

Occurrence of daily literacy routines

Use of a culturally sensitive and integrated curriculum

Use of assessment to guide instruction

Use of a variety of instructional means

Use of a variety of grouping patterns for activities and instruction

Recurrent, high-quality, deliberate input

Language facilitation techniques

---

raw scores, standard scores, percentile ranks), qualifications required for administration, and specific uses of the measure (e.g., for progress monitoring, to inform practice) as well as ways in which outcomes of the measure are interpreted and used for various purposes. See Table 1–3 for a summary of the measures of classroom language and literacy richness described here.

Measuring Structural Aspects of the Prekindergarten Classroom

Structural aspects of the environment focus on the availability of materials that support language and literacy development and the setup of the classroom. This construct reflects the availability of language and literacy materials in the classroom. It considers the provision and accessibility of literacy-related artifacts and materials associated with written language. It encompasses the quantity, quality, variety, and authenticity of these literacy props and objects.

Table 1–3. Summary of Measures of Classroom Language and Literacy Richness

Measure	Time	Administration	Relevant Subtest(s)	Scores	Constructs and Characteristics Addressed	Uses
Classroom Assessment Scoring System (CLASS; Pianta et al., 2005)	2–4 hours	Observation Rating	All (do not need to consider the Productivity or Behavior Management subscales)	Raw score	(1) Instructional Processes (2) Adult-Child and Peer Interactions (3) Language Facilitation Techniques	(1) Inform Instruction (2) Guide Program Improvement
Classroom Literacy Environmental Profile (CLEP; Wolfersberger et al., 2004)	40 min.	Observation Checklist	All	Raw score	(1) Classroom Setup (2) Available Materials (3) Instructional Processes	(1) Inform Classroom Setup (2) Inform Instruction (3) Guide Program Improvement

continues

Table 1-3. *continued*

Measure	Time	Administration	Relevant Subtest(s)	Scores	Constructs and Characteristics Addressed	Uses
Creative Curriculum Implementation Checklist (Teaching Strategies, Inc., 2003),	3 hrs.	Observation, Checklist, and Teacher Interview	All	Raw score	(1) Classroom Setup (2) Available Materials (3) Instructional Processes (4) Recurrent, High Quality, Deliberate Input (5) Language Facilitation Techniques	(1) Inform Classroom Setup (2) Inform Instruction (3) Guide Program Improvement
Early Childhood Environment Rating Scale (ECERS-R; Harms et al., 1998)	2 hrs.	Observation and Rating	All	Raw score	(1) Classroom Setup (2) Available Materials (3) Instructional Processes (4) Recurrent High Quality Deliberate Input	(1) Inform Classroom Setup (2) Inform Instruction (3) Guide Program Improvement

Measure	Time	Administration	Relevant Subtest(s)	Scores	Constructs and Characteristics Addressed	Uses
Early Language and Literacy Classroom Observation (ELLCO; Smith et al., 2002)	50 min.	Observation, Rating, and Teacher Interview	All	Raw score	(1) Classroom Setup (2) Available Materials (3) Instructional Processes (4) Recurrent, High Quality, Deliberate Input (5) Language Facilitation Techniques	(1) Inform Classroom Setup (2) Inform Instruction (3) Guide Program Improvement
Observation Measures of Instruction in Language and Literacy (OMLIT; Goodson et al., 2004)	2.5 hrs.	Observation and Rating	All	Raw score by item	(1) Classroom Setup (2) Available Materials (3) Instructional Processes	(1) Inform Classroom Setup (2) Inform Instruction (3) Guide Program Improvement

continues

Table 1-3. *continued*

Measure	Time	Administration	Relevant Subtest(s)	Scores	Constructs and Characteristics Addressed	Uses
Print Environment Assessment Form (Downhower & Beagle, 1998)	45 min.	Observation and Checklist	All	Raw	(1) Classroom Setup (2) Available Materials	(1) Inform Classroom Setup (2) Guide Program Improvement
Teacher Interaction and Language Rating Scale (TILRS; Girolametto et al., 2000)	1 hr.	Observation and Rating	All		(1) Recurrent, High-Quality, Deliberate Input (2) Language Facilitation Techniques	(1) Inform Instruction (2) Guide Program Improvement (3) Staff Development

The construct also measures how the physical arrangement, attractiveness, and organization of the classroom influence students' use of literacy materials and engagement in language- and literacy-related activities. Finally, it captures the degree to which the environment incorporates meaningful and relevant opportunities to use language and literacy in real-world manners.

Classroom Literacy Environment Profile (CLEP; Wolfersberger, Reutzel, Sudweeks, & Fawson, 2004)

The Classroom Literacy Environment Profile (CLEP; Wolfersberger et al., 2004) is designed to assess a teacher's effectiveness in implementing a print-rich literacy environment from both the structural and procedural perspectives. Subscale 1 of the CLEP addresses the provisioning of the classroom with literacy tools. Subscale 2 of the CLEP addresses the arrangement of classroom space and literacy tools, as well as procedural elements regarding the ability of the teacher to gain students' interest in literacy events and sustain students' interactions with literacy tools (Wolfersberger et al., 2004). Although the measure was designed for use in kindergarten through sixth-grade classrooms, a review of the items on the measure shows them to be closely aligned with measures such as the ELLCO (Smith et al., 2002) and Creative Curriculum Implementation Checklist (Teaching Strategies, Inc., 2003), which were designed for use in preschool classrooms. Although not specifically validated for use at the preschool level, the CLEP provides a means to "assess the *print-richness* of elementary and early childhood classrooms, as well as the properties of literacy tools found in these settings" (Wolfersberger et al., 2004).

The CLEP contains 33 items divided between the two subscales, *Provisioning the Classroom with Literacy Materials* and *Arranging Classroom Space and Literacy Tools, Gaining Students' Interest in Literacy Events, and Sustaining Students' Interactions with Literacy Tools*. Each item is assessed on a 7-point scale, which includes descriptions for the scale scores of 1, 3, 5, and 7. For example, item 1 measures the "quantity of literacy tools." A score of 1 is "No literacy tools are present." A score of 3 is "Literacy tools are limited to books, paper, pencils, AND crayons." A score of 5 is "Several literacy tools are present that contain print (e.g., books, organizational and informational print items), produce print (e.g., writing utensils and surfaces, publishing materials), AND support literacy events (e.g., technological resources, furnishings, storage and display containers, accessories)." A score of 7 is "Many literacy tools are present that contain print, are used to produce print, AND support literacy events" (Wolfersberger et al., 2004, p. 259). See Table 1–4 for the CLEP's definitions for the terms *literacy event*, *literacy product*, and *literacy tool*.

The CLEP is an observational measure that requires no interaction with students or teachers during the assessment. Thirty minutes is required to complete the rating scale in the classroom, with an additional 10 minutes required to score and interpret the scale. Examiners should have experience observing teachers in action, but no formal qualifications are required. The measure yields raw scores for each subscale, which are then divided by the number of items in the subscale to derive an average, which is used for interpretation. Interpretive ratings for each scale include *impoverished* (subscale average between 1.0 and 2.4), *minimal*

Table 1–4. CLEP Definitions

Literacy event	A communicative act in which reading, writing, speaking, and/or listening are integral to the participants' interactions and interpretive processes.
Literacy products	A concrete object or an observable event that occurs as the result of interaction with literacy tools.
Literacy tools	Physical objects present in the environment to support the acquisition of literacy (e.g., paper, pencils, professionally published books and magazines, adult- and child-authored materials, computers, and bookshelves).

Source: Reprinted with permission from "Developing and Validating the Classroom Literacy Environmental Profile (CLEP): A Tool for Examining the "Print Richness" of Early Childhood and Elementary Classrooms" by M. E. Wolfersberger, D. R. Reutzel, R. Sudweeks, and P. C. Fawson, 2004. *Journal of Literacy Research*, 36(2), 211–272.

(subscale average between 2.5 and 3.9), *satisfactory* (subscale average between 4.0 and 5.4), and *enriched* (subscale average between 5.5 and 7.0).

With regard to the classroom setup, the CLEP primarily addresses the arrangement and organization of the classroom. Items related to classroom arrangement assess the use of print for classroom organization (e.g., printed directions, labels, or schedules), presence and use of storage and display containers to support literacy events (e.g., easel for big books, pocket chart, flip chart, etc.), and types of classroom areas (with regard to their literacy related uses). CLEP items assessing classroom arrangement include the presence of furnishings identified to support literacy events (e.g., comfortable furniture in reading area, an "author's chair"); location, boundaries, and size of classroom areas (e.g., library center, listening center, and publishing center in close proximity with sufficient room); presence of a classroom library; and grouping of literacy tools (i.e., literacy tools in all areas of the classroom). The CLEP does not specifically address the attractiveness of the classroom setup or the degree to which the environment incorporates meaningful and related opportunities for use of language and literacy in real-world manners.

CLEP items that assess available literacy materials include quantity, utility (e.g., multiple uses), and appropriateness of literacy tools (e.g., books, papers, writing instruments) and accessories (e.g., pointers, book marks, mailboxes, flannel boards, puppets) Also assessed are quantity, genres, and difficulty levels of text materials. With regard to availability of materials to support writing, the CLEP considers variety in the availability of writing utensils and writing surfaces. Consideration is also given to the availability of tools to edit, assemble, and decorate whole class- and student-made literacy products. Availability of technological resources to support literacy is also addressed in one CLEP item. Finally, with regard to availability, the CLEP assesses the accessibility of literacy tools within the classroom.

Creative Curriculum Implementation Checklist (Teaching Strategies, Inc., 2003)

The Creative Curriculum Implementation Checklist (Teaching Strategies, Inc., 2003) is designed to assess the fidelity of implementation to the Creative Curriculum for Preschool (Dodge, Colker, & Heroman, 2002). We felt it important to include here as a measure of classroom language and literacy richness, as many aspects of the curriculum are closely aligned with the constructs we described previously as supporting characteristics of a language- and literacy-rich classroom. The Creative Curriculum Implementation Checklist can be used as a tool to inform teachers' instruction and classroom setup, as well as to evaluate their interactions with children. Additionally, administrators and supervisors can use the checklist to guide ongoing program improvement.

The checklist is divided into five sections: (1) physical environment; (2) structure; (3) teacher-child interactions; (4) assessment; and (5) family involvement. Most of the items within each section use an observational method (marking yes or no) to document existing elements of the curriculum implementation. It is important to note that the assessor should identify as present only those items or materials accessible by *children* (e.g., books on low shelves or work hung on the wall at children's eye level). Additionally, some sections also contain icons to indicate that the item should be discerned through an interview process with the teacher or through some physical documentation provided by the teacher (e.g., a copy of the weekly lesson plans).

The Creative Curriculum Implementation Checklist is an untimed observation. Not all items will be observable in a single visit. There are no formal published guidelines regarding the amount of time required to accurately complete the checklist, but our experience has been that a half to a full day in the classroom, plus additional time for the teacher interview, should be sufficient. Examiners should have experience observing teachers in action, but no formal qualifications are required. The assessment yields a raw score, which can be used to compare quality ratings over time.

The *physical environment* portion of the Creative Curriculum Implementation Checklist (Teaching Strategies, Inc., 2003) addresses how the teacher arranges the classroom environment as well as the availability of materials, furnishings, and equipment within the Creative Curriculum interest areas (i.e., classroom centers). This part of the tool includes a number of items characteristic of high quality language and literacy environments. For instance, assessment of the classroom environment includes questions about the location of centers to minimize interference (e.g., housing noisier centers away from the library center), the location and display of resources (e.g., books and CDs stored with the listening center, books shelved facing out), efforts to maximize children's independence (e.g., labeling shelves and containers to identify where most of the materials belong, and storing materials at child's level), and the children's comfort level (e.g., good lighting and comfortable furniture in the library center).

With regard to the availability of materials, questions in the physical environment portion of the checklist seek to determine if a variety of writing materials are available within the library center, whether a variety of writing surfaces are available in the center, and whether the center includes a variety of letter and word manipulatives (e.g., letter stamps, alphabet cards, magnetic letters). Two questions regarding content-related materials for literacy seek to determine whether reading and writing materials are present in several of the other classroom centers (e.g., blocks, dramatic play, discovery/science).

Early Childhood Environment Rating Scale (Revised Edition) (ECERS-R; Harms, Clifford, & Cryer, 1998)

The ECERS-R is designed to evaluate the preschool environment including spatial, programmatic, and interpersonal features that directly affect children and adults in early childhood settings. The original ECERS (Harms & Clifford, 1980) as well as this revised edition was intended for the evaluation of child care environments, with particular emphasis on children between 2½ and 5 years of age rather than elementary classrooms. Notably, there is an emphasis on aspects of the physical environment and safety elements of the classroom setting rather than instruction and content. However, we felt it important to include the ECERS-R in this chapter as it is widely used in the United States by teachers, administrators, and researchers as a measure of overall preschool environmental quality and, in some cases, in high-stakes settings such as eligibility for public funding (Perlman, Zellman, & Le, 2004).

The rating scale consists of 41 questions divided into seven subscales: (1) Space and Furnishings—8 questions, (2) Personal Care Routines—5 questions, (3) Language-Reasoning—4 questions

(4) Activities—10 questions, (5) Interaction—4 questions (6) Program structure—4 questions, and (7) Parents and Staff—6 questions. All of the subscales use the same 7-point Likert scale (1 = *inadequate*, 3 = *minimal*, 5 = *good*, 7 = *excellent*). In order to arrive at an appropriate rating, for each question there are indicators (some negative and some positive) for the 1 point, 3 point, 5 point, and 7 point scores and the ECERS-R manual gives specific details on how ratings should be assigned.

The ECERS-R is not a timed observation tool; however, the authors recommend that outside observers should allow at least 2 hours to complete the observation. The authors also urge observers to be aware of activities that may occur only at certain times of the day (e.g., gross motor play) and to be sure to schedule their observation accordingly. It is recognized that not all aspects of the observation schedule will be observed during the visit; therefore a 20-minute teacher interview is also recommended. Designated questions are provided for most items and should be asked only to decide whether a *higher* score should be assigned. Once all the scores for individual items have been gathered, an average score for each subsection is calculated; this is then recorded on the ECERS-R profile sheet so that quality measures (both raw scores and average scores) can be compared over time.

The Space and Furnishings section of the ECERS-R includes several items related to the classroom setup aspect of language and literacy richness. Items document the existence of soft, comfortable, and inviting furnishings in the classroom; organization and labeling of classroom materials; space for private/individual activities; display of children's work; display of books and pictures; and use of pictures and stories in the dramatic play center.

Only one item on the ECERS-R evaluates the availability of language- and literacy-related materials. The Books and Pictures item is given a rating of 1 (*inadequate*) if few or no books are present. The ratings of 5 (*good*) and 7 (*excellent*) require a wide selection of books including different genres, age appropriateness, provision and use of other language materials (e.g., poster, picture games, flannel boards), and books relevant to current themes or activities. This item also requires teacher processes illustrating that books are rotated to maintain interest and that informal (e.g., during free play or nap) reading of stories takes place in the classroom.

Early Language and Literacy Classroom Observation Toolkit (ELLCO; Smith, Dickinson, Sangeorge, & Anastasopoulos, 2002)

The ELLCO is a classroom observation tool designed to evaluate classroom practices and to provide professional feedback to teachers. It is composed of three mutually dependent constructs, to be completed in the following order: Literacy Environment Checklist, Classroom Observation and Teacher Interview, and Literacy Activities Rating Scale. The Literacy Environment Checklist provides an overall picture of the classroom, and serves to inform the assessor prior to the observation and teacher interview. The Literacy Activities Rating Scale assesses characteristics of literacy-related activities based on classroom observation.

The Literacy Environment Checklist assesses the setup and provision of the classroom literacy environment. Ideally, it is best to complete this portion of the checklist when children are not in the room because the observer must spend time walking around the classroom viewing, manipulating, and counting materials. If the checklist cannot be completed prior to the students' arrival, as recommended by the authors, it can be completed during recess, lunch, after the school day ends, or any other time children are not in the classroom. The checklist is organized into five subsections: Book Area (3 items), Book Selection (4 items), Book Use (5 items), Writing Materials (6 items), and Writing Around the Room (6 items; one item has two parts). Each item in this section of the ELLCO requires either a "yes/no" judgment or a "quantity" judgment. Items range in points from 0 to 3. For "yes/no" items, a "yes" answer receives one point. A score of 0 is entered for each "no" answer. For "quantity" items, points are assigned from 0 to 3 for each quantity range. For instance, item 6, "How many books convey factual information?" receives 0 points if no books convey factual information, 1 point if one or two books convey factual information, 2 points if three to five books convey factual information, and 3 points if six or more books convey factual information. The Literacy Environment Checklist portion of the ELLCO requires approximately 15 to 20 minutes to complete.

The Classroom Observation consists of 14 items rated on a 5-point Likert scale. The items are: Organization of the Classroom,

Contents of the Classroom, Presence and Use of Technology, Opportunities for Child Choice and Initiative, Classroom Management Strategies, Classroom Climate, Oral Language Facilitation, Presence of Books, Approaches to Book Reading (for prekindergarten and kindergarten-age children), Reading Instruction (for school-age children), Approaches to Children's Writing (for prekindergarten and kindergarten-age children), Writing Opportunities and Instruction (for school-age children), Approaches to Curriculum Integration, Recognizing Diversity in the Classroom, Facilitating Home Support for Literacy, and Approaches to Assessment. Detailed descriptions for the scores of 1 (*deficient*), 3 (*basic*), and 5 (*exemplary*) are provided to aid the assessor in determining the score for each item. There is also a place to make notations, which can be used for additional documentation or to provide clarification when calibrating scores between multiple assessors. Each item has an independent score, which is transferred to the scoring sheet at the back of the booklet. The items here are clustered under two headings: General Classroom Environment and Language, Literacy, and Curriculum. A grand total is then reached from these two subtotals.

The Teacher Interview follows the Classroom Observation. Each interview item includes a script for the question and a few sample probes that can be used if the question does not elicit a sufficient response. Interview questions are used only as needed to score items from the Classroom Observation portion of the assessment. For instance, if no technology use was witnessed during the classroom observation, the interview question "In what ways do you use technology in your classroom?" can be used to score the "Presence and Use of Technology" item of the Classroom Observation section. The classroom observation requires approximately 30 to 40 minutes to complete. An additional 10 minutes is required to complete the teacher interview.

Authors Smith, Dickinson, Sangeorge, and Anastasopoulos (2002) recommend that individuals intending to use the ELLCO have relevant experience teaching the targeted age range of prekindergarten through third grade. Assessors should also have a solid base of knowledge in early literacy and language development, specifically birth through age 8. ELLCO training is provided by the Center for Children and Families, Education Development

Center, Inc. Contact should be made through Paul H. Brookes Publishing Company. At least 9 hours is required to complete the training process. If possible, multiple assessors should code each classroom visit. Coding on the checklist and the observation items should occur independently, after which the assessors calibrate their scores through discussion of differences. Assessors are considered reliable with one another if on each item scores fall within one point of each other. If multiple assessors are observing the classroom, both observers should take part in the interview.

Both the Literacy Environment Checklist and Classroom Observation portions of the ELLCO contain items relating to the classroom setup component of the structural aspects of the classroom, although the Classroom Observation portion addresses only the "General Classroom Setup" and not the classroom setup as it relates to language and literacy. Additionally, 17 of the 24 items in the Literacy Environment Checklist portion of the ELLCO address the availability of materials relating to reading and writing. The items primarily encompass the quantity and variety of literacy-related materials. Also addressed is the incorporation of these materials into the classroom's distinct learning centers (e.g., science, dramatic play, blocks). These items consider both the provision and accessibility of the literacy materials. The Literacy Environment Checklist includes items that provide points for the existence of distinct areas for reading, listening, and writing. Points are also awarded for the organization of the book reading area, the comfort of the book reading area, and the display of teacher and children's writing samples.

Observation Measures of Language and Literacy Instruction in Early Childhood (OMLIT; Goodson, Layzer, & Smith, 2004)

The OMLIT was designed to assess the quality of the classroom by measuring the instructional processes and environmental resources of early childhood education classrooms. The OMLIT consists of five distinct observation instruments, which identify the type, quality, and available opportunities for supports in the classroom that promote children's language and literacy development. The five measures in the OMLIT battery include: the Classroom Literacy

Opportunities Checklist (CLOC), Snapshot of Classroom Activities (SNAP), Read Aloud Profile (RAP), Classroom Literacy Instruction Profile (CLIP), and Quality of Instruction in Literacy and Language (QUILL). The CLOC and SNAP gather information regarding the overall classroom environment, whereas the RAP, CLIP, and QUILL measure specific teacher behaviors and instructional practices used while engaged with children in various literacy activities. The early childhood education program should be observed for a minimum of 2½ hours. Preferably, a half-day program would be observed fully and a full-day program would be observed up to or through lunch. Each OMLIT measure is administered according to an established schedule, and a sample observation schedule for half-day and full-day programs is included in the training manual.

The SNAP briefly illustrates the general classroom activities taking place in the classroom and also describes the number of children and adults participating in each activity and the literacy resources and/or activities that are incorporated into each activity. Fifteen common classroom activities such as sensory play, block play, and alphabet activities are listed. Space is provided to write in other observed activities. No additional ratings are recorded for this measure.

The CLIP depicts the specific literacy activities taking place in the classroom and records the instructional methods the teacher uses. The observer gathers seven categories of information on the CLIP, including (1) the observed literacy activity (7 possible activities), (2) the literacy knowledge presented (8 choices), (3) the teacher's instructional style (6 choices), (4) the text support offered during instruction (9 possible supports), (5) the number of children participating in the activity (5 choices), (6) the types of child talk (4 choices), and (7) teacher involvement with children (3 options). Under the teacher's instructional style category, two of the options require a quality rating if selected: group discussion of more than one child or a discussion with a single child. In this case, the teacher's instructional style is rated using a 5-point Likert scale (1 = minimal, 3 = moderate, 5 = extensive). To arrive at an appropriate rating, indicators for a rating of 1 point, 3 points, or 5 points are provided for each question. Additionally, some indicators are provided for the in-between ratings of 2 and 4. The OMLIT training manual provides specific details on how ratings should be assigned. The SNAP and CLIP are completed every 15 minutes throughout the observation period; however, the CLIP is not completed until 5 minutes after the SNAP.

The RAP measures the teacher's dialogic reading practices during individual, small group, or whole class read-alouds throughout the day. This measure is administered whenever a read-aloud occurs. It consists of 12 items pertaining to the instructional strategies used during prereading (11 possibilities), while reading (14 possibilities), and post-reading (11 possibilities). The observer records which adult reads the book (e.g., teacher, assistant, or other) as well as which language the adult language uses (English, Spanish, other), the number of children participating (from 5 options), and book characteristics (1 option for each of six questions).

The CLOC is an inventory of the available literacy resources in the classroom. The QUILL rates the frequency and overall quality of literacy instruction and the additional supports provided to foster language and literacy development. Both the CLOC and the QUILL are completed once at the conclusion of the observation, and the entire observation period is considered when rating each item on these measures. The CLOC considers 55 items; however, a total score is not computed. The items are arranged among 11 subparts: physical layout (5 items), print environment (8 items), literacy toys and materials (2 items), books and reading area (12 items), listening area (3 items), writing supports (6 items), literacy materials outside of the reading and writing area (3 items), diversity in literacy materials (3 items), instructional technology (2 items), curriculum theme (7 items), and literacy resources outside of the classroom (4 items). Detailed descriptions aid the user in scoring each item from 1 to 3 based on the scale descriptions provided. For example, item 10 examines "labels for groups of toys, materials, or areas/centers in the classroom." A score of 1 would be assigned if there were no labels; 2 would be assigned for 1 to 6 labels; and 3 would be selected for 7 or more labels. The scales change based on the focus of the item. The OMLIT also provides observers space to write notes or comments. The QUILL consists of 10 items that observers rate using a 5-point Likert scale (1 = minimal, 3 = moderate, 5 = high). Observers also record a frequency rating for each item (none, minimal, moderate, or extensive). Multiple indicators for the 1 point, 3 point, and 5 point score are provided in order to inform an appropriate rating, and additional information is provided in the training manual.

The OMLIT training manual does not indicate what types of experience, training, or formal qualifications are required to administer this battery of measures. However, examiners should have some experience observing teachers in action and should be familiar with early literacy and language instructional practices. Each measure provides a raw score for each item.

The Classroom Learning Opportunities Checklist (CLOC) measure of the OMLIT includes items specifically related to the classroom setup construct. The *Physical Layout of Classroom* section contains items relating to the layout and arrangement of the classroom, but does not address any factors specific to language and literacy richness. However, the *Books and Reading Area* section of the measure seeks to determine the existence of a distinct reading area and the provision of comfortable furnishings in the reading area. Also addressed in this section are the display and accessibility of reading materials. Likewise, the *Writing Supports* section of the measure seeks to document the existence, setup, and provisioning of a distinct writing center. The *Listening Area* section seeks to document the existence and setup of a listening area. Additionally, the *Print Environment* section addresses the display of children's writing samples, functional print (e.g., calendars, schedules, rules, etc.), and environmental print. Also addressed are the use of labeling to indicate the locations of toys, materials, and classroom centers.

Print Environment Assessment Form (Dowhower & Beagle, 1998)

The Print Environment Assessment Form is a checklist designed to examine the physical print environment of early childhood classrooms from the structural perspective—the presence of literacy materials and classroom setup. Four subscales are used for analysis: (1) books, (2) writing supplies, (3) literacy centers, and (4) incidences of print. Subscale 1 addresses the quantity and variety of books as well as the books-to-child ratio. Subscale 2 addresses the quantity and variety of writing materials (e.g., paper, chalkboards), authentic props (e.g., clipboards), and tools (e.g., pencils, markers).

Subscale 3 addresses the set-up and available materials provided in literacy centers. Subscale 4 addresses the observable incidences of print produced by teacher and child throughout the classroom. In total the Print Environment Assessment Form addresses 131 categories of print divided among the four subscales. Most items within each section are assessed using an observational method (marking a + for items observed and a − for items not observed) as a means to document existing categories of print within the classroom. Additionally, the book subscale requires that the total number of books from each category (e.g., commercially published, child-authored) be counted and recorded. For example, the first item on the checklist is "commercially published storybooks." The observer would thus count the number of books in this category and record the total in the space provided. After completing the book subscale, the observer tallies the total number of books and computes the number of books available per child in the classroom.

The Print Environment Assessment Form is an observational measure that requires no interaction with students or teachers during the assessment process. Because this form follows a process similar to completing the Literacy Environment Checklist of the ELLCO (Smith et al., 2002), it may be easier to view, manipulate, and count materials when children are not present in the classroom, although this is not necessary. Approximately 45 minutes is required to fully examine the classroom and complete the assessment form. Additional time may be required for scoring. Examiners do not need to hold formal qualifications to complete this assessment form. The measure yields raw scores for each subscale, which reflect the total number of books and books per child as well as the total number of writing supplies, literacy center related materials, and incidences of print, respectively.

The Incidences of Print subscale includes items related to the classroom setup construct, and specifically address the display of literacy in the classroom. Between 5 and 15 items are included for each of five print categories. These categories include Directions (e.g., classroom rules, use of materials, recipes), Schedules (e.g., calendar, jobs, daily activities.), Labels (e.g., shelf contents, captioned work, signs designating classroom areas), Authentic Environmental Print (e.g., books, magazines, phone books, menus), and Communications (e.g., message boards, child authored letters, mailboxes).

The Literacy Centers subscale includes items concerning the provisioning of the literacy centers that are related to the classroom setup construct. For instance, there are items to document the provisioning of soft materials (e.g., furniture, pillows) in the literacy area. Additionally, organization of the classroom setup is addressed via items regarding existence of shelf labels, book check-out cards, and bulletin boards.

The Books, Writing Supplies, and Literacy Centers subscales of the Print Environment Assessment Form contain items related to the available materials construct of language and literacy richness. This subtest documents the number of commercially published storybooks, commercially published reference/informational books, commercially published poetry books, child-authored stories or books, and group- or class-authored stories or books in the classroom. These numbers are used to calculate the total quantity of books and the number of books per child. The Writing Supplies subtest documents specific items in the categories of paper (e.g., lined, unlined, colored), pencils (e.g., lead with eraser, markers, fine- and wide-tipped), tactile letters (e.g., plastic, magnetic, wooden), and writing center (e.g., alphabet chart, envelopes, ink pad).

Thus far we have described measures that assess (with varying degrees of detail and success) structural features of the classroom, which constitute one important aspect quality (i.e., the setup and provision of materials that support language and literacy). We now turn our attention to the procedural aspects of the classroom, (i.e., what the teacher says and does with the students to promote learning), which are also essential to providing a high-quality early learning environment.

Measuring Instructional Processes in the Prekindergarten Classroom

Instructional processes focus on what the teacher does before, during, and after instruction to enhance language and literacy development. This construct considers the teachers' selection of content and definition of the literacy learning objectives for both teacher-directed instruction and child-initiated activities. It also includes the extent to which children are engaged in these activities as a result of the teachers' instructional methods, which include use of multiple modalities, resources, and materials. This construct measures the teachers' use of strategies that develop concepts, actively involve students, and stimulate language and conversation. Also included in this construct is the degree to which classroom interactions (both adult-child and peer-peer) are fostered in a deliberate and recurrent manner and teacher-directiveness is curtailed in the context of the interactions.

Classroom Assessment Scoring System Preschool (CLASS; Pianta, La Paro, & Hamre, 2006)

The CLASS was designed as an observational measure to assess classroom quality in preschool and kindergarten through third grade classrooms. The CLASS consists of 11 classroom scales that are categorized into three broad domains (Emotional Support, Classroom Organization, and Instructional Support). The domain of *Emotional Support* includes the following scales: positive climate, negative climate, teacher sensitivity and regard for student perspectives. The domain of Classroom Organization includes the following: behavior management, productivity, and instructional learning formats. The domain of Instructional Support includes the following: concept development, quality of feedback, and language modeling.

Each of these three domains is designed to define and measure classroom and teacher-level quality. Specifically, the CLASS considers the quality of teachers' social and instructional interactions with students coupled with teachers' intentionality and student productivity in the overall CLASS ratings. The observer focuses exclusively on what teachers do with available materials and in the interactions they have with students.

There is one further global measure, Student Engagement, which seeks to capture the extent to which all students in the class are focused and participating in the activity facilitated by the teacher. It is anticipated that there is a relationship between the level of instructional/emotional support and the extent to which the students remain actively involved in an activity; however, the CLASS provides this as a separate measure to identify classrooms where children are disengaged in spite of receiving highly focused input.

The CLASS observation should commence at the start of the school day and continue for approximately 3 hours, or six observation cycles in which the observer watches for 20 minutes and codes (records ratings) for 10 minutes. The observer should discuss the morning's schedule with the teacher prior to conducting the observation. The schedule should allow for a minimum of four observation cycles (2 hours); however, as many as eight cycles can be used to judge classroom quality.

During the observation, the observer watches classroom activities for 20 consecutive minutes. Simultaneously, the observer takes notes regarding the teachers' instructional behaviors and interactions, which are then used during the last 10 minutes of the observation cycle to establish a final rating score for each of the 11 scales. After assigning ratings the observer begins a new observation cycle. Scores are given for each scale along a 7-point Likert scale with a *low* (1, 2), *mid* (3, 4, 5), and *high* (6, 7) range. A raw score is derived for each scale on the CLASS measure.

The CLASS can be administered only by individuals who have received in-depth training and who have passed a reliability test. The creators of this assessment recommend that individuals trained to use the CLASS routinely check reliability to help maintain their ability. The CLASS provides standardized information regarding classroom quality from preschool through third grade, which can be used by professionals for research, accountability efforts, program planning and evaluation, and professional development and supervision.

In this section and those following, we discuss each of the domains as they relate to the procedural and structural constructs of classroom quality described previously. The CLASS manual includes contact information pertaining to CLASS training as well as detailed descriptions and examples of the 11 scales listed above.

The CLASS has been designed to create a common vocabulary that can be used to describe the quality of classroom *processes* in terms of its emotional support, the quality of instruction, and overall level of organization. The process by which the teacher interacts responsively with the children and also encourages peer-peer interaction is at the core of the CLASS and can be evaluated in most of the emotional support scales. This domain observes the climate of the classroom (both positive and negative), teacher sensitivity, and the teacher's regard for student perspectives.

The Positive and Negative Climate scales reflect the overall emotional tone and the connection between the teacher and the students. So, a teacher who rarely engages in social conversations with children and gives no genuine praise or verbal affection will gain a low rating. Conversely, a teacher who is genuinely interested in what the students have to say and allows time for laughter and conversation will gain a high rating. Teacher Sensitivity encompasses their responsiveness to the emotional as well as academic needs of the children in the classroom. To gain a high score, teachers need to be consistently responsive and scaffold conversations with children to encourage them to initiate and maintain conversations. Regard for Student Perspectives captures the degree to which the teacher-child interactions are focused on the students' interests. A teacher who is flexible and able to incorporate students' interests into his or her plans and who creates opportunities for children to talk will gain a high score.

In the Concept Development scale, the CLASS considers supports the teacher utilizes to promote higher order thinking during instructional discussions and related activities. The Instructional Learning Formats scale examines the strategies the teacher uses during instruction and/or in the provision of activities, centers, as well as the materials that maximize student engagement and learning. The Quality of Feedback scale focuses on teacher feedback that expands children's learning and understanding. The CLASS measures Student Engagement by considering the extent to which all students are attentive and actively participating in the lesson or activity.

A final aspect of instructional process that is central to a high-quality preschool environment is that of language facilitation, which is addressed most fully in the Language Modeling scale of the CLASS. This scale captures not only the amount but also the quality of teachers' use of language stimulation strategies. Teachers receive a high score if they intentionally ask open-ended questions, repeat and extend children's utterances, and use appropriately advanced language and vocabulary. This aspect of classroom quality can also be evaluated on the Concept Development and Instructional Learning Formats scales of the CLASS. In each of these scales, teachers who display high-quality input will engage students through developmentally appropriate questioning to facilitate language and learning.

The CLASS is exceptionally well equipped to evaluate procedural aspects of both language and literacy richness of the preschool learning environment. However, it is not a tool for self-evaluation and requires training in order to reliably rate classroom quality.

Creative Curriculum Implementation Checklist (Teaching Strategies, Inc., 2003)

The instructional processes construct of classroom language and literacy richness is addressed in a number of sections in the Creative Curriculum Implementation Checklist. There is an entire section dedicated to teacher-child interactions (section III), which examines building relationships, guiding children's behavior and guiding children's learning, as well as the teacher's ability to interact with children during specific curricular activities such as literacy, mathematics, and the arts. In this section, the construct is addressed in terms of both specific teacher strategies, (e.g., "do teachers listen attentively to what each child has to say and respond respectfully at the children's eye level?") and intentional elements of the daily routine (e.g., "do teachers provide opportunities for children to engage in drama spontaneously, and in groups?")

The Implementation Checklist Creative Curriculum also has some questions that address the construct of teacher-child interactions such as assessing the use of both large and small group time to allow for interactive experiences (section II, part B). The Checklist evaluates many aspects of teacher-child interactions but does not seek to measure peer interactions, or more precisely the strategies that teachers should be using to facilitate peer interaction as part of a language-rich preschool environment.

With regard to measuring the process of language and literacy instruction, the Creative Curriculum Implementation Checklist considers what the teacher does *before* instruction through the provision of varied content-related materials; what the teacher does *during* instruction within the context of daily routines, large and small group time, and teacher-child interactions; and what the teacher does *after* instruction through the use of analysis and the application of child assessments.

The Creative Curriculum Implementation Checklist specifically focuses on classroom setup and the teacher's provision of materials, as discussed in earlier sections. The Physical Environment subtest does not, however, measure the extent to which a child is engaged in language and literacy learning as a result of the teacher's instructional methods, although concept development is addressed in this subtest as evidenced by the teacher's inclusion of a variety of materials ranging from simple to complex to meet the varying ability levels of students and attention to labeling materials.

The Teacher-Child Interaction section directly measures teachers' strategies that target language and literacy skills. The Creative Curriculum Implementation Checklist addresses these strategies through items designed to determine, for example, whether teachers comment on or describe what they see and whether they teach new words during play; whether they offer suggestions and props as well as join in play; and whether they read books to individuals, large, and small groups daily.

With regard to what the teacher does after instruction, the Creative Curriculum Implementation Checklist includes a section on assessment. In contrast to the other sections of the checklist, which require direct observation, this section reviews teacher documentation for evidence of instructional processes. The assessor examines teacher's methods of observation and documentation, analysis and evaluation of children's progress, and use of assessment to plan for individual and group lessons. Items include evidence of an existing system for collecting objective and factual observational data and work samples for each student demonstrated by a place to store observation notes and portfolios for each child; the use of various assessment data to write weekly plans; and the evaluation and tracking of child progress as indicated by labeling notes and work samples with relevant Creative Curriculum objectives, summarizing collected data using individual child profile forms, class summary worksheets, and/or updating the Creative Curriculum's companion assessment tool.

Early Language and Literacy Classroom Observation Toolkit (ELLCO; Smith et al., 2002)

In terms of evaluating procedural aspects of the preschool classroom, the ELLCO has a number of questions in the Classroom Observation section measure of instructional processes such as intentional teacher-child interactions and language facilitation. For example, in question 6 under "Classroom Climate," teachers receive an "exemplary" score if they respect children's contributions, listen attentively, and encourage children to listen to each other. A "basic" score represents teachers who generally listen to children but do not intentionally encourage children to talk to each other, and a "deficient" score represents classrooms where children are expected to listen to the teacher with few opportunities for conversation and where the teacher is "distant" or "tuned out." Different aspects of teacher-child interactions are not addressed specifically in the ELLCO (e.g., differentiating interactions for children at different developmental levels, using a variety of devices to keep a conversation going, avoiding rhetorical, test, or yes/no questions); therefore, it does not provide a detailed measurement of this aspect of preschool classroom quality.

With respect to the quality of language facilitation in the classroom, the ELLCO addresses this in question 7, for which teachers receive an "exemplary score" when they demonstrate awareness of the differentiated oral language skills of the children in their classroom, and they plan activities to broaden the children's intellectual development through expanded language and vocabulary development. Teachers receive a "basic" score when they do not appear to have specific goals for expanding language development in their curriculum but make some effort to expand vocabulary, and they receive a "deficient" score if they rarely encourage children to use oral language and do not make efforts to expand children's vocabulary.

Items from the General Classroom Environment and Language, Literacy, and Curriculum portions of the Classroom Observation of the ELLCO measure teacher processes related to book reading, and the instruction of reading and writing. The book reading items consider teachers' approaches to book reading, including discussions, the use of a variety of settings and groupings, and coordinating book readings with ongoing curriculum themes and learning objectives. Items regarding reading instruction evaluate the use of teaching strategies to support children's comprehension skills and instruction tailored to meet the needs of each student. Items about writing instruction take into account approaches to writing that provide and support instruction as well as modeling and presenting opportunities for introducing various purposes/functions of writing. Also addressed is the presence and use of technology to support children's developing language and literacy skills, and the provision of materials and facilitation of student's active engagement.

The ELLCO is a useful tool for the evaluation of some aspects of preschool classroom procedures. It briefly covers areas such as teacher-child interactions, language stimulation techniques, and the quality of literacy instruction; however, as with other classroom checklist style observational tools, its strengths would appear to be in the evaluation of structural aspects of the classroom.

Observation Measures of Language and Literacy Instruction in Early Childhood (OMLIT; Goodson et al., 2004)

The OMLIT incorporates a battery of measures specifically designed to measure teachers' language and literacy instruction. The SNAP offers a brief but informative snapshot of daily classroom activities and the literacy resources that are incorporated into each activity. The CLIP presents a description of the specific literacy activities taking place in the classroom and records the instructional methods used by the teacher. Seven categories of information are gathered on the CLIP, which target the observed literacy activity, literacy knowledge presented, the teacher's instructional style, text support offered during instruction, the number of children participating in the activity, types of child talk, and teacher involvement with children. The RAP measures the instructional characteristics, specifically dialogic reading practices, utilized during individual, small group, or whole class read-alouds throughout the day. It consists of 12 items pertaining to the instructional strategies used during the prereading, reading, and postreading. The QUILL rates the frequency and overall quality of literacy instruction and the additional supports provided to foster language and literacy development.

Early Childhood Environment Rating Scale (Revised Edition) (ECERS-R; Harms et al., 1998).

The ECERS-R has a small range of items that measure teacher process in terms of teacher-child interactions and language facilitation. In the Language and Reasoning section, "encouraging children to communicate" includes descriptors across the range of the Likert scale. However ratings of 1 through 5 describe the *materials* and *activities* that may or may not be present, whereas a rating of 7-point describes possible *strategies* used by the teacher to encourage children to hold extended conversations that stimulate language and reasoning. In this respect a teacher may receive a rating of "good" (5 points) for supplying materials/activities, and another teacher may receive a rating of "excellent" (7 points) for using a conversation-promoting device such as waiting and giving a child ample time to respond.

The Interaction subsection also has several questions that address the social affect of interactions between adults and children and between peers. These do not directly measure the number or quality of exchanges that expressly promote extended conversations, but seek to reflect the intentionality of the staff to promote language and extend childrens' thinking. As described earlier, the ECERS-R was designed primarily as a tool for measuring the *physical* attributes of the preschool classroom; therefore, it does not appear to provide the depth of analysis necessary to evaluate quality issues with regard to teachers' classroom interactions with children.

In terms of instructional processes in the classroom, the ECERS has a section called Program Structure, which addresses scheduling and planning aspects of the school day. This seeks to identify the *intentional* use of time (e.g., in transitions), class groupings (e.g., the use of both large and small group instructional time) and levels of supervision (e.g., a mixture of free-play and supervised instructional time to scaffold learning). The descriptions that accompany the rating scale place emphasis on the more *structural* elements of program planning (i.e., on the materials provided, rather than the quality of the teachers' instructional input); therefore, a teacher who displays "excellent" scheduling will facilitate smooth transitions by making sure that the materials are ready for the next activity regardless of whether he or she uses that transition time for instructional purposes.

For each of the different activity areas (e.g., art, music, sensory play, dramatic play, math/number, etc.), the ECERS-R is designed to evaluate only the more structural aspects of the classroom, rather than the instructional or process-oriented aspects of the teachers input. Therefore, a teacher could achieve an "excellent" rating for math/number by providing counting materials that are rotated on a regular basis. The nature of instructional support in terms of a developmentally differentiated activity set up for use with the *same* materials is not considered within the scope of this assessment tool.

Teacher Interaction and Language Rating Scale (TILRS; Girolametto, Weitzman, & Greenberg, 2000)

The Teacher Interaction and Language Rating Scale (TILRS) was developed as part of an evaluation system for The Hanen Program *Learning Language and Loving It.* The 3-day course is available to speech-language pathologists and early childhood educators and is designed to train and promote the use of language and communication facilitation techniques in the preschool classroom. Details of the course and prerequisite qualifications can be found at http://www.hanen.org .

The authors of the Hanen Program state that any allied professional can purchase and use the TILRS rating scale, although a clear understanding of the scale and familiarity with the definition of items is important before using it (personal communication, April 20, 2006). We decided to include the rating scale in this chapter, (Girolametto, & Weitzman, 2003) because it is one of the few tools designed solely to capture the quality and frequency of teacher-child conversational interactions in a preschool setting.

The rating scale is designed to rate professionals' skills from a prerecorded 5-minute videotape of a regular classroom observation. The program *Learning Language and Loving It* is focused primarily on facilitation techniques to be used with a small group of children; therefore, the videotape should capture the adult engaged with children in a small group activity.

The 11 items used to rate the teacher-child interaction can be subdivided into three broad categories; (1) Child Centered Strategies, (*Wait and Listen, Follow the Child's Lead, Join in and Play,* and *Be Face to Face*), (2) Interaction Promoting Strategies (*Use a Variety of Questions, Encourage Verbal Turn Taking, Scan*), and (3) Language Promoting Strategies (*Imitate, Label, Expand, Extend*). (For greater detail on the 11 items, see Weitzman and Greenberg [2000].) The 7-point Likert scale is used to rate the adult's performance on these 11 strategies on a scale ranging from 1—almost never, to 3—sometimes, to 5—frequently, to 7—consistently. There is an additional rating of N/A that can be used if the strategy under consideration is not applicable (e.g., for a book reading activity *Join In and Play* is not often possible).

The observer uses the observation guide (available through the Hanen Organization) to rate the adult's appropriate use of 11 techniques using the 7-point Likert scale. Each of the 11 subsections is scored separately so that an individual's performance on a particular technique can be compared over time. In total an observation should take no more than 20 minutes to complete; however, this will vary depending on how familiar the observer is with the strategy descriptions and the rating scale.

It is important to note that the TILRS is not designed to be used by individual professionals for the rating and monitoring of *their own* use of language-facilitating strategies in the class. Instead, it is designed to be used by (preferably) trained supervisors or speech-language pathology colleagues to identify strengths and needs in the teacher's or assistant's use of language promoting and communication promoting skills in the preschool classroom setting. A rating of 5 or more is considered satisfactory; thus by using the scale over time, improvements can be recorded as a measure of one aspect of classroom quality.

The TILRS is devoted to the evaluation of adults' intentional interactions with children for the purpose of facilitating language and adult-child and peer interactions The first two subsections (child-centered strategies and interaction-promoting strategies) refer directly to this construct and evaluate the teacher's use of seven specific, intentional behaviors to encourage verbal interchanges of four or more turns between adult and child.

The third and final section of the TILRS is designed specifically to evaluate teachers' language facilitation techniques. The particular strategies measured include the adult's ability to imitate the vocalizations of very early language learners; use a wide range of labels (i.e., nouns, verbs, adjectives); avoid nonspecific words such as "this" and "it"; expand children's utterances by repeating and correcting the grammar or adding another idea; and extend conversations with children by using comments or questions to inform, pretend, project, or talk about the future.

Although the TILRS contains very detailed measurements for the evaluation of preschool classroom interaction, assessment of other instructional elements of the curriculum (e.g., literacy or numeracy concept development) is beyond the scope of this assessment tool. It is also important to remember that the TILRS has been used primarily as a research tool has not yet undergone rigorous statistical analysis to evaluate its psychometric properties.

Special Considerations for Assessing Classroom Language and Literacy Richness

Assessing the language and literacy environment of early childhood classrooms is not without its limitations. Each of the measures described in this chapter is "observational" in nature or reliant on teachers' self-reporting of classroom processes. Although some are explicit about what constitutes evidence of a particular characteristic, others are defined more openly. This leaves room for differing interpretations and biased representation of the environment being evaluated. Some measures, such as the CLASS, require formal training and reliability procedures; others have no such means of ensuring quality and consistency between observers.

A further consideration is the reliability and validity of the assessment tools used to evaluate the quality or richness of a classroom environment. Despite widespread use, many of the measures described in this chapter have not been subjected to a thorough examination of their psychometric properties. This means that the individual constructs that each test claims to measure have not undergone factor analysis to ensure that each one is indeed unique. Resent research on the psychometric properties of the ECERS-R (Perlman et al., 2004), for instance, has found that it does not measure seven distinct aspects of quality as suggested, but instead measures one global aspect of quality. The overlap, or correlation, between the different items of the measures, was found to be strong, suggesting that only one dimension of the classroom is really being measured. Inevitably, certain aspects of an educational establishment are likely to cluster together; however, when every item is correlated, clearly some elements of the class are not being measured uniquely.

Evaluation of the language and literacy richness of classrooms also is limited by a gap in available literature (Pianta, 2003) and measures regarding the quality and type of literacy-related instruction. Consequently, none of the measures fully evaluates the procedural aspects of a language- and literacy-rich environment as we have described it in this chapter. Furthermore, none of the measures presented in this chapter addresses *all* the constructs of language and literacy richness. However, these measures can be used to monitor progress, demonstrate improvements, and aid in the design of effective language- and literacy-rich classrooms.

Interpreting the Results of Assessments of Classroom Language and Literacy Richness

The measures presented in this chapter provide opportunities for teachers, administrators, and researchers to set up improved learning environments, inform practice, and guide program improvements (see Table 1-3 for uses of each measure). As documented in our introduction to this chapter, research supports the principles that have been used to define many of the items on these measures of language and literacy richness. However, each of these measures provides only raw or average scores as there are yet no standards for scores on these measures. Additionally, many of the items on these measures merely document the presence or absence of specific features but do not determine whether and how children actually benefit from the features.

Ultimately, the interpretation one gives to the assessments of language and literacy richness in the preschool classroom depends on the intended use of the instrument. For example, the results may be used by administrators to identify the professional development needs of their staff; they may be used for research purposes to compare different practices or practitioners; or they may be used by policy makers to determine which services receive continued funding (or not) depending on the outcome. The latter scenario describes "high-stakes" testing, which is an increasing feature of educational reform in the United States (Meisels, 2006); therefore, a clear understanding of the strengths and pitfalls of quality measures is essential. In the case of the ECERS-R, which primarily addresses the structural aspects of the learning environment, improvements in the overall score of a classroom could be achieved simply by improving the quality and quantity of classroom materials. Although this is undeniably important, other aspects of the classroom would remain unchanged, such as the process items (e.g., the teacher's presentation of materials and information during instructional time). And it is precisely these process items of the ECERS-R that have been shown to consistently relate to children's gains in skills (Pianta, 2003).

Research on the effects of classroom language and literacy richness on child outcomes is relatively new. However, as we have discussed in this chapter, the positive impact of each characteristic of a language- and literacy-rich classroom is supported by available research. Although none of the measures discussed single-handedly assesses all of these characteristics, in combination, they do provide a means of determining the language- and literacy-richness of preschool classrooms.

References

Barker, R. G. (1968). *Ecological psychology: Concepts and methods for studying the environment of human behavior*. Stanford, CA: Stanford University Press.

Barnett, W. S. (1995). Long-term effects of early childhood programs on cognitive and school outcomes. *Future of Children*, 5, 25–50.

Bohannon, J., & Bonvillian, J. (1997). Theoretical approaches to language acquisition. In J. Berko Gleason (Ed.), *The development of language* (4th ed., pp. 259–316). Needham Heights, MA: Allyn & Bacon.

Bredekamp, S. (1987). *Developmentally appropriate practices in early childhood programs: Serving children from birth through age 8*. Washington, DC: National Association for the Education of Young Children.

Christie, J., Enz, B., & Vukelich, C. (2003). *Teaching language and literacy: Preschool through the elementary grades* (2nd ed.). Boston: Pearson Education.

Conti-Ramsden, G. (1990). Maternal recasts and other contingent replies to language impaired children. *Journal of Speech and Hearing Disorders*, 55, 262–274.

Dickinson, D. K. (2003). Are measures of "global quality" sufficient? *Educational Researcher*, *32*, 27–28.

Dickenson, D. K., & DiGisi, L. (1998). The many rewards of a literacy rich classroom. *Educational Leadership*, *55*(6), 23–26.

Dodge, D.T., L. Colker, & C. Heroman. 2002. *The creative curriculum for early childhood* (4th ed.). Washington, DC: Teaching Strategies.

Dowhower, S. L., & Beagle, K. G. (1998). The print environment in kindergartens: A study of conventional and holistic teachers and their classrooms in three settings. *Reading Research and Instruction*, *37*, 161–190.

Dunsmuir, S., & Blatchford, P. (2004). Predictors of writing competence in four to seven year old children. *British Journal of Educational Psychology*, *74*(3), 461–483.

Fractor, J., Woodruff, M., Martinez, M., & Teale, W. (1993). Let's not miss opportunities to promote voluntary reading: Classroom libraries in the elementary classroom. *The Reading Teacher*, *46*, 476–483.

Girolametto, L., Hoaken, L., Weitzman, E., & van Lieshout, R. (2000). Patterns of adult-child linguistic interaction in integrated day care groups. *Language, Speech and Hearing Services in Schools*, *31*, 155–168.

Girolametto, L., & Weitzman, E. (2002). Responsiveness of child care providers in interactions with toddlers and preschoolers. *Language, Speech and Hearing Services in Schools*, *33*, 268–281.

Girolametto, L., & Weitzman, E. (2003). Training day care staff to facilitate children's language. *American Journal of Speech-Language Pathology*, *12*, 299–311.

Girolametto, L., Weitzman, E., & Greenberg, J. (2000). *Teacher Interaction and Language Rating Scale.* Toronto, Ontario, Canada: The Hanen Centre.

Goodson, B. D., Layzer, C. J., & Smith, W. C. (2004). *Observation measures of language and literacy instruction in early childhood (OMLIT).* Cambridge, MA: Abt Associates.

Harms, T., & Clifford, R. (1980). *Early Childhood Environment Rating Scale.* New York: Teachers College Press.

Harms, T., Clifford, R., & Cryer, D. (1998). *Early Childhood Environment Rating Scale* (Rev. ed.). New York: Teachers College Press.

Hart, B., & Risley, T. (1995). *Meaningful differences in the everyday lives of American children.* Baltimore: Paul H. Brookes.

Heft, H. (2001). *Ecological psychology in context.* Mahwah, NJ: Lawrence Erlbaum Associates.

Helmke, A., & Schrader, F. W. (1988). Successful student practice during seatwork: Efficient management and active supervision are not enough. *Journal of Educational Research*, *82*, 70–75.

Hoffman, J. V. (2001). The TEX-IN3: *Text Inventory, Text In-Use and Text Interview Observation System.* Unpublished manuscript, University of Texas at Austin.

Howes, C., Phillipsen, L., & Peisner-Feinberg, C. (2000). The consistency and predictability of teacher-child relationships during the transition to kindergarten. *Journal of School Psychology, 38*(2), 113–132.

International Reading Association (IRA) and National Association for the Education of Young Children (NAEYC). (1998). *Learning to read and write: Developmentally appropriate practices for young children— A joint position statement of the IRA and NAEYC.* Washington, DC: Authors.

Johnston, P. H., & Rogers, R. (2002). Early literacy development: The case for "informed assessment." In S. B. Neuman & D. K. Dickinson (Eds.), *Handbook of early literacy research* (pp. 377–389). New York: The Guilford Press.

Justice, L. M. (2004). Creating language-rich preschool classroom environments. *Teaching Exceptional Children, 37,* 36–44.

La Paro, K. M., & Pianta, R. C. (2000). Predicting children's competence in the early school years: A meta-analytic review. *Review of Educational Research, 70*(4), 443–484.

Lonigan, C. J., & Whitehurst, G. J. (1998). Relative efficacy of parent and teacher involvement in a shared-reading intervention for preschool children from low-income backgrounds. *Early Childhood Research Quarterly, 17,* 265–292.

Matsumura, L. C., Patthey-Chavez, G. G., Valdes, R., & Garnier, H. (2002). Teacher feedback, writing assignment quality, and third-grade students' revision in higher and lower achieving schools. *The Elementary School Journal, 103,* 3–25.

McGee, L. M., & Richgels, D. J. (2003). *Designing early literacy programs: Strategies for at-risk preschool and kindergarten children.* New York: Guilford Press.

McGee, L. M., & Richgels, D. J. (2004). *Literacy's beginnings: Supporting young readers and writers* (4th ed.). Needham, MA: Allyn & Bacon.

McGill-Franzen, A., Allington, R. L., Yokoi, L., & Brooks, G. (1999). Putting books in the room seems necessary but not sufficient. *Journal of Educational Research, 93*(2), 67–74.

Meisels, S. J., (2006) *Accountability in early childhood: No easy answers.* Occasional Paper. Chicago: Erikson Institute for Advanced Study of Child Development.

Morrow, L. M. (1990). Preparing the classroom environment to promote literacy during play. *Early Childhood Research Quarterly, 5,* 537–554.

Morrow, L. M. (2005). *Literacy development in the early years: Helping children read and write* (5th ed.). Boston: Allyn & Bacon.

Morrow, L. M., & Smith, J. K. (1990). The effects of group size on interactive storybook reading. *Reading Research Quarterly, 25*(3), 213–231.

Morrow, L. M., & Weinstein, C. S. (1982). Increasing children's use of literature through program and physical design changes. *The Elementary School Journal*, *83*, 131–137.

National Association for the Education of Young Children (NAEYC). (1991). *Accreditation criteria and procedures of the National Academy of Early Childhood Programs.* Washington, DC: Author.

Neuman, S. B. (1996). Children engaging in storybook reading: The influence of access to print resources, opportunity and parental interaction. *Early Childhood Research Quarterly*, *11*, 495–514.

Neuman, S. B. (1999). Books make a difference: A study of access to literacy. *Reading Research Quarterly*, *34*, 286–311.

Neuman, S. B., & Roskos, K. (1989).Preschoolers' conceptions of literacy as reflected in their spontaneous play. In S. McCormick & J. Zutell (Eds.), *Cognitive and social perspectives for literacy research and instruction* (pp. 87–94). Chicago: National Reading Conference.

Neuman, S., & Roskos, K. (Eds.). (1990). *The influence of literacy-enriched play settings on preschoolers' engagement with written language.* Chicago: National Reading Conference.

Neuman, S., & Roskos, K. (1992). Literary objects as cultural tools: Effects on children's literacy behaviors. *Reading Research Quarterly*, *27*(3), 202–225.

Perlman, M., Zellman, G. L., & Le, V. (2004) Examining the psychometric properties of the Early Childhood Environment Rating Scale-Revised (ECERS-R). *Early Childhood Research Quarterly*, *19*, 398–412.

Pianta, R. C. (2003). *Standardized classroom observations from pre-K to third grade: A mechanism for improving quality classroom experiences during the P-3 years.* Retrieved May 5, 2006, from: http://www.fcdus.org/uploaddocs/standardizedclrmobsfrompre-kto3rdfinal.doc

Pianta, R. C., La Paro, K. M., & Hamre, B.K. (2005). *Classroom Assessment Scoring System [CLASS].* Charlottesville: University of Virginia, Charlottesville.

Roskos, K., & Christie, J. (2001). Examining the play–literacy interface: A critical review and future directions. *Journal of Early Childhood Literacy*, *1*, 59–89.

Smith, M. W., Dickinson, D. K., Sangeorge, A., & Anastasopoulos, L. (2002). *Early language and literacy classroom observation toolkit.* Baltimore: Paul H. Brookes.

Snow, C. E., Barnes, W. S., Chandler, J., Goodman, I. F., & Hemphill, L. (1991). *Home and school influences on literacy.* Cambridge, MA: Harvard University Press.

Snow, C. E., Burns, S., & Griffin, P. (Eds.). (1998). *Preventing reading difficulties in young children.* Washington, DC: National Academy Press.

Teaching Strategies, Inc. (2003). *Creative curriculum for preschool imple-mentation checklist.* Washington, DC: Author.

Tizzard, B., & Hughes, M. (1984). *Young children learning.* London: Fontana.

Vedeler, L. (1997). Dramatic play: A format for "literate" language? *The British Journal of Educational Psychology, 67,* 153-167.

Vukelich, C. (1990). Where's the paper? Literacy during dramatic play. *Childhood Education, 66,* 205-209.

Vukelich, C. (1991). Materials and modeling: Promoting literacy during play. In J. F. Christie (Ed.), *Play and early literacy development* (pp. 215-231). Albany, NY: SUNY Press.

Vukelich, C., & Christie, J. (2004). *Building a foundation for preschool literacy: Effective instruction for children's reading and writing development.* Newark, DE: International Reading Association.

Vygotsky, L. S. (1978). *Mind in society: The development of higher psychological processes.* Cambridge, MA: Harvard University Press.

Walpole, S., & McKenna, M. C. (2004). *The literacy coach's handbook: A guide to research-based practice.* New York: The Guilford Press.

Wolfersberger, M. E., Reutzel, D. R., Sudweeks, R., & Fawson, P. C. (2004). Developing and validating the classroom literacy environmental profile (CLEP): A tool for examining the "print richness" of early childhood and elementary classrooms. *Journal of Literacy Research, 36*(2), 211-272.

Weitzman, E., & Greenberg, J. (2002). *Learning language and loving it* (2nd ed.). Toronto: The Hanen Centre.

Chapter 2

Assessing Professionals' Knowledge and Skills

Marcia R. Davidson
Paula F. Moore

> *"Oh, magic hour, when a child first knows she can read printed words!"*
> —*A Tree Grows in Brooklyn*, 1943

The Importance of Teacher Knowledge to Emergent Literacy

Teacher knowledge is widely acknowledged to be of critical importance in the provision of effective emergent literacy instruction, yet the research base has not provided clarity with regard to what teachers must know about literacy and language in order to teach young children to read. In *Preventing Reading Difficulties in Young Children*, Snow, Burns, and Griffin (1998) called for enhanced teacher preparation so that more young children would become successful readers. Although a rich body of evidence identifies the critical skills children must have to learn to read, research that makes a strong connection between child learning outcomes and the requisite teacher knowledge and skills in emergent and early literacy is sparse. There is considerable research on teacher education and professional development that is "based in the wisdom of practice and in systematic reviews of successful preservice and inservice teacher education programs" (Snow, Griffin, & Burns, 2005, pp. 1-2). However, we currently do not have a strong research base that clearly links student learning outcomes to carefully manipulated variables in teacher preparation or professional development. Still, given the increasing demand for skilled teachers in early childhood, one cannot wait until the research base is able to fully inform teacher preparation programs. Thus, we must rely on recommendations and the emerging research base for preparing preschool teachers to effectively teach young children emergent and early literacy skills, and link the research evidence in our recursive efforts to improve and enhance the learning opportunities in teacher preparation and professional development.

This chapter addresses preschool teacher knowledge and skills in the teaching of literacy to young children. We will review the types of knowledge teachers acquire as they progress from novices to experts, describe current measures of teacher knowledge, and provide a template for a teacher knowledge assessment that encompasses the literacy and language knowledge we consider essential for teachers of young children.

Types of Knowledge Teachers Acquire in the Process of Developing Expertise

As teachers progress from novice to expert in their teaching experience, the notion of progressive differentiation (Snow et al., 2005) provides a framework for the process of building knowledge and skills in teaching. There are five steps in this process, with their relative emphases changing over time.

Declarative knowledge is the first step, typically being acquired during a teacher certification program. Declarative knowledge means knowledge about something, for example, the developmental processes of learning to read. The next step is a "situated" (Snow et al., 2005) procedural knowledge in which a novice teacher refines his or her knowledge through interactions with children or a mentor teacher. Situated procedural knowledge requires a teacher to know how to do something in a particular situation, for example, how to teach a small group of typically developing children the concept of rhyme during center time.

The third step in the progression from novice to expert teacher is stable procedural knowledge in which a teacher can successfully teach a typical group of children, but may need assistance in meeting the needs of children with unique needs. The fourth step is expert, adaptive knowledge, a role that includes leadership among teachers, as well as strong skills in teaching children with a variety of learning needs. Teachers who have acquired expert, adaptive knowledge incorporate research-based knowledge into their classrooms and mentor novice teachers.

Reflective, organized, analyzed knowledge is the fifth step in the process of developing teaching expertise. Teachers who reach this final phase are able to analyze what they have learned and evaluate its efficacy based on a rich knowledge of the research. These teachers are often leaders in professional development or consultants in their fields (Snow, et al., 2005).

All five steps in the process of developing teaching expertise are linked with a teacher's career progression (i.e., progressing from preservice or apprentice to novice to experienced to master teacher). The relative emphasis of the five steps is different at each level of a teacher's career progression, with preservice and apprentice teachers focusing largely on declarative knowledge and master teachers emphasizing reflective practice.

Although these steps provide a framework for following the development of teacher knowledge over time, current assessment tools typically focus on dimensions that are more static and reflect teacher knowledge at one point in time. The next section examines some of the challenges to developing measures of teacher knowledge of emergent literacy and language development.

Measures for Assessing Teacher Knowledge

One dilemma in attempting to develop measures of teacher knowledge or cognition is the phenomenon referred to as the Goldilocks effect (Katz & Raths, 1985 in Kagan, 1990). That is, some concepts of teaching are too large or vague to be applied in a concrete manner, and some are too small or specific to provide a reasonable application. As an example of the latter, providing an observer with a long list of specific teacher behaviors to identify constitutes breaking teaching into potentially uninformative narrow and discrete acts. Achieving a reasonable balance between skills that are too discrete to represent core knowledge and skills that are so broad that it is difficult to define them in observable terms is a challenge in assessing teacher knowledge.

In recent years, there has been increased interest in what teachers know about teaching reading and the structure of language. Recent federal legislation such as the No Child Left Behind Act emphasizes the importance of quality preschool classrooms and the role of effective literacy instruction in preventing reading difficulties. The role of scientific research-based practices is highlighted in initiatives such as Reading First and Early Reading First, and funding of these efforts requires states and local agencies to define a plan that incorporates current research findings, including effective classroom practices in emergent and early literacy instruction. However, there are no standardized measures for assessing preschool teachers' skills in contributing to young children's literacy acquisition that could be included in an accountability system that examines classroom quality. Still, a number of teacher knowledge assessments and classroom observation instruments are being studied currently. Some show great promise in informing the field about critical features in assessing the quality of emergent literacy instruction in preschool classrooms.

We begin with a review of current standards for teacher knowledge at the preschool level, as well as current research on what young children need to learn in order to become successful readers. Next, we consider several pencil-and-paper assessments of teacher content knowledge and practice. Finally, we recommend guidelines for an effective instrument to assess professionals in emergent literacy learning/teaching contexts.

A Framework for Examining Teacher Content Knowledge of Emergent Literacy Reading and Language

Although the disciplines of math and science have focused on teacher content knowledge for a number of years, teacher content knowledge in reading is a fairly new area of research. One explanation is that reading is not a discipline, making it difficult to define "content." Another possibility is that, because all teachers read competently, there has been less concern about reading than about math or science skills. Third, knowledge in reading traditionally has emphasized the psychology of reading, learning reading curricula, and the pedagogy of reading instruction (Phelps & Schilling, 2004).

There is new interest in the content knowledge required for the effective teaching of reading (Learning First Alliance/America Federation of Teachers, 1998; National Institute of Child Health and Human Development, 2000; National Reading Panel, 2000; Snow et al., 1998). Most of the current research focuses on teacher skills in teaching phonics and phonological awareness (e.g., McCutchen et al., 2002; McCutchen & Berninger, 1999; Moats, 2000). Findings from recent studies suggest that teachers lack understanding of a variety of important linguistic concepts such as an awareness of onset-rimes, phoneme segmentation, derivational affixes, inflected verbs, morphemes, and how spelling patterns represent sounds in words.

Because current research on how children learn to read includes substantial evidence for the importance of phonological awareness, word analysis/phonics, spelling, vocabulary, comprehension, and other components of the structure of language, it makes sense to expect that teachers understand this content well in order to teach it effectively. However, the assumption that being able to read competently equates to being able to teach another how to read competently simply ignores the great complexities in teaching children the prerequisite emergent literacy skills required to read words and to comprehend text at a later time. Teachers must have a conscious awareness of the details of emergent literacy, details that ordinarily represent tacit knowledge for adults. They then must know effective strategies for explicitly teaching these skills to young children. Being a proficient reader does not necessarily mean that one understands the structure of language or that one can unpack the process of reading in an explicit manner.

Content knowledge in the details of learning to read includes a variety of knowledge domains. For example, this book includes chapters addressing print knowledge, vocabulary, phonological awareness, narrative development, and literacy motivation. These topics require that teachers not only possess substantive declarative knowledge in these content domains, but also that they can apply this procedural knowledge appropriately in a variety of contexts. In a project that developed survey measures of the content knowledge of reading, Phelps and Schilling (2004) created three distinct components of teacher content knowledge required for teaching reading: knowledge of content, knowledge of students and content, and knowledge of teaching and content (p. 36). These categories differ primarily in the manner in which content knowledge is related to teaching. For example, if a teacher, Ms. Smith, knows what phonemic awareness is and she asks a child to tell her if the words "play" and "pat" begin with the same sound, she is demonstrating some level of content knowledge in phonemic awareness. However, to be an effective teacher, she must also be able to respond to a child, Jamie, when he says that "play" and "pat" do *not* begin with the same sound. She needs to know about Jamie's strengths and weaknesses and how to follow up to make sure he understands and accurately hears the individual sounds in words. That understanding is knowledge of students and content. Knowledge of teaching and content requires that Ms. Smith use her knowledge of content and her teaching skills to decide how to teach Jamie phonemic awareness skills. In their study, Phelps and Schilling (2004) found that it was important for teachers to know about children's current skills and abilities, their background knowledge, how to predict student responses, strategies to scaffold and build students' understanding, and how to determine how much practice students need to learn a concept. Teachers, they hypothesized, have to know the contexts, interactions, and practices that together define the effective teaching of reading. According to Phelps and Schilling (2004), the enterprise of teaching young children to read is necessarily complex, requiring a high level of teacher skills in three content domains, as illustrated in Table 2–1.

The authors developed a pilot teacher survey of 261 items from these three types of knowledge related to teaching reading. The survey was administered to 1,542 teachers in California, and after initial analyses, a follow-up survey with fewer items was administered to 599 teachers (most of whom had also participated in the pilot survey). The research questions focused on whether there were clearly identifiable dimensions that captured the content knowledge for teaching reading and whether it was possible to create a valid and reliable measure of this knowledge. Results indicated that the dimension of knowledge of teaching and content performed best in identifying more knowledgeable teachers,

Table 2-1. Three Domains of Teacher Content Knowledge Required for Teaching Reading

Knowledge of Content	*Knowledge of Students*	*Knowledge of Teaching and Content*
Knowledge of:	Interpreting students:	Teaching students to:
1. Phonemic awareness: initial sounds 2. Dialogic reading	3. Error in recognizing that beginning sounds are the same. 4. Responses to queries about a read-aloud.	5. Recognize words that begin with the same sound. 6. Provide elaborated responses to queries.

Source: Adapted from "Developing Measures of Content Knowledge for Teaching Reading," by G. Phelps & S. Schilling, 2004, *The Elementary School Journal, 105*(1), 31–47.

whereas the knowledge of content dimension worked better with less knowledgeable teachers. This is not surprising, as knowledgeable teachers are more likely to have a deeper understanding of teaching as it relates to the content being taught. The authors also found that content knowledge for reading is composed of several domains rather than a "general" reading domain. In their study, Phelps and Schilling identified word analysis and comprehension as defining two primary reading content domains for elementary teachers. This suggests that teachers must develop knowledge across a variety of domains comprising reading content. One example of emergent literacy content domains at the preschool level is the Head Start Child Outcomes Framework (2003), which is presented in detail later in this chapter.

Although the authors expected to find that knowledge of content and knowledge of teaching and content would overlap, that was not the case. They examined the data on one of the content dimensions of teaching reading and found that the knowledge of content as it applies to particular children in a specific teaching situation is different from a general knowledge of how to teach reading.

For teachers of young children, this study has important implications. It is likely that content knowledge alone will not be sufficient to represent the critical domains necessary for teaching young children emergent literacy skills. Knowing about the students, the general knowledge of teaching literacy to young children, and how to effectively teach specific content in a particular situation together comprise the critical domains of teacher knowledge and skills.

The next section examines several surveys of teacher knowledge that focus exclusively on content knowledge in the area of word analysis. These pencil-and-paper knowledge surveys of emergent literacy and language development include content considered to be essential knowledge for teaching reading in the primary elementary grades and the measures emphasize the importance of elements of the structure of language and word study. Although the measures included were not designed specifically for preschool teachers, the Teacher Knowledge and Skills Survey (Cunningham, 2003) has been piloted with preschool teachers.

Teacher knowledge surveys that address the content of reading often focus on the language and text variables critical to teaching young children to decode (Phelps & Schilling, 2004). Examples of item types from several surveys include the following topics: phoneme identification, phoneme segmentation, onset-rime differentiation, knowledge of morphemes, structural analysis, and so forth. (Cunningham, 2001; Moats, 1994). Researchers hypothesize that there may be an important relation between teacher performance on these knowledge assessments and student achievement. The assumption is that teachers who do not possess a substantive understanding of the structure of language will not be as effective in teaching young children these skills. A summary of several of the studies examining the relation between teacher content knowledge of reading and student achievement follows.

In a recent study (Spear-Swerling, Brucker, & Alfano, 2005), researchers administered a survey that addressed graduate teacher-education students' perceptions of their literacy-related knowledge followed by the completion of five tasks that measured their content knowledge in these areas. Level of preparation and teaching experience positively related to self-perceptions and knowledge, and teacher education students who reported high levels of reading-related background perceived themselves as more knowledgeable on three areas of knowledge: phonemic awareness and phonics, morpheme awareness and structural analysis, and general knowledge about reading and reading development. Students with more preparation and teaching experience also outperformed those with less preparation and experience on five early literacy knowledge tasks: general knowledge, morpheme task, pseudoword task, identification of phonetically irregular words task, and a grapho-phonemic segmentation task.

A teacher survey designed by Moats (1994; Moats & Foorman, 2003) found that few teachers possessed high levels of knowledge in either phonics or phonological awareness. Student achievement was not examined in these studies. In their 2003 study, Moats and Foorman found that teachers in grades K–4 had particular difficulties in differentiation of speech sounds from letters, often were unsuccessful in detecting the identity of phonemes in words, and did not understand spelling units such as digraphs, blends, or diphthongs. Syllable division was another problematic area for the teachers surveyed. In general, teachers lacked understanding of the ways in which the key components of reading instruction are related to one another.

The Teacher Knowledge and Attitude Survey (TKAS; Cunningham, 2001) addresses teacher content knowledge in literacy and is similar to the knowledge assessed in the Moats and Foorman survey, although it also includes a component that addresses teachers' knowledge of children's literature. Cunningham's survey was developed for teachers in grades K–3 and includes three domains of knowledge in early literacy: children's literature, phonological awareness, and phonics. Results of a study surveying 722 kindergarten through third grade elementary teachers from a large urban school district indicated that the knowledge base of the surveyed teachers in the three domains generally was not aligned with what current research indicates to be important early literacy content knowledge (Cunningham, Perry, Stanovich, & Stanovich, 2004).

Although student achievement was not addressed in this study, McCutcheon et al. (2002) demonstrated that kindergarten and first-grade teachers' increased understanding of phonology and spelling patterns positively influenced teachers' instructional practices and children's outcomes. Researchers provided training to teachers in phonological and orthographic awareness during a 2-week summer institute after which teachers were followed throughout the school year with assessment of teacher practices and student learning. Findings indicated that teachers' knowledge of the role of phonological and orthographic information in teaching early literacy skills improved as did their practice and student learning.

There is little research on teacher knowledge in the preschool setting. In a recent study (Davidson, Yang, & Cunningham, 2006), 28 preschool teachers completed a revised version of the Teacher Knowledge and Skills Survey (Cunningham, 2001) and a relationship between teacher knowledge and student achievement was not found. The hypothesis proposed earlier (Phelps & Schilling, 2004), that content knowledge differs from knowledge of the content and teaching may help in understanding why preschool teachers' scores on the Teacher Knowledge and Attitude Survey were not related to children's achievement outcomes. Teachers have to know how to take content knowledge and develop effective instruction with children who will likely demonstrate a range of skills and instructional needs. The interplay of content knowledge, knowledge of children, and the application of content knowledge in the context of effective instruction more accurately captures what is meant by teacher knowledge and skills than does content knowledge alone. Clearly, more research is needed to determine how teacher content knowledge informs and is affected by classroom teaching and knowledge of individual children.

Identifying the content knowledge in emergent literacy that is critical for preschool teachers is a first step in developing a framework for evaluating teacher knowledge and skills. One example of a content framework is the Head Start Child Outcomes Framework (Head Start, 2003), which includes four domain elements and nine indicators in language, literacy, and numeracy skills. The literacy skills are listed below:

Head Start Child Outcomes Framework: Literacy

- LANGUAGE DEVELOPMENT
  - Listening and Understanding
    - Demonstrates increasing ability to attend to and understand conversations, stories, songs, and poems.
    - Shows progress in understanding and following simple and multiple-step directions.

- Understands an increasingly complex and varied vocabulary.
- For non-English-speaking children, progresses in listening to and understanding English.
  - Speaking and Communicating
    - Develops increasing abilities to understand and use language to communicate information, experiences, ideas, feelings, opinions, needs, questions; and for other varied purposes.
    - Progresses in abilities to initiate and respond appropriately in conversation and discussions with peers and adults.
    - Uses an increasingly complex and varied spoken vocabulary.
    - Progresses in clarity of pronunciation and towards speaking in sentences of increasing length and grammatical complexity.
    - For non-English-speaking children, progresses in speaking English.

- LITERACY
  - Phonological Awareness
    - Shows increasing ability to discriminate and identify sounds in spoken language.
    - Shows growing awareness of beginning and ending sounds of words.
    - Progresses in recognizing matching sounds and rhymes in familiar words, games, songs, stories, and poems.
    - Shows growing ability to hear and discriminate separate syllables in words.
    - Associates sounds with written words, such as awareness that different words begin with the same sound.
  - Book Knowledge
    - Shows growing interest and involvement in listening to and discussing a variety of fiction and non-fiction books and poetry.
    - Shows growing interest in reading-related activities, such as asking to have a favorite book read; choosing to look at books; drawing pictures based on stories; asking to take books home; going to the library; and engaging in pretend-reading with other children.
    - Demonstrates progress in abilities to retell and dictate stories from books and experiences; to act out stories in dramatic play; and to predict what will happen next in a story.
    - Progresses in learning how to handle and care for books; knowing to view one page at a time in sequence from front to back; and understanding that a book has a title, author, and illustrator.

- ○ Print Awareness and Concepts
  - ▪ Shows increasing awareness of print in classroom home, and community settings.
  - ▪ Develops growing understanding of the different functions of forms of print such as signs, letters, newspapers, lists, messages, and menus.
  - ▪ Demonstrates increasing awareness of concepts of print, such as that reading in English moves from top to bottom and from left to right, that speech can be written down, and that print conveys a message.
  - ▪ Shows progress in recognizing the association between spoken and written words by following print as it is read aloud.
  - ▪ Recognizes a word as a unit of print, or awareness that letters are grouped to form words, and that words are separated by spaces.
- ○ Early Writing
  - ▪ Develops understanding that writing is a way of communicating for a variety of purposes.
  - ▪ Begins to represent stories and experiences through pictures, dictation, and in play.
  - ▪ Experiments with a growing variety of writing tools and materials, such as pencils, crayons, and computers.
  - ▪ Progresses from using scribbles, shapes, or pictures to represent ideas, to using letter-like symbols, to copying or writing familiar words such as their own name.
- ○ Alphabet Knowledge
  - ▪ Shows progress in associating the names of letters with their shapes and sounds.
  - ▪ Increases in ability to notice the beginning letters in familiar words.
  - ▪ Identifies at least 10 letters of the alphabet, especially those in their own name.
  - ▪ Knows that letters of the alphabet are a special category of visual graphics that can be individually named.

In addition to the Head Start Child Outcomes in Early Literacy listed above, the National Early Literacy Panel (Strickland & Shanahan, 2004) identified the key characteristics of children from birth to 7 that are most strongly related to later reading success: oral language development, phonological awareness, concepts about print, alphabet knowledge, and invented spelling, all of which are included in the Head Start Child Outcomes list. Preschool teachers need to know the content in each of the domains listed. Furthermore, preschool teachers need to demonstrate knowledge of teaching young children, that is, the knowledge of students mentioned in the Phelps and Schilling (2004) framework. For example, teachers need to know how to respond to young children's confusion with new concepts. They need to know how much practice children need to learn new skills and the requisite skills that need to be in place prior to introducing a new concept. Student knowledge in conjunction with knowledge of content and knowledge of teaching and content can be difficult to measure. One approach to assessing teacher knowledge and skills is an assessment that provides enough background information to allow the teacher respondent to identify the best response in a situated context. A measure that includes content knowledge, knowledge of students, and knowledge of teaching and content should provide a more balanced perspective of teacher knowledge and skills than content knowledge alone. Further, by combining these domains in a survey for teachers, it is likely to more accurately capture the skills of both beginning and more knowledgeable teachers. Appendix 2 includes an example of a teacher knowledge and skills survey that incorporates content knowledge through a series of selected and constructed response items and student and teaching knowledge through selected responses to specific case scenarios.

Special Considerations for Assessing Teacher Knowledge

The next section addresses the assessment of teacher knowledge through classroom observations. Because there are a number of observation instruments that focus on classroom quality, print-rich environments, and so forth, this section will focus specifically on two instruments that focus primarily on teacher knowledge and skills, the CLASS and the CLASSIC.

Classroom Observation Instruments

Observational measures at the preschool level typically involve rating the classroom on a variety of dimensions that evaluate quality. For example, the Early Childhood Environment Rating Scale

(ECERS-R Harms, Clifford, & Cryer, 1998) assesses the global quality of the classroom environment (Ferrar, 1996; Love, Meckstroth, & Sprachman, 1997). However, the ECERS-R does not provide any detailed observational data on teacher-student literacy interactions that may be important to young children's growth in key emergent literacy skills. Such information is critical to meet the increasing demand for accountability at all levels of education including preschool. Currently, accountability largely rests with assessing student achievement, but it is also important to identify teacher behaviors that contribute to strong student literacy outcomes.

Current research has established that high-quality instruction and interactions with adults in the classroom in prekindergarten settings have a positive impact on children's achievement (e.g., Barnett, 1995, 2004; Vellutino & Scanlon, 2001). Thus, it follows that, in a system of educational accountability that begins in the prekindergarten years, standardized measures of classroom quality should be in place.

Current research on classroom quality at the prekindergarten level reveals remarkable variability in quality and nature of teacher practices across classrooms with instructional quality being, on average, fairly low (Pianta & La Paro, 2003). Studies that have examined the prekindergarten classroom have found that a typical classroom provides "instruction delivered in a whole-group setting, a positive social environment, and low levels of child productivity and engagement in academic activities" (Pianta & La Paro, 2003, p. 9). Systematic tools that measure classroom quality and teacher behavior can provide benchmarks that target needs for professional development, curriculum, and resource allocation. One such instrument that was developed to study classroom quality as well as to link classroom practices to policy and training is the Classroom Assessment Scoring System (CLASS; Pianta, La Paro, & Hamre, 2005) Please see Chapter 1 of this volume for a thorough description of the CLASS. The CLASS is a broad system intended to evaluate classroom quality across content domains and is not limited to an evaluation of emergent literacy instruction.

Another measure for analyzing the quality of teacher-student interactions that focuses entirely on the reading and language arts components of instruction is the CLASSIC: the Classroom Language Arts Systematic Sampling and Instructional Coding (Scanlon, Gelzheiser, Fanuele, Sweeney, & Newcomer, 2003). The CLASSIC is an updated version of a classroom quality measure that has been used in early literacy research for several years (i.e., Scanlon & Vellutino, 1996, 1997; Vellutino & Scanlon, 2001). The purpose of this observation system is to provide several levels of detailed information about elementary-level teachers' language arts instruction and to collect data to address the following research purposes:

1. To identify those features of language arts instruction that are changed by professional development; and
2. To identify those features of language arts instruction that predict reading achievement among high-risk students (Scanlon et al., 2003, p. i).

The CLASSIC is a teacher observation system in which the observer codes seven levels of information about teacher instruction. The levels describe the structure of the classroom, the teacher's instructional block or lesson plan, materials the teacher utilizes, whom the teacher interacts with, the instructional activity, the teacher's specific instructional focus, and the students' response. The CLASSIC utilizes a modified time sampling procedure, which means that only a sample of the language arts instruction is coded. These samples are events that occur every 90 seconds. The observer is instructed by auditory cues provided through headphones to get ready; watch instruction; record verbatim the instructional event, usually entering the information on a laptop; and then code. Because the observer provides a verbatim record of the event, it allows coding decisions to be reviewed later by the observer or another coder.

This system has been used on an experimental basis in a preschool setting (Davidson et al., 2006). The observers found that many of the codes in the CLASSIC are appropriate for preschool settings. The CLASSIC allows for a fine-grained analysis of the quality of literacy instruction and is one of the few observation systems that addresses early literacy in great detail.

Interpreting the Results of Assessments of Teacher Knowledge

Few valid and reliable measures explicitly designed to assess teacher knowledge and skills in emergent literacy are available, and none has been demonstrated to have technical adequacy for teachers at the preschool level. Nonetheless, recent studies (e.g., Phelps & Schilling, 2004) provide important information about how to frame the assessment of teacher knowledge and the importance of considering items that include more than knowledge of content. The CLASSIC system provides the most detailed analysis of teaching behaviors during instruction, but it does not provide specific information regarding teacher content knowledge. The TKAS (Cunningham, 2001) and other content knowledge measures (e.g., Moats & Foorman, 2003) reflect teacher knowledge of the structure of language but are not designed to capture knowledge of teaching/pedagogy. We recommend that an instrument be developed that captures content knowledge, knowledge of students, and knowledge of teaching skills (i.e., knowledge of teaching and content) in a survey format. The sample assessment (see Appendix 2) includes a survey of content knowledge that reflects the content domains listed in the Head Start Framework (2003), scenarios written to emphasize either individual child interactions or more general group teaching knowledge and skills, and a detailed systematic modified time sampling classroom observation, namely the CLASSIC system.

The teacher knowledge assessment proposed focuses on three components of teacher knowledge, two of which include teacher judgment in the context of teaching. These types of teacher knowledge can also be described as declarative (content knowledge) and situated procedural (knowledge of students and knowledge of content and teaching). The developmental sequence of teaching knowledge described earlier (Snow et al., 2005) includes three additional phases: stable procedural knowledge; expert, adaptive knowledge; and reflective, organized, analyzed knowledge. These more refined, complex teacher skills may require additional assessment components, such as teacher responses to detailed case studies that include a sequence of scenarios with each requiring more knowledge and skills. Such an assessment could provide an evaluation of the phases of expertise in teacher knowledge and skills at the preschool level. However, defining these phases through case studies may require the development of sophisticated video scenarios, rather than paper-and-pencil tasks.

Current research on teacher knowledge in emergent literacy is clearly in its infancy. To date, no published measures provide a comprehensive evaluation of teacher knowledge and its relation to child outcomes at the preschool level. We have provided a prototype for consideration in the hope that further research will provide insights and data that will improve the quality of preservice and inservice teacher education, practicing teachers, and, most importantly, the reading skills of our young children.

References

Adams, M. J. (1990). *Beginning to read: Thinking and learning about print.* Cambridge, MA: MIT Press.

Barnett, S. W. (1995). Long-term effects of early childhood programs on cognitive and school outcomes. *The Future of Children, 5,* 25–50.

Barnett, S. W. (2004). Better teachers, better preschools: Student achievement linked to teacher qualifications. *Preschool Policy Matters, 2,* 1–12.

Cunningham, A. C. (2001). *Teacher Knowledge and Attitude Survey: Revised.* (Unpublished measure). Berkeley, CA: University of California-Berkeley.

Cunningham, A. C., Perry, K. E., Stanovich, K. E., & Stanovich, P. J. (2004). Disciplinary knowledge of K–3 teachers and their knowledge calibration in the domain of early literacy. *Annals of Dyslexia, 54*(1), 139–167.

Davidson, M. R., Yang, J., & Cunningham, A. C. (2006). Effective preschool literacy curricula: *A randomized trial study of "Ready, Set, Leap."* (manuscript in review)

Ferrar, H. (1996). *Places for growing: How to improve your child care center.* Princeton, NJ: Mathematica Policy Research

Harms, T., Clifford, R. M., & Cryer, D. (1998). *Early Childhood Environment Rating Scale* (Rev. ed.). New York: Teachers College Press.

Head Start. (2003). *The Head Start Child Outcomes framework. Head Start Bulletin,* No. 76. Washington, DC: U.S. Department of Health and Human Services. Retrieved July 2, 2006 from: http://www.headstart info.org/publications/hsbulletin76/hsb76_09.htm

International Reading Association. (2000). Excellent reading teachers: A position statement of the International Reading Association. *Reading Teacher, 54*(2), 235–240.

Kagan, D. M. (1990). Ways of evaluating teacher cognition: Inferences concerning the Goldilocks principle. *Review of Educational Research, 60*(3), 419–469.

Katz, L. G., & Raths, J. D. (1985). A framework for research on teacher education programs. *Journal of Teacher Education, 36*(6), 9–15.

Love, J. M., Meckstroth, A., & Sprachman, S. (1997). *Measuring the quality of program environments in Head Start and other early child-*

hood programs: A review and recommendations for future research (Contract RN 94094001). Washington, DC: U.S. Department of Education, National Center for Educational Statistics.

McCutchen, D., Abbott, R. D., Green, L. B., Beretvas, S. N., Cox, S., Quiroga, T., Potter, N. S., & Gray, A. L. (2002). Beginning literacy: Links among teacher knowledge, teacher practice, and student learning. *Journal of Learning Disabilities, 35*(1), 69-87.

McCutchen, D., & Berninger, V. (1999). Those who know, teach well: Helping teachers master literacy-related subject-matter knowledge. *Learning Disabilities Research and Practice, 14*(4), 215-226.

Moats, L. (1994). The missing foundation in teacher education: Knowledge of the structure of spoken and written language. *Annals of Dyslexia, 44*, 81-102.

Moats, L. (2000). *Speech to print: Language essentials for teachers.* Baltimore: Paul H. Brookes.

Moats, L. C., & Foorman, B. R. (2003). Measuring teachers' content knowledge of language and reading. *Annals of Dyslexia, 53*, 23-45.

Moore, P., & Lyon, A. (2005). *New essentials for teaching reading in preK-2: Comprehension, vocabulary, fluency.* New York: Scholastic.

National Institute of Child Health and Human Development (NICHD). (December 2000). Report of The National Reading Panel, Reports of the Subgroups. *Teaching children to read: An evidence-based assessment of the scientific research literature on reading and its implications for reading instruction.* (NIH Pub. No. 00-4754). Washington, DC: Author.

Phelps, G., & Schilling, S. (2004). Developing measures of content knowledge for teaching reading. *The Elementary School Journal, 105*(1), 31-47.

Rey, M., & Rey, H.A. (1966). *Curious George goes to the hospital.* Boston: Houghton-Mifflin.

Pianta, R., & La Paro, K. (2003). Improving early school success. *Educational Leadership, 60*, 27-29.

Pianta, R. C., La Paro, K. M., & Hamre, B. K. (2005). *Classroom Assessment Scoring System (CLASS).* Charlottesville: University of Virginia.

Scanlon, D. M., & Vellutino, F. R. (1996). Prerequisite skills, early instruction, and success in first grade reading: Selected results from a longitudinal study. *Mental Retardation and Developmental Disabilities, 2*, 54-63.

Scanlon, D. M., & Vellutino, F. R. (1997). A comparison of the instructional backgrounds and cognitive profiles of poor, average, and good readers who were initially identified as at risk for reading failure. *Scientific Studies of Reading, 1*(3), 191-215.

Scanlon, D., Gelzheiser, L., Fanuele, D., Sweeney, J., & Newcomer, L. (2003). *CLASSIC: Classroom Language Arts Systematic Sampling and Instructional Coding*. Albany, NY: Child Research and Study Center, The University at Albany State University of New York.

Snow, C. E., Burns, M. S., & Griffin, P. (Eds.). (1998). *Preventing reading difficulties in young children*. Washington, DC: National Academy Press.

Snow, C. E., Burns, M. S., & Griffin, P. (Eds.). (2005). *Knowledge to support the teaching of reading: Preparing teachers for a changing world*. San Francisco: Jossey-Bass.

Spear-Swerling, L., Brucker, P. O., & Alfano, M. P. (2005). Teachers' literacy-related knowledge and self-perception, and experience. *Annals of Dyslexia, 55*(2), 266–296.

Strickland, D. S., & Shanahan, T. (2004, March). Laying the groundwork for literacy. *Educational Leadership*, pp. 74–77.

Vellutino, F. R., & Scanlon, D. M. (2001). Emergent literacy skills, early instruction, and individual differences as determinants of difficulties in learning to read: The case for early intervention. In S.B. Neuman & D.K. Dickinson (Eds.), *Handbook of early literacy research* (pp. 295–332). New York: Guilford Press.

APPENDIX 2

Sample Teacher Assessment

Part I: Knowledge of Content Survey

Administration of an instrument such as TKAS (Cunningham, 2001) or the Moats and Foorman (2003) survey of teacher knowledge. Additional items that address the content included in the Head Start Child Outcomes Framework should be included.

Part II: Observation of Teacher Skills

CLASSIC teacher observation system (Scanlon et al., 2003)

Part III: Knowledge of Students

Scenarios that require a teacher to judge possible teaching responses to children in a learning context. An example that illustrates the importance of the knowledge of children is provided in the scenario below.

Scenario 1

Instructional Context: Interactive Writing in the context of centers

Grouping: Small Group

Time of Year: November

Instructional Goal: Concepts About Print

The first hour of the day in Mrs. Payne's preschool classroom is spent in free choice centers. Mrs. Payne and her helper circulate around to the centers and provide instruction as appropriate. Two days ago the class had listened to *Curious George Goes to the Hospital* (Rey, 1966) and had been visited by a local pediatrician. Mrs. Payne turned the housekeeping center into a hospital and encouraged the children to role-play using their new understandings of the role of doctors and nurses. Now, Maria and Charlotte want to make a sign at the entrance of the hospital that says: Quiet! I am sick. Following are hypothetical interactions between Mrs. Payne and the children that provide Mrs. Payne with opportunities to teach the girls more about how print works.

Select the best teacher response from the list below and provide a rationale for your selection.

a. Mrs. Payne writes the sign for the children as they dictate what they want it to say. She models left-to-right movement, spacing, and proper letter formation. She asks the children to reread the sign as she points to each word to make sure she has written exactly what the girls want.

b. Mrs. Payne asks Maria and Charlotte to clap out how many words there will be on the sign. She makes lines on the paper, moving from left-to-right, to show the girls where the words would go. She leaves large spaces between the words and talks about leaving spaces to make the sign easy to read. Then, Mrs. Payne writes the word *Quiet!* and tells the girls she will use an exclamation point to make it very clear that they want the other children to be *very* quiet. She then shows the girls how the word I is an uppercase letter. They practice making uppercase I in the air, then she lets Charlotte write the uppercase I on the sign. As she writes the word *am* Mrs. Payne says: "I hear a sound in am that starts like your name, Maria. Listen: /a/ /m/. Can you hear the /m/?" Mrs. Payne invites Maria to write her m to complete the word am. Finally, Mrs. Payne writes the work *sick*, invites the girls to reread the sign with her, and they hang the sign at the entrance to the center.

c. Mrs. Payne asks the children what they want the sign to say. She lets each girl choose a writing tool. Maria chooses a large marker and Charlotte chooses a crayon. Mrs. Payne suggests that each girl make a sign so that they can put one at the entrance to the hospital center and one inside the center. Mrs. Payne helps each girl to hear sounds and match them to letters.

She reminds them where to start leach letter and to leave spaces between words. Maria's sign read: "kwt!!! I m sk." Charlotte's sign read: 'K Im sk."

Provide a rationale for your response.

Scenario 2

Setting: Teacher, Ms D., is sitting on the floor with 3 students and the class pet guinea pig

Instructional Context: Small group informal setting

Time of Year: February

Instructional Goal: To develop conversation about the class pet

It is 9:00 in Ms. D's preschool classroom. Rosita, Tiffany, and Tyrone are sitting on the floor watching the class pet, a guinea pig named Dandy. The children are waiting for Dandy to finish his breakfast of seeds so they can hold him. The children watch Dandy's every move with great interest. Ms. D allows each child to hold him for a few moments and then she returns him to his cage. She walks over to Rosita and begins a conversation with her. Which of the following teacher interactions is most effective?

a. Ms. D (T) approaches Rosita and says:

T: Rosita, do you like Dandy?

R: Yeah, he's cute.

T: Do you have a pet?

R: No.

T: Would you like to draw a picture of Dandy?

R: Yes! (goes to table and Ms. D provides crayons and paper)

b. Ms. D approaches Rosita and says,

T: My, Dandy is a funny little fellow. What do you think of him?

R: He makes me laugh.

T: What do you think he likes to do all day?

R: Play and play . . . and eat.

T: Do you think he has any brothers or sisters? What would they be like?

R: I don't know.

T: Let's go get some crayons and paper and draw a picture of Dandy. Draw what he likes to eat and where he lives, too.

c. Ms. D approaches Rosita and says,

T: I think Dandy really likes you. What do you think?

R: Oh, yes. He's so cute.

T: What do you like best about him?

R: He's so furry. He's funny,

T: What does his fur feel like?

R: Oh . . . I don't know.

T: Can you think of other animals with fur like Dandy?

R: Oh, my dog. He furry. And my cat is soft.

T: Tell me about your pets at home. What do they like to do best?

R: Oh, my dog likes to chase kitty.

T: Where does he chase the cat? What does the cat do?

Explain why you chose the response you did.

Part IV: Knowledge of Teaching and Content

The scenarios provided below serve as examples of items to include.

Scenario 3

Instructional Context: Big book shared reading

Grouping: Whole group

Time of Year: September

Instructional Goal: To foster children's motivation for and enjoyment of reading

Miss Davies begins Big Book reading with her preschoolers almost as soon as they enter her room. She knows that the enlarged books, resting on a low easel, provide an ideal format to foster early literacy learning and engage the children in books. The large print and pictures make it easy for the children gathered on the floor to see and follow along with the engaging stories, and she can easily point out features of the pictures and print with a pointer while sitting on a low chair facing the class.

Today, Miss Davies is reading the Big Book version of *Mrs. Wishy-Washy* by Joy Cowley (Wright Group, 1990). It is the simple story of a harried farm wife who just cannot keep the naughty farm animals clean. She scrubs them up in a large washtub, "wishy-washy, wishy-washy," but they immediately run back to frolic in the "lovely mud." Much to the delight of 4-year-old humor, when Mrs. Wishy-Washy tries to get the muddy pig into the washtub, his hind end hangs out provocatively, facing the readers. Recurring refrains, *wishy-washy, wishy-washy,* and repetitive sentence structure, "*In went the duck. In went the cow. In went the pig,*" make it easy for the children to immediately join in with the reading.

Following are some ways that Miss Davies might use the Big Book, *Mrs. Wishy-Washy*, to continue fostering motivation for and engagement in the reading.

Given that it is early in the school year, which one is probably best suited for this purpose? Explain why.

a. Miss Davies suggests that the children act out the story following the reading. Children are selected to "play" the various roles and a laundry basket is recruited to be the washtub. Then, Miss Davies suggests that acting out the story could be one of the free choice centers, and she puts the laundry basket and the Big Book in an ongoing "Play Center" where a puppet theater and flannel board are also located.

b. After reading Mrs. Wishy-Washy's horrified exclamation when she sees the muddy animals, "Just **LOOK** at you!" Miss Davies thinks out loud, "Look at those naughty animals. Now I've got to wash them up!"

c. Miss Davies suggests that the children and she rewrite the Big Book using different animals as characters. They create their rewrite on chart paper, with student illustrations, and assemble it into a new Big Book that will be read and reread by the class.

Explain why you chose the teacher response you did.

Scenario 4

Setting: Teacher, Mr. J., is sitting at the front of the class with all 12 students. Next to him is an easel with chart paper. Children are sitting on their mats around the teacher's chair.

Instructional Context: Large group activity with the month's theme of Transportation.

Time of Year: February

Instructional Goal: To learn to count the sounds in 2- and 3-letter words.

T: Boys and girls, we are going to think about all the ways we can travel to different places. In the mornings, I take the bus to our school. Let's think about the word "bus." What letter does "bus" begin with?

C: B.

T: Yes! B. What sound does B make?

C: /b/

T: Yes! B makes a /b/ sound. Let's write bus on our board. (T prints on chart paper for all children to see.) 'Bus' starts with what letter?

C: (all respond) B!

T: That's right. What makes the /ʌ/ sound?

C: (no response at first, then one child says "a.")

T: No, the /ʌ/ sound is made with a U. Now what's the other letter in "bus"?

C: Is it /s/?

T: /s/ is the sound that S makes. Good! Now, how many sounds are in "bus"?

Which summary below best represents the strengths and weaknesses of the above instructional interactions?

a. Mr. J began his lesson too quickly without sufficiently motivating the children to respond to his questions about letters and sounds. The lesson was very appropriate in that he alternated between letter names and sounds and encouraged the children to think hard. He did not call on individual children, but allowed them to respond spontaneously.

b. Mr. J began by setting the stage for an activity about transportation. He related the theme to his own experience which can be very helpful to children. He selected the word 'bus,' but should have included at least two other words representing transportation to make sure that children had a broad range of practice in identifying the letters and the sounds they make.

c. Mr. J did an excellent job of introducing letter names and sounds and then transitioned to the number of sounds in a word. He did not begin by asking the children more general questions about transportation to generate more interest in their part. He should have initiated a lively discussion about transportation before launching into the spelling and sounds of "bus." His questions were direct and children were immediately corrected when necessary.

d. Mr. J provided a motivating context for learning about the sounds in words. He used the word "bus" as the first example and all of the sounds can be easily heard in that word. He did not model the sounds for the children and he mixed up letter names and sounds. The last question is a completely new activity with no modeling or lead in.

e. Mr. J began the group activity in a lively way, but should have had several words already written on the chart for the children to see (e.g., car, train, bus). Then, he could have talked them through each word and they could have counted the sounds together. The activity would have been more powerful if each child had been asked to copy the words from the chart and say the sounds in them

Explain why you chose the response you did.

Chapter Three

Assessing Home Supports for Literacy

Tricia A. Zucker
Staci L. Grant

The Importance of Home Literacy to Emergent Literacy

We live in a society in which the standards for literacy have risen sharply over the last century, in part because "literacy is the energy supply of the Information Age" (Brandt, 2001, p. 171). Increased demands for literacy often translate into a greater focus on the role of family as a key sponsor of literacy development. Families, like any sponsor of literacy, can "enable, support, teach, and model, as well as recruit, regulate, suppress, or withhold literacy" (Brandt, 2001, p. 19). In particular, young children's emergent and early literacy development is affected by the presence of supports for literacy in the home environment, and the degree to which literacy is part of family activities.

Home literacy support is commonly defined as the level to which families provide an environment that fosters a child's literacy development (Snow, Burns, & Griffin, 1998). Although many educators have long recognized that family is the foundation of learning and literacy development, research concentrating on family literacy as an educational construct is fairly new (Purcell-Gates, 2000). Recent family literacy research focuses on identifying students most at risk for reading difficulties by assessing aspects of the home environment (Burchinal, Peisner-Feinberg, Pianta, & Howes, 2002; National Center for Education Statistics, 1999; Snow et al., 1998) or studying how different facets of the home literacy environment affect language and literacy achievement (Dickinson & Tabors, 1991; Evans, Shaw, & Bell, 2000; Leseman & de Jong, 1998; Pan, Rowe, Singer & Snow, 2005; Sénéchal, 2006).

Assessing a child's home literacy background is valuable to educators because the home context influences and supports emergent and early literacy development. This view is grounded in an ecological perspective of child development (Bronfrenbrenner & Morris, 1998) as nested in multiple influential settings ranging from micro (e.g., the home and classroom) to macro (e.g., the cultural context). An ecological perspective acknowledges the role of key players in young children's microsystems and acknowledges the importance of quality interactions in immediate environments such as home and school. When educators collaborate with caregivers they can support sustainable changes in a child's literacy trajectory because two key constituents in a child's life, caregivers and teachers, work in tandem to promote literacy. An extensive body of literature explores methods for promoting culturally responsive family literacy programs and partnerships that respect and value each family's unique culture (see Auerbach, 1995; Paratore, 2002). Such respectful partnerships may even serve as a protective factor for children at risk for developing reading difficulties.

The home literacy context varies dramatically among American children. For instance, notable variability can exist in opportunities for extended conversations, engaging in storybook reading, and occasions to use print in authentic home tasks such as writing a letter to grandparents or composing and reading e-mails from distant relatives. Adams (1990) describes how children from middle-income homes may have experienced between 1,000 to 1,700 hours of one-on-one storybook reading before entering first grade, whereas Whitehurst and colleagues (1994) estimate that many children from low-income families can experience as few as 25 total hours of one-on-one storybook reading before school entry. Purcell-Gates' (1996) observations in low-income homes revealed considerable variability ranging from one family who exposed their child to 4.21 reading and writing events per hour to another family that only exposed their child to 0.04 reading and writing events per hour. Thus, sizable variability can exist in home literacy supports both within and between income levels.

Although factors such as income level and maternal education are often moderately correlated with children's language and literacy outcomes even as children mature (Burchinal et al., 2002; Leseman & de Jong, 1998), measures of these factors are not explored directly in this chapter because these are areas in which educators typically have less influence than other domains. Further, many scholars argue that income alone cannot explain the difference in home literacy environments (Heath, 1983; Serpell, Sonnenschein, Baker, & Ganapathy, 2002; Taylor & Dorsey-Gaines, 1988). Thus, we focus our discussion on research and assessments related to areas of home literacy where educators can most directly foster literacy or influence change in the home literacy environment.

Current policies and initiatives acknowledge that families and the home environment can contribute to young children's literacy development. Since the National Academy of Science report, *Preventing Reading Difficulties in Young Children* (Snow et al., 1998), home and family risk factors are at the forefront of our national agenda. This report concludes that children may be at risk for developing reading difficulties if they have one or more of the following risk factors associated with the home environment: being from low-income families or poor neighborhoods, having limited English proficiency, speaking a dialect that differs from the one used in school, having parents with histories of reading difficulties, or acquiring limited knowledge and skills from home literacy experiences. These risk factors are some of the most significant ways home literacy contexts vary among American children.

Both in response to and before this report was commissioned, policies have been in place to support and reinforce positive home literacy practices for at-risk populations. At the policy level, family literacy has been defined in the No Child Left Behind Act (Title IX, General Provisions, Section 20), the Adult Education and Family Literacy Act, Even Start, Head Start, and the Reading Excellence Act with similar descriptions such as: services that make sustainable changes in a family through interactive literacy activities, parent training regarding how to be the primary teacher and education partner for their children, and education for the child (Peyton,

1999). The current Bush administration has promoted family literacy through the Good Start, Grow Smart Initiative, which continues Head Start and Even Start programs while also supporting families through informative parent guidebooks and a monthly television program with education information called *News Parents Can Use.* Smaller scale programs exist throughout the country such as Reach Out and Read, a program in which pediatricians "prescribe" a book to read at checkups by giving the family a new book (Needlman, Klass, & Zuckerman, 2006). Yet, despite the quantity and comprehensiveness of many of these family literacy programs, a tremendous gap remains in the literacy knowledge and experiences American children bring to their first years of school (Britto, Fuligni, & Brooks-Gunn, 2006; Neuman, 2006).

This chapter provides overviews of five home literacy constructs that influence or predict reading acquisition and then reviews measures that may be useful for assessing home supports related to each construct. We systematically searched for valid and reliable measures that educators may find useful when working with emergent and early readers and their families. Nonetheless, other useful home literacy measures are available elsewhere that could not be included due to space limitations. After considering several available measures of home literacy, we discuss considerations for assessing special populations and suggestions for interpreting assessment results.

Measures for Assessing Home Literacy

Before enumerating the details of each measure of home literacy, we briefly discuss the major constructs that are presumably being measured by these assessments. These broad areas include: (1) measuring parents' beliefs and knowledge, (2) measuring home activities such as parent-child shared storybook reading, (3) measuring home activities other than storybook reading, (4) measuring home environmental context, and (5) measuring oral language and vocabulary supports. Research shows that considering multiple areas or facets of home literacy simultaneously is more informative than considering any of these areas in isolation (Leseman & de Jong, 1998).

Measuring Parents' Beliefs and Knowledge

Parents' beliefs about reading, knowledge of literacy development, and expectations for literacy achievement appear to work "behind the scenes" to support a child's literacy development (Snow et al., 1998). Parents may demonstrate their beliefs about and motivation for reading in observable ways through their own reading habits. Consequently, children may be more likely to value reading if they see their parents reading. Likewise, the degree to which parents express their expectations for their children's literacy achievement and respond to their children's initiations for reading may influence children's attitudes and motivation toward reading (Britto et al., 2006; Snow et al., 1998; Strickland, 2001). In this same manner, measures of maternal knowledge of child rearing and typical developmental milestones may be associated with the quality of the home environment (Benasich & Brooks-Gunn, 1996). However, exactly how parental knowledge and beliefs influence child outcomes is somewhat unclear because of differences across cultural and ethnic groups and evidence of both direct and indirect influences of maternal knowledge on child outcomes (Benasich & Brooks-Gunn, 1996; Serpell et al., 2002).

Parental knowledge and beliefs may provide a mechanism for changing children's literacy outcomes, thereby making assessments of these constructs valuable to educators. Parents' knowledge can be measured with many methods; however, within this chapter we focus on assessments of parents' knowledge of literacy development because research has shown that aspects of parental knowledge mediate their teaching style and beliefs about how their child can learn (Benasich & Brooks-Gunn, 1996; McGillicuddy-Delisi, 1982). We review measures of parents' beliefs about literacy that investigate the scope and frequency of parents' personal reading, parents' perceptions of how children should learn to read, and parents' orientation toward literacy. Chapter 10 of this volume, Assessing Literacy Motivation and Orientation, reviews measures for assessing the child's orientation to literacy. Thus, our discussion focuses on how parents' beliefs, attitudes, motivation, and orientation toward literacy may influence children's literacy development. We examine six measures for assessing parents' beliefs and knowledge (for a summary see Table 3–1).

Table 3–1. Measuring Parents' Beliefs and Knowledge

Measure	Use	Time (Approximate)	Administration
Parental Perceptions Interview	To assess parent opinions of literacy development. To assess parent perceptions of importance of literacy artifacts in the home.	30 minutes	Individual parent
Parent Reading Beliefs Inventory (PRBI)	To measure parents' feelings of self-efficacy in the informal teaching role.	15–30 minutes	Individual parent or groups of parents
Approaches to Beginning Reading and Reading Instruction (ABRRI)	To assess whether parents espouse a bottom-up or top-down view of learning to read.	10–15 minutes	Individual parent
Parents' Orientation to Literacy	To assess whether parents espouse an entertainment or skills view of literacy.	15 minutes	Individual parent
Parents' Symbolic Job Content and Parents' Literacy	To assess the literacy content of parents' occupation and the range of parent's informational and recreational literacy practices.	15 minutes	Individual parent
Author Recognition Test (ART) and Magazine Recognition Test (MRT)	To assess parents' exposure to print and determine extent to which parents may model reading behaviors. The ART measures knowledge of best-selling authors. The MRT measures knowledge of popular magazine titles.	10 minutes	Individual or group of parents

Parental beliefs may moderate some aspects of early literacy development. Rodriguez and Olswang (2003) define beliefs as "constructions of reality that incorporate one's knowledge and do not require evidence of their truthfulness" (p. 453). Some researchers suggest that parental beliefs may be based on their individual experiences as a child and as a parent (McGillicuddy-DeLisi, 1982). Others assert that all parents hold beliefs about skills children should master and suitable timelines for mastery (Sonnenschein, Brody, & Munsterman, 1995). These beliefs may be mediated by the literacy and education level of the parent, cultural beliefs, or socioeconomic status.

Assessing parental beliefs and knowledge is important because emerging evidence suggests parents' ways of thinking shape home literacy practices. Positive parental beliefs about early academics are associated with frequent literacy events in the home (DeBaryshe, 1995; DeBaryshe & Binder, 1994; Sonnenschein et al., 1995). DeBaryshe and Binder (1994) found a strong association between parental reading beliefs and positive home reading practices as measured by both parent report and home observation. In their study of 150 parents of preschoolers, DeBaryshe and Binder (1994) found that parents who scored higher on the Parent Reading Beliefs Inventory (PRBI) read to their children often, owned several books, frequently modeled reading, and established reading practices and routines at an early age. Parents with higher scores on the PRBI also demonstrated more positive interactions with their children during storybook reading.

Parents' beliefs about literacy may be linked to their self-efficacy or perception of their ability to affect their child's literacy trajectory as well as to their view of what constitutes helpful literacy practices. Fitzgerald, Spiegel, and Cunningham (1991) found that parents with both high and low literacy levels were optimistic that literacy learning can begin in the preschool years; however, they found key differences between beliefs of parents with high and low levels of literacy. These differences included: (1) parents with lower literacy levels perceived literacy artifacts and events in the home to be more important as compared to perceptions of high literacy parents; (2) high-literacy parents embraced natural literacy artifacts and activities but disapproved of skill-oriented materials and activities; (3) high-literacy parents felt that modeling reading was more important when compared to the beliefs of low-literacy parents;

(4) low-literacy parents offered fewer explanations than high-literacy parents about why children can have varying levels of academic success in school; and (5) low-literacy parents offered fewer suggestions than high-literacy parents about how parents can promote academic success. Fitzgerald et al. (1991) concluded that low-literacy parents might believe that literacy development is important but may feel a sense of helplessness in fostering that development, whereas parents with higher levels of literacy believe they have more influence over their child's literacy development.

Another factor that influences parental beliefs about literacy development is culture. Rodriguez and Olswang (2003) point out that American schools uphold beliefs and values that often differ from the beliefs and values held by families from diverse cultural backgrounds. Children from nonmainstream backgrounds thus may enter school at a disadvantage as compared to their peers whose family values are consistent with those endorsed at school. For example, Purcell-Gates' (1995) ethnographic case study of a white, urban Appalachian family details how they functioned daily without print—a stark difference between home and school literacy values. Thus, even after receiving 2 years of schooling, print lacked linguistic meaning for this child because of the family's stance toward printed words. In another ethnographic case study, Heath (1983) details the home lives of families in two communities in the Piedmont Carolinas in which children learned to use language and literacy in vastly different ways depending on their family structure and societal values. For example, one community valued reading and intentionally accumulated reading material for young children, whereas in the other community children had no books and parents engaged in reading only when tasks such as shopping or paying bills required it. Differences in home literacy backgrounds must be taken into account to provide emergent literacy instruction matched to each child's needs (Adams, 1990).

As previously stated, we will not examine measures of socioeconomic status as a stand-alone variable in part because "from the perspective of literacy development, psychosocial features of a family's intimate culture are more informative than economic indices of the family's material resources" (Serpell et al., 2002). Yet, research suggests that income level may influence noteworthy differences in parents' orientation to literacy. For instance, several studies found differences in parent views of reading related to income level (Serpell et al., 2002; for a summary see Wasik, Dobbins, & Herrmann, 2001). Middle-income parents viewed reading as a source of entertainment, whereas low-income parents viewed reading as work or a skill that needed to be practiced. Serpell et al. (2002) found that parents who espoused an entertainment orientation toward literacy positively influenced their child's reading achievement, whereas embracing a skills orientation toward literacy was a prohibitive factor in the child's literacy development.

Multiple facets of parents' beliefs appear to shape young children's home literacy experiences. Another consideration is the level to which parents hold progressive parenting beliefs that include less authoritarian and more child-centered approaches to parenting. Progressive beliefs are associated with more advanced receptive language scores and basic reading skills (Burchinal et al., 2002). Further, the affect and control during mother-child interactions as well as the quality of the mother's instruction during problem-solving tasks are stronger and more consistent predictors of kindergarten social adjustment than the preschool teacher-child relationship (Pianta, Nimetz, & Bennett, 1997). Related measures of secure attachment between the mother and child, or trusting relationship, appear to influence the quality of literacy interactions such as shared storybook reading (Bus, 2001). In summary, parents' beliefs and knowledge shape children's earliest interactions with literacy and the nature of their home literacy environment in complex ways.

Parental Perceptions Interview

The first measure we review is a parent interview used in the research of Fitzgerald et al. (1991) to assess parental perceptions of literacy development. These researchers used a parent interview to examine the relationship between a parent's literacy level and a parent's perceptions of the importance of literacy artifacts and events. No estimate for time to administer is given; however the interview probably requires 15 to 30 minutes to administer. The interview is designed for parents of preschool-age children. The interviewer begins by asking the parent: "Why do you think some children learn to read and write while in school and others don't?" and "Do you think there is anything parents of two- to four-year-olds might do to help their children learn to read and write better when they start school? If yes, what?" (Fitzgerald et al., 1991, p. 194). After the interviewer asks these open-ended questions, he or she reads a list of items children might have at home in the years before they go to school. The interviewer directs the parents to give their opinion on the importance of having each item at home to prepare children to do well in school.

Parents rate each item on a 4-point scale including 1: *not important*, 2: *slightly important*, 3: *important*, and 4: *very important*. Nine distractor items, which are not related to literacy development, are included to minimize the tendency of adults to select socially desirable responses. Table 3–2 shows interview questions. Questions are divided into two scales: the importance of literacy artifacts and the importance of literacy events and interactions. The importance of literacy events and interactions is further divided into the subscales: child-focused events and adult-focused events. The interview is available in English; however, it may be useful if translated to other languages. The 4-point scale is used to score parents' responses. Parent answers are averaged across the two scales to calculate a total score. Distractor items are not included in scoring. Higher scores indicate beliefs that literacy artifacts and events are important. Interviewers should be trained in interview and scoring procedures before administration.

Parent Reading Belief Inventory

DeBaryshe and Binder (1994) designed the Parent Reading Belief Inventory (PRBI) to measure parents' beliefs about emergent and beginning literacy related to six central tenets: (a) adult-child conversation, (b) literacy awareness in the context of everyday activities, (c) daily exposure to book-related materials, (d) children's role in discussing the meaning of the books they read, (e) the motivating and child-centered nature of book reading, and (f) emphasizing meaning versus code skills during book reading. Table 3–3 contains PRBI items. High scores on the PRBI indicate that parents believe they are important to their children's learning, children should be actively involved in reading, children should read for fun and knowledge rather than instructional purposes, parents should find time and resources to read to their children, and language skills are influenced by language environment.

Table 3-2. Parental Perceptions Interview

Instructions: Rate each items as (1) *Not Important*, (2) *Slightly Important*, (3) *Important*, (4) *Very Important*. For the first 12 items read the directions: I'm going to read a list of some things children might have at home in the years before they go to school. Please tell me how important you think it is for children to have each one at home before they go to school in order for them to do well in reading and writing when they go to school. You may think some of these things have nothing to do with reading or writing, you may think some are not important, some are slightly important, important, or very important. Also, I'd just like to emphasize that I'm interested in your opinion about theses things for children in general. For the next 17 items the directions are similar, except they emphasize what children might do at home. The final eight emphasize things children might see adults doing at home.

Item	Rating Scale			
1. Alphabet letter blocks or magnetic letters at home	1	2	3	4
2. Flashcards with letters or pictures and words in the home	1	2	3	4
3. Balloons at home (D)[a]	1	2	3	4
4. Paper to write on	1	2	3	4
5. Pens, pencils, markers	1	2	3	4
6. Bubble-blowing sets (D)[a]	1	2	3	4
7. Chalkboard or other kind of board children can write on	1	2	3	4
8. Computer-type toys that have children read or spell	1	2	3	4
9. Stuffed animals (D)[a]	1	2	3	4
10. Children's books and magazines	1	2	3	4
11. Preschool workbooks	1	2	3	4
12. Comic books	1	2	3	4
13. Books with records or cassettes that go with them	1	2	3	4
14. Children's encyclopedia or dictionary	1	2	3	4
15. Musical instruments in the home	1	2	3	4
16. Daily newspaper, or books or magazines for grown-ups	1	2	3	4

continues

91

Table 3–2. *continued*

Item	Rating Scale			
17. Children visit the public library	1	2	3	4
18. Children hear stories on records, cassettes, or videos at home	1	2	3	4
19. Children pretend to read story books	1	2	3	4
20. Children play in a sandbox (D)[a]	1	2	3	4
21. Children watch "Sesame Street," "Reading Rainbow," or other similar TV shows at home	1	2	3	4
22. Children talk about written letters and words	1	2	3	4
23. Children try to tell or write stories	1	2	3	4
24. Read or look at children's magazines or books by themselves	1	2	3	4
25. Children talk about stories read to them	1	2	3	4
26. Children help to write letters and/or cards	1	2	3	4
27. Children receive letters or cards, or open mail	1	2	3	4
28. Have an older person write words or alphabet letters for the child	1	2	3	4
29. Children have races (D)[a]	1	2	3	4
30. Children "play school" with reading and writing activities	1	2	3	4
31. There's an older person at home who teaches children about reading and writing skills	1	2	3	4
32. Children listen to stories read to them at home	1	2	3	4
33. Children recite the alphabet	1	2	3	4
34. Children say sounds for alphabet letters	1	2	3	4
35. Children learn to color within the lines (D)[a]	1	2	3	4

Table 3–2. *continued*

Item	Rating Scale			
36. Children recognize store signs or traffic signs	1	2	3	4
37. Adults reading books, magazine, newspaper at home	1	2	3	4
38. Adults using *TV Guide*	1	2	3	4
39. Adults using written recipes	1	2	3	4
40. Adults doing the laundry (D)[a]	1	2	3	4
41. Adults following written directions, such as on a box to put something together	1	2	3	4
42. Adults receiving or writing letters	1	2	3	4
43. Making shopping lists	1	2	3	4
44. Leaving notes for family members	1	2	3	4
45. Adults raking leaves (D)[a]	1	2	3	4
46. Adults having their own library cards	1	2	3	4

Open Ended Questions:

1. Why do you think some children learn to read and write well in school and others don't?

2. Do you think there is anything parents of two- to four-year olds might do to help their children learn to read and write better when they start school? (If yes, what?)

3. For both questions ask: "Is there anything else?" until the parent says no.

Note. [a]Distractor items.

Source: Adapted from "The Relationship Between Parental Literacy Level and Perceptions of Emergent Literacy," by J. Fitzgerald, D. L. Spiegel, and J. W. Cunningham, 1991, *Journal of Reading Behavior, 23*, pp. 194–195. Copyright 1991 by Lawrence Erlbaum Associates, Inc. Adapted with permission of the publisher and authors.

Table 3–3. Examples of Parent Reading Belief Inventory Items

Scale	Example of Item Content
Affect	I find it boring or difficult to read to my child.
Participation	When we read, I want my child to help me tell the story.
Resources	Even if I would like to, I'm just too busy and too tired to read to my child.
	I don't read to my child because there is no room and no quiet place in the house.
Efficacy	As a parent, I play an important role in my child's development.
	When my child goes to school, the teacher will teach my child everything my child needs to know so I don't need to worry.
Knowledge	Reading helps children learn about things they never see in real life
	My child learns lessons and morals from the stories we read.
Environment	Some children are natural talkers, others are silent. Parents do not have much influence over this.
	Children inherit their language ability from their parents, it's in their genes.
Reading Instruction	I read to my child so he/she will learn the letters and how to read simple sentences.
	My child is too young to learn about Reading.

Note: Parents rate these questions on the following scale: (1) Strongly agree, (2) Agree, (3) Disagree, and (4) Strongly Disagree.

Source: Reproduced from "Development of an Instrument for Measuring Parental Beliefs About Reading Aloud to Young Children," by B. D. DeBaryshe and J. C. Binder, 1994, *Perceptual Motor Skills, 78,* p. 1306. Copyright 1994 by Perceptual and Motor Skills. Reprinted with permission of authors and publisher.

The PRBI is a 42-item scale in which parents rate their level of agreement to statements about their own attitudes and beliefs from *strongly agree* to *strongly disagree*. Time to administer is not reported; however, administration probably requires 15 to 30 minutes. The PRBI is appropriate for parents of preschool-age children and can be administered either to individuals or groups of parents. The PRBI also can be administered orally to parents with minimal reading skills. Each item on the PRBI corresponds to one of seven scales. The scales include: teaching efficacy, positive affect, verbal participation, reading instruction, knowledge base, resources, and environmental input. The PRBI is available in English; however, it may be useful in other languages if translated. These scales form a single factor (parental reading beliefs). Therefore, DeBaryshe and Binder (1994) suggest that each item be included in a total score calculation. No qualifications for administration are stated. DeBaryshe and Binder (1994) note that the PRBI is a reliable and valid measure of parental reading beliefs.

Approaches to Beginning Reading and Reading Instruction

The Approaches to Beginning Reading and Reading Instruction (ABRRI) was designed by Evans, Barraball, and Eberle (1998) and later used by Evans, Fox, Cremaso, and McKinnon (2004) to determine parental approaches to reading instruction at home and parental views on beginning reading. The ABRRI also measures whether parents subscribe to a bottom-up or top-down view of reading. Evans et al. (2004) describe a bottom-up view as "a code driven view in which skilled reading entails the ability to rapidly process the visual cues of letters and letter patterns to get at the meaning of the passage" (p. 132). In contrast, a top-down view is "a knowledge driven view in which skilled readers rely on their broad knowledge of the world, the language, and the text to make sense of the passage without attending to all of the letters on the page" (p. 132). A bottom-up view is generally associated with phonics, whereas a bottom-up view is aligned with whole-language approaches. Educators can use the ABRRI to compare parental approaches to beginning reading instruction with teacher approaches.

The ABRRI contains 14 items that reflect different activities, materials, and goals in a beginning reading program. The phrasing of the ABRRI can be easily understood by both parents and teachers. An estimate of the amount of time it takes to complete the ABRRI is not given; however, Evans et al. (2004) describe it as a quick measure of parental beliefs. The items on the ABRRI are rated on a 5-point scale ranging from 1: *little importance* to 5: *greatest importance*. Table 3–4 shows ABRRI items. This measure is designed for parents of emergent and beginning readers to complete individually.

Table 3–4. ABRRI Parent Questionnaire with Teacher Version in Parentheses

---

1. Different authorities in reading tend to favor emphasizing different goals as aspects of reading in first grade. The following is a list culled from different authorities. Rate each of these goals on a scale from 1 to 10 according to the emphasis you place on it in encouraging reading in your home "(teacher version—according to its emphasis in your reading program as it is implemented)." A rating of 1 indicates no emphasis and a rating of 10 indicates strongest emphasis.

	No Emphasis						Strongest Emphasis		
A. Developing broad reading interests	1 2 3 4 5 6 7 8 9 10									
B. Developing the confidence to guess at or predict printed words based on a variety of clues	1 2 3 4 5 6 7 8 9 10									
C. Developing the ability to sound out words independently	1 2 3 4 5 6 7 8 9 10									
D. Developing accurate oral reading	1 2 3 4 5 6 7 8 9 10									
E. Developing oral language as a basis for written language (writing and reading)	1 2 3 4 5 6 7 8 9 10									
F. Developing skill in associating the sounds in spoken words with the letters and letter combinations used to represent them	1 2 3 4 5 6 7 8 9 10									
G. Developing a core sight vocabulary through repeated presentation of a certain set of words	1 2 3 4 5 6 7 8 9 10									

---

2. On a scale of 1 to 10, rate the following approaches to word recognition according to the emphasis that they receive in your home "(teacher version—in your reading program)." Assign a 1 to approach(es) that receive(s) no emphasis, and a rating of 10 to the approach(es) which receive(s) the strongest emphasis

Table 3–4. *continued*

	No Emphasis								Strongest Emphasis
A. Phonic generalizations using rules (such as a final "e" makes the first vowel sound long, etc.)	1	2	3	4	5	6	7	8	9	10
B. Context and meaning cues (recognizing unknown words by "what makes sense" from the surrounding known words and picture clues on page)	1	2	3	4	5	6	7	8	9	10
C. Phonetic analysis (recognizing words by "sounding out" letters and groups of letters)	1	2	3	4	5	6	7	8	9	10
D. Inference cues (recognizing unknown words by inferring from one's general knowledge base)	1	2	3	4	5	6	7	8	9	10
E. Whole word recognition (recognizing words through repeated practice with a given set of words)	1	2	3	4	5	6	7	8	9	10

3. Two basic conceptions of reading guide research and theory in the area. One theory referred to as "top down" holds that the reader brings to text his or her knowledge, understanding of syntax and vocabulary, and samples what is on the page to make predictions and confirm predictions about the printed text. The other theory referred to as "bottom-up" holds that the reader acquires a set of automatic subskills through practice that allow him or her to rapidly decipher the symbols (letters) on the page that represent spoken language, to arrive at the meaning of the text. Is your view of reading as expressed in your behaviors and activities when helping your child to read, "(teacher version—in your classroom activities and teacher methods)" more top down or more bottom-up?

Top-down _____

Bottom-up _____

Source: Reprinted from "Parental Responses to Miscues During Child-to-Parent Book Reading," by M. A. Evans, L. Barraball, and T. Eberle, 1998, *Journal of Applied Developmental Psychology, 19*(1), pp. 83–84. Copyright 1998 by Elsevier, Ltd. Reprinted with permission of the publisher.

The ABRRI is available in English. A high score on an item represents high agreement with and endorsement of the item's approach. Examiners also use the open-ended questions to determine if the parents hold a bottom-up or top-down view of reading. Evans et al. (1998) used the ABRRI to compare parents' views on reading with their child's teachers' view on reading and to determine how parent views influence how parents read to their children. There are no stated qualifications for the examiner.

Parents' Orientation to Literacy

The purpose of this interview is to assess parents' orientation to literacy and determine whether parents endorse an entertainment or skills orientation (i.e., theme) themetoward learning to read. Serpell et al. (2002) employed this interview in conjunction with other measures to estimate parents' orientation to literacy, but only the interview detailed in Table 3-5 is discussed in this chapter. An entertainment orientation (i.e., theme) suggests literacy is an enjoyable or pleasurable activity whereas a skills orientation suggests literacy is a skill to be worked at or practiced. A third orientation is included in Table 3-5, the everyday life theme, referring to a view that literacy is an essential part of daily living for tasks such as paying bills or writing letters or e-mails. Serpell et al. (2002) caution that the everyday life theme is less predictive of literacy development than the entertainment and skills themes. Thus, less weight should be given to responses related to the everyday life theme when interpreting the outcomes.

Outcomes are interpreted using a 5-point scale as a total for each theme to determine which orientation theme parents espouse. This interview probably requires 15 to 20 minutes to administer and is useful for parents with preschool or kindergarten children. The interview should take place with the parent who spends the most time engaged in literacy activities with the child. It was designed for English-speaking, low- and middle-income African American and European American parents, but may be useful with other populations as well. There are no special qualifications for the examiner; however, Serpell et al. (2002) note that the items should be presented in a sequence that alternates across the three themes, rather than presenting the questions in the order shown in Table 3-5.

Table 3–5. Parents' Orientation to Literacy

Examiner introduction[a]: Begin by asking the parent to consider these questions for preschool and kindergarten children. Say, "Which things do you think are important for a child to become a good reader?"

	Not Important			Very Important	
Entertainment theme:					
• Show children that reading books is fun	1	2	3	4	5
• Encourage children to pick out books about things they have interest in	1	2	3	4	5
• Encourage children to read and look at books in their spare time	1	2	3	4	5
• Encourage children to pick out books about fictional characters they like	1	2	3	4	5
Skills theme:					
• Encourage children to recognize letters	1	2	3	4	5
• Encourage children to recite the alphabet	1	2	3	4	5
• Encourage children to read words from lists or cards	1	2	3	4	5
• Encourage children to learn letter–sound correspondences	1	2	3	4	5
Everyday life theme:					
• Show children how reading is useful in going to the store	1	2	3	4	5
• Show children that reading can be used for getting places	1	2	3	4	5
• Show children that reading is necessary for understanding bills and letters	1	2	3	4	5
• Show children that reading is useful for preparing packaged foods	1	2	3	4	5

Note: [a]Do not ask questions in order listed. Alternate with questions from the entertainment theme, skills theme, and everyday life theme.

Source: Adapted with permission from "Intimate Culture of Families in the Early Socialization of Literacy," by R. Serpell, S. Sonnenschein, L. Baker, and H. Ganapathy, 2002, *Journal of Family Psychology, 16,* p. 394. Copyright 2002 by the American Psychological Association.

Parents' Symbolic Job Content and Parents' Literacy

Characteristics of the literacy opportunities parents provide to young children may relate to the contexts of literacy parents use for daily work or entertainment. Leseman and de Jong (1998) measured parents' literacy uses as context variables in their home literacy work with three ethnically diverse populations in the Netherlands. These context variables included parents' symbolic job content (the amount of literacy-related tasks required by parents' jobs), parents' literacy practices, parents' education level, and the predominant home language. We describe the first two context variables in this chapter (see Leseman & de Jong, 1998 for parental education and home language assessments). We discuss parents' symbolic job content because it was strongly associated with the socio-emotional quality and instructional quality of home literacy activities as measured during observations (Leseman & de Jong, 1998). We also describe parents' informational and recreational literacy uses because they are strongly related to the frequency of literacy opportunities offered to children in the home.

Leseman and de Jong's (1998) measure of symbolic or literate content of the parents' most recent job involves a parent interview that is coded like a questionnaire with a 4-point scale ranging from 1 *never* to 4 *very often/daily*. Parents report information about their daily job activities such as the extent to which they use manual tools or heavy machinery as compared to the extent to which they engage in written tasks using computers (see Table 3-6 for items). During the same interview, the examiner asks questions to assess parents' informational literacy and recreational literacy practices. These questions assess how often parents use different genres of literacy in their job, education, or daily leisure activities (see Table 3-6). The examiner rates the responses using a 3-point scale ranging from 1 *(almost) never* to 3 *often*.

The outcomes of this interview are interpreted as an average 4-point or 3-point score depending on the scale used for questions. A higher average indicates a more literate lifestyle. The time required to complete this interview is probably under 15 minutes. Leseman and de Jong (1998) employed this measure with parents of 4- to 7-year-old children, but it may be appropriate for parents with children of different ages as well. The original questionnaire was created in Dutch, but we present the English translation.

Table 3–6. Job Content and Literacy Questionnaire

Job Content Questionnaire[a]

How often in your job do you have to work with or deal with . . .

1. Mechanical tools such as broom, brush, floor-cloth, wrench, hammer? 1...2...3...4
2. Electrical tools such as vacuum cleaner, food-blender, welding-electrode? 1...2...3...4
3. Big, heavy machines such as a truck, crane, harvesting machine? 1...2...3...4
4. Paperwork such as letters, tickets, cash-book? 1...2...3...4
5. Conference minutes and written reports? 1...2...3...4
6. Written analytical reports, policy documents? 1...2...3...4
7. Modern computer technology? 1...2...3...4
8. Professional magazines, journals, or books? 1...2...3...4
9. Additional courses (with written materials) to keep up with job requirements? 1...2...3...4

Total ___ ÷ 36 = ___ [a] **4 = 4-point Average**

Parents' Informational Literacy[b]	*Parents' Recreational Literacy*[b]
How often do you usually (in a year) read . . .	How often do you usually (in a year) read . . .
1. Books about scientific subjects? 1...2...3	1. Espionage novels? 1...2...3
2. Books about animals and plants? 1...2...3	2. Police, private investigator novels? 1...2...3
3. (Auto-)biographies? 1...2...3	3. Romantic novels, romance? 1...2...3
4. Textbooks, educational books? 1...2...3	4. Books about holiday countries? 1...2...3
5. Books about art? 1...2...3	5. Regional novels? 1...2...3
6. Books about history? 1...2...3	6. War, adventure novels? 1...2...3
7. Modern (literary) literature or poetry? 1...2...3	7. Local newspaper articles on your town or neighborhood? 1...2...3

continues

Table 3–6. *continued*

Parents' Informational Literacy[b]	Parents' Recreational Literacy[b]
8. Encyclopedia? 1...2...3	8. Little ads in your newspaper or free advertising magazine? 1...2...3
9. Books about other countries? 1...2...3	9. Gossip articles on TV stars and other celebrities? 1...2...3
10. Magazine or newspaper articles about international politics? 1...2...3	10. Sports news? 1...2...3
11. Economic news? 1...2...3	11. Advertisements of the local supermarket? 1...2...3
12. Book reviews? 1...2...3	12. Newspaper or magazine articles about fashion? 1...2...3
13. Art reviews? 1...2...3	13. Newspaper reports on crime and accidents? 1...2...3
14. Articles about scientific topics? 1...2...3	14. Articles about TV programs? 1...2...3
Total ___ ÷ 42 = ___ [b] 3 = 3-point Average	15. TV schedule in the newspaper or TV guide? 1...2...3
	16. Information on opportunities for leisure activities? 1...2...3
	Total ___ ÷ 48 = ___ [b] 3 = 3-point Average

Note: [a]All symbolic job content items scored on a 4-point scale ranging from 1 *never* to 4 *very often/daily*. [b]All parent literacy items scored on a 3-point scale ranging from 1 *(almost) never* to 3 *often*.

Source: Adapted from "Home Literacy: Opportunity, Instruction, Cooperation, and Social-Emotional Quality Predicting Early Reading Achievement," by P. P. M. Leseman and P. F de Jong, 1998, *Reading Research Quarterly, 33*, p. 317. Copyright 1998 by the International Reading Association. Adapted with permission from the publisher and author.

Scores are computed as a mean of both parents' job content or by using the score of the parent who is employed. There are no stated qualifications for the examiner.

Author Recognition Test and Magazine Recognition Test

Stanovich and West (1989) developed the Author Recognition Test (ART) as a measure of exposure to print and recreational reading activity. The ART measures knowledge of best-selling authors. Educators can create an updated adaptation of this measure with current authors to use as a proxy for the amount of time parents may read in the home and thereby model literate behaviors. The analogous Magazine Recognition Test (MRT) measures knowledge of popular magazine titles. Stanovich and West's (1989) ART contained a list of 100 author names in alphabetical order. Half of the names were popular author names from best-seller lists and a variety of genres, whereas another 50 were foils (names from the editorial board of an academic journal). One key feature of this measure is that it circumvents the problem of social desirability, or the tendency of people to select answers on questionnaires or self-report measures that are most socially acceptable. Because this measure contains foils, it eliminates the possibility for adults to exaggerate how much they engage in reading.

When administering the ART or MRT, participants are asked to check names of authors they are familiar with by placing a check next to the name. The instructions prevent guessing because they include a caution that some names are not real, and that participants should only check names they know to be real authors or magazines. This simple measure probably can be administered in less than 10 minutes and was initially designed for use with adults. The ART and MRT can be administered to groups or individuals. The scores are interpreted as the number of correct targets identified, minus the number of foils checked. There are no special qualifications required of the examiner. Table 3–7 shows the names of the real authors used in Stanovich and West's (1989) ART.

Measuring Literacy Activities in the Home— Parent-Child Storybook Reading

Parents are often encouraged to read to their child daily (e.g., Armbruster, Lehr, & Osborn, 2003; Snow et al., 1998). A recent national survey suggests that many parents have responded to this message because over 90% of 3- to-5-year-old children whose mothers had at

Table 3-7. Author Recognition Test (ART)

Instructions: Before administering the test, say: "Some of the authors/titles on this list are the names of popular authors/real magazines and some are not. Read the list and check the ones you know are authors/magazines, but do not guess because some are not real authors/titles so guessing will be easily detected."

Names [real authors]	[sample foils]
Maya Angelou	Fred Mael
Isaac Asimov	Marvin Widen
Pete Axthelm	Judith Mayer-Smith
Jean Auel	
James Baldwin	
Judy Blume	
Barbara Taylor Bradford	
Anthony Burgess	
Edgar Rice Burroughs	
Barbara Carland	
Arthur C. Clarke	
James Clawell	
Jackie Collins	
Michael Crichton	
Len Deighton	
Ian Fleming	
Dick Francis	
Nancy Friday	
Andrew Greeley	
Bob Greene	
Robert Heinlein	
Frank Herbert	
Seymour Hersh	
S. E. Hinton	
Erica Jong	
Stephen King	
Judith Krantz	

Table 3-7. *continued*

Names [real authors]	[sample foils]
Louis L'Amour	
Elmore Leonard	
Doris Lessing	
Robert Lucllum	
Colleen McCullough	
James Michener	
Desmond Morris	
Toni Morrison	
John Naisbitt	
Lewis Patten	
Sylvia Porter	
Jane Bryant Quinn	
Mike Royko	
Sidney Sheldon	
Red Smith	
Danielle Steel	
Lewis Thomas	
Alvin Toffler	
J. R. R. Tolkien	
Irving Wallace	
Alice Walker	
Joseph Wambaugh	
Garry Wills	

Proportion Correct: ____# Correct detections – ____# Foils checked = ____ Derived score

Note: Only real authors used in Stanovich and West's (1989) ART are shown in this table. To use an author recognition test as a measure of print exposure, 50 actual authors and 50 foils need to be included in the measure.

Source: Reprinted from "Exposure to Print and Orthographic Processing," by K. E. Stanovich and R. F. West, 1989, *Reading Research Quarterly*, *24*, p. 431. Copyright 1989 by the International Reading Association. Reprinted with permission of the publisher and author.

least a college degree were read to three or more times a week (National Center for Education Statistics, 1999). However, for children whose mothers had less than a high school education only 63% of this population was read to three times a week or more (National Center for Education Statistics, 1999). Variability in frequency and quality of parent-child storybook reading makes this an important construct for educators to assess. Knowledge of existing home storybook reading routines assists educators in suggesting and modeling strategies for building language and literacy skills in the context of this common early childhood activity (Justice & Ezell, 2000).

Adult-mediated literacy events such as parent-child storybook reading appear to have a substantial influence on children's language development (Leseman & de Jong, 1998; Neuman, 1996; Payne, Whitehurst, & Angell, 1994) and literacy development (Justice & Ezell, 2000; Neuman, 1996). For instance, parents who include a print focus during shared reading may accelerate the early literacy skills of preschool children (Justice & Ezell, 2000). Chapter 5 of this book, Assessing the Quality of Shared Storybook Reading, provides a detailed account of the influences of storybook reading on children's language and literacy development and provides measures for assessing quality of storybook reading in the classroom setting. Thus, our discussion of shared storybook reading focuses on findings from home literacy research, and we present four measures for assessing frequency and characteristics of parent-child storybook reading (for a summary of these measures see Table 3–8). A substantial body of literature has investigated storybook reading. Thus, many tools for assessing the quality of storybook reading are available elsewhere. Because of the considerable amount of research in this domain, we discuss the activity of parent-child storybook reading separately from general measures of home literacy activities, although these constructs are interrelated.

The details of how the adult mediates storybook reading by going beyond reading the text (extratextual utterances: comments, conversations, and questions) may determine the value of shared storybook reading. A great deal of research has analyzed parents' extratextual utterances during storybook reading. This work indicates that certain types of parent-child talk may be more beneficial than others for developing language and literacy. For instance, DeTemple (2001) found that a high percentage of immediate talk

Table 3-8. Measuring Literacy Activities in the Home–Parent-Child Storybook Reading

Measure	Use	Time (Approximate)	Administration
Title Recognition Test (TRT)	To assess parent's exposure to children's books as a proxy for frequency of storybook reading at home.	10 minutes	Individual or group of parents
Family Routines: Reading Aloud	To assess the degree to which reading aloud is a routine activity in the home.	15 minutes	Individual parent
Home-School Coding System	To measure the type and timing of talk during storybook reading	15–30 minutes[a]	Single parent-child dyad
Coding of Parent's Print-Referencing Behaviors	To measure parent's verbal and nonverbal print-referencing behaviors during storybook reading.	15–30 minutes[a]	Single parent-child dyad

[a]Time for administration varies depending on length of text used and quantity of extratextual talk

(comments, labeling, and yes-no questions that are closely tied to the text) during shared storybook reading was associated with low scores on kindergarten literacy outcomes. In contrast, a higher percentage of nonimmediate talk (comments, questions, inferences, and predictions that use the text as a springboard for talk that is not immediately visible in the text or illustrations) during reading was associated with higher scores on kindergarten literacy measures. Britto, Brooks-Gunn, and Griffin (2006) also analyzed maternal speaking and teaching patterns during storybook reading and a puzzle task. Their work suggests that when mothers provide preschool children with support and high levels of interaction during book reading and other teaching activities children demonstrate greater school readiness and expressive language skills as compared to children who receive less maternal engagement.

Similarly, Hammettt, van Kleeck, and Huberty (2003) examined the extratextual utterances of middle- to upper-middle income mothers and fathers during book sharing. Using cluster analysis, they described notable variability in the quantity of extratextual talk of these parents. Most of the parents in their sample fell into a cluster using an average of only 17 extratextual utterances; however another cluster of parents used an average of 69 occasions of talk during reading. Hammett and colleagues' (2003) analysis indicated variations in the style of talk used by each cluster as well. For example, one cluster of parents made several utterances related to print and book conventions, whereas others focused more on story content at different levels of abstraction. The majority of parents in this study chose to focus mostly on text reading and contributed only a limited number of utterances outside of read-ing the text. This observation that parents tend to stick to the words in the text differs from the interactive reading style promoted by intervention programs such as Whitehurst and colleagues' dialogic reading.

Dialogic reading appears to be a promising interactive storybook reading strategy in which the child takes a lead role in directing the conversation around the pictures in the book. Parents are trained to use open-ended questions and to rephrase and extend the child's utterances to promote language development and model extended discourse during book reading. Dialogic reading is "based on the assumption that practice, feedback, and appropriately scaffolded interactions facilitate language development" (Arnold,

Lonigan, Whitehurst, & Epstein, 1994, p. 236). Even when parents were trained in dialogic reading strategies through inexpensive videotape training, children who received dialogic reading interventions made gains in their language skills (Arnold et al., 1994). Similarly, adult-mediated, elaborated discussion of word meanings during storybook reading in school settings showed a more promising impact on word learning than repeated exposure to words without elaboration, especially for children with low levels of vocabulary (Justice, Meier, & Walpole, 2005).

Parent-child storybook reading offers an opportunity for parents to build children's emergent literacy skills through extratextual references about print. The work of Justice and Ezell (2000) encourages adult print referencing during parent-child storybook reading to build metalinguistic skills of thinking and talking about print. Print referencing requires that adults use verbal and nonverbal cues that direct the child's attention to print through questions, comments, requests about print, and pointing to or tracking print. Justice and Ezell provided a 15-minute training session for individual parents, which included watching a video of print-referencing behaviors, modeling of print referencing by the researcher, and a practice session with the child. The researcher provided feedback to parents regarding their use of print-referencing behaviors after the practice session and then asked parents to use these behaviors during a 4-week home reading program. Results showed significant gains for the experimental group in several emergent literacy outcomes such as ability to identify words in print, to segment one-, two- or three- word phrases, and to demonstrate awareness of print concepts. Further, parents in the experimental group reported positive perceptions about the impact of print-focused reading sessions on early language and literacy skills.

Other research has analyzed the impact of text structure in parent-child interactions during storybook reading and children's questions and comments during reading. Neuman (1996) found that predictable texts tended to elicit book-focused conversations about the text such as the child chiming in at familiar words or phrases. In contrast, narrative texts tended to elicit more cognitively demanding talk related to story meaning and making connections to the text. Patterned or predictive texts were valuable for some parents who lacked proficiency in reading because the repetition and rhyme appeared to scaffold parent-child interactions (Neuman,

1996). Yaden, Smolkin, and Conlon (1989) analyzed the spontaneous questions children asked during parent-child reading and noted tentative findings that reading fewer high-quality children's books may limit the child's interest and scope of questions. Yaden et al. (1989) determined that the majority of children's questions (40–50%) were about pictures, and the next most frequent questions were about story meaning, followed by questions about word meaning. They found a consistent trend that children asked few spontaneous questions about the graphic forms of print. When children did ask about print, their questions usually occurred when reading texts with speech balloons and alphabet books.

A meta-analysis by Bus, van IJzendoorn, and Pellegrini (1995) concluded that time spent reading storybooks in the home carried a modest predictive value, accounting for approximately 8% of the variance, in children's future literacy skills. Yet other researchers describe less promising findings for shared book reading at home. Evans et al. (2000) used a children's book title recognition checklist as a proxy for frequency of home shared-reading and found no contribution of home book reading to prediction of kindergarten print and language skills after controlling for age, parent education, and cognitive ability. They suggested that letter name, letter sounds, phonological sensitivity, and receptive vocabulary are not improved through common, uncoached storybook reading. Rather, Evans et al. (2000) found that parent reports of home activities involving letters and sounds was a stronger predictor of kindergarten print-related and phonological skills. However, Sénéchal (2006) found that early storybook exposure predicted kindergarten vocabulary and explained 11% of the variance in fourth-grade reports of frequency of reading for pleasure. In other words, parent-child storybook reading influences different literacy skills than parent teaching.

Scholars and politicians suggest that parents are the first and arguably the most important teachers (e.g., Britto et al., 2006; U.S. Department of Education, 2005) in a child's life because of the plethora of natural learning experiences parents can foster through activities such as shared storybook reading. Educators can find opportunities to show parents how to involve children in storybook reading and how to scaffold for their children during reading if parents are unsure of what to do during storybook reading (Edwards, 1995). Teachers also can provide parents with free publications about how to help their child learn to read by ordering booklets from the U.S. Department of Education Web site (http://www.ed.gov/parents/ read/resources/edpicks.jhtml?src=qc) and sharing these at parent-teacher conferences or school sponsored literacy workshops.

Title Recognition Test

Like the ART and MRT used with adults, Cunningham and Stanovich (1990) designed the Title Recognition Test (TRT) for use with children as a quick measure of print exposure and recreational reading. This checklist contained titles of real children's books and foils in the same design as the ART and MRT. This format circumvents the problem of social desirability because children can only select the titles of books they know are real. Cunningham and Stanovich (1990) created this measure for use with third- and fourth-grade students; however, many researchers have adapted the design for use in home literacy research with parents of emergent and early readers. For instance, Sénéchal, LeFevre, Thomas, and Daley (1998) administered a measure comparable to the TRT to parents. When a checklist of popular children's books is used with parents, it can serve as a proxy for adults' exposure to and presumably reading of children's books to their child in the home. Table 3-9 shows the titles and foils used by Sénéchal and colleagues (1998) and the percentage of parents who recognized these titles. Educators should adapt TRT checklists to match the age and available books in their population.

When administering a TRT to parents, participants are asked to check names of children's books they are familiar with by placing a check next to the name. The instructions prevent guessing because the examiner notes that some titles are not real, and that participants should only check titles they know are real. This simple measure probably can be administered in less than 10 minutes and was designed for use with adults. The TRT can be administered to groups or individuals. The scores are interpreted as the number of correct targets identified, minus the number of foils checked. There are no special qualifications required for the examiner. For additional examples of children's book title checklists for parents, see Fritjers, Barron, and Brunello (2000). For a checklist used with teachers, see Cunningham and Stanovich (2004).

Table 3-9. Children's Title Checklist

Instructions: Before administering the test, say: "Some of the titles on this list are the names of popular children's books and some are not. Read the list and check the ones you know are children's books, but do not guess because some are not real books so guessing can be easily detected."

Titles	*Foils*
A Difficult Day	Big Old Trucks
Alexander and the Terrible, Horrible, No Good, Very Bad Day	Clarissa's Patch
	Eleanor and the Magic Bag
Alligator Pie	Hello Morning Hello Day
A Pocket for Corduroy	How Stephen Found a Pet
Bears on Wheels	How Wishes Come True
Busiest Firefighters Ever	I Hear a Knock at My Window
Caps for Sale	Kimberly's Horse
Curious George	Martha Rabbit's Family
Farmer Joe's Hot Day	Rachel's Real Dilemma
Franklin in the Dark	Snowflakes Are Falling
Go Dog Go	Terry Toad
Goodnight Moon	The Paper Boat's Trip
Green Eggs and Ham	The Toy Trunk
Happy Birthday Moon	Tracy Tickles
Harry the Dirty Dog	Three Cheers for Gloria
In the Kitchen	What Do I Hear Now?
I Was So Mad	Worry No Longer
Jelly Belly	Winter Fun on Snowy Days
Just Me and My Dad	Zack's House
Love You Forever	
Matthew and the Midnight Tow Truck	
Mortimer	

Table 3-9. *continued*

Titles	Foils
Murmel, Murmel, Murmel	
Polar Express	
Red Is Best	
Saggy Baggy Elephant	
Scuffy the Tugboat	
Shy Little Kitten	
The Poky Little Puppy	
The Runaway Bunny	
The Snowy Day	
The Very Hungry Caterpillar	
This is My Family	
Thomas' Snow Suit	
Tootle	
Velveteen Rabbit	
We're Going on a Bear Hunt	
Where the Wild Things Are	
Whispering Rabbit	
Wonderful Pigs of Jillian Jiggs	

Scoring: ____ Proportion correct detections − ____ Proportion foils checked = ____ Derived score

Note: When developing a title recognition test for use with parents consider age-appropriate texts and texts available in your community.

Source: From "Differential Effects of Home Literacy Experiences on the Development of Oral and Written Language," by M. Sénéchal, J. LeFevre, E. M. Thomas, and K. E. Daley, 1998, *Reading Research Quarterly, 33,* p 114. Copyright 1998 by the International Reading Association. Reprinted with permission of the publisher and author.

Family Routines: Reading Aloud

To assess how reoccurring family activities or established routines might provide opportunities for advancing young children's literacy skills, Serpell et al. (2002) created a Reading Aloud scale. This scale frames questions in a less presumptuous manner than some other self-report measures in an effort to minimize the tendency to select socially desirable responses. Therefore, this may provide a better estimate of home storybook reading than some questionnaires that simply ask parents to report how often they read to their child. Parents are asked to check one response for each of the seven items on a 4-point scale ranging from 1 *not at all true* to 4 *very true* for their family (see Table 3–10).

The outcomes are interpreted by assigning a 4-point value from 1 *low* to 4 *high* for each response after the parent has completed the form. The higher the score, the more routinized reading aloud is for this family. The time for administration is probably 15 minutes or less. This measure was administered to parents of kindergarten and first-grade children by Serpell et al. (2002), but may be useful for parents of preschool children also. The measure can be administered to an individual parent or a group. The measure is available in English, but may be useful for other languages if translated. Score types range from 1 to 4 with a higher score indicating a more routinized activity for this family. No special qualifications are required for the examiner.

Home-School Coding System

De Temple's (1993) Home School Coding System (as cited in Britto et al., 2006) is a scheme for coding transcripts of parental speech during home book reading. This coding scheme allows educators to analyze extratextual utterances for functionality and nature of talk that occurs during storybook reading. Britto et al. (2006) concluded that mothers who provide high levels of support before, during, and after reading fostered school readiness and expressive oral language. Along with this interactive style of book reading, a relationship was found between higher school readiness and language scores in children and mothers who used more decontextualized language, asked more labeling questions, and gave more positive feedback to the child. Five codes for labeling parental

Table 3–10. Family Routines: Reading Aloud (Serpell et al., 2002)

Reading Aloud

For our family really true	sort of true					_For our family_ really true	sort of true
_4_	_3_	1. Some families regularly read aloud together.	BUT	Other families rarely read aloud together.		_2_	_1_
_4_	_3_	2. In some families, the same parent or older child always reads aloud to the youngest child.	BUT	In other families, different people read aloud to the child at different times depending on who is available.		_2_	_1_
_1_	_2_	3. In some families, the timing of reading aloud is flexible. People read aloud when they get the (a) chance.	BUT	In other families, reading aloud is very definitely scheduled; it happens at the same time every day.		_3_	_4_
_—_	_—_	4. In some families, people feel strongly about reading aloud together.	BUT	In other families, it is not that important whether people read aloud or not.		_—_	_—_

continues

115

Table 3–10. *continued*

Reading Aloud

For our family really true	sort of true				*For our family* really true	sort of true
—	—	5. In some families, reading aloud is just so others can hear.	BUT	In other families, reading aloud is more than just information; it has special meaning.	—	—
—	—	6. In some families, reading aloud has always been and will always be a regular family event.	BUT	In other families, the time at which people read aloud has changed over the years as children grow up and schedules change.	—	—
—	—	7. In some families, there is little planning around reading aloud.	BUT	In other families, reading aloud is planned in advance.	—	—

Note. Sample coding values from 1 (low) to 4 (high) should be removed from the scale before used by respondents. Respondents only mark one side of the continuum for each question.

Source: From "Intimate Culture of Families in the Early Socialization of Literacy," by R. Serpell, S. Sonnenschein, L. Baker, and H. Ganapathy, 2002, *Journal of Family Psychology, 16*, p. 404. Copyright 2002 by the American Psychological Association. Reprinted with permission of the publisher and author.

utterances are detailed in Table 3–11, including: (1) timing of parental talk, (2) decontextualized language, (3) expressive language use, (4) labeling questions, and (5) positive feedback.

Higher rates of talk in these five categories indicate a more supportive parental reading style that can potentially improve children's literacy outcomes. The time required to videotape a parent-child reading session is probably 15 to 30 minutes, depending on the length of the book and the amount of conversation. Substantially more time will be required to transcribe and code transcripts of parent-child interactions (see Appendix A of Britto et al., 2006, for complete transcription and coding procedure). This coding scheme was used with 3-year-old children in Britto et al. (2006), but a similar system has been used with children through the early school years (Beals, DeTemple, & Dickinson, 1994). Reading sessions should occur with single parent-child dyads in the home or at school. The coding system is only available in English, but may be useful with other languages if translated. Score types include frequencies and percentages of talk in each category. Examiners may benefit from training to reliably code all parent utterances into the same categories.

Coding of Parent's Print-Referencing Behaviors

Print is seldom a focus during shared storybook reading because "adults reading to young children rarely reference print verbally (e.g., questioning about print) or nonverbally (e.g., pointing to print)" (Justice & Ezell, 2000, p. 258). Likewise, children seldom ask questions about print; most of their questions relate to the illustrations (Yaden et al., 1989). Therefore, this assessment is probably most useful when working with parents who have been coached or trained to use print-referencing behaviors during reading to accelerate their child's print awareness (see Justice & Ezell, 2000). This coding system provides a systematic method for examining parents' behaviors during reading. Justice and Ezell (2000) videotaped parent-child dyads' shared reading session and used transcripts for analysis. Table 3–12 contains a template assessors can use to code parent's verbal and nonverbal print-referencing behaviors during storybook reading.

Parent's extratextual talk and gestures are coded as three types of cues: 1: *verbal print reference*, 2: *nonverbal print reference*, or 3: *other nonprint references* (see Table 3–12 for examples).

Table 3-11. Home-School Coding System

Coding Label	Description	Example	Examiner Notes
Timing of parental talk	Did parental talk occur before, during, or after reading?	*Before:* "Would you like to turn the pages?" *During:* "This is the title of the book." *After:* "Did you like the book?"	
Decontextualized language use	Parental talk that goes beyond the text or illustrations to make predictions, inferences, or connections to the child's life. This also includes providing definitions or explanations. This category does *not* include immediate or contextual talk which uses information that is readily available from the text or illustrations.	*Inference:* Child asks, "Why is she crying?" and parent offers an inferential response. *Text-child connection:* "Remember when we went in grandma's car?" (a connection to illustration of a car in the book)	

118

Coding Label	Description	Example	Examiner Notes
Expressive language use	Parental talk that includes a diverse range of content and functions of talk. A wide range of functions of talk could include: requesting responses from child, giving responses to child, and making spontaneous comments. A diverse range in content could include multiple topics or a number of different words.	*Multiple functions:* Request response—"What is that?" Giving response—"Good!" Making a gesture—Parent points to picture Making a comment—"This is the dog's nose."	
Labeling questions	Talk in which the parent requests information that requires the child to name, label, or point to an illustration or word in the book.	"What is that?" "Show me . . . "	
Positive feedback	Parent gives an approving reaction to a previous utterance made by the child.	"Good." "Right."	

Source: Adapted from "Maternal Reading and Teaching Patterns: Associations with School Readiness in Low-Income African American Families," by P. R. Britto, J. Brooks-Gunn, and T. M. Griffin, 2006, *Reading Research Quarterly, 41,* pp. 74–75. Copyright 2006 by the International Reading Association. Adapted with permission of the publisher.

Table 3–12. Print Referencing During Storybook Reading

Behavior	Cue	Example	Notes
Verbal print reference	*Requests about print*	Show me where it says "splash."	
	Questions about print	What do you think this word says?	
	Comments about print	This word says "splash!"	
Nonverbal print reference	*Pointing to print*	Adult points to word "splash."	
	Tracking print	Adult runs finger under words when reading.	
Other nonprint references	*Requests, questions comments, and gestures unrelated to print*	Adult prompts related to illustrations or story events.	
		Adult points to illustrations.	

Source: Adapted from "Enhancing Children's Print and Word Awareness Through Home-Based Parent Intervention," by L. M. Justice and H. K. Ezell, 2000, *American Journal of Speech-Language Pathology, 9*, p. 261 and from "Use of Storybook Reading to Increase Print Awareness in At-Risk Children," by L. M. Justice and H. K. Ezell, 2002, *American Journal of Speech-Language Pathology, 11*, p. 22. Adapted with permission of the publisher and author.

The first two types of print-referencing cues include three types of print-related talk:

(a) print conventions (e.g., parts of the book—"Where is the front of this book?" or directionality—"Show me which way I need to read."), (b) concept of word (e.g., word isolation—"Show me just one word on this page." or distinguishing the white spaces—"How many words are on this page?"), and (c) alphabet knowledge (e.g., letter recognition—"Where is the letter B on this page?" or letter sounds—"What letter makes the /d/ sound in 'duck'?") (Justice & Ezell, 2002, p. 22).

Once coding is complete, the outcomes are interpreted first as the raw frequency with which parents used verbal and nonverbal references to print during the session. A second calculation is necessary to account for individual differences in length of the book reading session. The raw frequency is divided by the length of the book reading session to determine the rate with which each parent used print-referencing behaviors.

The time required for administration varies depending on length of text used and quantity of extratextual talk, but shared reading sessions will probably take between 15 to 30 minutes. This coding system is appropriate for use with single parent-child dyads at a home or in a school setting. The assessment was designed for use with 4-year-old children (Justice & Ezell, 2000) but may be useful with slightly older or younger children. This coding system was used with English-speaking parents and children, but it may be useful with other languages. There are not formal qualifications for the examiner; however, examiners may benefit from training to reliably code all parent behaviors into the same categories.

Measuring Literacy Activities in the Home— Other Than Storybook Reading

Families can support literacy development at home by providing a variety of opportunities for literacy activities such as writing, reading print, learning about letters and language, or playing with words. However, not all children have equal experiences and interactions with literacy and print (Purcell-Gates, 2000) despite the fact that we live in a literate society. Therefore, assessing children's requisite knowledge of literacy as acquired through home activities provides educators with useful information about their prior experiences.

Measures of home literacy activities usually attempt to gauge the frequency of home activities and the quality of interactions that take place during literacy activities. Other chapters within this volume review measures of knowledge and skills such as phonological and print awareness that may be supported by home literacy activities. For example, Chapter 7 of this volume (Assessing Print

Knowledge) provides measures for assessing children's letter recognition and written print awareness. Thus, our discussion focuses on assessing activities in the home that may support print knowledge such as parent teaching of letters and sounds or parent scaffolding during writing. We consider five measures for assessing home literacy activities (for an overview see Table 3–13).

Home literacy activities are a key component in home literacy research because many scholars espouse a Vygotskian view that caregivers can motivate learning through scaffolded language interactions (e.g., Beals, 2001; Katz, 2001; Snow, 1991) and literacy interactions (e.g., Britto et al., 2006; Leseman & de Jong, 1998). Both parents and teachers recognize, "What the child can do in cooperation today he can do alone tomorrow" (Vygotsky, 1962, p. 104); therefore, opportunities for scaffolded literacy events in the home support emergent and early literacy development. Parents and caregivers have a unique opportunity to mediate and support both informal and formal literacy activities.

Formal and informal home literacy activities appear to influence different aspects of children's literacy development. Informal activities such as shared storybook reading influence vocabulary development, conceptual knowledge (Storch & Whitehurst, 2001) and oral-language skills, but not written-language skills (Sénéchal et al. 1998). Formal parent teaching activities such as teaching letter sounds influence letter name and sound knowledge, phonological awareness, (Storch & Whitehurst, 2001) and written-language skills, but not oral-language skills (Sénéchal et al., 1998). Some parents act as tutors in the teaching of letter names and sounds, decoding skills, and activities that support invented spelling and writing in the home.

Some research elucidates the distinction between formal parent teaching activities in the home and more informal activities such as shared storybook reading. A study by Evans et al. (2000) found that formal, parent-initiated activities involving letters, such as teaching letter names and sounds and printing letters, was a strong predictor, accounting for 5 to 10% of variance in kindergarten print-related literacy skills, whereas shared book reading made no contribution to the prediction of kindergarten print-related skills. Evans et al. (2000) concluded that print-related and oral language skills are not enhanced or developed by general, "uncoached" informal reading activities when parent education level is statistically controlled (pp. 71–72). Similarly, Sénéchal et al.

Table 3–13. Measuring Literacy Activities in the Home—Other Than Storybook Reading

Measure	Use	Time (Approximate)	Administration
Home Literacy Questionnaire of Formal and Informal Literacy Experiences	To measure parental report of informal literacy activities (e.g., storybook reading) and formal parent teaching activities (e.g., teaching letters) in the home.	5–10 minutes	Individual or group of parents
Early Childhood Longitudinal Study-K (ECLS-K) Parent Interview	To assess opportunities for literacy activities in the home.	10 minutes	Individual parent
Family Involvement Questionnaire (FIQ)	To assess multiple dimensions of family involvement in learning activities including: school-based involvement, home-school conferencing, and home-based involvement.	15 minutes	Individual or group of parents
Early Literacy Parent Questionnaire	To measure parent report of their child's emergent and early literacy skill development.	15 minutes	Individual or group of parents
Graphophonemic Mediation of Mother-Child Joint Writing	To assess how much mediation and support a mother provides to her child during writing tasks.	20–30 minutes	Single parent-child dyad

(1998) found that the frequency of formal parent teaching of reading and writing explained 7% of the variance kindergarten in written-language skills. A follow-up study by Sénéchal (2006) revealed that parent teaching continued to influence later reading, specifically explaining 18% of the variance in fourth-grade reading fluency. In terms of informal teaching experiences at home, 11% of variance in the frequency children reported reading for pleasure in the fourth grade was predicted by informal activities such as storybook reading. Informal components also made a significant contribution to Grade 4 reading comprehension measures (see Sénéchal, 2006).

Before examining assessments of home literacy activities, we briefly summarize the purposes of several home literacy activities and how these may support emergent and early literacy development. By growing up in an environment where print is valued, children may become aware of print conventions such as directionality of print in texts from left-to-right and top-to-bottom, distinguishing pictures from print, use of punctuation, and boundaries of letters and words (Adams, 1990). Although awareness of print concepts is less predictive of later reading achievement than other skills such as knowledge of letter sounds, knowledge of print conventions helps to demystify how print works (Neuman & Roskos, 2005). These skills are essential for knowing how to deal with texts; thus, home supports for developing print awareness are beneficial.

Children who can consciously attend to the sounds (as distinct from the meanings) of words have phonemic awareness—a strong predictor of prereaders' later first-grade reading achievement (Adams, 1990; National Reading Panel Report, 2000; Scarborough, 2001). Children may develop sensitivity to the units of sound through many home activities such as teaching songs and nursery rhymes or playing language games (Snow et al., 1998). Maclean, Bryant, and Bradley (1987) suggest that both middle- and low-income British parents unwittingly foster growth of phonological skills in children through informal linguistic routines such as learning nursery rhymes. Maclean et al. (1987) demonstrated that a simple measure of children's knowledge of nursery rhymes is strongly related to phonological skills. Employing a more formal approach to parent teaching activities, Justice, Kaderavek, Bowles, and Grimm (2005) used parent teaching of early phonological awareness skills such as rhyme and alliteration with storybook reading. Parents reported high marks for their interest in implementing this phonological skills practice and children's rhyme awareness was accelerated (Justice et al., 2005).

Some parents choose to teach letter names and sounds, decoding skills, and invented spelling or writing in the home. Interest in assessing home supports for letter learning emerges from the fact that knowing letters is a strong predictor of prereaders' later reading achievement (Adams, 1990; Scarborough, 2001). Adams (1990) suggests that, if children learn to recognize letters before beginning formal education, they may have an easier time learning letter sounds and word spellings. When children are taught letter names by their parents they may know more letters than their peers (Ehri & Roberts, 2006; National Center for Education Statistics, 1999). Children who receive parental instruction in learning letter sounds demonstrate higher invented spelling scores in preschool and kindergarten (Ehri & Roberts, 2006).

The home is an opportune location for practicing invented spelling and simultaneously developing phonemic awareness through functional or purposeful writing experiences (Richgels, 2001). Yet, before suggesting that parents teach writing at home, it is important to consider that writing is a more difficult concept for children to grasp than oral speech because it requires an additional step of producing inner speech, then translating it into writing (Vygotsky, 1962). Further, parents may need guidance in coaching their child in appropriate developmental spelling (for a summary see Bear, Invernizzi, Templeton, & Johnston, 2004) and appropriate expectations for fine motor development. Nonetheless, assessing characteristics of mother-child joint writing sessions using the Graphophonemic Mediation scale (Aram & Levin, 2002) showed that the level of maternal mediation of writing was strongly related to children's basic literacy skills. Maternal mediation of joint writing predicted 41% of word writing and recognition outcomes as well as 26% of phonological awareness scores (Aram & Levin, 2002).

Assessments of home literacy activities provide educators with valuable information about home supports for literacy development. Before encouraging parents to utilize formal parent teaching activities educators need to consider each family's unique culture and how multiple realities of home literacy contexts may support successful literacy development (Snow, 1991). The family's culture, preferences, and literacy routines, should guide home literacy programs and interventions (Klingner & Edwards, 2006; Wasik et al.,

2001). Again, free publications are available for educators to inform parents of activities they can do in the home to support language and literacy development from the Web sites of the U.S. Department of Education (www.ed.gov) or the National Institute for Literacy (www.nifl.gov/partnershipforreading).

Home Literacy Questionnaire of Formal and Informal Literacy Experiences

Sénéchal and colleagues (Sénéchal et al., 1998; Sénéchal, Ouellette, & Rodney, 2006) utilized a simple, yet informative parent questionnaire to assess two distinct categories of children's experiences with printed materials: informal and formal literacy experiences. Sénéchal et al. (1998) found that parent reports of engaging their children in informal literacy experiences such as storybook reading were not closely associated with parent reports of formal literacy experiences such as teaching children how to read and print. A second measure of storybook exposure, a children's storybook title recognition test, was employed in Sénéchal et al. (1998) and Sénéchal (2006) but is not discussed in this chapter because it is similar to the TRT reviewed previously. The informal and formal literacy experiences questionnaire is detailed in Table 3–14.

Outcomes for these questions are interpreted on 5- and 8-point scales depending on the nature of the question (see Table 3–14). Question 3 should be converted to a 5-point scale for calculating the total score. The time for administration is probably under 5 minutes. The measure is designed for parents of kindergarten and first-grade children. It can be administered to groups or individual parents. The questionnaire in Table 3–14 is divided into informal components in the upper half and formal teaching components in the lower half. The measure is written for English-speaking parents, but may be useful in other languages if translated. Scores are calculated as total score for informal, formal, and grand total. No special qualifications are required for the examiner.

Early Childhood Longitudinal Study Parent Interview

The Early Childhood Longitudinal Study (ECLS) is an ongoing, longitudinal study of the kindergarten class of 1998–99 that follows

Table 3–14. Home Literacy Questionnaire of Formal and Informal Literacy Experiences

---

Parent Questionnaire

Please mark the number that best describes you and your child's behavior or home.

Storybook exposure

1. How often do you read storybooks to your child in a typical week at bedtime?
   ___never ___once ___2 ___3 ___4 ___5 ___6 ___7 times
   ___more, please estimate:

2. How often do you read storybooks to your child in a typical week at other times?
   ___never ___once ___2 ___3 ___4 ___5 ___6 ___7 times
   ___more, please estimate:

Number of children's books

3. Please estimate the number of children's books that are available in your home?
   ___none ___1–20 ___21–40 ___41–60 ___61–80 ___more, please estimate:

Please circle the number that you think best describes your child's behavior

Frequency of reading requests

4. During a typical week, how often does your child ask to be read to? Choose a number from 1 to 5, where 1 means never and 5 means very often.

My child asks to be read to:	Never	Seldom	Sometimes	Often	Very often
	1	2	3	4	5

Frequency of child library visits

5. How often does your child go to the library? Choose a number from 1 to 5, where 1 means never and 5 means very often.

My child goes to the library:	Never	Seldom	Sometimes	Often	Very often
	1	2	3	4	5

continues

Table 3–14. *continued*

Reading Onset

6. How old was your child when you started reading picture books to him or her?

(please estimate age) _____

Total (Questions 1–6): _____

Frequency of parent teaching

During a typical week how often do you engage in the following activities? Choose a number from 1 to 5, where 1 means never and 5 means very often.

I teach my child:

	Never	Seldom	Sometimes	Often	Very often
7. how to name the letters of the alphabet:	1	2	3	4	5
8. how to read words:	1	2	3	4	5
9. how to print words:	1	2	3	4	5

Total (Questions 7–9): _____

Grand Total: _____

Source: Adapted from "Differential Effects of Home Literacy Experiences on the Development of Oral and Written Language," by M. Sénéchal, J. LeFevre, F. M. Thomas, and K. E. Daley, 1998, *Reading Research Quarterly,* *33*, p. 113. Copyright 1998 by the International Reading Association. Adapted with permission of the publisher and author.

a cohort through 12th grade. The study, which is sponsored by the U.S. Department of Education and the National Center for Education Statistics, analyzes a range of family, school, community, and individual factors that influence children's academic progress. The ECLS (1999) kindergarten Fall Parent Interview procedures may provide useful, basic information for early literacy educators. The full instrument is available at http://nces.ed.gov/ecls/KinderInstru ments.asp along with other public domain instruments.

The outcomes for this measure are interpreted using a 4-point scale to indicate frequency of activities for most items. The exceptions are two questions that ask for an estimate of number of books and items in the household. Time for administration is probably under 10 minutes. The measure is appropriate for parents of kindergarten children. This measure is administered to parents in an individual, oral format in person or over the phone. The Fall Home Environment, Activities, and Cognitive Stimulation subtest is relevant to home literacy. Items from this subtest are summarized in Table 3–15. The interview questions are provided in English, but may be useful for other languages if translated. Scores are interpreted using either the 4-point scale or the estimated quantities given by parents. No special qualifications are required for the examiner.

Family Involvement Questionnaire (FIQ)

A multidimensional scale of family involvement in early childhood education was designed by Fantuzzo, Tighe, and Childs (2000) to establish construct validity of the Family Involvement Questionnaire (FIQ) and analyze whether there were differences in family involvement as a function of demographic variables and early childhood program variables. This measure assesses variables outside of literacy, but does include several items indirectly related to reading and writing tasks. The questionnaire contains three involvement constructs: school-based involvement, home-school conferencing, and home-based involvement. Sample FIQ items are detailed in Table 3–16. Fantuzzo et al. (2000) reported that parents with education beyond high school engaged in higher levels of school-based involvement and home-school conferencing. They also found that two parent families reported higher levels of home-school conferencing and home-based involvement than single-parent families.

Table 3–15. ECLS-K Parent Interview

Examiner states the purpose: I'd like to talk with you about {CHILD}'s activities with family members.

In a typical week, how often do you or any other family member do the following things with {CHILD}?

RESPONSES: 1 = not at all, 2 = once or twice, 3 = 3–6 times, 4 = every day, 7 = refused, 9 = don't know

- Read books to {CHILD}? Would you say not at all, once or twice, 3–6 times, or every day?

continues

Table 3–15. *continued*

- Tell stories to {CHILD}?
- Sing songs with {CHILD}?
- Help {CHILD} to do arts and crafts?
- Involve {CHILD} in household chores, like cooking, cleaning, setting the table, or caring for pets?
- Play games or do puzzles with {CHILD}?
- Talk about nature or do science projects with {CHILD}?
- Build something or play with construction toys with {CHILD}?
- Play a sport or exercise together?

    _____ = TOTAL

- About how many children's books does {CHILD} have in your home now, including library books?
    _____ Enter # of books; ___ Refused; ___ Don't know

- About how many children's records, audiotapes, or CDs do you have at home, including any from the library? Please only include what you have for children.
    _____ Enter # of records, tapes, or CDs; ___ Refused; ___ Don't know

- Now please think about the past week. How often did {CHILD} look at picture books outside of school in the past week? Would you say: Never = 1, once or twice = 2, 3 to 6 times a week = 3, or 4 = every day? 7 = refused, 9 = don't know

- In the past week, how often did {CHILD} read to or pretend to read to {himself/herself} or to others outside of school? Would you say: Never = 1, once or twice = 2, 3 to 6 times a week = 3, or 4 = every day? 7 = refused, 9 = don't know

- Now think about the year before {CHILD} started kindergarten. Did {CHILD} watch Sesame Street either at home or someplace else, at least once a week for a period of three months or more? Yes = 1, No = 2, Have no TV = 3, Refused = 7, Don't know = 9

Note: Full ECLS-K Parent Interview available at http://nces.ed.gov/ecls/KinderInstruments.asp

Source: Adapted from *ECLS-K Fall Parent Interview*, by the Early Childhood Longitudinal Study (ECLS), 1998, p. HEQ-1–HEQ-2. Public domain instrument developed by the Early Childhood Longitudinal Study with support of National Center for Education Statistics and U. S. Department of Education.

Table 3–16. Family Involvement Questionnaire

Instructions: Ask the primary caregiver to rate the nature and extent of their involvement in their child's early educational experiences for each item.

School-Based Involvement	Rarely	Sometimes	Often	Always
1. I volunteer in my child's classroom	1	2	3	4
2. I participate in parent and family social activities with the teacher	1	2	3	4
3. I participate in planning classroom activities with the teacher	1	2	3	4
4. I go on class trips with my child	1	2	3	4
5. I talk with other parents about school meetings and events	1	2	3	4
6. I participate in planning school trips for my child	1	2	3	4
7. I meet with other parents from my child's class outside of school	1	2	3	4
8. I hear teachers tell my child how much they love learning	1	2	3	4
9. I participate in fundraising activities in my child's school	1	2	3	4
10. I feel that parents in my child's classroom support each other	1	2	3	4

continues

Table 3–16. *continued*

Home-Based Involvement	Rarely	Sometimes	Often	Always
11. I spend time working with my child on number skills	1	2	3	4
12. I spend time working with my child on reading/writing skills	1	2	3	4
13. I talk to my child about how much I love learning new things	1	2	3	4
14. I bring home learning materials for my child (videos, etc.)	1	2	3	4
15. I spend time with my child working on creative activities	1	2	3	4
16. I share stories with my child about when I was in school	1	2	3	4
17. I see that my child has a place for books and school materials	1	2	3	4
18. I take my child places in the community to learn special things (i.e., zoo, museum)	1	2	3	4
19. I maintain clear rules at my home that my child should obey	1	2	3	4
20. I talk about my child's learning efforts in front of relatives	1	2	3	4
21. I review my child's school work	1	2	3	4
22. I keep a regular morning and bedtime schedule for my child	1	2	3	4
23. I praise my child for school work in front of the teacher	1	2	3	4

Home-School Conferencing

	Rarely	Sometimes	Often	Always
24. I talk to the teacher about how my child gets along with his/her classmates at school	1	2	3	4
25. I talk with my child's teacher about classroom rules	1	2	3	4
26. I talk with my child's teacher about his/her difficulties at school	1	2	3	4
27. I talk with my child's teacher about school work to practice at home	1	2	3	4
28. I talk to my child's teacher about my child's accomplishments	1	2	3	4
29. I talk to my child's teacher about his/her daily routine	1	2	3	4
30. I attend conferences with the teacher to talk about my child's learning or behavior	1	2	3	4
31. The teacher and I write notes about my child or school activities	1	2	3	4
32. I schedule meetings with administration to talk about problems or to gain information	1	2	3	4
33. I talk with my child's teacher on the telephone	1	2	3	4
34. I talk with my child's teacher about personal or family matters	1	2	3	4

Note. To protect the integrity of the FIQ scale, only an abstraction of items is shown.

Source: Sample items reprinted from "Family Involvement Questionnaire: A Multivariate Assessment of Family Participation in Early Childhood Education," by J. Fantuzzo, E. Tighe, and S. Childs, *Journal of Educational Psychology, 92,* p. 370. Copyright 2000 by the American Psychological Association. Adapted with permission of the publisher and author.

Fantuzzo et al. (2000) interpreted the outcomes for purposes of establishing validity and studying associations with family background variables; however, educators can interpret outcomes as an average for each construct or as an indicator of developmentally appropriate levels of parental involvement across grade levels or programs. The questionnaire can be administered in less than 15 minutes. The FIQ is designed for parents of preschool, kindergarten, and first grade children. Administration of the questionnaire can occur in individual or group formats. Parents respond to the 42 items related to specific involvement behaviors with a 4-point Likert scale (1: *rarely*, 2: *sometimes*, 3: *often*, 4: *always*). The FIQ is constructed in English. Scores are computed as an average across constructs or across a program. No specific training is required for administration of the FIQ.

The Early Literacy Parent Questionnaire

Boudreau (2005) concluded that using parent reports to measure emergent and early literacy skills is effective because parent reports were closely related to more formal measures in the following literacy domains: phonological awareness, response to print in the environment, alphabet knowledge, interactions around books, writing, orientation to literacy, and parent practices. Boudreau's (2005) Early Literacy Parent Questionnaire can be used to gather preliminary data about a child before a formal assessment by a speech-language pathologist or reading specialist; screen for areas that require more in-depth assessment; collect information from a variety of sources for reports or planning intervention; and provide insight into literacy behaviors in a naturalistic context. The results of the questionnaire are interpreted using a 5-point scale, where 1 represents lack of a trait and 5 represents high frequency of a trait. Early Literacy Parent Questionnaire items are detailed in Table 3–17.

No estimate of time to complete the questionnaire was reported; however, Boudreau reported allowing 2 weeks for participants to complete and return the questionnaire at their leisure. The Early Literacy Parent Questionnaire is designed specifically for use with parents of preschool-age children. The parent who spends the most time with the child should complete the instrument.

Table 3–17. Early Literacy Parent Questionnaire

Please answer the following questions by circling your response on the scale provided and filling in information.

Reading Books

1. Does your child ask you to read to him/her?

   Never/Rarely   On occasion   Weekly   Daily   Several times
   per day

2. How often do you read to your child?

   On occasion   Once a month   Weekly   Several times   Daily
   per week

   On average, how many hours per week? _____

   Do you have a designated time for reading? _____

   How many books do you typically read at one sitting? _____

3. Does your child independently point to or talk about pictures when you read stories?

   Not currently   Has but rarely   Occasionally
   A few times per story   Very frequently during story

4. Does your child ask questions about characters or events during story reading?

   Not currently   Has but rarely   Occasionally
   A few times per story   Very frequently during story

5. Does your child pretend to read the story in a book (such as sitting with a book and producing speech that is similar to the actual story in the book)?

   Never/Rarely   On occasion   Weekly   Daily   Several times
   per day

   Are there specific books she/he will typically do this with?

   _____

   What are some of your child's favorite books?

   _____

6. Does your child make up stories and tell them?

   Never/Rarely   On occasion   Weekly   Daily   Several times
   per day

continues

Table 3–17. *continued*

7. Does your child fill in words or lines from a story when reading with you? (when reading a book he/she knows well, says the next line or word before you read it)

    Not currently   Has but rarely   Occasionally
    A few times per story   Very frequently during reading

8. Do you attempt to teach the names of the letters in the alphabet and/or alphabet sounds when reading?

    Not currently   Has but rarely   Occasionally
    A few times per story   Very frequently during story

9. In comparison to other activities how would you rate your child's interest in books?

1	2	3	4	5
Activity least liked			Favorite activity	

Response to Print

10. Do you point out signs and words such as restaurant names or street signs to your child (i.e., McDonald's arches, Pepsi logo, etc.)?

    Not currently   Have but rarely   Occasionally   Weekly   Daily

11. Does your child show interest in adult reading materials (i.e., newspaper, TV Guide, magazine, etc.) in the environment (such as asking you to read it; asking what words say, etc.)?

    Never/Rarely   On occasion   Weekly   Daily   Several times
                                                                 per day

12. Does your child ask for help in reading words such as signs on the street or words on food packages?

    Never/Rarely   On occasion   Weekly   Daily   Several times
                                                                 per day

13. Does your child identify words in the environment (such as food packaging, signs of stores and restaurants, etc.) in your environment by him- or herself?

    Never/Rarely   On occasion   Weekly   Daily   Several times
                                                                 per day

    When does this occur? _____

    Which signs or words does your child know?

    _____

Table 3–17. *continued*

14. Does your child read any words by sight (or common words they have memorized and can identify, such as mom, cat, etc.)?

    Not currently   On occasion   Knows a word
    Knows several words   Knows many words

Language Awareness

15. Do you play rhyming games with your child?

    Not currently   Have but rarely   Occasionally   Weekly   Daily

    Can you child rhyme words? _____

16. Does your child try to play rhyming games with you or others?

    Not currently   Has but rarely   Occasionally   Weekly   Daily

17. Does your child produce rhymes by him- or herself?

    Never/Rarely   On occasion   Weekly   Daily   Several times
                                                   per day

18. Does your child notice and say something when she/he hears words that rhyme? (i.e., That rhymes!)

    Not currently   Has but rarely   Occasionally   Frequently
    Very Frequently

19. Does your child tell nursery rhymes (such as Jack and Jill or Little Bo Peep)?

    Not currently   Has but rarely   Occasionally   Weekly   Daily

    Which ones does she/he know? _____

20. Does your child sing simple songs?

    Never/Rarely   On occasion   Weekly   Daily   Several times
                                                   per day

    Which ones does she/he know? _____

Interest in Letters

21. Does your child name letters of the alphabet?

    Never/Rarely   On occasion   Weekly   Daily   Several times
                                                   per day

    How many does he/she know? _____

continues

Table 3–17. *continued*

---

22. Does your child attempt to make sounds for alphabet letters?

    Not currently   Has but rarely   Occasionally   Frequently   Very Frequently

    How many does he/she know? _____

23. Can your child identify some letters of the alphabet? (such as pointing to the letter "A" when you ask him/her to?)

    Not currently   Has but rarely   Occasionally   Frequently   Very Frequently

    Which letters does he/she know? _____

Writing

24. Does your child draw?

    Never/Rarely   On occasion   Weekly   Daily   Several times per day

25. Does your child write letters?

    Never/Rarely   On occasion   Weekly   Daily   Several times per day

26. Does your child ask you to write for him/her?

    Never/Rarely   On occasion   Weekly   Daily   Several times per day

27. Does your child ask you how to spell items?

    Never/Rarely   On occasion   Weekly   Daily   Several times per day

28. Does your child write words?

    Not currently   Has but rarely   Occasionally   Weekly   Daily

---

Additional Interests

29. Does your child watch video stories on a VCR (i.e., Lion King or other stories)?

    Never/Rarely   On occasion   Weekly   Daily   Several times per day

    How many hours per week does s/he watch them? _____

    Does your child own any stories on video, and if so, which ones?

    _____

    _____

Table 3-17. *continued*

---

30. Does your child watch TV?

    Never/Rarely On occasion Weekly Daily Several times per day

    How many hours per day? _____

    What is the show watched most frequently?

---

31. Does your child go to the library to select books?

    Rarely Every few months Monthly Bimonthly Weekly

32. Do you have a computer at home? Yes No

    If so, does your child use it? _____

    Average number of hours per week _____

    What programs does he/she enjoy?

Additional Questions

33. At what age did you begin reading to your child? _____

34. How many books does your child own? _____

35. How many books do you own? _____

36. Do you receive any published reading materials at home, such as newspaper, magazines, and so forth? Which ones?

Source: From "Use of a Parent Questionnaire in Emergent and Early Literacy Assessment of Preschool Children," by D. Boudreau, 2005, *Language, Speech, and Hearing Services in Schools, 36,* pp. 45–47. Copyright 2005 by the American Speech-Language-Hearing Association. All rights reserved. Adapted with permission of the publisher and author.

This questionnaire is currently available in English; however it may be useful in other languages if translated. Each item on the questionnaire is assigned a point value ranging from 1 to 5. The five construct scores are tallied to determine a total score for each area of literacy knowledge. There are no stated qualifications for administration.

Graphophonemic Mediation of Mother-Child Joint Writing

Aram and Levin (2002) assessed mother-child joint writing of Hebrew words during two tasks using the Graphophonemic Mediation Scale. The first task was a structured activity in which the mother guided the child in writing eight dictated words while showing the child a or picture illustrating each word. The second task was an unstructured activity in which the mother guided her child in writing a guest list for the child's imaginary birthday party. For this unstructured task, names were generated by both the mother and the child. This scale indicates how much graphophonemic mediation or scaffolding a mother gives her child during a joint writing task. The Graphophonemic Mediation of Mother-Child Joint Writing scale is summarized in Table 3–18.

Scores are interpreted on a 6-point scale showing how much scaffolding and support the mother provides her child during writing. The time required for administration is probably 20 to 30 minutes depending on how many words are dictated and whether or not both a structured and unstructured task are employed. The Graphophonemic Mediation scale is designed for use with preschool- and kindergarten-age children. To employ the Graphophonemic Mediation scale, videotapes of writing events were evaluated using a 6-point scale to rank maternal writing support. Every time the child writes a letter it is scored as an event. The original language of the assessment activities was Hebrew; however, similar activities can be analyzed for English writing using this 6-point scale. The maternal mediation scores are determined by pausing the video after each letter, scoring the event, and then calculating an average score across all the letters for the activity. Aram and Levin (2002) found no significant difference in the scores for structured and unstructured tasks; therefore, scores obtained in both activities were averaged to provide a total maternal mediation score. Scores can be interpreted as a mean for each activity or across both activities. The activities are designed for a parent-child dyad. Examiners may benefit from training to code each event reliably.

Table 3–18. Graphophonemic Mediation of Mother-Child Joint Writing

---

Graphophonemic Mediation Scale

Score each event (the mediation of each letter) by determining which level best represents how the parent guided the child.

---

1. Mother wrote down all the letters of the word for the child.
   Example: The child sits on his mother's lap holding the pencil. The mother holds the child's hand, murmurs the word to herself, and writes the word while leading the child's hand. The child looks at his mother and at the written word.

2. Mother wrote down all the letters of the word as a model for copying.
   Example: The mother writes the word silently. The child copied the word beneath the mother's model, looking at her mother for reassurance after printing each letter.

3. Mother dictated a letter.
   Example: Writing the letter *n* in the word *man*.
   Mother: Now write *n* (the last letter name).
   The child writes the letter after getting some help regarding its shape.

4. Mother retrieved a phonological unit (syllable, subsyllable, or phoneme) and immediately dictated the required letter name.
   Example: Writing the *n* in *can*.
   Mother: /c-a-n/, /nnn/, like at the end of Kristin (name) (stressing the last phoneme). It's *n* (letter name).
   The child writes the letter.

5. Mother retrieved a phonological unit (syllable, subsyllable, or phoneme) and encouraged or helped the child to link this unit with the letter name.
   Example: Writing the *s* in *bus*.
   Mother: /b-u-s/ /s/ /s/. What is it?
   Child: C? (letter name)
   Mother: No, *c* sounds like /k/ or /s/.
   Child: S? (letter name)
   Mother: Right. *S* is for /s/.

continues

Table 3–18. *continued*

6. Mother encouraged or helped the child to retrieve a phonological unit (syllable, subsyllable, or phoneme) and to link it with a letter name.
   Example: Writing the letter *t* in *stop.*
   Mother: What do you hear next?
   Child: /t/
   Mother: How do we write it?
   Child: *T* (letter name)
   Mother: Great!

Source: Adapted from "Mother-Child Joint Writing and Storybook Reading: Relations with Literacy Among Low SES Kindergartners," by D. Aram and I. Levin, 2002, *Merrill-Palmer Quarterly, 48*(2), pp. 207–208. Copyright 2002 by Wayne State University Press. Adapted with permission of the publisher. Web site: http://wsupress@wayne.edu.

Measuring the Home Environment

Families can support literacy development by simply having and using literacy materials such as books and writing instruments in the home environment (Snow et al., 1998). The home literacy environment is commonly defined as "the variety of resources and opportunities provided to children as well as parental skills, abilities, dispositions, and resources that determine the provision of these opportunities for children" (Burgess, 2005, p. 250). This definition and research suggests that home literacy is a multifaceted phenomenon (Leseman & de Jong, 1998). Leseman and de Jong (1998) found that measuring home literacy required considering the characteristics of several facets: frequency of literacy opportunities, quality of instruction during literacy interactions, cooperation and co-construction of literacy concepts, and social-emotional quality during literacy interactions. Thus, many measures of home environment attempt to calculate a complex, global measure of the home by probing for such things as the quantity and quality of books or reading materials, visits to the library, stimulating toys and learning materials, parental responsiveness, structure and organization in the home, and general emotional climate in the home.

Several researchers have established that there is a relationship between the home literacy environment and emergent literacy skills in preschool children (Boudreau, 2005; Jordan, Snow, & Porche, 2000; Roberts, Jurgens, & Burchinal, 2005; Storch & Whitehurst, 2001). For instance, Boudreau (2005) found that early readers were significantly more likely than nonreaders to have parents who read magazines and newspapers, suggesting that exposure to literate behaviors in the home environment positively influences literacy development. In the long term, measures of the home environment are modestly correlated with later language, cognitive, and academic skills (Roberts et al., 2005; Snow et al., 1998). Our discussion of the home environment focuses on literacy materials and literacy experiences available in the home as well as characteristics of these literacy opportunities in the home environment. We describe five measures for assessing the home literacy environment (for a summary see Table 3-19).

Although home environments can change over time or in response to macrolevel influences outside of the home, at the microlevel, a supportive and responsive home environment is critical for young children. Supportive, print-rich environments include objects such as magnetic refrigerator letters, posters, writing materials, newspapers, and books in the home (Snow et al., 1998). Presence of print and literacy materials in the home can influence emergent, pretend reading and other literacy skills because children who have regular access to books at home or at local libraries spend more time in emergent reading activities before school begins (Strickland, 2001).

Yet, consider how the home environment can be affected by macrosystems of poor neighborhoods. Neuman and Celano (2001) studied access to print in middle- and low-income neighborhoods, revealing unequal access to resources such as public spaces conducive to reading and volume of print such as signs, labels, and logos. Even when libraries are present in poor neighborhoods, not all libraries contain equal quality of books and multimedia capabilities

Table 3–19. Measuring the Home Environment

Measure	Use	Time (Approximate)	Administration
Home Observation for Measurement of the Environment (HOME) Inventory	To screen for potential environmental risk. The HOME measures aspects of the literacy environment as well as environmental characteristics beyond literacy.	Less than 60 minutes	Observation of home environment and conversation with parents
Project on Human Development in Chicago Neighborhoods (PHDCN) Homelife Interview	To assess environmental risk in the home for children ages 3- through 15-years-old.	15–20 minutes	Individual parent
Home Visit Guide	To help early literacy professionals identify literacy practices unique to the child's family and to provide an opportunity to establish a relationship with the family.	As much time as needed to gain insight on the home environment	Observation of home environment
Get Ready to Read Home Literacy Environment Checklist	To measure presence of elements of a supportive home literacy environment.	Approximately 15 minutes	Individual parent
Home Literacy Environment Questionnaire (HLEQ)	To evaluate the quality of different aspects of the home literacy environment.	15–20 minutes	Individual parent

(Strickland, 2001). Stanovich and colleagues (Cunningham & Stanovich, 1990, 1997) suggest that differential access to and exposure to print can have long-term consequences because children who have less exposure to print are initially less likely to become skilled readers, resulting in less motivation to read more, which produces a downward spiral where children with limited exposure to print gain less and less proficiency and exposure to print than their more advantaged peers.

The degree of literacy support in the home environment can vary significantly between families and groups. Burgess (2005) reports considerable variability in home literacy measures for factors such as number of children's books in the home (range = 0 to 1,500), age of onset of shared reading (range = birth to 6 years), and amount of television watched per day (range = 0 to 12 hours). This study also revealed that teenage mothers generally provided a less supportive home literacy environment than nonteenage mothers with a notable difference in number of television hours children watched after controlling for various demographic variables (Burgess, 2005). Variability in parent responsiveness can be associated with other factors such as culture (Leseman & de Jong, 1998). Still, the home literacy environment appears to be a vital component in literacy development in many cultures. For instance, Umek, Podlesek, and Fckonja (2005) used the Home Literacy Environment Questionnaire to reveal that 4-year-old Slovenian children's language competence was related to aspects of the home literacy environment such as frequent trips to the library, visits to the puppet theater or cinema, and frequency of interactive reading. These variations in home literacy environments demonstrate that the overall home environment can be a source of support or, perhaps unwittingly, deter emergent and early literacy development.

In the next section, several measures of the home environment are presented. Many of the items in these assessments overlap with characteristics and skills of other home literacy constructs. For example, a widely used measure for assessing the home literacy environment, the Home Observation for Measurement of the Environment (HOME), probes for "emotional support and cognitive stimulation children receive through their home environment, planned events, and family surroundings" (Linver, Brooks-Gunn, & Cabrera, 2004, p. 99). These investigations appear to include an implicit measure of parent beliefs and knowledge as well as other factors such as literacy activities in the home.

Despite the overlap with other constructs in this chapter, we elected not to break apart these instruments into separate constructs because the items typically are not clustered by subgroups that could be easily separated from the rest of the assessment. This may prove useful because global measures of the home environment may be more sensitive predictors of literacy development as these assessments may tap into multiple constructs. For instance, a longitudinal study (Roberts et al., 2005) of African American families used both the infant/toddler and early childhood version of the HOME scale and found this global measure to be a more consistent and powerful predictor of children's language and literacy skills than measures of specific literacy practices (i.e., frequency of storybook reading, child enjoyment of reading, maternal sensitivity, and maternal book reading strategies). Taken together, this research indicates that the responsiveness and supportiveness of the home environment is a key factor in supporting literacy development and a worthwhile domain for educators to assess.

Home Observation for Measurement of the Environment (HOME) Inventory

Caldwell and Bradley (1984) designed the HOME Inventory as a screening tool for identifying potential environmental risk. As you can see from the HOME items in Table 3–20, this measure is not specific to literacy. The HOME can be used with a variety of populations (Roberts et al., 2005). The time for full-scale administration is 60 minutes; however, when only two of the subscales are used to assess home literacy environment, administration time should be significantly less than 60 minutes. There are three versions of the HOME; however, the HOME Inventory for Families of Preschool-Age Children (ages 3–6) is most appropriate for the preschool population. Information for the HOME inventory is gathered by observation in the home along with parent report of environmental aspects that are not likely to be observed during a home visit. The observation should take place at a time when the child is home and awake (Boehm, 1993). Administration of the HOME should be relaxed and casual to reduce intimidation and increase the probability of realistic responses (Bradley & Caldwell, 1979).

Table 3–20. Home Observation for Measurement of the Environment (HOME) Inventory Items

---

Early Childhood HOME (ages 4–5 years)

Learning stimulation
 1. Child has toys which teach color, size, and shape
 2. Child has three or more puzzles
 3. Child has record player and at least five children's records
 4. Child has toys permitting free expression
 5. Child has toys or games requiring refined movement
 6. Child has toys or games that help teach numbers
 7. Child has at least 10 children's books
 8. At least 10 books are visible in the apartment
 9. Family buys and reads a daily newspaper
10. Family subscribes to at least one magazine
11. Child is encouraged to learn shapes

Language stimulation
12. Child has toys that help teach the names of animals
13. Child is encouraged to learn the alphabet
14. Parent teachers child simple verbal manners (please, thank you)
15. Mother uses correct grammar and pronunciation
16. Parent encourages child to talk and takes time to listen
17. Parent's voice conveys positive feeling to child
18. Child is permitted choice in breakfast or lunch menu

Physical environment
19. Building appears safe
20. Outside play environment appears safe
21. Interior of apartment is not dark or perceptually monotonous
22. Neighborhood is aesthetically pleasing
23. House has 100 sq ft of living space per person
24. Rooms are not overcrowded with furniture
25. House is reasonably clean and minimally cluttered

Warmth and acceptance
26. Parent holds child close 10–15 minutes per day
27. Parent converses with child at least twice during visit
28. Parent answers child's questions or requests verbally
29. Parent usually responds verbally to child's speech
30. Parent spontaneously praises child's qualities twice during visit

continues

147

Table 3-20. *continued*

31. Parent caresses, kisses, or cuddles child during visit
32. Parent helps child demonstrate some achievement during visit

Academic stimulation
33. Child is encouraged to learn colors
34. Child is encouraged to learn patterned speech (songs, etc.)
35. Child is encouraged to learn spatial relationships
36. Child is encouraged to learn numbers
37. Child is encouraged to learn to read a few words

Modeling
38. Some delay of food gratification is expected
39. TV is used judiciously
40. Parent introduces visitor to child
41. Child can express negative feelings without reprisal
42. Child can hit parent without harsh reprisal

Variety in experience
43. Child has real or toy musical instrument
44. Child is taken on outing by family member at least every other week
45. Child has been taken on a trip of more than 50 miles during the last year
46. Child has been taken to a museum during the past year
47. Parent encouraged child to put away toys without help
48. Parent uses complex sentence structure and vocabulary
49. Child's artwork is displayed someplace in the house
50. Child eats at least one meal per day with mother and father
51. Parent lets child choose some foods or brands at grocery store

Acceptance
52. Parent does not scold or derogate child more than once
53. Parent does not use physical restraint during visit
54. Parent neither slaps nor spanks child during visit
55. No more than one instance of physical punishment during last week

Source: From "The Home Observation for Measurement of the Environment (HOME) Inventory: The Derivation of Conceptually Designed Subscales," by M. R. Linver, J. Brooks-Gunn, & N. Cabrera, 2004, *Parenting: Science and Practice*, 4(2&3), pp. 102–103. Copyright 2004 by Lawrence Erlbaum Associates, Inc. Reproduced with permission of the authors and publisher.

The subscales of the HOME that are applicable to measuring home literacy environment are the Learning Stimulation and Variety of Experience subscales. The HOME is available and normed in English. Items on the HOME are scored as yes or no. The observer is not required to determine quality of each item, just whether the indicator is present or not present in the home. To score the HOME, the assessor sums the items on each subscale and converts the score to a percentile in order to determine how a particular family's HOME score compares to a normed population. No qualifications for administration are mentioned.

Project on Human Development in Chicago Neighborhoods Homelife Interview

The Project on Human Development in Chicago Neighborhoods (PHDCN) Homelife Interview was adapted from the HOME inventory described previously. Leventhal, Selner-O'Hagan, Brooks-Gunn, Bingenheimer, and Earls (2004) designed this interview to assess environmental risk in children from age 3 to 15. The Homelife Interview has six domains, one of which can be used to assess literacy environment of emergent and beginning readers: the Provision of Learning Activities scale. This subtest measures the presence of age-appropriate materials that encourage school readiness. Table 3-21 details items for this Homelife Interview subtest. This subtest of the Homelife Interview is appropriate for parents of children between the ages of 3 and 6. No estimate administration time estimate is reported; however, it probably requires between 15 and 20 minutes. This semistructured interview contains a scale for rating parent reports.

This scale comprises three dimensions: developmental stimulation, literacy support, and outings and activities. The developmental stimulation dimension measures the quantity and quality of enrichment opportunities in the home. The literacy support dimension taps for presence of books and printed materials and whether or not parents encourage age-appropriate reading. Finally, the outings and activities dimension gauges family involvement in and encouragement of activities occurring outside the home. The Homelife Interview is available in English. Scores on the interview are reported as percentile ranks. No qualifications for administration are stated.

Table 3–21. PHDCN Homelife Interview Questions

Developmental Stimulation
Access to toy or real musical instrument
Access to toys to learn colors
Access to toys to learn shapes
Access to toys to learn numbers
Access to toys to learn animal names/behaviors
Access to toys to learn spatial relations
Access to at least three puzzles
Access to toys to learn patterned speech
Access to toys permitting free expression
Access to toys for refined hand movements
Parent has rules about homework and checks to see done
Parent assisted child w/homework every other week
Parent talks daily with child about day
Parent discussed TV w/child in the past two weeks
Parent discussed current events w/child in the past two weeks

Access to Reading
Parent/family member reads to child three times/week
Child has access to toys to learn the alphabet
Child has access to 10 books
Child has three or more books of own
At least 10 books are present and visible
Child has access to a dictionary

Outings/Activities
Parent engages in outdoor recreate w/ child
Child goes on outing every other week
Child has gone to museum past year
Child has gone on trip >50 miles from home past year
Child included in family's hobby
Child taken trip on plane, train, bus past year
Child seen live musical/theater perform past year

Source: Reprinted from "The Homelife Interview from the Project on Human Development in Chicago Neighborhoods: Assessment of Parenting and Home Environment for 3- to 15-Year-Olds," by T. Leventhal, M. B. Selner-O'Hagan, J. Brooks-Gunn, J. B. Bingenheimer, and F. J. Earls, 2004, *Parenting: Science and Practice,* 4(2&3), p. 223. Copyright 2004 by Lawrence Erlbaum Associates, Inc. Reproduced with permission of authors and publisher.

Home Visit Guide

The Home Visit Guide designed by Barone, Mallette, and Xu (2005) supports home observation because visits can help educators identify literacy practices unique to the child's family and it provides an opportunity to establish a relationship with the family (see Table 3-22). Time required to complete home observation varies based on the family and the topics discussed. Because the goal of the home visit is to gain insight into the child's home environment that can inform instruction observers should spend as much time as is necessary. The Home Visit Guide is designed for use with parents of emergent and beginning readers.

When using the Home Visit Guide, the teacher should spend time observing the environment for the items specified in the guide. The teacher or observer should also engage the family in a conversation about home literacy practices during the visit. Any information that is not gained through the observation and conversation can be obtained through targeted questions. Other questions and items for observation can be added to the informal home environment assessment based on the needs of the program and the needs of the child. The Home Visit Guide is available in English but it could be useful in other language if translated. There are no scoring procedures for the Home Visit Guide, but the instrument provides anecdotal information to inform literacy instruction. There are no stated qualifications for examiners.

Get Ready to Read Home Literacy Environment Checklist

The Web site www.GetReadytoRead.org provides a free Home Literacy Environment Checklist (National Center for Learning Disabilities, 2004). The Web site suggests that parents use the items they marked as false on the checklist as a guide to improve the home literacy environment for their child. The checklist should take 15 minutes or less to complete and is appropriate for parents of preschool-age children. The checklist has 37 items (answered as true or false) grouped into four subscales: literacy materials in the home, home literacy practices, adult modeling of literacy skills, and academic and literacy support provided to the child by a family member. The checklist is available in English but could be translated

Table 3-22. Informal Observation of the Home Literacy
Environment

Family _____ Date _____

Literacy environment

List observed print materials, in English and/or a native
language (e.g., books, TV schedule, papers for writing, ads,
Bible or other religious text, bills, student's work, etc.):

List observed nonprint materials, in English and/or in a native
language (e.g., PlayStation, Game Boy, TV, VCR, DVD player,
computer, etc):

(*Note:* For both print and nonprint materials, ask family
members about things that you have not observed. For
example, you may not see a computer in a living room, but
this does not necessarily mean that the family does not own a
computer.)

School-related literacy practices

Reading, in English and/or in a native language (e.g., an
assigned book):

Writing, in English and/or in a native language (e.g., an
assigned essay):

Word study, in English and/or in a native language (e.g.,
studying spelling words):

Non-school-related literacy practices

Functional and survival, in English and/or a native language
(e.g., reading ads to identify items on sale):

Table 3–22. *continued*

Spiritual, in English and/or in a native language (e.g., reading Bible or other religious text):

Entertainment, in English and/or in a native language (e.g., reading a TV schedule, watching a TV show):

Source: From *Teaching Early Literacy: Development, Assessment, and Instruction*, by D. M. Barone, M. H. Mallette, and S. H. Xu, 2005, New York: Guilford Press. Copyright 2005 by Guilford Press. Reproduced with permission of the publisher.

into other languages. After the parent completes the checklist, they sum the number of items marked true and compare their score to a scale that provides qualitative descriptors of the home literacy environment. The scale rates the home literacy environment as follows:

> 30–37 true: The home literacy environment has most of the necessary supportive elements; 20–29 true: The home literacy environment has many supportive elements; 11–19 true: The home literacy environment has some supportive elements; and 0–10 true: The home literacy environment needs improvement (National Center for Learning Disabilities, 2004, p. 2).

No qualifications for administration are given.

Home Literacy Environment Questionnaire

Umek and colleagues' (2005) Home Literacy Environment Questionnaire (HLEQ) is used to measure the quality of the home literacy environment. Outcomes of the HLEQ may predict the child's language competence. The HLEQ contains 33 items and probably takes between 15 and 20 minutes to complete. The questionnaire is appropriate for parents of preschool- and kindergarten-age children. Parents are asked to respond to questions that evaluate the quality of different aspects of the home literacy environment on a

6-point scale with response options ranging from *never* to *always*. The HLEQ contains five subscales: (1) Stimulation to Use Language and Explanation, (2) Reading Books to Child and Visiting Puppet Theater (or other theatrical productions), (3) Joint Activities and Conversation, (4) Interactive Reading, and (5) Zone-of-Proximal-Development-Stimulation.

The full HLEQ instrument is currently available only in Slovene, but its authors suggest the full measure will be translated to English soon. Table 3–23 details the HLEQ items in English as published in Umek et al. (2005). Administration time and scoring procedures are not specified. We recommend using the scale as a guide for identifying strength and weaknesses in the home literacy environment. For example, items in which parent responses are at the high end of the scale are strengths of the home environment and items at the low end are areas for improvement. No qualifications are specified for administering the HLEQ.

Measuring Oral Language and Vocabulary Supports at Home

When families talk often with their child and expose their child to sophisticated vocabulary they build important listening and speaking skills. These verbal abilities influence many strands of literacy development including comprehension, vocabulary, sentence recall, story recall, discourse, syntax, and concepts of print (Neuman & Roskos, 2005; Scarborough, 2001). Given this influence, it is reasonable that young children's verbal abilities are a reliable predictor of later reading achievement (Catts & Hogan, 2003; Neuman & Roskos, 2005; Scarborough, 2001; Snow et al., 1998). In the long term, some scholars assert that preschoolers' development of decontextualized language skills at home can support reading comprehension in the later grades when children read for meaning because, at this later stage, vocabulary and syntactical knowledge are essential for comprehension (Sénéchal et al., 2006; Snow, 1991). In the short term, Payne et al. (1994) suggest that 12 to 18.5% of the variance in the language development of 4-year-old children can be accounted for by the home literacy environment as measured by caregiver report. Thus, language and literacy appear to operate in tandem to support young children's development.

Table 3–23. Home Literacy Environment Questionnaire (HLEQ) Items

Stimulation to use language, explanation

I complete and expand my child's utterances (e.g. "The boy is crying." with "Yes, the boy is crying because he hurt himself.")

When I talk to my child, I use grammatically correct sentences.

I talk to my child about how she has spent her day.

I answer my child's questions and offer explanations, even if she repeats a question many times.

I try to explain things that I believe my child understands.

I praise my child when I notice progress in her speech.

I encourage my child to talk to peers and adults.

If I do not understand my child, I ask her to repeat her utterance.

I answer my child's questions consistently.

I correct my child's use of the dual and plural, and encourage her to use them correctly.

I correct my child's use of the past and the future tenses, and encourage her to use them correctly.

Reading books to the child, visiting the library and puppet theater

I read picture books with my child.

I read to my child whenever she wants me to.

I go to the library with my child.

At the library, my child borrows the books that she wants.

I go to the puppet theater or cinema with my child.

I talk to my child about the puppet show or the movie that she has seen.

I buy my child books or picture books as gifts.

I read books to my child.

Joint activities and conversation

I encourage my child to narrate when looking at pictures.

When I play with my child, I name and describe different objects and toys.

I play with my child at least half an hour a day.

I watch TV with my child.

I talk to my child about what she has seen on TV.

I talk to my child about what she would like to do.

continues

Table 3–23. *continued*

Interactive reading

I allow my child to interrupt me and ask questions while I'm reading to her.

I allow my child to create her own stories while I'm reading to her.

When reading to my child, I talk to her about the content of the book.

Zone-of-proximal-development stimulation

I teach my child to count.

I encourage my child to learn to read a few words (e.g., her name).

I encourage my child to learn letters (e.g., I show her letters in books, I teach her the letters in her name).

When talking to my child, I use long and complicated sentences (e.g., complete sentences, compound sentences, subordinate clauses).

When talking to my child, I try to speak in a manner similar to hers (e.g., I call objects as she does, I use childish speech).

Source: From "Assessing the Home Literacy Environment," by L. M. Umek, A. Podlesek, and U. Fekonja, 2005, *European Journal of Psychological Assessment, 21*(4), pp. 274–275. Copyright 2005 by Hogrefe & Huber Publishers. Reprinted with permission of the publisher.

Verbal abilities develop through a variety of language- and knowledge-building experiences that often occur in the home. For instance, stimulating verbal interactions during dinner, when reading storybooks, or during familiar routines, contribute to children's oral language development. Both the quantity and variety of words used by parents appear to be major factors affecting the size of a child's vocabulary (Hart & Risley, 1995; Huttenlocher, Vasilyeva, Cymerman, & Levine, 2002). Similarly, discourse patterns and narrative structure may be influenced by the family and home environment (Heath, 1983; Snow et al., 1998). Chapter 9 of this book, Assessing Vocabulary Knowledge, provides a detailed account of how oral language and vocabulary development and assessment. Thus, our discussion of home language focuses on key findings from home literacy research that are connected to children's oral language and vocabulary. We present four measures for assessing characteristics of the home language environment (for an overview see Table 3–24) such as the quality of parent language input and features of parent-child verbal interactions.

Differences in language patterns in the home environment present a source of substantial variability for American children. Children from low-income homes or homes where English is not the dominant language may have limited exposure to decontextualized language and the formal register of English at home (Payne, 2001). Hart and Risley (1995) found that poor and uneducated families offer a similar array of language experiences to their children as middle-class families; however, the quantity of verbal interactions in these homes was much less than in middle-class homes. This is considered a risk factor (Snow et al., 1998) because having fewer verbal interactions decreases the potential for vocabulary growth, which is essential to many reading outcomes. Research with low-income families revealed the quantity of maternal input was not as strongly correlated to toddler's vocabulary development as the lexical diversity of maternal talk and mother's use of nonverbal gestures such as pointing during parent-child interactions (Pan et al., 2005). Tabors and Snow (2001) suggest that the quality of parent-child language interactions is particularly important in bilingual families to ensure that the first language is used to develop a firm foundation for learning to speak and read a second language.

Much research exploring caregiver and family talk has analyzed language during specific home activities such as during play or meals. Katz (2001) found a relationship between kindergarten language and literacy skills and pretend talk during mother-child play, where pretend talk is defined as a form of extended discourse containing pretend elements and a nonliteral approach to play. Preschoolers' engagement in or exposure to narrative talk and explanatory talk (such as logical explanations or cause-effect explanations) during family mealtimes was associated with literacy outcomes, such as story comprehension and the ability to define words in kindergarten. Similarly, observational measures of parent-child book reading by DeTemple (2001) as part of Home-School Study of Language and Literacy revealed that mother's use of "nonimmediate talk" or decontextualized talk was strongly and positively associated with children's scores on several measures of kindergarten literacy (p. 41). Conversely a negative relationship was found between mothers who used more immediate talk, or talk closely tied to the illustrations or words in the text, and early literacy measures.

Table 3-24. Measuring Oral Language and Vocabulary Supports at Home

Measure	Use	Time	Administration
Family Talk: Development of Decontextualized Language Skills	To measure the quantity and quality of talk during various home settings: during storybook reading, play, retellings, and mealtimes.	Varies[a]	Single focal child interacting with one parent or family
Hart and Risley (1995) Language Coding Scheme	To measure and classify the type of talk within the home environment.	Varies[a]	Single focal child interacting with one parent or family
Huttenlocher et al. (2002) Coding Protocol	To measure and classify lexical density of parental input and child's language.	Varies[a]	Single focal child interacting with one parent
Our Word Expressive Vocabulary Test	To assess child's expressive knowledge of unique words in text learned from parent-child storybook reading.	Approximately 15 minutes	Single parent-child dyad

Note. [a]Varies depending on length of observation or interaction

Findings that emphasize the quality and type of the caregiver's language input align with more specialized studies of how children learn specific elements of language such as verbs. More frequent use of verbs by the mother and more diverse syntactic environments in which mothers use verbs (e.g., using multiple types of syntactic frames for verbs) predicts the child's subsequent frequency of verb use and the child's ability to create more syntactically flexible uses of the verb (Naigles & Hoff-Ginsberg, 1998). A promising finding comes from the work of Landry, Smith, and colleagues (for a summary see, Landry & Smith, 2006) who used interventions aimed at changing parents' responsive behaviors in language-rich activities such as toy play and storybook reading. They found that coaching mothers and encouraging self-evaluation of responsiveness from videotapes of play and reading led to a strong increase in rich language input and ability to use more specific vocabulary. Similarly, a program called It Takes Two to Talk by the Hanen Centre in Toronto, Canada is designed to increase verbal interactions with parents and children in the home. Due to space limitations the video evaluation tool is not described in this chapter; however, for more information about this extensive program and assessments, see Pepper, Weitzman, and McDade, 2004 or www.hanen.org. In summary, both the quantity and quality of language a young child is exposed to in the home environment significantly influences early language and literacy development.

Family Talk: Development of Decontextualized Language Skills

The Home-School Study of Language and Literacy longitudinal study contains useful methods for analyzing the type of talk between a child and their family members. DeTemple and Beals (1991) explain four specific home activities that were used to analyze talk between child and their caregivers: (1) book reading talk, (2) elicited reports, (3) toy play talk, and (4) mealtime talk. Detailed procedures for soliciting each type of activity and scoring to calculate the Information Index are described in Table 3–25.

The Information Index indicates the degree of support the child required to respond to questions or requests for information. An Information Index score greater than 1 indicates that the child had no difficulty responding to the caregiver and offered more information than was requested. An Information Index score less than 1 indicates

Table 3–25. Family Talk: Development of Decontextualized Language Skills

Activity Description	Analysis of Talk and Scoring
Book Reading	*(a) Information Index:*
1. Ask the caregiver and child to look at and read one book brought by the examiner.	▪ Count the number of times the caregiver requested information from the child including additional prompts when the child did not respond to the initial request.
2. Record the reading and any extratextual conversation.	▪ Assign one point for each time the child answers the caregiver's response and does not provide additional information.
3. Ask the caregiver and child to look at and read a second book. This book is provided by the caregiver unless the caregiver did not provide one.	▪ Assign an additional point to the child's response if the child spontaneously provides additional information.
	Calculate Information Index: _____ # times child gave information ÷ _____ # of caregiver's requests for information = _____
4. Transcribe the recording and code for (a) Information Index score, and (b) Immediate and nonimmediate talk.	*(b) Immediate talk coding:*
	▪ comments,
	▪ labeling,
	▪ yes-no questions, and
	▪ talk that is closely tied to the text
	Nonimmediate talk coding:
	▪ comments that build world knowledge
	▪ comments, questions, and inferences that use the text as a springboard for talk that is not immediately visible in the text or illustrations
	▪ predictions that use the text as a springboard for talk
	Calculate Decontextualized Talk %: (_____ # nonimmediate utterances by caregiver ÷ _____ # of caregivers total utterances) × 100 = _____ %

Activity Description	Analysis of Talk and Scoring
Elicited Reports 1. Ask the caregiver to elicit a report of an event that the child participated in. 2. Record the story. 3. Caregivers generally suggest an event that both the caregiver and child attended and then ask a series of questions about the location, participants, and major occurrences. 4. Transcribe the recording and code for (c) Information Index score, and (d) number of spontaneously offered comments by the child.	*(c) Information Index:* ▪ Count the number of times the caregiver requested information from the child while eliciting the narrative. This includes additional prompts when the child did not respond to the initial request. ○ Caregivers may use various strategies to elicit a response such as: repeating a question, reducing the level of demand on the child in asking the question, moving from an open-ended question (e.g., "What did we do yesterday?") to a more specific question (e.g., "What did we do at the park yesterday?"), or moving to a yes-no question (e.g., "Did we play on the swings?"). ▪ Assign one point for each time the child answers the caregiver's response and does not provide additional information. ▪ Assign an additional point to the child's response if he/she spontaneously provided additional information. *Calculate Information Index:* _____ # times child gave information ÷ _____ # of caregiver's requests for information = _____ *(d) Amount of Spontaneous Comments:* ▪ Calculate the number and proportion of child utterances in which he/she gives information without prompting, or spontaneously. *Calculate Spontaneous Information %:* (_____ # utterances by child ÷ _____ # of child utterances providing spontaneous information) × 100 = _____ %

161

continues

Table 3–25. *continued*

Activity Description	Analysis of Talk and Scoring
Toy Play 1. Examiner brings a variety of toys to the home such as: a tea set, small animals, cars, people, and blocks. 2. Ask the caregiver and child to play with the toys. Record their conversation. 3. Transcribe the toy play session and code (e) Information Index and (f) for amount of pretend play. This kind of talk is of interest because it discusses less than tangible concepts requiring more explicit language to clarify the context for the other.	*(e) Information Index:* ▪ Count the number of times the caregiver requested information from the child during toy play including additional prompts when the child did not respond to the initial request. ▪ Assign one point for each time the child answers the caregiver's response and does not provide additional information. ▪ Assign an additional point to the child's response if he/she spontaneously provided additional information. *Calculate Information Index:* _____ # times child gave information ÷ _____ # of caregiver's requests for information = _____ *(f) Pretend Play Talk:* ▪ Pretend play is any fantasy talk and can include talking in voices of the characters in the constructed story. This includes talk with pretend elements or a nonliteral approach to features in the environment. 　∘ This does not include nonpretend talk that maintains a literal approach to actions and toys. 　∘ This does not include talk that is nontoy play talk or utterances about events or concerns that are unrelated to the immediate play setting. ▪ Calculate the number and proportion of utterances in which the caregiver or child uses pretend play. *Calculate Caregiver Pretend Talk %:* _____ # pretend play utterances by caregiver ÷ _____ # of total caregiver utterances) × 100 = _____ %

162

Activity Description	Analysis of Talk and Scoring
	Calculate Child Pretend Talk %: _____ # pretend play utterances by child ÷ _____ # of total child utterances) × 100 = _____ %
Mealtime Conversation	(g) *Narrative Talk:*
1. Ask the caregiver to record a more naturalistic talk setting—a family mealtime. Explain procedures for using audio devices and returning the tape to examiner. Consider including an information sheet in which the caregiver can note which family members were present during the meal and note whether or not they consider the recording to represent a typical mealtime.	▪ This is one type of extended discourse which can be constructed by an individual family member or co-constructed between family member(s) and the child. Narratives usually take shape over several turns of conversation.
	▪ Code talk as narrative if it tells about an event that has happened in the past or will happen in the future (an event taking place in another time and/or place).
	Calculate CHILD Narrative Talk %: _____ # Narrative talk utterances by child ÷ _____ # total utterances by child) × 100 = _____ %
	Calculate CAREGIVER 1 (_____) *Narrative Talk %:* _____ # Narrative talk utterances by caregiver 1 ÷ _____ # total utterances by caregiver 1) × 100 = _____ %
	Calculate CAREGIVER 2 (_____) *Narrative Talk %:* _____ # Narrative talk utterances by caregiver 2 ÷ _____ # total utterances by caregiver 2) × 100 = _____ %
2. Examiner leaves tape with family and concludes home visit.	*Calculate OTHER Family Member* (_____) *Narrative Talk %:* _____ # Narrative talk utterances by family member ÷ _____ # total utterances by family member) × 100 = _____ %
3. When tape is returned, transcribe talk and calculate the (g) Narrative Talk, and (h) Explanatory Talk frequencies and percentages for each family member present.	TOTAL
	Calculate TOTAL FAMILY Narrative Talk %: (_____)# Narrative talk utterances by all family at meal ÷ _____ # total utterances by all family at meal) × 100 = _____ %

continues

Table 3–25. *continued*

Activity Description	Analysis of Talk and Scoring
	(h) Explanatory Talk:
	▪ Explanatory talk requests and/or makes some kind of logical connection between objects, events, concepts, or conclusions.
	▪ Code talk as explanatory if it is an explanation of people's actions or speech.
	▪ Code talk as explanatory if it contains cause-effect explanations.
	▪ Code talk as explanatory if it contains definitions or descriptions of words and objects as an explanation.
	Calculate CHILD Explanatory Talk %: _____ # Explanatory talk utterances by child ÷ _____ # total utterances by child) × 100 = _____ %
	Calculate CAREGIVER 1 (_____) *Explanatory Talk %:* _____ # Explanatory talk utterances by caregiver 1 ÷ _____ # total utterances by caregiver 1) × 100 = _____ %
	Calculate CAREGIVER 2 (_____) *Explanatory Talk %:* (_____ # Explanatory talk utterances by caregiver 2 ÷ _____ # total utterances by caregiver 2) × 100 = _____ %
	OTHER Family Member (_____) *Explanatory Talk %:* _____ # Explanatory talk utterances by family member ÷ _____ # total utterances by family member) × 100 = _____ %
	TOTAL
	Calculate TOTAL FAMILY Explanatory Talk %: _____ # Explanatory talk utterances by all family at meal ÷ _____ # total utterances by all family at meal) × 100 = _____ %

Source: Based on *Beginning Literacy with Language: Young Children Learning at Home and School,* edited by D. K. Dickinson and P. O. Tabors, 2001, Paul H. Brooks.

that the child had greater difficulty in responding to the question and required support from the adult.

Each activity also contains a second layer of coding to analyze talk specific to that home context. We briefly discuss each additional level of coding for book reading, elicited reports, toy play, and mealtime talk. Analysis of the book reading activity includes an additional measure of immediate and nonimmediate talk. This measure indicates the number of nonimmediate or decontextualized utterances made by the mother or caregiver during reading. The elicited report analysis includes a second coding for amount of spontaneously given information that the child provides beyond the mother's request. Toy play talk is analyzed with an additional layer of coding for pretend play talk or fantasy talk, which is less tangible and requires more explicit language than nonpretend talk. Finally, the analysis of mealtime talk requires coding utterances by all family members present and then coding for the quantity and proportion of narrative and explanatory talk. Narrative talk is conversation about past or future events and explanatory talk is conversation that clarifies logical connections. These kinds of decontextualized talk promote language development and reading comprehension (Beals, 2001).

The time required for the parent and child to carry out the first three tasks is probably 45 to 60 minutes, depending on the length of engagement with each activity. The fourth activity, mealtime talk, is recorded after the examiner has left the home and the parents return the tape of the dinnertime conversation at a later visit or via mail. Time required for transcription, coding, and analysis was not specified by DeTemple and Beals (1991) or in Dickinson and Tabors (2001). This analysis is appropriate for families with children ages 3 to 5 years old. To assess these interactions, all conversations during activities are audiotaped and transcribed to calculate the Information Index. No language specifications are given for this measure. The scoring system for this measure is the Information Index. This is a ratio of the number of times the child gave information (including responses to questions and spontaneous comments beyond the mother's request) to the number of requests the caregiver made to elicit information. Examiners may benefit from training in appropriate methods for prompting caregivers to produce these tasks. Examiner training may also be useful to reliably code data from transcriptions.

Hart and Risley Language Coding Scheme

The Hart and Risley (1995) coding scheme can be used to analyze family interaction styles by focusing on factors of parental speech that are strongly related to children's vocabulary usage and growth. Hart and Risley studied 42 American families and examined five categories of family interactions that were significantly related to children's language outcomes: (1) Language Diversity, (2) Feedback Tone, (3) Symbolic Emphasis, (4) Guidance Style, and (5) Responsiveness. Although all categories were related to children's language accomplishments, only two of these categories are discussed in this chapter due to space limitations (see Hart & Risley, 1995, for a detailed description of their coding procedures). The Language Diversity and Guidance Style coding schemes are explained in Table 3–26. Examiners observe family interactions in the home for 1 hour and then code family talk using this coding system.

The outcomes for the Language Diversity category are interpreted as the "variety of experiences that a parent talks about to the child," as reflected by "the number of words the parent uses" (Hart & Risley, 1995, p. 150). This is important because a larger range of experiences with a word can help the child refine his or her understanding of the word's meaning. The outcomes of the Guidance Style category are interpreted as the child's typical experiences with parent directives, such as "how often a child is asked rather than told what to do" (Hart & Risley, 1995, p. 153). Parental prompts that guide rather than tell imply parental confidence in the child's motives and are strongly related to the child's vocabulary growth.

Throughout Hart and Risley's study, the time required to obtain a single observation was 1 hour in order to observe interactions that were truly representative of the family when not in the presence of an observer. After observing, considerably more time will be required for transcription and coding. These coding schemes were applied to children between 7 months and 3 years of age in Hart and Risley's work. To assess family talk and interactions, the researcher coded behaviors of the parent and target child while audiotaping the session. This coding scheme was designed for use in English. Within the context of the study scores types included averages, ranges, cumulative number of words, and cumulative instances. Examiners using this scheme will need training in how to establish and maintain rapport with families during the observation and how

Table 3-26. Language Diversity and Guidance Style Coding System

Category of Significant Family Experience	Quality Features Coded in Data Variables	Examples
Language Diversity: sum of different nouns plus different modifiers used per hour	**Vocabulary:** all words, all different words (nouns, modifiers, verbs, functors)	**nouns:** person, place, thing, or idea—cat, boy, dog **verbs:** action or state of being—run, jump, eat **modifiers:** adjectives and adverbs—pretty, happy, nicely **functors:** all other words—determiners, articles, quantifiers, pronouns, prepositions, and conjunctions
Guidance Style: Auxiliary-fronted yes/no questions divided by auxiliary-fronted yes/no questions plus imperatives per hour	**Discourse Functions:** declaratives, imperatives, interrogatives (wh-questions, yes/no questions, auxiliary-fronted yes/no questions)	**declarative sentence:** all sentences (utterances containing a verb) that are not imperatives **imperative sentence:** "You do it," or "Do it" **questions:** wh- questions asking "who," "what," "where," "when," "why," or "how"; questions answerable with "yes," or "no"; other question alternatives (e.g., "Is it a cat or dog?"); a code was added to yes/no questions for auxiliary fronting when a verb appeared before the noun (e.g., "Do you want it?" rather than "You want it?" or "Want it?").

Source: Adapted from *Meaningful Differences in the Everyday Experience of Young American Children,* by B. Hart and T. R. Risley, 1995, pp. 139 and 149. Copyright 1995 by Paul H. Brookes Publishing Co., Inc. Adapted with permission of the publisher.

to code verbal and nonverbal behaviors. Examiners should possess a solid understanding of syntactic structures to code transcripts accurately.

Huttenlocher et al. Language Coding Scheme

A child's language environment and the complexity of speech the child encounters in environments such as home and school are related to children's speech production and language development (Huttenlocher et al., 2002). To study this relationship Huttenlocher et al. recorded parent and child talk and then coded all complete sentences within transcriptions of these interactions as either simple or complex sentences. To classify each sentence Huttenlocher and colleagues determined that "Simple sentences contained only one clause . . . Complex sentences contained more than one clause" (p. 346). Yet, the distinction between a simple and complex sentence was not always clear; therefore, Huttenlocher et al. established a coding scheme detailed in Table 3–27. In additional analyses Huttenlocher et al. included a second coding scheme to further examine the number of noun phrase utterances (although we do not discuss this in detail due to space limitations). A complete treatment of how to apply this second coding system, which classifies multiclause sentences, is included in Huttenlocher et al.

After all utterances are coded as simple or complex sentences, the proportion of complex sentences is determined by dividing the number of complex sentences by the total number of complete sentences. This calculation is made for both the parent's and the child's talk. A higher proportion of complex parental utterances is associated with more complex speech production in the child. Huttenlocher et al. (2002) collected speech samples that contained 5 hours of the child's talk throughout their interactions at home and school; however, a smaller amount of talk could probably be analyzed reliably for sentence complexity. Perhaps 1 hour of talk, as collected in the Hart and Risley (1995) observations, is a sufficient amount of time for assessment. This coding system was applied to the talk of individual 4-year-old children and their parents. Speech samples were obtained by either videotaping the child or asking children to wear vests with microphones that recorded everything they said or heard at home and school. The outcome measures in Huttenlocher et al. were interpreted as the proportion of complex

Table 3–27. Language Coding Scheme From Huttenlocher et al. (2002)

Code	Sentence Classification	Examples
Code as [NO]	**Incomplete sentence** is an utterance that does not contain both a subject and a verb.	"the dog [NO]" "pretty sky [NO]" "that one [NO]"
Code as [XX]	Inaudible utterances are also incomplete sentences.	"This XXX [NO]."
Code as *simple* [S] or *complex* [C] (see descriptions below)	**Complete sentences** are utterances that contain both a subject and verb, including:	
	▪ imperatives with an understood second person subject	"Sit down."
	▪ copula deletion (because the copula is optional in some cases in African American English dialect)	"He tired."
Code as [S]	**Simple sentences** are simple utterances that contain one clause. This category includes several varieties:	"John made a mistake [S]." "He gave the book to the girl [S]."
	▪ utterances that contain modal verbs, such as *can, could, had better, may, might, must, ought to, shall, should, will,* and *would*	"The girl can hit the ball [S]." "He will play piano [S]." "Jamila ought to [S]."

continues

Table 3-27. *continued*

Code	Sentence Classification	Examples
Code as [S] *continued*	• utterances that contain marginal modals and a verb, such as *used to + V[a], ought to + V, has/have to + V, had better + V, would rather + V, might/could + V, may/can + V, need to + V*	"They used to play [S]." "I would rather sit [S]."
	• utterances that contain quasimodals and a verb, such as *going to + V, gonna + V, go + V, let's + V, supposed to + V, to come + V, to be able to + V*	"I'm gonna eat it all [S]." "Are you going to come [S?]"
	• tag questions that only contain one prior verb	"You went to the store, didn't you [S]?" "You are going, aren't you [S]?"
	• sentences with a conjoined subject or object	"Sam and Harry watched TV [S]." "He ate mashed potatoes and chicken [S]."
Code as [C]	**Complex sentences** are complex utterances that contain two or more clauses. This category includes several varieties:	"He thought John made a mistake [C]." "He gave the book to the girl who lived down the street [C]."
	• sentences that contain infinitival forms with an additional verb	"Carol has to clean her room [C]." "They need to take a vacation [C]."

Code	Sentence Classification	Examples
Code as [C] *continued*	▪ sentences that use "let" verbs following by a pronoun with another predication	"Let's tell him about it [C]." "Let me ask her the question [C]."
	▪ sentences that contain gerund forms (the *–ing* form) with an additional verb. Gerunds are verbs, although they take the place of a noun in these sentences	"Start picking up your toys [C]." "Swinging is really hard [C]."
	▪ sentences that use conjunctions (*for, and, nor, but, or, yet, so, as, then*) between clauses. They may have single or multiple subjects	"He read the book, but he didn't finish it [C]." "Miguel is eating, and John is cleaning up [C]."

Scoring:

Calculate the proportion of complex sentences

Parent speech: _____ # of complex sentences ÷ _____ # total complete sentences = _____

Child speech: _____ # of complex sentences ÷ _____ # total complete sentences = _____

Note. [a]V stands for verb.

Source: Adapted from "Language Input and Child Syntax," by J. Huttenlocher, M. Vasilyeva, E. Cymerman, and S. Levine, 2002, *Cognitive Psychology, 45,* p. 346–347. Copyright 2002 by Elsevier Science. Adapted with permission from Elsevier.

sentences children produced. This was calculated by dividing the number of complex sentences by the total number of complete sentences. The coding system was designed for use with English-speaking parents and children. Scores can be calculated in raw scores, means, and as proportions to total utterances. The examiner will need a through understanding of syntactic complexity to code transcriptions accurately.

Our Word—Expressive Vocabulary Test

The Our Word is an expressive vocabulary measure designed by Whitehurst and colleagues (1994) to assess unique vocabulary gained from shared storybook reading with parents. Whitehurst et al. designed this assessment by selecting 37 black-and-white photocopies of text illustrations from books used in a study of dialogic reading techniques. These pictures were selected because they contained novel vocabulary (e.g., a picture of an oar) that children may have learned the meaning of during storybook reading, especially if the parent employed the dialogic reading strategies promoted in this intervention. Educators can design a similar measure to assess expressive vocabulary gains by using the same technique of isolating pictures from a shared book reading text and asking the child to identify the object. This assessment could be expanded beyond the format used by Whitehurst et al. to include a request for the child to define the word or purpose of an object. This extension would allow educators to assess what level of word meaning the child acquired during the interactive reading session.

Outcomes from the Our Word (Whitehurst et al., 1994) can be interpreted as a gains score from pretest to posttest. One point is given for each rare picture identified correctly at pre- and post-test. Gains in expressive vocabulary may be attributable to a successful interactive parent-child reading session. The time to administer the Our Word at pretest is probably under 5 minutes. Then, approximately 15 minutes will be required for the parent and child to complete interactive storybook reading. Finally, another 5 minutes will be required for post-test. Educators should determine if they are interested in administering the Our Word immediately after reading, or if they are interested in administering the post-test measure after time has lapsed to measure whether children's gains in word learning are retained for a designated period of time. This measure was designed for use with 3-year-old children. To administer the test, the assessor asks the child, "What is this?" or "What is this part of the picture?" The child's responses are recorded and scored immediately. Individual administration is required. Score types include raw scores and gain scores from pre- to post-test. There are no specified qualifications for the examiner.

Special Considerations for Assessing Home Literacy

Before one begins to assess home literacy supports, several factors should be considered. The first step is to provide parents with a description of your purpose so that parents know why you are conducting the assessment. According to Rhodes (1993), it is helpful to preface home literacy assessments with a description of how the assessment information will help you to know the child better and plan literacy instruction more effectively. If you have other purposes for your assessment, it is important for you to make parents aware of those purposes too. Other factors to consider before assessing home literacy include: family structure, family culture, socioeconomic status, parental literacy level, and language spoken at home.

Family structure can vary greatly, making this important information for educators to have before assessing home literacy. Some children live with one or both parents; other children live with grandparents, foster parents, or adoptive parents. Some households include immediate family, and other households include immediate and extended family (e.g., aunts, uncles, grandparents). Barone et al. (2005) explain that gaining knowledge of family structure helps educators understand the child's unique family structure and culture, identify a key contact person, and determine what languages are spoken in the home. Figure 3–1 contains a family interview that educators can use to determine family structure. The interview can be completed face-to-face or can be sent home for parents to return. Some families may not feel comfortable divulging details about their family structure. In cases such as these, the families' wishes should be respected; however, educators can still ask for a contact person for discussing the child's literacy development.

Child's name_____ Date_____

In the spaces below, list all family members who reside in the home with the child. Circle or highlight the name of the contact person for the family. In the "Relationship to child" column, the following abbreviations may be used: M, mother; F, father; B, brother; S, sister; GM, grandmother; GF, grandfather; A, aunt; U, uncle; C, cousin; N, niece; Ne nephew; SM, stepmother; SF, stepfather; FM, foster mother; FF, fosterfather; AM, adoptive mother; AF, adoptive father.

Name of family member	Relationship to child	Languages spoken

Are there family members or friends who are not residents in the home with the child, but with whom the child maintained a close relationship? If so, list them below. The abbreviations given above may be used in the "Relationship to child" column, as well as the following: CG, caregiver; GodM, godmother; GodF, godfather; Ff, friend.

Name of family member	Relationship to child	Languages spoken

Figure 3–1. Parent Interview to Determine Family Structure. From *Teaching Early Literacy*, by D. M. Barone, M. H. Mallette, & S. H. Xu, 2005, p., New York: Guilford Press. 172. Copyright 2005 by The Guilford Press. Reproduced with permission of the publisher.

Questions a teacher may ask to obtain further information on family structure.

1. Who takes care of the child at home? _____

   _____

2. Who helps the child with homework? _____

   _____

3. Who reads to/with the child? _____

   _____

4. Who plays with the child? _____ _____

   _____

5. Who watches TV or plays games with the child? _____

   _____

6. Who talks to/with the child? _____

   _____

7. Other questions: _____

   _____

Figure 3–1. *continued*

When educators and families are from different cultures, there is the potential for misunderstandings and misconceptions about the other's culture. According to Rodriguez (2000), the first step to assessing home literacy in a culturally sensitive manner is to be aware of and reflect on your own cultural beliefs and practices. Once assessors are aware of and comfortable with their own cultural practices, they must accept their degree of comfort with diverse populations and take steps to address their comfort level. Next, assessors should educate themselves on the culture of the families they will be working with if different from their own.

Family involvement in children's literacy development may vary across cultures. Barone and colleagues (2005) note that educators may misinterpret a family's limited participation in school activities as the family not valuing their child's education; however, this may not be the case. Some cultures feel it is the parent's job to educate their children in terms of moral development and the teacher's job to educate their children in terms of academic development. Families who hold this belief may feel hesitant to offer input on their child's academic development. Educators can be sensitive to this belief if they are aware of it before assessment and home-school partnerships begin. Likewise, some answers families give to literacy assessments may be based on cultural norms (Rodriguez, 2000). For example, the age at which a child is first exposed to books may be based on such norms. Educators who are aware of cultural norms can interpret the assessment with care and sensitivity and can create respectful home-school partnerships.

Socioeconomic status (SES) is another factor that can influence administration and interpretation of home literacy assessments. Some low-income families may play a different role in their child's literacy development than higher income families; however, this should not be misunderstood as disinterest in their child's education. Factors such as lack of transportation and work schedules can affect family members' abilities to participate in home literacy assessments. Family members without transportation may find it difficult to attend parent-teacher conferences or come to school to talk with educators about home literacy. Educators can accommodate parents by conducting assessments over the telephone or by scheduling a home visit with the family.

Assessments that require an emphasis on written evidence may alienate parents who are not literate (Crutchley, 2000). If family members are not literate or have limited literacy skills, early literacy professionals can mediate by completing the assessment in the style of an interview to remove reading requirements from the assessment process. An interview format also allows educators to further clarify items or directions as needed. Rhodes (1993) suggests sometimes giving a parent with low literacy the option to take the assessment home because this allows them to obtain assistance with the assessment from someone with whom they feel comfortable. Decisions to not complete a home literacy assessment should be respected and educators should take steps to obtain the information in other ways such as talking to the child.

Whenever possible, to obtain valid results, assessments should be completed in the language that the parent speaks at home. If a family member speaks both English and another language, early literacy professionals should ask parents what language is most comfortable for completing assessments. In some oral assessment situations, a translator should be obtained. For both the educator and translator, it is important to take time to establish a rapport with the family member before the assessment begins. Once you have considered all of the above factors, you are ready to begin the assessment process.

Interpreting Results of Home Literacy Assessments

Having reviewed several assessments for measuring home literacy, we now consider the question of how this assessment information can be used and its possible implications for practice. This is not a simple question because early childhood development is multi-faceted (Meisels, 2006) and home literacy is multifaceted as well (Leseman & de Jong, 1998). Thus, the advice of Meisels (2006) related to assessing young children's academic status applies to assessing home literacy:

> No brief test of young children's achievement administered in a sum-mative way can capture the complexity of pre-K children's growth. Just as a single facet of a reflective surface can never provide an accurate reflection of a complex phenomenon, so a one-dimensional early childhood test of achievement will give off a distorted image of what it is intended to measure (p. 16).

Employing multiple measures of home literacy supports and con-sidering global measures of home literacy environment may provide the most accurate assessment information (Leseman & de Jong, 1998; Roberts et al., 2005).

Further, carefully considering your purpose for assessing home literacy supports can guide selection of well-aligned assessments. Common purposes for assessing home supports include: (a) infor-mation is required about children's opportunities to learn before entering your program or class, (b) home literacy outcomes can be used to evaluate the quality of programs for increasing parental involvement in home literacy, (c) home literacy variables can be used to determine if particular aspects of the program worked for children of a particular family or home literacy background, or (d) home literacy variables can help determine whether home factors or program factors are more closely associated with particular child outcomes. Of course, some assessments can be employed to satisfy more than one purpose.

When interpreting results of home literacy assessments, several limitations must be taken into consideration. First, the validity of results from any self-report measure may be confounded by the factor of social desirability, which has been considered "one of the most serious problems with standard questionnaires about reading activity" (Stanovich & West, 1989, p. 406). Social desirability is the tendency to exaggerate engagement in activities that society generally perceives to be positive, such as reading to your child. This tendency to overestimate socially desirable responses constitutes a serious flaw in measurement accuracy that should be accounted for when employing any of self-report measures discussed throughout this chapter. A small number of the self-report measures in this chapter are designed to circumvent the problem of social desirability.

Observations of literacy behaviors in naturalistic settings such as the home environment may give more accurate information about home literacy practices. Yet, it is possible that families may alter their typical behaviors because they are being observed. For instance, "there is . . . the possibility that mothers who know that they are being observed may alter their usual manner during book reading, so that it adheres more closely to their notions of the most acceptable way of interacting with a preschooler" (Scarborough & Dobrich, 1994, p. 255). Nevertheless, observational assessments may provide an accurate estimate of home literacy supports and activities.

Another limitation to consider is the issue of generalizability of empirical findings. Much of the research reviewed in this chapter was conducted with small or unique populations. Thus, generalizing to other samples with different characteristics should be done carefully.

Overall, it appears that home literacy practices can facilitate later reading achievement (Purcell-Gates, 2000). Therefore, educators may be interested in promoting home-school activities or partnerships relevant to the needs of their population or individual children. Before initiating home literacy programs, educators should be aware that an ideological debate about how family literacy programs ought to operate currently exists. Purcell-Gates (2000) summarizes how some take issue with family literacy programs that either implicitly or explicitly take a stance that a family or parent needs to change behaviors to be considered acceptable. Instead, a culturally responsive family literacy program in which parents and educators collaborate to create respectful partnerships is suggested (see Auerbach, 1995). The assessments in this chapter can be employed in culturally responsive ways especially when families are viewed as an asset for fostering sustainable changes to a child's development (Bronfrenbrenner & Morris, 1998) and for planning responsive interventions for at-risk children (Klingner & Edwards, 2006).

Concluding Thoughts

This chapter has examined how a child's home environment supports or deters literacy and the aspects of the home context that exert the greatest influence on children's emergent and early literacy development. Several measures that may be useful in assessing five home literacy constructs: parent's beliefs and knowledge, parent-child storybook reading, home literacy activities, the home environment, and home language environment were presented. Information gleaned from these assessments can inform questions of how educators can involve caregivers in fostering home supports for literacy. For early childhood educators, the first years of school are an ideal time for initiating or building on parents' home literacy involvement. Purcell-Gates (1996) describes how the momentum of both school and home literacy activities foster one another by noting, "We see a complex pattern of schooling influence with literacy knowledge emanating directly from the school instruction and activities as well as from home-based activities that were put into increased play by the onset of schooling" (p. 426). Consider how schools might increase the natural momentum of building home supports for literacy if reliable measures are employed to direct resources and support for essential home literacy activities.

References

Adams, M. J. (1990). *Beginning to read: Thinking and learning about print*. Cambridge, MA: Massachusetts Institute of Technology.

Aram, D., & Levin, I. (2002). Mother-child joint writing and storybook reading: Relations with literacy among low SES kindergartners. *Merrill-Palmer Quarterly, 48*, 202–224.

Armbruster, B. B., Lehr, F., & Osborn, J. (2003). *Proven ideas from research for parents: A child becomes a reader: Kindergarten through grade 3*. Portsmouth, NH: RMC Research Corporation.

Arnold, D. H., Lonigan, C. J., Whitehurst, G. J., & Epstein, J. N. (1994). Accelerating language development through picture book reading: Replication and extension to a videotape training format. *Journal of Educational Psychology, 86*, 235–243.

Auerbach, E. R. (1995). Which way for family literacy: Intervention or empowerment? In L. M. Morrow (Ed.), *Family literacy: Connections in schools and communities* (pp. 11–27). New Brunswick, NJ: International Reading Association.

Barone, D. M., Mallette, M. H., & Xu, S. H. (2005). *Teaching early literacy: Development, assessment, and instruction*. New York: Guilford Press.

Beals, D. E. (2001). Eating and reading: Links between family conversations with preschoolers and later language and literacy. In D. K. Dickinson & P. O. Tabors (Eds.), *Beginning literacy with language: Young children learning at home and school* (pp. 75–92). Baltimore: Brookes.

Beals, D. E., DeTemple, J. M., & Dickinson, D. K. (1994). Talking and listening that support early literacy development of children from low-income families. In D. K. Dickinson (Ed.), *Bridges to literacy: Children, families, and schools* (pp. 19–40). Cambridge, MA: Blackwell.

Bear, D. R., Invernizzi, M., Templeton, S., & Johnston, F. (2004). *Words their way: Word study for phonics, vocabulary, and spelling instruction*. Upper Saddle River, NJ: Pearson.

Benasich, A. A., & Brooks-Gunn, J. (1996). Maternal attitudes and knowledge of child-rearing: Associations with family and child outcomes. *Child Development, 67*, 1186–1205.

Boehm, A. E. (1993). HOME. *09 Mental Measurements Yearbook*. Abstract retrieved January 29, 2006, from Mental Measurements database.

Boudreau, D. (2005). Use of a parent questionnaire in emergent and early literacy assessment of preschool children. *Language, Speech, and Hearing in Schools, 36*, 33–47.

Bradley, R. H., & Caldwell, B. M. (1979). Home observation for measurement of the environment: A revision of the preschool scale. *American Journal of Mental Deficiency, 84*, 235–244.

Brandt, D. (2001). *Literacy in American lives*. Cambridge, UK: Cambridge University Press.

Britto, P. R., Brooks-Gunn, J., & Griffin, T. M. (2006). Maternal reading and teaching patterns: Associations with school readiness in low-income African American families. *Reading Research Quarterly, 41*, 68–89.

Britto, P. R., Fuligini, A. S., Brooks-Gunn, J. (2006). Reading ahead: Effective interventions for young children's early literacy development. In D. K. Dickinson & S. B. Neuman (Eds.), *Handbook of early literacy research* (Vol. 2, pp. 311–333). New York: Guilford Press.

Bronfrenbrenner, U., & Morris, P. A. (1998). The ecology of developmental processes. In W. Damon & R. M. Lerner (Eds.), *Handbook of child psychology* (5th ed., pp. 993–1028). New York: Wiley.

Burchinal, M. R., Peisner-Feinberg, E., Pianta, R., & Howes, C. (2002). Development of academic skills from preschool through second grade: Family and classroom predictors of developmental trajectories. *Journal of School Psychology, 40*, 415–436.

Burgess, S. (2005). The preschool home literacy environment provided by teenage mothers. *Early Childhood Development and Care, 175*, 249–258.

Bus, A. G. (2001). Joint caregiver-child storybook reading: A route to literacy development. In S. B. Neuman & D. K. Dickinson (Eds.) *Handbook of early literacy research* (Vol. 1, pp. 179–191). New York: Guilford.

Bus, A. G., van IJzendorn, M. H., & Pellegrini, A. D. (1995). Joint book reading makes for success in learning to read: A meta-analysis on intergenerational transmission of literacy. *Review of Educational Research, 65*, 1–21.

Caldwell, B. M., & Bradley, R. H. (1984). *Home observation for measurement of the environment*. Little Rock: University of Arkansas.

Catts, H. W., & Hogan, T. P. (2003). Language basis of reading disabilities and implications for early identification and remediation. *Reading Psychology, 24*, 223–246.

Crutchley, A. (2000). Bilingual children in language units: Does having "well-informed" parents make a difference? *International Journal of Language and Communication Disorders, 35*, 65–81.

Cunningham, A. E., & Stanovich, K. E. (1990). Assessing print exposure and orthographic processing skill: A quick measure of reading experience. *Journal of Educational Psychology, 82*, 733–740.

Cunningham, A. E., & Stanovich, K. E. (1997). Early reading acquisition and its relation to reading experience and ability 10 years later. *Developmental Psychology, 33*, 934–994.

Cunningham, A. E., & Stanovich, K. E. (2004). Disciplinary knowledge of K–3 teachers and their knowledge calibration in the domain of early literacy. *Annals of Dyslexia, 54*, 139–167.

DeBaryshe, B. D. (1995). Maternal belief systems: Linchpin in the home reading process. *Journal of Applied Developmental Psychology, 16,* 1–20.

DeBaryshe, B. D., & Binder, J. C. (1994). Development of an instrument for measuring parental beliefs about reading aloud to young children. *Perceptual and Motor Skills, 78,* 1303–1311.

DeTemple, J. M. (1993). *Coding system for home book reading.* Cambridge, MA: Harvard University Graduate School of Education.

DeTemple, J. M. (2001). Parents and children reading books together. In D. K. Dickinson & P. O. Tabors (Eds.), *Beginning literacy with language: Young children learning at home and school.* Baltimore: Brookes.

DeTemple, J. M., & Beals, D. E. (1991). Family talk: Sources of support for the development of decontextualized language skills. *Journal of Research in Childhood Education, 6,* 11–19.

Dickinson, D. K., & Tabors, P. O. (1991). Early literacy: Linkages between home, school, and literacy achievement at age five. *Journal of Research in Childhood Education, 6,* 30–46.

Dickinson, D. K., & Tabors, P. O. (Eds.). (2001). *Beginning literacy with language: Young children learning at home and school.* Baltimore: Brookes.

Early Childhood Longitudinal Study. (1999). *Early Childhood Longitudinal Study-K fall parent interview.* Retrieved May 28, 2006, from http://nces.ed.gov/ecls/pdf/kindergarten/fallparent.pdf

Edwards, P. A. (1995). Combining parents' and teachers' thoughts about storybook reading at home and school. In L. M. Morrow (Ed.), *Family literacy: Connections in schools and communities* (pp. 54–69). New Brunswick, NJ: International Reading Association.

Ehri, L. C., & Roberts, T. (2006). The roots of learning to read and write: Acquisition of letters and phonemic awareness. In D. K. Dickinson & S. B. Neuman (Eds.), *Handbook of early literacy research* (Vol. 2, pp. 113–131). New York: Guilford Press.

Evans, M. A., Barraball, L., & Eberle, T. (1998). Parental responses to miscues during child-to-parent book reading. *Journal of Applied Developmental Psychology, 19*(1), 67–84.

Evans, M. A., Fox, M., Cremaso, L., & McKinnon, L. (2004). Beginning reading: The views of parents and teachers of young children. *Journal of Educational Psychology, 96*(1), 130–141.

Evans, M. A., Shaw, D., & Bell, M. (2000). Home literacy activities and their influence on early literacy skills. *Canadian Journal of Experimental Psychology, 52,* 65–75.

Fantuzzo, J., Tighe, E., & Childs, S. (2000). Family Involvement Questionnaire: A multivariate analysis of family participation in early childhood education. *Journal of Educational Psychology, 92,* 367–376.

Fitzgerald, J., Spiegel, D. L., & Cunningham, J. W. (1991). The relationship between parental literacy level and perceptions of emergent literacy. *Journal of Reading Behavior, 23*, 191–213.

Fritjers, J. C., Barron, R. W., & Brunello, M. (2000). Direct and mediated influences of home literacy and literacy interest on prereaders' oral vocabulary and early written language skill. *Journal of Educational Psychology, 92*, 466–477.

Hammettt, L. A., van Kleeck, A., & Huberty, C. J. (2003). Patterns of parents' extratextual interactions during book sharing with preschool children: A cluster analysis study. *Reading Research Quarterly, 38*, 442–468.

Hart, B., & Risley, T. R. (1995). *Meaningful differences in the everyday experiences of young American children.* Baltimore: Brookes.

Heath, S. B. (1983). *Ways with words: Language, life, and work in communities and classrooms.* Cambridge, UK: Cambridge University Press.

Huttenlocher, J., Vasilyeva, M., Cymerman, E., & Levine, S. (2002). Language input and child syntax. *Cognitive Psychology, 45*, 337–374.

Jordan, G. E., Snow, C. E., & Porche, M. V. (2000). Project EASE: The effect of a family literacy project on kindergarten students' early literacy skills. *Reading Research Quarterly, 35*, 524–546.

Justice, L. M., & Ezell, H. K. (2000). Enhancing children's print and word awareness through home-based parent intervention. *American Journal of Speech-Language Pathology, 9*, 257–269.

Justice, L. M., & Ezell, H. K. (2002). Use of storybook reading to increase print awareness in at-risk children. *American Journal of Speech-Language Pathology, 11*, 17–29.

Justice, L. M., Kaderavek, J., Bowles, R., & Grimm, K. (2005). Language impairment, parent-child shared reading, and phonological awareness: A feasibility study. *Topics in Early Childhood Special Education, 25*, 143–156.

Justice, L. M., Meier, J., & Walpole, S. (2005). Learning new words from storybooks: An efficacy study with at-risk kindergartners. *Language, Speech, and Hearing Services in Schools, 36*, 17–32.

Katz, J. R. (2001). Playing at home: The talk of pretend play. In D. K. Dickinson & P. O. Tabors (Eds.), *Beginning literacy with language: Young children learning at home and school.* Baltimore: Brookes.

Klingner, J. K., & Edwards, P. A. (2006). Cultural considerations with Response to Intervention models. *Reading Research Quarterly, 41*, 108–117.

Landry, S. H., & Smith, K. E. (2006). The influence of parenting on emergent literacy skills. In D. K. Dickinson & S. B. Neuman (Eds.), *Handbook of early literacy research* (Vol. 2, pp. 135–148). New York: Guilford.

Leseman, P. P. M., & de Jong, P. F. (1998). Home literacy: Opportunity, instruction, cooperation, and social-emotional quality predicting early reading achievement. *Reading Research Quarterly, 33*, 294–318.

Leventhal, T., Selner-O'Hagan, M. B., Brooks-Gunn, J., Bingenheimer, J. B., & Earls, F. J. (2004). The Homelife interview from the Project on Human Development in Chicago Neighborhoods: Assessment of parenting and home environment for 3- to 15-year-olds. *Parenting: Science and Practice, 4*, 211–241.

Linver, M. R., Brooks-Gunn, J., & Cabrera, N. (2004). The Home Observation for Measurement of the Environment (HOME): The derivation of conceptually designed subscales. *Parenting: Science and Practice, 4*, 99–114.

Maclean, M., Bryant, P., & Bradley, L. (1987). Rhymes, nursery rhymes, and reading in early childhood. *Merrill-Palmer Quarterly, 33*, 255–281.

McGillicuddy-DeLisi, A. V. (1982). Parental beliefs about developmental processes. *Human Development, 25*, 192–200.

Meisels, S. J. (2006). *Accountability in early childhood: No easy answers* (Erikson Institute Occasional Paper No. 6). Chicago: Herr Research Centers for Children and Social Policy at Erikson Institute.

Naigles, L. R., & Hoff-Ginsberg, E. (1998). Why are some verbs learned before other verbs? Effects of input frequency and structure on children's early verb use. *Journal of Child Language, 25*, 95–120.

National Center for Education Statistics. (1999). *Home literacy activities and signs of children's emerging literacy, 1993 and 1999*. (NCES Publication No. NCES 2000-026rev). Washington, DC: U.S. Department of Education.

National Center for Learning Disabilities. (2004). *Home literacy environment checklist*. Retrieved February 12, 2006, from http://www.get readytoread.org

National Reading Panel Report. (2000). *Teaching children to read*. Washington, DC: National Institute of Child Health and Development.

Needlman, R., Klass, P., & Zuckerman, B. (2006). A pediatric approach to early literacy. In D. K. Dickinson & S. B. Neuman (Eds.), *Handbook of early literacy research* (Vol. 2, pp. 333–346). New York: Guilford Press.

Neuman, S. B. (1996). Children engaging in storybook reading: The influence of access to print resources, opportunity, and parental interaction. *Early Childhood Research Quarterly, 11*, 495–513.

Neuman, S. B. (2006). The knowledge gap: Implications for early education. In D. K. Dickinson & S. B. Neuman (Eds.), *Handbook of early literacy research* (Vol. 2, pp. 29–40). New York: Guilford Press.

Neuman, S. B., & Celano, D. (2001). Access to print in low-income and middle-income communities: An ecological study of four neighborhoods. *Reading Research Quarterly, 36*, 8–26.

Neuman, S. B., & Roskos, K. (2005). The state of pre-kindergarten standards. *Early Childhood Research Quarterly, 20*, 124–145.

Pan, B. A., Rowe, M. L., Singer, J. D., & Snow, C. E. (2005). Maternal correlates of growth in toddler vocabulary production. *Child Development, 76,* 763–782.

Paratore, J. R. (2002). Home and school together: Helping beginning readers succeed. In A. E. Farstrup & S. J. Samuels (Eds.), *What research has to say about reading instruction.* Newark, DE: International Reading Association.

Payne, R. K. (2001). *A framework for understanding poverty.* Highlands, TX: aha! Process.

Payne, A. C., Whitehurst, G. J., & Angell, A. L. (1994). The role of home literacy environment in the development of language ability in preschool children from low-income families. *Early Childhood Research Quarterly, 9,* 427–440

Pepper, J., Weitzman, E., & McDade, A. (2004). *It takes two to talk: The Hanen program for parents.* Toronto, ON: The Hanen Centre.

Peyton, T. (1999). *Family literacy legislation and initiatives in eleven states.* Louisville, KY: National Center for Family Literacy.

Pianta, R. C., Nimetz, S. L., & Bennett, E. (1997). Mother-child relationships, teacher-child relationships, and school outcomes in preschool and kindergarten. *Early Childhood Research Quarterly, 12,* 263–280.

Purcell-Gates, V. (1995). *Other people's words: The cycle of low literacy.* Cambridge, MA: Harvard University Press.

Purcell-Gates, V. (1996). Stories, coupons, and the *TV Guide*: Relationships between home literacy experiences and emergent literacy knowledge. *Reading Research Quarterly, 31,* 406–428.

Purcell-Gates, V. (2000). Family literacy. In M. L. Kamil, P. B. Mosenthal, P.D Pearson, & R. Barr (Eds.), *Handbook of reading research* (Vol. 3, pp. 853–870). Mahwah, NJ: Erlbaum.

Rhodes, L. K. (1993). *Literacy assessment: A handbook of instruments.* Portsmouth, NH: Heinemann.

Richgels, D. J. (2001). Invented spelling, phonemic awareness, and reading and writing instruction. In S. B. Neuman & D. Dickinson (Eds.), *Handbook of early literacy research* (Vol. 1, pp. 142–155). New York: Guilford Press.

Roberts, J., Jurgens, J., & Burchinal, M. (2005). The role of home literacy practices in preschool children's language and emergent literacy skills. *Journal of Speech, Language, and Hearing Research, 48,* 345–359.

Rodriguez, C. (2000). Culturally sensitive psychological assessment. In I. A. Canino & J. Spurlock (Eds.), *Culturally diverse children and adolescents* (pp. 84–102). New York: Guilford.

Rodriguez, B. L., & Olswang, L. B. (2003). Mexican-American and Anglo-American mothers' beliefs and values about child rearing, education, and language impairment. *American Journal of Speech-Language Pathology*, *12*, 452–462.

Scarborough, H. S. (2001). Connecting early language and literacy to later reading (dis)abilities: Evidence, theory, and practice. In S. B. Neuman & D. Dickinson (Eds.), *Handbook of early literacy research* (Vol. 1, pp. 97–110). New York: Guilford.

Scarborough, H. S., & Dobrich, W. (1994). On the efficacy of reading to preschoolers. *Developmental Review*, *14*, 245–302.

Sénéchal, M. (2006). Testing the Home Literacy Model: Parent involvement in kindergarten is differentially related to grade 4 reading comprehension, fluency, and reading for pleasure. *Scientific Studies of Reading*, *10*, 59–87.

Sénéchal, M., LeFevre, J., Thomas, E. M., & Daley, K. E. (1998). Differential effects of home literacy experiences on the development of oral and written language. *Reading Research Quarterly*, *33*, 96–116.

Sénéchal, M., Ouellette, G., & Rodney, D. (2006). The misunderstood giant: On the predictive role of early vocabulary to future reading. In D. K. Dickinson & S. B. Neuman (Eds.), *Handbook of early literacy research* (Vol. 2, pp. 173–182). New York: Guilford Press.

Serpell, R., Sonnenschein, S., Baker, L., Ganapathy, H. (2002). Intimate culture of families in the early socialization of literacy. *Journal of Family Psychology*, *16*, 391–405.

Snow, C. E. (1991). The theoretical basis for relationships between language and literacy in development. *Journal of Research in Childhood Education*, *6*, 5–10.

Snow, C. E., Burns, M. S., & Griffin, P. (Eds.). (1998). *Preventing reading difficulties in young children*. Washington, DC: US Government Printing Office.

Sonnenschein, S., Brody, G., & Munsterman, K. (1995). The influence of family beliefs and practices on children's early reading development. In L. Baker, P. Afflerbach, & D. Reinking (Eds.), *Developing engaged readers in school and home communities*. Mahwah, NJ: Erlbaum.

Stanovich, K. E., & West, R. F. (1989). Exposure to print and orthographic processing. *Reading Research Quarterly*, *24*, 402–433.

Storch, S. A., & Whitehurst, G. J. (2001). The role of family and home in the literacy development of children from low-income backgrounds. *New Directions for Child and Adolescent Development*, *92*, 53–72.

Strickland, D. S. (2001). Early intervention for African American children considered to be at risk. In S. B. Neuman & D. Dickinson (Eds.), *Handbook of early literacy research* (Vol. 1, pp. 322–332). New York: Guilford.

Tabors, P. O., & Snow, C. E. (2001). Young bilingual children and early literacy development. In S. B. Neuman & D. K. Dickinson (Eds.), *Handbook of early literacy research* (Vol. 1, pp. 159–178). New York: Guilford.

Taylor, D., & Dorsey-Gaines, C. (1988). *Growing up literate: Learning from inner-city families*. Portsmouth, NH: Heinemann

Umek, L. M., Podlesek, A., & Fekonja, U. (2005). Assessing the home literacy environment: Relationships to child language, comprehension, and expression. *European Journal of Psychological Assessment, 21,* 271–281.

U.S. Department of Education. (2005). *Helping your child become a reader*. Washington, DC: Office of Communications and Outreach.

Vygotsky, L. S. (1962). *Thought and language*. Cambridge, MA: M.I.T. Press.

Wasik, B. H., Dobbins, D. R., & Herrmann, S. (2001). Intergenerational family literacy: Concepts, research, and practice. In S. B Neuman & D. K. Dickinson (Eds.), *Handbook of early literacy research* (Vol. 1, pp. 159–178). New York: Guilford Press.

Whitehurst, G. J., Arnold, D. S., Epstein, J. N., Angell, A. L., Smith, M., & Fischel, J. E. (1994). A picture book reading intervention in day care and home for children from low-income families. *Developmental Psychology, 30,* 679–689.

Yaden, D. B., Smolkin, L. B., & Conlon, A. (1989). Preschoolers' questions about pictures, print conventions, and story text during reading aloud at home. *Reading Research Quarterly, 24,* 188–214.

Chapter Four

Assessing Implementation of Literacy Curricula

Sharon Walpole
Katrin L. Blamey

In this chapter, we argue that assessing children's literacy development without assessing the instructional environment in which they are learning is problematic. We present tools that all those interested in emergent literacy achievement—researchers, administrators, professional developers, and teachers—can use to assess teacher fidelity to curricula in a given emergent literacy environment. We begin with generic or general tools that could be used in any curriculum and then move to tools specific to a given curriculum. We present both existing, published tools and strategies for designing tools. We end the chapter with recommendations for using the results of these assessments to guide continuous improvement in literacy teaching and learning in emergent literacy settings.

The Importance of Assessing Implementation of Literacy Curricula to Emergent Literacy

It may seem surprising to include a chapter on assessment of curriculum implementation in this book, but assessment of implementation is key to program development and reform. Without specific knowledge of the quality of curriculum implementation, it is very difficult to interpret the results of the many assessments of language and literacy achievement presented in other chapters. Continuous improvement in any educational environment depends on deep understanding of the learning opportunities offered to children *and* ongoing monitoring of their literacy learning within that environment.

Many preschools and kindergartens are in the process of designing and implementing curriculum innovation. One part of any curriculum innovation is planning for, establishing, and monitoring fidelity. Fidelity is the degree to which an individual implements the innovation as envisioned and the degree to which implementation is consistent across individuals. The issue of establishment of fidelity is important (and problematic) in many areas of the social sciences, and it is of special importance to research efforts designed to test the effectiveness of interventions. Neither correlational nor causal claims for the effectiveness of any educational practice can be made without assurances that the practice was actually used as intended by the target participants, but such evidence is not always provided—even in research studies.

We assume that readers of this chapter will be designing, implementing, or assessing instruction in emergent literacy environments and that their work likely includes the introduction of an innovation or intervention. The research literature is filled with cautions in such work. Detrich (1999) indicates that several factors influence fidelity—goodness of fit of the intervention to the environment, general teacher buy-in, availability of resources related to the intervention, and the match between the innovation and previous experience and practice.

Dane and Schneider (1998) reviewed published studies from 1980 to 1994 in diverse areas of prevention research to document the extent to which the researchers included program fidelity or integrity measures (which they defined as exposure, adherence, quality of delivery, program differentiation, and participant responsiveness) in their analyses. The review was sobering: only 39 of 162 studies included such documentation. Given the importance of establishment of fidelity to interpreting the outcomes of such studies, researchers need to plan for it and measure it; given the potential long-term effects of high-quality emergent literacy instruction on children's later achievement, those designing or implementing new curricula have an even more urgent charge. Part of the job can be accomplished in planning. We agree with Dane and Schneider that implementers of instruction need a training manual, training, and supervision at the very least. We also argue that assessment of fidelity of curriculum innovations should be intimately linked with the design of professional support systems. Data to indicate that innovations are not implemented with fidelity may be interesting theoretically, but in the practical (and important) world of real-life emergent literacy environments, teachers must be provided professional support until they have the knowledge and skills necessary to implement programs with fidelity.

Our general questions about fidelity can be answered with formal and informal measures, both commercially available and adopted from research studies, within the framework of innovation configuration (Hord, 1986; National Staff Development Council, 2003). Innovation configuration models assume that any innovation that is planned for a particular setting will be accomplished as part of a process involving both individual and institutional characteristics and adaptations. To that end, the innovation will be operationalized somewhat differently by different individuals in one site and also across multiple sites. Some adaptations will be judged to be acceptable differences that represent the range of choices made during implementation; others will constitute differences that, in fact, create a new innovation. Understanding, documenting, and analyzing those differences is the goal of assessment of instructional fidelity; providing support to teachers whose implementation involves unacceptable adaptations provides direction to professional development programs.

An example of a published innovation configuration related to professional development might help make innovation configurations more concrete. The National Staff Development Council (2003), an organization which supports the design and implementation of high-quality professional development systems, published a set of standards for staff development that includes attention to context, process, and content. They then used the process of innovation configuration to create implementation guides specific to all levels of stakeholders (teachers, principals, central office staff members, superintendents, and school boards). Table 4–1 presents one portion of that work. Clearly, the tool itself anticipates varying degrees of implementation across individuals, including one (Level 4) that is unacceptable. Collection of implementation data through innovation configurations can guide both interpretation of student data and professional support plans in any institution.

Table 4–1. Sample Innovation Configuration to Measure a Teacher's Professional Learning

Desired Outcome 7.1: Participates in a variety of appropriate staff development designs aligned with expected improvement outcomes			
Level 1	**Level 2**	**Level 3**	**Level 4**
Engages in collaborative interactions in learning teams and participates in a variety of activities that are aligned with expected improvement outcomes (e.g., collaborative lesson design, professional networks, analyzing student work, problem solving sessions, curriculum development).	Selects and engages in a variety of staff development activities such as study groups, individually guided school improvement/ curriculum improvement, action research, or classroom observation/ feedback that are aligned with expected improvement outcomes.	Attends workshops to gain information about new programs and receives classroom-based coaching to assist with implementation of new strategies and activities that may be aligned with expected improvement outcomes.	Experiences a single model or inappropriate models of professional development that are not aligned with expected outcomes.

Source: Used with permission of the National Staff Development Council, www.nsdc.org, 2006. All rights reserved.

Assessment of curriculum implementation, especially when it involves some sort of innovation, is complicated and especially important in the complex world of emergent literacy instruction. Classroom quality is important for preschool-age students' development of emergent literacy skills (Burchinal, Roberts, Hooper, & Zeisel, 2000; National Institute of Child Health and Human Development, 2000). Yet, despite the importance of high-quality programs, researchers have documented problems in ensuring high-quality instruction in preschool settings (Dickinson, McCabe, & Clark-Chiarelli, 2004; Snow, Tabors, & Dickinson, 2001). Thus, current policymakers are beginning to set standards for preschool programs. One example of this standardization has occurred in several states, which have implemented childhood quality rating systems (QRS) to monitor the quality of childcare programs (Stoney, 2004). A QRS, much like an innovation configuration, consists of a framework of expectations that participants can use to evaluate their fidelity to external standards and identify areas of weakness for improvement. For example, Kentucky created the STARS for KIDS NOW QRS to evaluate both licensed and home childcare programs on a volunteer basis (http://www.education.ky.gov). The STARS for KIDS NOW rating system scores childcare programs on a four-star scale in seven areas: staff-to-child ratios, group size, curriculum, parent involvement, training and education of staff, regulatory compliance, and personnel practices. To achieve four stars on the curriculum component, a childcare program must implement four family involvement activities, post daily schedules and program activities, maintain an average program score of 6 or more on an Environmental Rating Scale (ERS) created by the state, and possess state-approved national accreditation. The evaluation project initiated by the state to determine the impact of the STARS for KIDS NOW QRS found that participation in the program was related to overall center quality. For further information on states using the QRS model, please visit the National Child Care Information Center Web page, http://www.nccic.org/poptopics/qrsimpactqualitycc.html.

In addition to individual state projects, national efforts are underway to design and test the efficacy of specific curricular innovations during the preschool years. Early Reading First (2006) is an innovation funded as part of the reauthorization of the Elementary and Secondary Education Act in 2002. Seventy-five million dollars were appropriated in 2002 and in 2003 to improve the curricula in preschools serving children from poor families. The legislation specifically targets innovations and professional support for teachers to implement them. The purpose of the project is to enhance young children's early language and literacy skills by improving teaching quality. Those efforts target instructional materials and practices, storybook reading, and monitoring of progress, but individual sites must select and implement their own curricular innovations. To judge the efficacy of these efforts, assessment of implementation of the curricula used in the Early Reading First projects is an essential component.

Early Reading First is not the only timely setting for developing and testing measures of literacy curricula for young children. The Institute of Education Sciences has funded a series of investigations called Preschool Curriculum Evaluation Research (PCER, 2006), with the charge of rigorous evaluation of existing preschool curricula. The design of the PCER evaluation specifically targets implementation by literally asking this question: What effects do level of implementation and participation have on curriculum effectiveness? Individual research teams are carefully monitoring the effects of different curricular innovations in preschools and also coordinating their efforts by working across sites to assess the global qualities of classrooms, teacher-child interactions, teaching style, and class-size ratios.

The PCER project provides evidence that evaluating and monitoring implementation of high-quality literacy curricula in preschool settings is not only a good idea for children's development but is quickly becoming a national mandate. As we await the results of these coordinated efforts, local preschools will also be implementing curricular innovations and conducting their own site-based examinations of the effects of those innovations on the children they are serving. In the rest of this chapter, we provide guidance for researchers, administrators, teacher leaders, and teachers who are working to ensure high-quality implementation of literacy curricula, particularly in emergent literacy settings.

General Measures and Procedures for Examining Curriculum Fidelity

How can we assess the implementation fidelity of literacy curricula by preschool teachers? In this section we describe an initial procedure, content analysis, which we consider an essential first step in *any* fidelity measurement system. Content analysis establishes deep understanding on the part of the observer. Then we describe several measures an individual might choose to use in different places for different purposes. Measures might be categorized by type: content analyses, teacher surveys and logs, interviews, and both formal and informal observations. Choice among these options will depend, to a large extent, on the match between existing tools and the curriculum being implemented and on the resources available to the evaluator. Measures might also be categorized by purpose: refining the curriculum itself, planning professional support in the form of direct training or implementation manuals, or analyzing the relationship between the curriculum and specific indices of student achievement. In many instances, as new curricula are being developed and tested, professionals must craft their own evaluation instruments during the course of implementation. A careful review of existing tools and procedures can make that process much more productive.

Our presentation addresses three questions that are important to researchers and practitioners working to implement high-quality curricula in emergent literacy settings, which we believe must be answered in order to assess implementation of literacy curricula:

1. To what extent is the curriculum as a whole consistent with general standards for quality?
2. To what extent are teachers implementing the specific components of the curriculum?
3. To what extent is teacher implementation of high quality?

Establishing the General Quality of the Curriculum

We define quality in any curricular innovation as the presence or absence of specific indicators. General implementation measures are stronger if they are derived from externally determined criteria for excellence in the domain of interest. General standards measures are necessarily broad, and they provide evidence of balance and breadth rather than depth. General standards measures, then, impose outside standards and can be used to begin to compare implementation across multiple curricula.

We have located one general approach and several standardized tools for measuring general curriculum quality in preschool or kindergarten classrooms. Table 4–2 provides a preview of their characteristics. We describe each in turn by first presenting available information on the design and characteristics of the assessment, and then on how the data are collected and summarized.

Content Analyses

An essential first strategy for assessing the quality of literacy curricula is a thorough content analysis. A content analysis is simply a page-by-page reading and cataloging of the contents of the entire curriculum. Content analysis provides deep understanding of what the curriculum actually includes, in terms of both general characteristics and of its specific goals-based scope and sequence of lessons. Understanding exactly what the curriculum requires of teachers and children is absolutely essential to any deep understanding of its implementation, but if investigators conduct a content analysis using an external set of criteria, they gain added insight about the degree to which the curriculum is consistent with content-specific standards.

One useful strategy for evaluating preschool or kindergarten curricula is to compare them to early childhood standards. The National Association for the Education of Young Children (NAEYC, 2006) established standards for early childhood programs. One standard is devoted to curriculum. The association defines curriculum as "the goals for the knowledge and skills to be acquired by children and the plans for learning experiences through which such knowledge and skills will be achieved." The general standard indicates that "the program implements a curriculum that is consistent with its goals for children and promotes learning and development in each of the following areas: social, emotional, physical, language, and cognitive." The rationale for the standard has direct implications for the conduct of a content analysis:

> A curriculum that draws on research assists teachers in identifying important concepts and skills as well as effective methods for fostering children's learning and development. When informed by teachers' knowledge of individual children, a well-articulated curriculum guides teachers so they can provide children with experiences that foster growth across a broad range of developmental and content areas.

Table 4–2. Measuring General Implementation of the Curriculum

Assessment	Use	Grade	Time	Names of Subtests
Content Analysis	Analysis and cataloguing of curriculum page-by-page	Appropriate for all grade levels	Several days	
Quality Learning Instrument	Assesses curriculum quality from the child's perspective	Kindergarten	2 days	1. Motivation 2. Concentration 3. Independence 4. Confidence 5. Well-Being 6. Social Interaction 7. Respect 8. Multiple Skill Acquisition 9. Higher Order Thinking Skills
Early Language and Literacy Classroom Observation (ELLCO)	Assesses the literacy practices and materials used in classrooms	PreK–3rd	1–1½ hours	1. Literacy Environment Checklist 2. Classroom Observation and Teacher Interview 3. Literacy Activities Rating Scale

continues

Table 4-2. *continued*

Assessment	Use	Grade	Time	Names of Subtests
Early Childhood Environment Rating Scale, Revised (ECERS-R)	Assesses preschool and childcare programs	PreK–K	2½–3 hours	1. Space and Furnishings 2. Personal Care Routines 3. Language-Reasoning 4. Activities 5. Interactions 6. Program Structure 7. Parents and Staff
Assessment of Practices in Early Elementary Classrooms (APEEC)	Assesses developmentally appropriate instruction in classrooms for students with and without disabilities	K–3	1 full day's instruction	1. Physical Environment 2. Instructional Context 3. Social Context

A curriculum also helps ensure that the teacher is intentional in planning a daily schedule that (a) maximizes children's learning through effective use of time, materials used for play, self-initiated learning, and creative expression as well as (b) offers opportunities for children to learn individually and in groups according to their developmental needs and interests (NAEC, 2006).

Figure 4-1 provides a set of questions constructed directly from this standard, which could be used in a standards-based content analysis of an early childhood curriculum. The procedure for using

---

What Evidence Can We Find That This Curriculum:

Helps teachers identify important skills and concepts?

Helps teachers identify effective methods for fostering learning and development?

Guides teachers to provide children with experiences that foster growth across a broad range of developmental and content areas?

Helps teachers plan a daily schedule that maximizes children's learning through effective use of time, materials used for play, self-initiated learning, and creative expression?

Helps teachers plan a daily schedule that offers opportunities for children to learn individually and in groups according to their developmental needs and interests?

Figure 4-1. Questions based on NAEYC Standards to Guide Content Analysis.

these questions is easy to describe but requires time and work to implement. A team works together to review the curriculum manuals provided for the innovation, specifically looks for direct evidence of each item in the standards, and then describes it fully. If evidence is not easily located, the curriculum itself does not conform to the standards, and that may be cause either to supplement it or to consider a different curriculum.

Content analysis is appropriate for different individuals at different times. If school- or center-based staff members are considering adoption of a curriculum, they would be well advised to conduct content analyses of several different curricula. Professional developers, too, can use the content analysis procedure to establish deep understanding of the curriculum they are charged to support with teachers. Finally, teachers, especially in the early stages of curriculum implementation, might use content analysis techniques to build deep understanding of both individual curriculum components and of the interrelatedness of multiple components.

For kindergarten curricula, content analysis can be used to compare any curriculum to a publicly available curriculum map constructed by Simmons and Kame'enui (1999) for the Institute for the Development of Educational Achievement (IDEA.) Table 4–3 presents two major constructs (phonemic awareness and oral vocabulary) along with indicators in the curriculum map for the first half of kindergarten. Other constructs in the map include alphabetic principle and passage understanding. This curriculum map can be used to guide a content analysis of the language and literacy portion of any kindergarten curriculum. Investigators could conduct a page-by-page analysis and document the presence (or absence) of direction to teachers to accomplish each item and also the type and amount of instruction, practice, and application offered to children.

A similar content analysis procedure for assessing the design of kindergarten curricula is used to implement the *Consumer's Guide to Evaluating a Core Reading Program Grades K-3: A Critical Elements Analysis* (Simmons & Kame'enui, 2003). That tool is designed for teams of reviewers to conduct a thorough review, sometimes looking within a sequence of two or three lessons, sometimes in the scope and sequence provided by the publisher, and sometimes in a series of 10 consecutive lessons. Items in the guide are quite specific, and the designers provide research citations for

Table 4–3. Curriculum Map for Kindergarten

General Target	Specific Component	Indicators
Phonemic Awareness	Sound and word discrimination	Tells whether items are the same or different Identifies different word Identifies different sound
	Rhyming	Tells whether items rhyme Produces rhyming words
	Blending	Blends syllables and onsets and rimes Blends individual sounds
	Segmenting	Counts words Counts syllables Says syllables Identifies initial sounds in words Identifies all sounds in words
Oral Vocabulary	Concept naming	Names pictures of common concepts Uses words to describe location, size, color, and shape Uses names and labels for basic concepts
	Categorization	Sorts pictures of basic concepts into categories
	Vocabulary development and use	Learns new vocabulary through storybook readings Listens to new vocabulary in multiple contexts Uses new vocabulary in multiple contexts

Source: Adapted with permission from *Curriculum Maps: Mapping Instruction to Achieve Instructional Priorities in Beginning Reading Kindergarten–Grade 3*, by Deborah C. Simmons & E. C. Kame'enui, 1999. Copyright 1999 by Deborah C. Simmons.

many of them. Table 4–4 provides items in the kindergarten analysis that refer to listening comprehension.

Assessment of curriculum implementation may (perhaps must) begin with deep understanding of the curriculum itself; there is no substitute for some sort of content analysis to accomplish that. In choosing to implement a content analysis, we offer these three pieces of advice:

1. Use a set of standards or a procedure designed specifically for the age group you are working with; do not apply kindergarten standards to preschool programs or first-grade standards to kindergarten programs.
2. Even when external applications of a content analysis to a specific curriculum are publicly available, there is no substitute for a school-based team using the procedure directly to build deep knowledge. We advocate using the procedure of content analysis rather than using the results of content analyses conducted by others.

Table 4–4. Items in Listening Comprehension Content Analysis for Kindergarten

---

High-Priority Items: Listening Comprehension

Models and systematically reviews critical comprehension strategies (literal comprehension, retelling).

Models and guides the students through story structure, thinking out loud as the elements are being identified.

Strategically selects and reinforces critical vocabulary during story reading.

Provides plentiful opportunities to listen to and explore narrative and expository text forms and to engage in interactive discussion of the messages and meanings of the text.

Source: Adapted with permission from *A Consumer's Guide to Evaluating a Core Reading Program Grades K-3: A Critical Elements Analysis,* by Deborah C. Simmons & E. C. Kame'enui, 2003, p. 14. Copyright 2003 by Deborah C. Simons.

3. Consider a team-based approach so that more than one person is offering insights and so that some of the work can be divided.

Content analysis is a useful first step in any deep assessment of implementation. However, like most strategies in the area of early childhood education, it is necessary but insufficient. Some type of observation of the curriculum in action will be necessary. We next describe four observation tools that could be implemented in a variety of settings. We describe them here because, like content analysis based on external standards, these observation tools entail application of external, general criteria or goals and can be used with any curricular innovation in an emergent literacy setting.

The Quality Learning Instrument (QLI)

Designed in Northern Ireland for the first year of formal schooling, the Quality Learning Instrument (QLI) targets program quality from the perspective of the children in either formal or play-based environments (Walsh & Gardner, 2001). Designers preselected nine indicators of quality (motivation, concentration, independence, confidence, well-being, social interaction, respect, multiple skill acquisition, and higher order thinking skills) and treated them as themes to guide observational note-taking. Within each indicator, observers focused attention on the children, the adults, and the environment and constructed indicators of high and low levels of quality. This particular instrument is currently being used in a large-scale evaluation project in Northern Ireland.

The Early Language and Literacy Classroom Observation Literacy Environment Checklist

The Early Language and Literacy Classroom Observation (ELLCO; Smith, Dickinson, Sangeorge, & Anastapoulos, 2002) Toolkit is a psychometrically sound instrument used to assess literacy practices and materials used in preschool through third grade classrooms. The ELLCO Toolkit has been used by researchers to document program implementation, by administrators to monitor school improvement, by supervisors to analyze classroom performance, and by professional developers to observe and offer feedback on intervention implementation. The developers of the tool recommend that those who administer the ELLCO have both knowledge of literacy development and experience teaching in emergent literacy environments (Smith et al., 2002). Moreover, additional training in administering the tool is encouraged in order to ensure its reliability and validity. The authors have developed a 9-hour program conducted by the Center for Children and Families, Education Development Center in Massachusetts to train future users of the ELLCO (see http://www.brookespublishing.com for information regarding training).

The ELLCO takes between 1 and 1½ hours to administer and consists of three components: (1) Literacy Environment Checklist (15–20 minutes), (2) Classroom Observation and Teacher Interview (20–45 minute observation, 10 minute interview), and (3) Literacy Activities Rating Scale (10 minutes).

As the first of the three components, the Literacy Environment Checklist simply inventories the curriculum items related to literacy in the classroom. In a way, it is like a content analysis procedure applied to the environment. The checklist consists of 24 items, all of which ask the observer to familiarize him- or herself with the environment and content (types of books, availability of writing materials) of the classroom. The checklist is designed as follows: 3 items on the organization of the classroom book area, 4 items on the book selection available to students, 5 items on the accessibility of books to students, 6 items on the variety of writing materials available to students, and 6 items on the display of student and teacher writing in the classroom. Preferably the checklist is administered when the observer can move around the classroom for 15 to 20 minutes without interrupting instruction; therefore, the designers recommend using the checklist at a time when students are not present in the classroom.

Each of the 24 items in the Literacy Environment Checklist consists of a primary question and a secondary question. For each of five categories—book area, book selection, book use, writing materials, and writing around the room—the observer calculates a score by summing the number of points for the items related to the category. For example, to determine a numeric score for the book area category, the observer totals the scores on three items. The book area total can be written as 3 points earned out of 3 possible points. Once each individual category has been summed, the totals for each category are summed to determine a total numeric score for the literacy environment. The highest number of points available for the literacy environment is 41.

The ELLCO Classroom Observation and Teacher Interview component provides "specific criteria about language and literacy practices in classrooms that are the basis for critical distinctions in quality" (Smith et al., 2002). The Classroom Observation consists of 14 items conceptually grouped into two categories: (1) General Classroom Environment and (2) Language, Literacy, and Curriculum. The General Classroom Environment category comprises 6 items: (1) Organization of the Classroom, (2) Contents of the Classroom, (3) Presence and Use of Technology, (4) Opportunities for Child Choice and Initiative, (5) Classroom Management Strategies, and (6) Classroom Climate. The Language, Literacy, and Curriculum category consists of 8 items: (1) Oral Language Facilitation, (2) Presence of Books, (3) Approaches to Book Reading, (4) Approaches to Children's Writing, (5) Approaches to Curriculum Integration, (6) Recognizing Diversity in the Classroom, (7) Facilitating Home Support for Literacy, and (8) Approaches to Assessment. The Classroom Observation should be conducted during classroom time allotted for literacy instruction, after the Literacy Environment Checklist has been completed. During the observation, the observer's goal should be to understand the big picture of reading instruction in the classroom, examining how teaching, learning, and the environment work together to support the literacy program. In total the observation should take between 30 and 40 minutes to conduct.

For each item of the observation, there is a 5-point Likert scale with 1 describing the lowest level of quality and 5 describing the highest. To facilitate the observer's scoring process, the scale includes a summary statement and a series of bulleted points to describe exemplary characteristics of each level of sophistication. For example, the Organization of the Classroom item can be scored from 1 (deficient) to 5 (exemplary). The summary statement for a score of 5 states, "There is **strong** evidence of an intentional approach to the organization of the physical environment" (Smith et al., 2002). One bullet point to elaborate a score of 5 states, "Furnishings are appropriately sized for young children and are in good repair. The classroom does not appear barren or crowded with furnishings" (Smith et al., 2002).

Because each of the 14 items can earn a maximum of 5 points, the highest number of points available for the observation is 70.

Immediately following the observation, the observer schedules a 10-minute interview with the classroom teacher to supplement data gathered during the observation (Smith et al., 2002). The Teacher Interview consists of 6 questions with follow-up probes in case the observer needs more information after the teacher's initial answer. Because an observer may not observe all the activities the Classroom Observation asks for in one class period, the interview serves as a means of gaining supplemental information to assist in scoring the observation. However, the designers note that, when inconsistencies arise between what is observed and what is discussed, preference should always be given to what is seen during the observation.

The third section of the ELLCO is the Literacy Activities Rating Scale, which requires approximately 10 minutes to complete. The designers describe the purpose of this component as, "collecting information on the number of book-reading sessions and writing activities that take place during the course of the classroom visit" (Smith et al., 2002). The scale consists of 9 items divided into Book Reading (5 items) and Writing (4 items) categories. Each item consists of a question and a scoring tool. Depending on the question, the scoring tool may ask the observer to record number of books, time spent reading, or indicate the presence or absence of a reading or writing feature with a yes/no response. As with the Literacy Environment Checklist, each answer in the Literacy Activities Rating Scale has been assigned a numeric score. Once the observer has scored each of the 9 items, subtotals for the Book Reading and Writing categories can be determined. Finally, a total score is derived by summing the two subtotals.

ELLCO points do not constitute "adequate" or "inadequate" implementation. Rather, the ELLCO is especially useful for assessing curriculum implementation if it is used in a pre- and postinnovation design. Specifically, leaders of a preschool or kindergarten curriculum innovation might collect data with the ELLCO Literacy Environment Checklist before the innovation is begun in order to establish a baseline during the initial implementation to identify areas for improvement and professional development and later to establish the extent to which the curricular innovation was associated with positive changes in the language and literacy environment.

The Revised Early Childhood Environment Rating Scale (ECERS-R)

The revised Early Childhood Environment Rating Scale (ECERS-R) is an observation tool used to assess programs for children, preschool through kindergarten (Harms, Clifford, & Cryer, 2005). First published in 1980, the original ECERS was revised to incorporate new ways of thinking about early childhood education evident from research conducted since 1980. Both the ECERS and the ECERS-R have been used by teachers as a form of self-assessment, by administrators and professional developers for implementation monitoring, and by researchers for determining intervention effects (Harms et al., 2005). Moreover, several researchers have used the ECERS-R as a measure of program quality, establishing its validity and reliability (Peisner-Feinberg, & Burchinal, 1997; Rossbach, Clifford, & Harms, 1991; Whitebrook, Howes, & Phillips, 1990). Translations of the ECERS-R exist in Italian, Swedish, German, Portuguese, Spanish, and Icelandic (Harms et al., 2005). The designers of ECERS-R recommend those who administer it receive proper training from either an experienced trainer or a video training package (available through Teachers College Press) before using the scale for evaluation.

The ECERS-R requires between 2½ and 3 hours to administer and comprises 43 items grouped into seven subscales: Space and Furnishings, Personal Care Routines, Language-Reasoning, Activities, Interactions, Program Structure, and Parents and Staff. Each subscale consists of several topic-related rubrics for scoring. For example, the Space and Furnishings subscale includes rubrics for evaluating indoor space; furniture for routine care, play, and learning; furnishings for relaxation and comfort; room arrangement for play; space for privacy; child-related display; space for gross motor play; and gross motor equipment. The form of the rubric is consistent throughout the scale; each rubric is scored on a 7-point scale with 1 designating inadequate, 3 designating minimal, 5 designating good, and 7 designating excellent. Each score is accompanied by a series of bullets describing characteristics one would find in classrooms at each level. For example, the inadequate score for indoor space is described with the following bullets: insufficient space for children, adults, and furnishings; space lacks adequate lighting, ventilation, temperature control, or sound-absorbing materials; space in poor repair; and space poorly maintained. Accompanying each bullet descriptor on the score sheet is a box for the observer to check yes or no; the rubric score depends on the number of boxes checked under each descriptor. In addition to the descriptions of common characteristics for each score, the scale includes notes for clarification. These notes provide definitions so that scorers agree on what constitutes terms such as "poor repair" and "reasonably clean." Also included in the scale are questions that the observer can ask the classroom teacher after the observation in order to clarify any unresolved issues or to gain further information. For example, when rating the accessibility of blocks for children's play, the observer may need to ask the teacher a follow-up question, such as "How often is block play available?" (Harms et al., 2005).

To score the ECERS-R, the observer sums the scores for each rubric in the subscale and divides by the total score possible. The total number possible for each subscale is as follows: Space and Furnishings (8), Personal Care Routines (6), Language-Reasoning (4), Activities (10), Interaction (5), Program Structure (4), and Parents and Staff (6). To find a total score, the observer sums the subscale scores and divides by the total number of rubrics (43). In addition, the score sheet includes a chart for calculating which activities made up a "substantial portion of the day" and a graph for creating a visual display of strengths and weaknesses observed.

Assessment of Practices in Early Elementary Classrooms (APEEC)

The Assessment of Practices in Early Elementary Classrooms (APEEC; Hemmeter, Maxwell, Ault, & Schuster, 2001) was designed as a measure of the extent to which teachers were implementing developmentally appropriate practices in the primary grades. The tool, which entails both observation and interview, can be used in kindergarten though Grade 3 classrooms, including classrooms serving children with special needs. Three broad areas are assessed: physical environment, curriculum and instruction, and social context. Within those three broad areas, there are 40 individual items, with specific descriptors at 1, 3, 5, and 7 on a 7-point Likert scale.

The procedure for observation is clear. The observer is directed to arrive before the children, and to stay for the entire day.

A 20- to 30-minute interview is scheduled at or near the end of the day. Individual items are rated either from observation (O), from interview (I), or both. The observer reads each indicator and assigns a score of T (true) or NT (not true) and then determines the score for that item; there are specific examples and clear definitions on the rating sheet. The designers suggest that a score of 1 be interpreted as inadequate, 3 as minimal, 5 as good, and 7 as excellent. A total score is determined by summing the item scores and dividing by the total number of items.

The QLI, ELLCO, ECERS-R, and APEEC are similar in that all four provide formal (but general) measures of curriculum implementation, and they rely on observations and interviews conducted by a person or a team that has first learned to conduct observations reliably. Because these observation tools do not provide normative scores, they are not useful for documenting a specific level of implementation that constitutes "adequate" fidelity. However, they are especially useful for assessing change in instruction that comes as the result of initiation of an innovation in the curriculum or for documenting the degree to which classrooms are similar and different within and across sites. They can be administered multiple times, and can be used to document change over time. They also can be used to identify areas of need and to guide professional development for teachers if implementation is unacceptably low (based on the judgment of the site leaders) or inconsistent across classrooms. A similar tool, the Program Administration Scale (Talan & Bloom, 2004), can be used to document general qualities of the leadership and management (rather than the instruction) in an early childhood program.

Informal measures, especially those that rely on content analysis, provide a different type of window into implementation; they assume that evaluating the extent to which a particular curriculum is implemented with fidelity demands specific and deep understanding of the components of the curriculum, and they provide access to research-based standards to allow for comparison. Although potentially time-consuming, we think that there is no real substitute for content analysis as a first step toward assessment of implementation. Regardless of the tools that a researcher might choose to measure implementation, deep knowledge of the curriculum as envisioned by its designers is a necessary prerequisite.

Measuring Teacher Implementation of Specific Components of a Specific Curriculum

We began our review of implementation assessments by inviting comparisons of the curriculum to general indicators of quality as presented either in standards or in research using the process of content analysis or observation/interview. Guidance provided by either of these procedures is necessary but not sufficient in program evaluation and improvement. Whether or not teachers are implementing specific components of the site's curriculum is a logical next step, and it demands curriculum-specific strategies. That means that individuals will either have to use tools provided by the designers of the curriculum innovation (researchers or publishers) or design the tools themselves. Below we present choices in assessing implementation of program components; we have elected to organize them in order of ease of data collection, which unfortunately means that they are also in inverse order of general quality of data collected—when fidelity data are collected very easily, they often lack nuance. Table 4-5 presents a preview of each of the methods we discuss, including strategies for data collection and evaluation.

Teacher Activity Logs

Collecting teacher self-report data is one strategy for documenting implementation of any curriculum. In general, this option is low-cost in terms of evaluation expense; teachers can report their time and activities in ways that are consistent with curricular goals. A description of the use of teacher logs as a tool for this type of data collection comes from Taylor, Pearson, Clark, and Walpole (2000), who devised a form for teachers to report the amount of time that they spent in various components of reading instruction each day. The logs included conceptual areas (word recognition instruction, comprehension strategy instruction) as well as grouping configurations (whole-class, small-group, or independent). In the research study, data from the logs were used in combination with direct observations to describe instruction across schools; they also were used to document relationships between instructional decisions and achievement. To design and use a log of time and activities, site

Table 4–5. Measuring Teacher Implementation of Specific Components of a Specific Curriculum

Assessment	Use	Grade	Time
Teacher logs	Collect data on the type of activities implemented	Appropriate for all grade levels	Determined by need
Generic observations	Document how any curriculum is enacted	Appropriate for all grade levels	Usually last for duration of reading instruction
Publisher checklists	Document the degree to which a specific curriculum is enacted as designed	Appropriate for all grade levels for which the curriculum is being used	Widely variable
Formal innovation configuration	Identify teacher actions consistent and inconsistent with the curriculum	Appropriate for all grade levels	Can be applied to units of curricular instruction

leaders can simply construct a grid to capture choices in a day's or week's instruction and ask teachers to record the number of minutes they actually spend in each of the activities of interest.

Teacher logs are potentially efficient and effective ways to collect data on the type of activities implemented. The strength of such an approach is that the designer of the log can tailor it directly to the design of the curriculum innovation, providing a simple, low-cost data set to look within and across classrooms. Logs can be used to capture reports either of time spent or of content focus. For example, researchers in a recent study of preschool curriculum innovation used teacher logs as part of their measurement of curricular fidelity. They copied specific lesson plans from the teacher's guide for the program and asked teachers to indicate any portions of the lesson in which their instruction was different from the plan. However, self-report data are also potentially unreliable, especially if they are the only sources of data used to evaluate program fidelity. In addition, it is only possible to document quantity of instruction; instructional quality cannot be measured adequately through self-report data.

Open-Ended Observations

It is unlikely that any curriculum in early childhood education can be implemented across multiple sites exactly as specified by the developers. All innovations must be contextualized to fit the time, space, and personnel available. Understanding the modifications that are necessary is essential to studying the effectiveness of any program, and documenting modifications is an essential aspect of establishing curriculum implementation. Initial teacher implementation can be verified with observations that are designed for and implemented in one site with observation tools designed to document the program as enacted there. Walpole and McKenna (2004) present two general options for the design of such observations. The observation can be conducted in real time (as in set intervals of time, perhaps every 5 minutes) to capture teacher language or activity and student language or activity. Alternatively, the observations can be conducted by domain, with specific content or processes within the curriculum listed in a checklist that can be used to document their presence or absence in a given instructional period.

Curriculum-Specific Implementation Checklists

Another low-cost, high-utility fidelity measure is a checklist that is matched directly to the curriculum being implemented. Such an approach is site-specific; it does not make sense to use a checklist produced to match one program to evaluate fidelity in a different program. To investigate the characteristics of implementation checklists, we targeted several specific preschool curriculum innovations—those involved in PCER, the federal evaluation of preschool curricula described previously. Our descriptions of the structure of these checklists should in no way be construed as endorsement of the effectiveness of the curricula; that is an empirical question, which is currently being answered by researchers. In addition, we provide descriptions of these checklists (rather than including them directly) because they are available only in conjunction with the actual curriculum materials or from researchers studying those curricula. However, understanding their structure will help to build understanding of the potential for such checklists in a comprehensive curriculum evaluation program.

One comprehensive checklist was designed to accompany the Creative Curriculum for Preschool. The checklist (www.teachingstrategies.com) is similar to the procedures that were described in the ECERS-R and the ELLCO. The checklist includes five general areas and many indicators for each. Table 4–6 is a summary of the areas addressed in the checklist.

Table 4–6. Categories Measured in Creative Curriculum Implementation Checklist

General Category	Specific Indicators
Physical environment	Overall environment
	Specific child interest areas (e.g., blocks, library)
	Content-specific materials (e.g., literacy, math)
Structure	Schedules and routines
	Time for large and small-group activities
	Choice time
	Transitions
	Weekly plans
Teacher-Child Interactions	Relationships
	Guiding behavior
	Guiding learning
Assessment	Observation
	Evaluating progress
	Planning
Family Involvement	

Source: Teaching Strategies, Inc. (http://www.teachingstrategies.com)

The procedure for observation is unambiguous (and again harkens back to the general procedures discussed earlier.) The observer is directed to observe an entire instructional day, as this is a comprehensive curriculum, from initial greeting of the children, without interrupting the teacher and then to conduct an interview after instruction, with the teacher providing assessment data for five children. The entire procedure is guided with a series of over 100 questions that begin with the stem "Do teachers . . . ?" Some items can be documented through physical evidence, some by listening to the teacher during instruction, and others are addressed during the interview. A total score is calculated for each of the subsections listed in Table 4–6.

Another team constructed a fidelity checklist for Project Construct. They estimate that it would take 2½ to 3 hours to complete the procedure through observation and also allow the observer to ask questions later, if needed. The checklist includes 59 items and allows for documentation of "no evidence," "some evidence," or "extensive evidence." The first category, with 7 total items, is Physical Environment and Schedule. Language Development and Symbolic Expression (with a total of 14 items) is also considered, as is Mathematical and Scientific Thinking (5 items), Social and Personal Development (6 items), and Assessment (2 items). The largest observation category (21 items) is Constructivist Teaching Practices. Examples in that section include items about time to choose activities, support for child problem-solving, and individual conferencing during activities. The research team on this project has computed correlations and internal consistency statistics for these subscales and also correlated values from this measure with ECERS-R.

The designers of Curiosity Corner provide a form for teacher self-assessment and also a form for implementation visits. The self-assessment begins with three general categories (managing the classroom, cooperative learning, and assessment) and then moves to the specific components of the curriculum (e.g., greetings and reading, clues and questions, rhyme time, and story time). In each area, there are two columns: what the teacher does and what the students do. This self-assessment is designed to support teachers who are considering their own fidelity to the curriculum and could be used before an implementation visit, where someone else observes their implementation.

In a Curiosity Corner implementation visit, observers have a clear focus. They have a rubric representing four levels of implementation, each level representing progress toward full implementation. There are three subscales: environment (10 items), general indicators (17 items), and curriculum components (19 items). The language of the checklist is intimately tied to the language of the curriculum, making it simple to communicate results to someone with deep knowledge of Curiosity Corner, either from a design, research, or teaching perspective.

Formal Innovation Configurations

For home-grown or experimental curricula, leaders might need to develop their own curriculum-specific checklist. We recommend that they use the procedure of innovation configuration. Innovation configuration is a perfect frame for the design of a curriculum-specific implementation assessment system. The process of design of a complete innovation configuration (Hord, 1986) develops deep understanding of the ideal program components and also of implementation variations that are acceptable and those that are unacceptable. The process begins with the materials themselves and with the people responsible for providing initial training. In both instances, the important question is simple: What are the major components of this curriculum if it is implemented exactly as intended? In a preschool language and literacy curriculum, those components might include, for example, whole- and small-group sharing to promote oral language, storybook reading, literacy skills development, and dramatic play, each scheduled for a specific amount of time during the day.

The next step in the design of an innovation configuration is to interview and observe a small number of individuals enacting the curriculum. At this stage, the major components of the curriculum can be described more directly and variations in those components documented. As these variations are documented, they become items in a checklist of teacher or student actions organized around the major program components. Finally, after this period of refinement, the checklist can be used across classrooms to identify the choices that individuals are making as they implement the curriculum and to provide feedback and assistance in areas where choices are inconsistent with the requirements of the program.

The approaches described above capture the degree to which teachers are attempting to implement the curriculum as envisioned by its designers; yet this is a far cry from establishing that they are doing so in a truly expert manner. In early childhood, the quality of teacher interaction with children, particularly language-based interaction with children, is essential to true program fidelity. However, capturing such information is much easier said than done.

Measuring Quality of Implementation

Although some of the measures above include judgments about quality, they are really more useful for documenting the presence or absence of particular components of the curriculum. The tools described below go a step farther—they document both presence and quality of specific instructional practices. However, they are only useful to the extent that they target quality teaching and learning in ways consistent with the curriculum being implemented. Table 4–7 offers a summary of the tools discussed below.

Teacher Interaction and Language Rating Scale

The Hanen Centre (http://www.hanen.org) trains teachers to improve their strategies for eliciting and developing children's language. Their rating scale, the Teacher Interaction and Language Rating Scale (Girolametto, Weitzman, & Greenberg, 2000), was developed to measure teachers' language interactions before and after they participated in Hanen training. Raters use the scale by watching a videotape prepared by the teacher. The scale targets 11 specific language interactions (e.g., join in and play, use a variety of questions, encourage turn taking) rated on a 7-point Likert scale. Scores of 1 to 3 indicate that the individual needs improvement in an area; a score of 4 is interpreted to mean that an individual needs fine-tuning in an area; and scores of 5 to 7 indicate that the individual uses the strategy consistently and needs no further support. The scale (and its interpretation) are designed with multiple observations in mind and for the possibility that an individual might need (and receive) support in improving performance.

Table 4-7. Measuring Quality of Implementation

Assessment	Use	Grade	Time	Names of Subtests
Teacher Interaction and Language Rating Scale (TILRS)	Assesses teacher strategies for language development	Not specified	Teacher-determined language interaction, videotapec	Items target 11 specific strategies associated with the Hanen Centre's program
Teacher Performance Appraisal System (TPAS)	Assesses teacher instructional performance	Not specified	Duration o⁼ reading instruction	1. Time management 2. Student behavior management 3. Instructional presentations 4. Instructional monitoring 5. Instructional feedback 6. Facilitating instruction 7. Communication 8. Performing noninstructional duties
Scale for Coaching Instructional Effectiveness (SCIE)	Assesses teacher instructional performance	Not specified	Duration of reading instruction	1. Planning and organization 2. Instruction 3. Classroom management
Key Reading Instructional Activities for REA	Assesses use of instructional activities in classroom	Kindergarten	Duration of reading instruction	1. Daily activities 2. Weekly or periodic activities

217

Teacher Performance Appraisal System (TPAS)

One way to assess quality of implementation is to view teacher instruction through a lens consistent with teacher quality research. The revised Teacher Performance Appraisal System (TPAS) was designed as a tool for supervisors and administrators to measure the competence of teachers (Bradshaw, Glatthorn, & Buckner, 2000). The tool is used to rate teacher performance based on data collected from observation, discussion, and classroom artifacts. The tool consists of eight major functions: management of instructional time, management of student behavior, instructional presentation, instructional monitoring, instructional feedback, facilitating instruction, communicating within the educational environment, and performing noninstructional duties. Each major function is accompanied by a list of teacher behaviors describing the function, a space for recording rater comments, and a scale to record whether the teacher is above standard, at standard, below standard, or unsatisfactory. Rather than a numeric total, a summary of the appraisal is given in the form of written comments by the appraiser to be shared with the teacher during a formal discussion. The TPAS, as its name suggests, is appropriate when the goal of assessment of fidelity is tied to teacher evaluation.

Scale for Coaching Instructional Effectiveness (SCIE)

In other settings, assessments of teacher quality might be conducted in a purely formative system, one designed to promote collegial cooperation and peer interaction for a group of adults working together to implement an instructional innovation. The Scale for Coaching Instructional Effectiveness (SCIE) was designed and field tested as an observational tool for peer coaches to use to record strengths and weaknesses in their peer's instruction (Hasbrouck, 1997; Hasbrouck & Christen, 1997). The scale consists of 15 items divided into three categories: planning and organization, instruction, and classroom management. In addition, the 15 items are further divided into 51 subitems. To administer the SCIE, an observer observes a complete classroom lesson, making notes of teacher and student behavior. Immediately after observing, the observer uses his or her notes to rate the lesson on the 15 items. Each item consists of a specific observable behavior and a point system for scoring the behavior. For example, under the category of Starting Lesson, one observable behavior measured is Starts Lesson Promptly and Purposefully; this behavior can earn 2 points (excellent quality), 1 point (good/fair quality), 0 points (not implemented and should have been), and NtOb (not observed). To determine a final score for the scale, the observer first sums the points within each subscale to determine a total for each of the three categories and then sums the three subtotals for the categories to determine a scale total. A summary form provides space for the observer to record total scores and for the teacher to record future goals.

Key Reading Instructional Activities for Reading Excellence Act (REA)

The Key Reading Instructional Activities for REA is an observation system used to assess the literacy instruction in kindergarten classrooms. The instrument was developed as part of a collaborative evaluation project between the Utah State Office of Education and the Institute for Behavioral Research in Creativity (IBRIC) for the purpose of evaluating the extent to which classroom teachers were implementing scientifically based reading instruction in Utah's Reading Excellence Act project (Nelson, Fox, & Gardner, 2002). Subsequently, it has been used by state-level evaluators who are measuring implementation of Reading First Initiatives in kindergarten classrooms To ensure reliability, the IBRIC performed rigorous psychometric analyses on the instrument, yielding an internal consistency of 0.85 and an interrater reliability between 0.89 and 0.95. The instrument consists of two components: daily activities and weekly/periodic activities.

To administer the Key Reading Instructional Activities for REA tool, an observer gains permission from a teacher to observe the entirety of a day's reading instruction; total observation time, then, is determined by the characteristics of the local curriculum implementation, but might be estimated at 2 hours. Throughout the observation, the observer records notes on both teacher behaviors and student responses. Immediately following the observation, the observer uses his or her notes to complete the observation form; therefore, the observer must be familiar with the form prior to observing reading instruction. The first section of the form asks the observer to record daily activities in eight areas: Oral Language

Activities, Reading Aloud, Book Exploration, Writing Activities, Thematic Activities, Print-Related Activities, Phonemic Analysis Activities, and Word-Directed Activities. For each area, there are multiple items describing observable teacher behavior and two scales. The first asks the observer to mark if the activity was actually observed, if clear evidence existed that the class had completed the activity during a time outside of the observation, or if the activity was not observed and there was no evidence that the activity had ever been completed. The second scale asks the observer to evaluate the instructional quality as excellent, good, or needs improvement. Within the form, there are also several items asking the observer to comment on student response. For example, under the Oral Language Activities area, a student response item asks the observer to mark the number of students who listen attentively by checking none, some, most, or almost all.

The second section asks the observer to record weekly or periodic activities in seven areas: Reading Aloud, Book Exploration, Writing Activities, Thematic Activities, Print-Related Activities, Phonemic Analysis Activities, and Word-Directed Activities. Unlike the first section, which must be completed based solely on the classroom observation, the second section can be completed using data from observations, interviews with teachers, and review of the classroom environment. Like the first section, the second section has two scales for recording. The first scale asks the observer to mark yes or no to indicate that there is evidence that the activity exists. The second scale requires the observer to judge instructional quality by checking excellent, good, or needs improvement. A total score for each of the instructional areas can be obtained by comparing the total points score from the observation to the total number of possible points for the area. The points score was created by the designers to reflect both the occurrence and the quality of the instruction.

The Key Reading Instructional Activities for REA was designed to assess implementation of a specific curricular innovation in kindergarten; however, it is still useful in those kindergarten curricular innovations that draw from the same research base and target similar daily activities. Like the ELLCO, this tool includes assessment of the literacy environment, but unlike the ELLCO, it also includes observer-determined measures of quality. Such insights are particularly useful in the design of professional development for teachers and in the measurement of the effects of a curriculum innovation on teacher practice. As with the measures described above as general measures, these measures of quality are best administered before the innovation, in the early stages, and then later; the tools are flexible enough to allow as many scored observations as appropriate in the site.

Special Considerations for Assessing Implementation of Literacy Curricula

We have described a collection of tools and strategies for assessing implementation of literacy curricula—measuring fidelity—that are appropriate in a variety of emergent literacy environments. To say that each is appropriate in a variety of environments is not to say that all are appropriate in any one environment. In fact, there are several issues to consider in choosing tools and strategies for a specific environment. These include issues of time, training, confidentiality and trust, and the match of the tools and strategies to the goals of the assessment.

Designing a fantastic system for assessing curriculum implementation is not useful if it cannot be fully implemented with the resources available. In an ideal world, we would encourage the use of specific tools at specific intervals. First, conduct a content analysis to help choose one curriculum or intervention from a "short list" of potential ones. Engaging in content analysis early on ensures that the curriculum itself is coherent and matched to standards that are important in the environment and that those making decisions about implementation and assessment do so with deep understanding. Next, the team might choose a general measure, one of the formal observation/interview systems we have described, and schedule it early in the project and then again after teachers have received training to check that there are indicators of growth. As soon as the teachers begin teaching, a curriculum-specific checklist (either one developed with the curriculum or an innovation configuration) should guide teachers and trainers to areas where fidelity is weak so that they can address them quickly, and it should be administered periodically until fidelity is reached. Finally, the initial general measure can be readministered, ensuring that attention to the checklist or innovation configuration guided participants toward larger goals. Such a system is costly, in terms of both time and money, and should be entertained only if resources are available.

In many settings, where resources are scarce, training teachers to implement the specific curriculum with fidelity must be the only goal. In that case, curriculum-specific checklists or innovation configurations can be used to guide and evaluate training. If there is no plan for training, we suggest that there is no sense in measuring fidelity; the only likely outcome of such a plan is evidence that teachers cannot implement the curriculum consistently and with fidelity. Teachers can use checklists in many ways, and we suggest that they see the tools before they are evaluated with the tools.

We work extensively with literacy coaches. Literacy coaches are site-based professional development providers. The general job of a literacy coach is to help to choose an instructional intervention, design a system for measuring its effects on student achievement, and craft and implement a comprehensive system for providing teacher support. In essence, then, they must both measure fidelity and react to measurements of fidelity. Increasing fidelity to emergent literacy curricula requires trust among teachers and between teachers and teacher leaders. Assessment of fidelity without feedback is likely to breed mistrust. Teachers may feel that administrators, coaches, or researchers are spying on them or that they are evaluating them with a critical (rather than helpful) eye. With those issues in mind, we end this chapter with a discussion of strategies for interpreting the results of assessment of implementation.

Interpreting the Results of Assessments of Implementation of Literacy Curricula

Although this is the end of the chapter, it should be the beginning of the design stage for those who are interested in assessment of implementation. The goal of the assessment influences the interpretation of data and the choice of tools and strategies. The overarching goal of anyone involved in emergent literacy is support of student achievement, but there are many ways to contribute to that goal.

Researchers might contribute by designing and testing the relationship between specific innovations or interventions and specific student outcome data. If that is the case, they might need to choose among two types of tools: general and specific. The general tools we described early in the chapter, particularly those with established validity and reliability data, may be a start. They also might use or construct curriculum-specific fidelity measures so that they can monitor implementation of specific aspects of the curriculum. In fact, researchers involved in the PCER project are doing just that. They are using tailored measures within their individual curricula and also general tools across sites. Once a research study has begun, though, it may not be feasible to provide feedback to teachers; the data might be interpreted to decide which teachers to include in an analysis of effects. Such a charge assumes that researchers might have knowledge of low implementation but not be able to use it to improve instruction—at least not until after the study is finished.

Professional developers, site-based administrators, literacy coaches, and teachers have no such responsibility to avoid sharing information gathered from assessments of instructional fidelity. In fact, their responsibility lies in the opposite direction. Those who are charged with the support of emergent literacy teachers must share results of implementation assessments with the stakeholders most able to benefit, the teachers who are working to implement effective instructional practices. We urge individuals in this position to do so clearly and with tact, and to use the information they gain from such assessments to design and implement support systems that serve all teachers and, ultimately, the children they serve.

References

Bradshaw, L. K., Glatthorn, A. A., & Buckner, K. (2000). *The evaluation of beginning teachers: A report on the validation of the revised teacher performance appraisal system for beginning teachers.* Submitted to the North Carolina Department of Public Instruction. Retrieved February 17, 2006 from: http://www.dpi.state.nc.us/evalpsemployees/vldrptbt. pdf#search='Teacher%20Performance%2 0Appraisal%20System

Burchinal, M. R., Roberts, J. E., Hooper, S., & Zeisel, S. A. (2000). Cumulative risk and early cognitive development: A comparison of statistical risk models. *Developmental Psychology, 36,* 793-807.

Dane, A. V., & Schneider, B. H. (1998). Program integrity in primary and early secondary prevention: Are implementation effects out of control? *Clinical Psychology Review, 18,* 23-45.

Detrich, R. (1999). Increasing treatment fidelity my matching interventions to contextual variables within the educational setting. *The School Psychology Review, 28,* 608-620.

Dickinson, D. K., McCabe, A., & Clark-Chiarelli, N. (2004). Preschool-based prevention of reading disability. In C. A. Stone, E. R. Silliman, B. J. Ehren, & K. Apel (Eds.), *Handbook of language and literacy: Development and disorders* (pp. 209–227). New York: Guilford.

Early Reading First. Retrieved May 1, 2006 from: http://www.ed.gov/programs/earlyreading/index.html

Girolametto, L., Weitzman, E., & Greenberg, J. (2000). *Teacher interaction and language rating scale.* Toronto, Ontario: Hanen Early Language Program.

Harms, T., & Clifford, R. (1980). *The Early Childhood Environment Rating Scale* (ECERS). New York: Teachers College Press.

Harms, T., Clifford, R. M., & Cryer, D. (2005). *Early Childhood Environment Rating Scale* (Rev. ed.). New York: Teachers College Press.

Hasbrouck, J. E. (1997). Mediated peer coaching for training preservice teachers. *The Journal of Special Education, 31,* 251–271.

Hasbrouck, J. E., & Christen, M. H. (1997). Providing peer coaching in inclusive classrooms: A tool for consulting teachers. *Intervention in School and Clinic, 32,* 172–177.

Hemmeter, M. L., Maxwell, K. L., Ault, M. J., & Schuster, J. W. (2001). *Assessment of practices in early elementary classrooms (APEEC).* New York: Teachers College Press.

Hord, S. (1986). *A manual for using innovation configurations to assess teacher development programs.* Austin, TX: Southwest Educational Development Laboratory.

National Association for the Education of Young Children. Retrieved May 1, 2006 from: http://www.naeyc.org/

National Child Care Information Center. Retrieved May 1, 2006 from: http://www.nccic.org/

National Institute of Child Health and Human Development Early Child Care Research Network (2000). The relation of child care to cognitive and language development. *Child Development, 71,* 960–980.

National Staff Development Council. (2003). *Moving NSDC's staff development standards into practice: Innovation configurations.* Oxford, OH: Author.

Nelson, D. E., Fox, D. G., & Gardner, J. L. (2002). *An evaluation of the Utah reading excellence act project—Year two of school implementation.* Salt Lake City, UT: The Institute for Behavioral Research in Creativity.

Peisner-Feinberg, E., & Buchinal, M. (1997). Relations between preschool children's child care experiences and concurrent development: The cost, quality, and outcomes study. *Merrill-Palmer Quarterly, 43*(3), 451–477.

Preschool Curriculum Evaluation Research (PCER). Retrieved May 1, 2006 from: http://pcer.rti.org/

Rossbach, H. G., Clifford, R. M., & Harms, T. (1991). *Dimensions of learning environments: Cross-national validation of the Early Childhood Environment Rating Scale.* Paper presented at the annual meeting of the American Educational Research Association, Chicago.

Simmons, D. C., & Kame'enui, E. J. (1999). *Curriculum maps: Mapping instruction to achieve instructional priorities in beginning reading kindergarten–grade 3.* Retrieved May 2, 2006 from: http://reading. uoregon.edu/appendices/maps.php

Simmons, D. C., & Kame'enui, E. J. (2003). *A consumer's guide to evaluating a core reading program grades K–3: A critical elements analysis.* Retrieved May 2, 2006 from: http://reading.uoregon.edu/curricula/ con_guide.php

Smith, M. W., Dickinson, D. K., Sangeorge, A., & Anastasopoulos, L. (2002). *User's Guide to the Early Language & Literacy Classroom Observation (ELLCO) Toolkit.* Baltimore: Paul H. Brookes.

Snow, C. E., Tabors, P. O., & Dickinson, D. K. (2001). Language development in the preschool years. In D. K. Dickinson & P. O. Tabors (Eds.), *Beginning literacy with language: Young children learning at home and school* (pp. 1–26). Baltimore: Paul H. Brooks.

STARS for Kids Now. Retrieved May 1, 2006 from: http://www.education. ky.gov

Stoney, L. (2004). *Financing quality rating systems: Lessons learned.* United Way of America

Success by 6. Retrieved February 3, 2006 from: http://www.earlychild hoodfinance.org/handouts/Louise_Stoney_QRS_Financing_Paper.pdf# search='Financing%20quality%20rating%20systems.

Talan, T. N., & Bloom, P. J. (2004). *Program administration scale.* New York: Teachers College Press.

Taylor, B. M., Pearson, P. D., Clark, K., & Walpole, S. (2000). Effective schools and accomplished teachers: Lessons about primary-grade reading instruction in low-income schools. *The Elementary School Journal,* *101*(2), 121–165.

Walpole, S., & McKenna, M. C. (2004). *The literacy coach's handbook: A guide to research-based practice.* New York: Guilford Press.

Walsh, G., & Gardner, J. (2005). Assessing the quality of early years learning environments. *Early Childhood Research and Practice,* 7, 1–18.

Whitebrook, M., Howes, C., & Phillips, D. (1990). *Who cares? Child care teachers and the quality of care in America.* Final report of the National Child Care Staffing Study. Oakland, CA: Child Care Employee Project.

Chapter Five

Assessing the Quality of Storybook Reading

Margaret M. Sutton
Amy E. Sofka
Kathryn E. Bojczyk
Stephanie M. Curenton

The Importance of Quality Storybook Reading for Emergent Literacy

Reading to children is a central activity in many preschool classrooms. This makes sense, considering that it is thought to be the single most important activity for building children's skills required for learning to read (Hoffman, Roser, & Battle, 1993). It is commonly recognized that the more often a child is exposed to reading during the preschool years, the more academically successful that child will be when he or she begins formal schooling. For that reason, most research on shared storybook reading has focused on the merit of the *frequency* of storybook sharing between a child and an adult, usually parents and teachers, as the leading activity to promote early language and literacy skills that are prerequisites to independent reading. Researchers place value on measuring the frequency with which adults engage in storybook reading with children because prior research has found that children who frequently are exposed to storybook reading, whether at home or school, are more likely to use complex sentences, have increased literal and inferential comprehension skills, gain greater story concept development, acquire increased letter and symbol recognition, and develop positive attitudes about reading (Silvern, 1985). In fact, the number of hours a child is read to during the preschool years has been found to be one of the better predictors of the child's reading achievement in school (Mason, Stewart, Peterman & Dunning, 1992; Wells, 1985) and oral language ability (Wells, 1985).

Although researchers sometimes disagree about the precise outcomes resulting from the frequency with which children and adults engage in shared storybook reading, they do agree that a relationship exists between the regularity of a child's book reading experiences and his or her receptive vocabulary, verbal precocity, and knowledge of print (Bus, van IJzendoorn, & Pellegrini, 1995; Crain-Thoreson & Dale, 1992; DeBaryshe, 1993; Scarborough & Dobrich, 1994; Wells, 1985). This raises the question as to what exactly transpires during the adult-child storybook reading process to facilitate development in children's emergent literacy and language skills. In other words, what are the distinctive characteristics of the interaction between an adult reading and children listening that lead to children's growth in their receptive and expressive vocabulary and print knowledge?

For many children, successfully promoting their early language and literacy abilities, and creating a lifetime love of reading, requires more than the adult "read" and the child passively "listen." For example, it seems implausible that a disinterested adult reading an amusing storybook to a child repeatedly will advance a child's language skills or engage his or her interest as much as a supportive adult would reading a boring book in one session. In order for a child to reap the most benefit from storybook reading, the adult reader should simplify, extend, and/or explain concepts *while* reading, rather than simply reading the text as the child listens passively (e.g., Beals, DeTemple, & Dickinson, 1994; Reese, 1995; Teale & Sulzby, 1987). When readers comment on or pose questions about novel words, fascinating characters, or unusual illustrations or situations, they invite the listener to meaningfully connect with the story. Storybook reading naturally provides children with vicarious experiences by way of new words and concepts to which they otherwise may not have been exposed, and at the same time reinforces fundamental concepts about language and print.

Definition of Quality Storybook Reading

Frequency of reading benefits young children in many ways, yet the concept of frequency does not capture many aspects of the rich context of shared storybook reading. Researchers, parents, and educators seem to agree that reading aloud to children on a regular basis is important, but the majority of studies have only focused on child outcomes (e.g., Dickinson & Smith, 1994; Elley, 1989; Karweit, 1989) and not the *specifics* of how to successfully read with preschool children to help them achieve the most benefits. A knowledgeable, enthusiastic, and sensitive reader is more likely to have a captive and entertained audience and set in motion the acquisition of necessary language and literacy skills children need for later reading achievement.

When considering a definition of quality shared storybook reading, three specific domains are apparent: (1) the talent and skills of the adult to facilitate concept and skill development in a stimulating manner; (2) the socio-emotional aspect of the relationship between the adult and the child; and (3) the adult's ability to engage the child during the reading session. These three domains are interrelated and, in combination, they contribute to the quality of the book reading and learning experiences for the preliterate child. Because the notion of quality with respect to shared storybook reading is fairly new, currently there are few measures that address the quality of storybook reading in a group setting. In this chapter, we discuss two measures designed to address storybook reading quality in a group setting and two measures created for dyads. For a discussion of measuring storybook reading quality during one-on-one interactions, see Chapter 3 of this book, Measuring Literacy Activities in the Home: Parent-Child Storybook Reading, which addresses the frequency and characteristics of parent-child book reading (for an overview of these measures, see Table-3–8).

Promoting Concept and Skill Development During Storybook Reading

Children do not learn to read simply by listening to someone else read, just as they do not learn to play a musical instrument by listening to someone else play. Adults must encourage children's active participation during storybook reading in order to support important foundational language and literacy skills during the reading. Adults can be taught explicitly to point, question, or comment about the text in a storybook, thereby making the story an excellent tool for facilitating print-concept knowledge, word awareness, and alphabet knowledge in preliterate children (Justice & Ezell, 2000, 2002, 2004).

The context of shared book reading also presents an excellent environment for teaching language skills as it provides a genuine framework for rich conversations (Crain-Thoreson & Dale, 1992) and opportunities for learning decontextualized language (language referring to context outside of the immediate situation) and vocabulary (e.g., Curenton & Justice, 2004; Dickinson & Snow, 1987; Snow, 1983; Westby, 1991). A knowledgeable reader invites dialogue with the listener beyond the information presented in the text by illuminating and expanding the storybook content, illustrations, and unusual vocabulary (Kaderavek & Sulzby, 2000; van Kleeck, Vander Woude, & Hammett, 2006), such as when the reader defines an interesting word, describes an unusual picture or print, or asks questions that lead to a conversation. Hart and Risley (1995) found that, during storybook reading, children who engage with adults in conversations that extend beyond the explicit story messages perform better on vocabulary measures than those who only listen to the text of the story (see also Haden, Reese, & Fivush, 1996; van Kleeck et al., 2006). Children's oral language skills have also been shown to be related to several aspects of conventional literacy, such as reading and writing, and success with this type of conversation arises from children's meaningful language exchanges during the preschool years (Dickinson, DeTemple, Hirschler, & Smith, 1992) and prepares them for later cognitively challenging abstract concepts (van Kleeck, Stahl, & Bauer, 1997).

The majority of past book-reading studies applied to language have been with mothers, although researchers have studied the importance of the *quality* of shared book-reading interactions in the classroom (e.g., Bus, Belsky, van IJzendoorn, & Crnik, 1997). For example, a preschool teacher who asks questions, responds to children's input, and intersperses reading with back and forth discussion with the children about the story, will have children more likely to quickly gain important prerequisite emergent literacy skills (Flood, 1977; Ninio, 1983; Teale 1983) than children who are not encouraged to be actively involved in the story. Another popular technique to encourage language during book reading is *dialogic reading* (Whitehurst et al., 1988), where the adult prompts, questions, expands, and repeats the child's words until the child is eventually able to tell the story with minimal assistance. Children develop important conversational skills when they are actively involved in storytelling, and dialogic reading provides one such opportunity by creating a situation where the child serves as the storyteller and the adult serves as the listener. The idea behind this type of dialogue is to encourage active participation from the children in hopes of developing their expressive and receptive language skills, and literacy understandings necessary for formal schooling. This is especially important for children who come to school with limited storybook reading experiences.

In order for a child to understand and enjoy the story when an adult is reading, it is important that the child understand at least 90% of the story vocabulary (Ezell & Justice, 2005). This leaves a wonderful teaching opportunity for the 10% of words in the text with which the children are unfamiliar. A popular and effective way to introduce new vocabulary during storybook reading is to find a way to relate new vocabulary words to the child's experiences. Wasik and Bond (2001) created an interactive book-reading intervention to provide children with opportunities to learn and use new vocabulary in a meaningful context. Teachers were trained to reinforce vocabulary by presenting concrete objects that represented words in the text, ask open-ended questions about the story, and engage children in conversations about the books, all of which increased the children's receptive and expressive vocabulary. This study demonstrated the importance of not only introducing and discussing new vocabulary during shared book reading, but also providing concrete supports (e.g., picture, gesture) as well as connecting to the child's semantic network by linking the word to other related words.

A high-quality storybook reading also utilizes opportunities to naturally instruct the child in print functions, print direction, words, letters, and text orientation through brief discussion and by physically pointing to the text features, while at the same time making the story enjoyable and engaging. For example, while reading, an adult can easily point out familiar words or letters or have the children count the letters or words, find the top or bottom of the page, or point to the place on the page where one begins to read (Justice & Ezell, 2002). These interactive strategies will also likely increase the chances that the children will remain actively engaged throughout the reading, another important component in creating a quality storybook reading session.

Scaffolding is evident in a high-quality, interactive read-aloud when the reader adjusts his or her reading behaviors based on the child's needs. These behaviors include expanding on concepts, extending information, clarifying, and questioning to help a child understand and comprehend the story or vocabulary. Scaffolding can be used to assist a child in specific concepts and skills, although to do so the reader must be aware of the child's ability and skill level and adjust the level of support to accommodate the child's increasing skill level (e.g., Baker, Sonnenchein, & Gilat, 1996; Wood & Middleton, 1975). These adjustments that teachers make to help children understand new concepts are critical, especially considering the broad range of experiences and background knowledge children bring into preschool classrooms (Ezell & Justice, 2005). Examples of additional interactive strategies include encouraging physical participation, such as having a child turn the pages or point; verbal participation, such as questioning and commenting about the story, illustrations, or print; and/or relating the story to the child's personal experiences.

Socio-Emotional Quality of Shared Storybook Reading

High quality shared book reading requires cooperation, collaboration, and engagement of the reader and child, as well as the reader's ability to create communication opportunities for young children as they talk about the text and the illustrations (Kaderavek & Justice, 2000). When thoughtful, frequent discussion during storybook reading is initiated by a trusted and caring adult, it not only increases a child's interest in reading, but plays an important role in children's vocabulary development at the end of kindergarten, even after controlling for other aspects of classroom quality (van Kleeck et al., 2002). Adults need to be aware that children learn best when adult interactions are responsive to their language and include positive feedback and guidance (Hart & Risley, 1995; Snow, 1994; Yoder, Warren, McCarthern, & Leew, 1998). This means asking and answering children's questions, encouraging them to actively participate, and reinforcing their attempts to engage in the story. This type of back-and-forth lively conversation makes the storybook exciting and engaging for the children.

Girolametto and Weitzman (2002) found that when adults are consistently responsive to children's initiations, teach respectful turn-taking skills, and include uninvolved children in storybook reading activities, children talk more and produce more word combinations than when caregivers are not responsive to their initiations. For this reason, it is important to remember that, if the goal is teaching expressive and receptive language skills to young children, the child benefits the most from a sensitive and responsive interaction style.

Child Engagement During Storybook Reading

Children's interest in reading is a necessary prerequisite to the prospective rewards gained in language and literacy skills through shared book reading. Regardless of what the adult brings to the reading, the child must be interested in listening to the story. Children demonstrate interest and engagement in a variety of ways. They may listen intently and quietly because they are captivated by the story or they may be loudly expressive and physically active. In terms of assessment, child engagement during book reading is most often portrayed in terms of the child's verbal and nonverbal participation during the book reading. By observing variations in a child's posture, eye contact, facial expression, physical positioning, and sustained attention, the adult can decide whether or not the child is actively or passively engaged. This is important because heightened interest and participation during book reading can lead to more learning (Beals & DeTemple, 1992) and children who are actively engaged in reading a book with an adult learn more vocabulary than children who are passively engaged (Sénéchal, Thomas, & Monker, 1995).

A child's disposition to read and interact with books and the readers' inclination to facilitate a child's literacy development heavily influences whether or not a child will become a successful reader (Whitehurst & Lonigan, 1998; Whitehurst, et al., 1999). Calling on children, whether as a group or individually, is an excellent way to achieve interactive engagement. It is important for preschool teachers to bear in mind that, in order to maintain active engagement when reading storybooks, they should make an effort to ask open-ended questions, have the children physically interact with the book, individually and as a group, as well as respond to all children's communication efforts in order to create an atmosphere that supports conversations.

Summary

There are many observable characteristics of adult's reading behaviors, including individual instructional techniques, emotional tone while reading, and the ability to spark and maintain the child's interest. These attributes can be assessed on a continuum ranging from low to high quality. In the following sections, several measures of quality book reading are discussed in relation to how each evaluates the behaviors and strategies that adults use that are characteristic of a quality shared book reading session. Each of the measures is described according to its significance within one of three domains: (1) the adult's ability to teach concepts and skills, (2) the socio-emotional characteristics of the relationship between the reader and child, and (3) child engagement.

 We have included four measures that assess the overall quality of storybook reading. They are: the Observation Measure of the Language and Literacy Instruction–Read Aloud Profile (OMLIT-RAP; Goodson, Layzer, Smith, & Rimdzius, 2006); the Observation Measure of the Language and Literacy Instruction–Read Aloud Profile Together (OMLIT-RAPT; Goodson, Layzer, Smith, & Rimdzius, 2006); the Adult/Child Interactive Reading Inventory (ACIRI; DeBruin-Parecki, 2006); and the Book Reading Assessment Scoring System (BRASS; Justice, Sutton, Sofka, McGinty, & Pianta, 2006). One observational measure of book reading that examines child engagement and persistence during reading, the Rating of Orientation to Book Reading (ROB; Kaderavek & Sulzby, 1998), also has been included. Features of each assessment, are described in Table 5-1.

Table 5-1. Summary of Observational Storybook Reading Measures

Measure	Time	Type of Administration	Scores	Focus
Observation Measure of Language and Literacy Instruction–Read Aloud Profile (OMLIT-RAP; Goodson, Layzer, Smith, & Rimdzius, 2006)	5–30 minutes	Group	Binary coding (Adult receives credit for exhibiting certain behaviors during prereading, reading, and postreading) Five-point rating scale	Print concepts Comprehension Phonological/ orthographic awareness Higher order thinking Vocabulary Use of open-ended questions Postreading activities
Observation Measure of Language and Literacy Instruction–Read Aloud Profile Together (OMLIT-RAPT; Goodson, Layzer, Smith, & Rimdzius, 2006)	5–30 minutes	Individual	Binary coding (Adult and child receive credit for exhibiting certain behaviors during prereading, reading, and postreading) Five-point rating scale	Print concepts Comprehension Phonological/ orthographic awareness Higher order thinking Vocabulary Use of open-ended questions Depth of conversation

continues

235

Table 5-1. *continued*

Measure	Time	Type of Administration	Scores	Focus
Adult/Child Interactive Reading Inventory (ACIRI; DeBruin-Parecki, 2006)	15–20 minutes	Group Individual	Three-point rating scale	Comprehension Literacy strategies Print motivation
Book Reading Assessment Scoring System (BRASS; Justice et al., 2006)	5–30 minutes	Group	Seven-point rating scale	Book reading experience Session climate Teacher sensitivity Language encouragement and enrichment Child engagement
Rating of Orientation to Book Reading (Kaderavek & Sulzby, 1998)	5–30 minutes	Individual	Four-point rating scale	Child engagement

Assessing the Quality of Concept and Skill Development During Shared Storybook Reading

Four key components of emergent literacy skills can be addressed through shared storybook reading: (1) oral language, (2) print motivation, (3) phonological awareness, and (4) print knowledge. The degree to which adults introduce these concepts and skills during shared book reading can be evaluated using the following four measures: The Observation Measure of Language and Literacy Instruction–Read Aloud Profile (OMLIT-RAP; Goodson et al., 2006); the Observation Measure of Language andLiteracyInstruction–Read Aloud Profile Together (OMLIT-RAPT; Goodson et al., 2006); the Adult/Child Interactive Reading Inventory (ACIRI; DeBruin-Parecki, 2006); and the Book Reading Assessment Scoring System (BRASS; Justice et al., 2006).

Observation Measure of Language and Literacy Instruction: Read-Aloud Profile (OMLIT-RAP; Goodson, Layzer, Smith, & Rimdzius, 2006).

The Observation Measure of Language and Literacy Instruction (OMLIT; Goodson et al., 2006) was developed to capture the instructional processes and environments of early childhood classrooms as part of the Even Start Classroom Literacy Interventions and Outcomes (CLIO) study for the U.S. Department of Education. The OMLIT-Read Aloud Profile (OMLIT-RAP) is one of the five observational instruments within the Observation Measure of Language and Literacy Instruction (OMLIT). The OMLIT-RAP is designed to capture the quality and interactive instructional characteristics of an adult reading aloud to children in an early childhood classroom. It is intended to assist researchers in identifying the behaviors and strategies that an adult uses during story reading. The OMLIT-RAP is coded whenever a read-aloud occurs involving an adult and children during the observation period.

The focus during the prereading stage is the adult's instructional strategy before he or she begins to read the text or talk about the illustrations and story. For example, the adult pointing to and discussing the title, author, illustrator, letters, or words on the front cover would be coded. During the reading stage, the adult's style of reading and instruction is coded. These include, but are not limited to, how often the reader highlights new vocabulary, comments on letters or sounds, and asks questions about the story. After the read-aloud is completed, the adult's instructional practices (i.e. extension activities to support comprehension) are coded; this is considered the postreading stage.

The observer also completes three summary ratings of overall quality of the book reading after the read-aloud is completed. Ratings are made on a scale ranging from 1 (minimal) to 5 (extensive) on the following three indicators: (1) the extent to which new vocabulary words are introduced and supported through various comprehension strategies; (2) the number of open-ended questions asked by the adult to stimulate children to engage in higher order processes such as prediction, explanation, or analysis; and (3) the quality of any postreading activities in extending and supporting children's comprehension of the text.

Each stage of the read-aloud—prereading, reading, and postreading—is coded for behaviors that encompass specific strategies to facilitate children's early language and literacy skills. All of the behaviors listed in each stage of the read-aloud are coded in binary fashion; the reader receives credit if he or she demonstrates the targeted behaviors and/or strategies and does not receive credit if the behaviors and/or strategies are not present. For example, if the adult does not track the print during the story, he or she would not receive credit for Print Concepts during the reading stage. The overarching quality indicators of story-related vocabulary, open-ended questions, and quality of post-reading activities are coded on a 5-point scale. See Table 5–2 for a full description of these behaviors and strategies, and see Exhibit 6.2 of the OMLIT-RAP in Appendix 5–A.

Observation Measure of Language and Literacy Instruction—Read Aloud Profile Together (OMLIT-RAPT; Goodson, Layzer, Smith, & Rimdzius, 2006)

The OMLIT–Read Aloud Profile Together (OMLIT-RAPT; Goodson et al., 2006) measures caregiver and child behaviors during storybook reading, as well as quality indicators for the read-aloud based on adult technique. Although the OMLIT-RAP and the OMLIT-RAPT measure many of the same prereading, reading, and post-

Table 5–2. Concepts and Skills Development Using the Observation Measure of Literacy and Language Instruction-Read Aloud Profile (OMLIT-RAP)

Concepts and Skills Development	Adult Strategies Coded
Print Concepts	Discussing story features (e.g., author, title)—to be coded under prereading stage. Discussing print features. Pointing to story features (e.g., text, illustrations). Tracking print while reading.
Comprehension	Discussing background information Incorporating and/or relating to children's experiences. Highlighting new vocabulary. Directing children's attention to illustrations and text. Expanding on children's comments. Answering children's questions. Asking children recall questions. Using picture walk where applicable. Relating to classroom activities. Reviewing and reinforcing new vocabulary. Summarizing with and without children's involvement. Using nonoral activities to extend learning.
Phonological/ Orthographic Awareness	Commenting on letters, sounds, and their relation.
Language Through Higher Order Thinking	Asking story-related questions about a child's experiences outside of the classroom. Asking story-related, open-ended questions that require expansion of answers and abstract thinking.

continues

Table 5-2. *continued*

Concepts and Skills Development	Adult Strategies Coded
Story-Related Vocabulary	Number of story-related vocabulary words introduced/discussed.
	Number of supports provided (e.g., concrete support and semantic network linking).
Use of Open-Ended Questions	Number of open-ended questions asked.
	Level of support provided for child's answer (e.g., restating question, scaffolding, and allowing response time).
Depth of Postreading	Extension activities to reinforce comprehension.
	Length of time in postreading discussion.

Source: Goodson, Layzer, Smith, and Rimdzius (2006).

reading activities, the OMLIT-RAPT also measures child behaviors in addition to adult behaviors, and is specifically designed for coding dyads, such as a parent and child engaged in storybook reading.

Each section is rated on a scale ranging from 1 through 5. Descriptions of the coded behaviors and strategies are presented in Table 5-3. The first quality indicator is the caregiver's introduction and discussion of story-related vocabulary and whether or not semantic or concrete support accompanies the correct definition. The caregiver's use of open-ended questions is the second quality indicator on the OMLIT-RAPT. This is evaluated according to the number of open-ended questions the caregiver asks the child during the reading, and whether or not the caregiver consistently provides encouragement to the child to facilitate a response to the questions asked.

Table 5–3. Concepts and Skills Development Using the Observation Measure of Literacy and Language Instruction-Read Aloud Profile Together (OMLIT-RAPT)

Concepts and Skills Development	Adult and Child Strategies Coded
Print Concepts	**ADULT:** Directing children's attention to book features (i.e., author, title, illustrator). Tracking print while reading. Discussing print features—to be coded under prereading stage. **CHILD:** Pointing out print features of book (e.g., words, letters). Labeling pictures. Making comments/asking questions about text. Trying to "read" book.
Comprehension	**ADULT:** Introducing and highlighting new vocabulary. Discussing background information. Incorporating child's experiences. Directing child's attention to illustrations and text. Expanding child's comments. Answering child's questions. Asking child recall questions. Using picture walk where applicable. Relating to classroom activities. Relating to the child's experience. Reviewing and reinforcing new vocabulary to be coded during postreading. Answering child's questions. Expanding on child's comments.

continues

Table 5–3. *continued*

Concepts and Skills Development	Adult and Child Strategies Coded
Comprehension *continued*	Summarizing with and without children's involvement. Using nonoral activities to extend learning. **CHILD:** Verbally responding to questions about the book. Asking questions about the book. Repeating words or parts of story.
Phonological/ Orthographic Awareness	**ADULT:** Commenting on letters, sounds, and their relationship.
Language Through Higher Order Thinking	**ADULT:** Asking story-related, open-ended questions that require expansion of answers and abstract thinking. Asking story-related questions about a child's experiences outside of the classroom. **CHILD:** Verbally responding to caregiver questions about the book. Commenting on story/illustrations. Expanding on caregiver comments about the book. Asking questions about the book. Repeating words or parts of story. Trying to "read" book.
Story-Related Vocabulary	**ADULT:** Number of story-related vocabulary words introduced/discussed. Number of supports provided (e.g., concrete support and semantic network linking).

Table 5–3. *continued*

Concepts and Skills Development	Adult and Child Strategies Coded
Use of Open-Ended Questions	**ADULT:** Number of open-ended questions asked. Level of support provided for child's answer (e.g., restating question, scaffolding, and allowing response time).
Depth of Parent-Child Discussion	**ADULT:** Using extension activities to reinforce comprehension. Length of time in postreading discussion.

Source: Goodson, Layzer, Smith, and Rimdzius (2006).

Caregiver depth of discussion during the reading is the third quality indicator on the OMLIT-RAPT. This is coded based on examination of the length and depth of the discussion between the caregiver and the child, as well as how many back-and-forth discussion points, or feedback loops, occur during the reading.

Adult/Child Interactive Reading Inventory (ACIRI; DeBruin-Parecki, 2006)

The ACIRI was designed to assist teachers in assessing the quality of book-reading sessions engaged in by parents and their children. In so doing, teachers are able to help parents work with their children to better develop fundamental literacy skills necessary for achievement. The ACIRI is useful not only for evaluating the parent/child dyad, but also can also be used at a more global level to evaluate the success of family literacy programs that have a mission of improving interactive book reading between parents and children. The ACIRI is available in both English and Spanish.

The ACIRI is composed of three constructs: Enhancing Attention to Text, Promoting Interactive Reading and Supporting Comprehension, and Using Literacy Strategies. Under each construct, there are four subcategories that describe both adult and child behavior. These subcategories for adults and children map onto each other. For Enhancing Attention to Text, the four categories cover physical space while reading, interest in the text, manipulation of the book, and acknowledgment of the interactive nature of reading together. For Promoting Interactive Reading and Supporting Comprehension, the four categories cover questioning and answering, identification, and extension of text into child's own experiences. For using Literacy Strategies, the four categories pertain to explicit attention to print/pictures, prediction, recall, and elaboration. Prior to evaluating a book-reading session, the author requests that all users become familiar with the specifics of each construct and subcategory in order to maintain strong reliability. A description of strategies that adults use to promote interactive reading and comprehension concepts and skills is presented in Table 5–4.

The 4-point scale is as follows: 0 signifying "no evidence" of the specific behavior; 1 signifying "infrequently" observed behaviors; 2 for behaviors observed "some of the time;" and 3 for behaviors observed "most of the time." Both the adult and child are scored on this scale for the four subcategories, and then a mean is calculated for each construct. A total mean score is then calculated for the adult and for the child.

The categories within both adult behavior and child behavior related to early literacy concept and skill development are: Promoting Interactive Reading and Supporting Comprehension, and Using Literacy Strategies. Four types of behaviors are coded under each category. Under Promoting Interactive Reading for adult behavior the four subcategories are: Poses and asks for *questions* on the story's content; points to pictures and text to facilitate *word identification* and *comprehension*; relates the book to the child's own experiences and ties child's comments back to the story's content to facilitate *comprehension*; and takes time to answer the child's questions or encourages further questioning. The child is coded for responding to the adult's cues or for offering his or her own ideas by answering questions about the text; responding to adult cues on word or picture identification or offering his or her own information; relating content to his or her own experiences; and asking

Table 5–4. Concepts and Skills Development Using the Adult-Child Interactive Reading Inventory (ACIRI)

Concepts and Skills Development	*Strategies and Activities Coded*
Promoting Interactive Reading and Supporting Comprehension, Using Literacy Strategies	**ADULT:** Asking and soliciting questions. Highlighting pictures and words. Relating story to children's experiences. Answering questions posed by child. Highlighting visual cues (i.e., words and pictures related to the story). Soliciting predictions. Promoting recall of story elements. Elaborating and extending child's responses. **CHILD:** Responding to adult's questions. Responding to adult's prompts and/or identifying pictures and/or words on his or her own. Attempting to relate story to own experiences. Responding to adult's prompts and/or identifies visual cues related to the story by himself. Making predictions based on picture cues. Recalling information from the story when asked. Offering ideas about the story on his or her own.

Source: DeBruin-Parecki (2006).

questions concerning the story and related topics. Each of these four subcategories falls under child behavior and is coded as such.

The coding section for Using Literacy Strategies again focuses primarily on *comprehension*. Four subcategories under adult behaviors include identifying visual cues to promote understanding of the text, prompting predictions, asking the child to recall story elements, and elaborating and extending the child's ideas (see Table 5-4). Coded child behaviors include responding to the adult concerning visual cues to text or pictures, predicting what will occur next in the story, recalling information that has already been covered, and volunteering information as the shared reading continues. A sample scoring sheet of the ACIRI can be found in Appendix 5-B.

Book Reading Assessment Scoring System (BRASS Justice, Sutton, Sofka, McGinty & Pianta, 2006)

The Book Reading Assessment Scoring System (BRASS; Justice et al., 2006) is an objective observational tool that measures the overall quality and characteristics of an adult reading a storybook to a group of preschool children. The BRASS is based on the Classroom Assessment Scoring System (CLASS-PreK Pianta, La Paro, & Hamre, 2006), an observational instrument developed to measure the social and instructional interactions that take place between a teacher and children in an early childhood classroom. The BRASS also measures the social and instructional interactions that take place between the teacher and children but is specific to book reading sessions in preschool classrooms; however, the measure can be applied to any shared storybook reading. The BRASS comprises five constructs that encompass the overall quality of the book reading: Book Reading Experience, Session Climate, Teacher Sensitivity, Language Encouragement and Enrichment, and Child Engagement. The BRASS is useful for teachers, administrators, and researchers who wish to study the behaviors and characteristics of quality book reading, as well as assess those behaviors and characteristics.

Scoring for the five quality constructs involves coding on a 7-point Likert scale with results falling in the low (1-2), mid (3-5), or high (6-7) range. The behaviors that fall into each range are described explicitly in the manual for each construct. Examples of teacher and child behaviors for each range are also included to help with coding.

The category of Language Encouragement and Enrichment is included in this chapter's description of concepts and skills given that it is coded to capture the quality and amount of teachers' use of language stimulation and facilitation techniques during book reading to enhance children's early language acquisition. This construct is similar to the Language Modeling construct of the Classroom Assessment Scoring System (CLASS: Pianta et al., 2006). It is divided into three sections, the teacher's questioning techniques (i.e. the number of open-ended questions asked), how often the teacher repeats and/or extends children's responses, and the teacher's use of advanced language (i.e., new vocabulary, clarifying difficult concepts). A teacher would be given a score in the low-range (1–2) if he or she did not ask the children any open-ended questions, did not repeat or extend children's responses, and did not highlight or discuss new vocabulary and/or concepts. Teachers who read the story text straight through without any elaboration would score in the low-range. Teachers who ask a variety of open-ended questions, repeat and extend children's responses, use self and parallel-talk, and emphasize novel concepts, and vocabulary *throughout* the reading session would score in the high-range. Strategies for facilitating language development are presented in Table 5–5.

Table 5–5. Concepts and Skills Development Using the Book Reading Assessment Scoring System (BRASS)

Concepts and Skills Development	*Strategies Coded*
Language	Teacher asking open-ended questions.
	Teacher extending and/or repeating the children's responses.
	Teacher using advanced language with children.
	Teacher engaging in self- and/or parallel talk.
	Teacher questioning and encouraging children to engage in higher level thinking and reasoning.

Source: Justice, Sutton, Sofka, McGinty, and Pianta (2006).

Assessing the Socio-Emotional Quality of Storybook Reading

The Book Reading Assessment Scoring System (BRASS; Justice, Sutton, Sofka, McGinty, & Pianta, 2006)

The BRASS measures the socio-emotional domain of book reading through three scales: Book Reading Experience; Session Climate; and Teacher Sensitivity. Low-range is coded 1 to 2, mid-range is coded 3 to 5, and high-range is coded 6 to 7. Under book-reading experience, there are three subcategories: Attention to Story Book Features; Techniques to Elicit Child Participation; and Physical Delivery. This scale examines the teacher's techniques to make the reading interactive and engaging (e.g., calling on individual children, varying voice and tone, using motions to illustrate the story for dramatic effect). A teacher who consistently asks questions to individual children, adds additional information about the story, varies voice and tone to suit the story, and is enthusiastic would score in the high-range (6–7). The following subcategories are considered when coding for Session Climate: interactions, positive affect, and respect. This scale reflects the emotional tone of the book-reading session and the connection between the teachers and the children. The teacher's display of enjoyment (i.e., smiling, genuine praise, eye contact, using children's names and respectful tone) throughout the book reading is included under this rating. This BRASS construct, Session Climate, is adapted from the Classroom Assessment Scoring System (CLASS-PreK; Pianta et al., 2006) particularly the scale titled Positive Climate. Teacher Sensitivity encompasses the following: responsiveness, scaffolding, and quality of feedback. This construct includes the teacher's responsiveness to children's needs and awareness of the children's academic functioning (Pianta e.g., 2006). In order for a teacher to score in the high range, the teacher must consistently provide feedback to the children's questions and statements and focus on the process of learning to help the children understand novel or difficult concepts. Scaffolding is an important feature of teacher sensitivity, where the teacher is providing support and asking questions consistent with children's abilities and needs. The strategies the BRASS defines under socio-emotional quality are presented in Table 5–6.

Table 5–6. Socio-Emotional Assessment Using the Book Reading Assessment Scoring System (BRASS)

Socio-Emotional	*Strategies and Activities Coded*
Book Reading Experience	Attending and elaborating on story book features.
	Eliciting child participation and providing opportunities for the child to interact physically with the book.
	Using physical motions and varying voice to make the reading exciting.
Session Climate	Enjoying interactions with the children (i.e., smiling, laughing, showing affection).
	Using eye contact, having a positive affect, giving authentic praise, using children's names.
Teacher Sensitivity	Responding to the children consistently.
	Asking questions and making comments that are interesting to the children.
	Scaffolding for the children according to their needs.
	Providing feedback to help the children gain a deeper understanding.

Source: Justice et al. (2006).

Assessing Child Engagement During Storybook Reading

The Adult/Child Interactive Reading Inventory (ACIRI; DeBruin-Parecki, 2006)

A measure of child engagement is found in the ACIRI under the construct of Enhancing Attention to Print. For a full description of the ACIRI, please see discussion under Assessing Concept and Skills Development in Shared Storybook Reading.

There are four subcategories under Enhancing Attention to Print and notes are taken during the observation in order to code for the following specific behaviors: The adult encourages and maintains close proximity to the child; the adult uses positive reinforcement and encouragement, as well as child-appropriate language, to facilitate the child's interest and engagement; the adult provides the child with the opportunity to manipulate the book; and the adult is sure to have the book and pictures accessible ("book sharing") to the child. When coding for the child's behaviors, the following characteristics are considered: The child pursues and maintains close proximity to the adult; the child's motivation and engagement are sustained; the child volunteers to manipulate the book or responds when asked; and the child shares the book on his or her own or when asked. For description of these adult and child behaviors, see Table 5–7.

Table 5–7. Child Engagement Using the Adult/Child Interactive Reading Inventory (ACIRI)

Child Engagement	Strategies and Activities Coded
Enhancing Attention to Print	**ADULT:**
	Encouraging and maintaining close proximity to the child during the book reading.
	Using positive reinforcement, encouraging, and using child-appropriate language to facilitate child's interest and motivation.
	Allowing the child to manipulate the book.
	Making the book accessible to the child at all times.
	CHILD:
	Pursuing and maintaining close proximity to the adult.
	Sustaining motivation and engagement.
	Manipulating the book on his or her own, or when asked.
	Engaging in book sharing on his or her own or when asked.

Source: DeBruin-Parecki (2006).

Book Reading Assessment Scoring System (BRASS; Justice, Sutton, Sofka, McGinty, & Pianta, 2006)

The BRASS measures child engagement with its child engagement construct to capture the degree to which all students in the book-reading session are focused and participating. On this scale, the difference between active versus passive engagement is particularly important (Pianta et al., 2006). A session would score in the 1 to 2 point range if the majority of children appeared actively disengaged or distracted, and this was sustained throughout the book reading session. A score of 3 to 5 would be coded if a majority of the children were passively engaged, listening to, or watching the teacher. A score of 6 to 7 would apply if most children were actively engaged—frequently volunteering information and comments or responding consistently to teacher prompts. This high level of engagement should be sustained throughout the duration of the book reading for the maximum rating. For a full description of the BRASS, please see discussion under Assessing the Quality of Concept and Skill Development in Shared Storybook Reading.

The Kaderavek and Sulzby Rating of Orientation to Book Reading (ROB; Kaderavek & Sulzby, 1998)

The Kaderavek and Sulzby Rating of Orientation to Book Reading (ROB; Kaderavek & Sulzby, 1998) uses two scales with which to measure a child's engagement during book reading: persistence and engagement. The ROB was developed to globally assess children's orientation to book reading by observing their verbal and nonverbal participatory behaviors during a book reading session. The children are ranked on a 4-point rating scale. The scale differentiates children exhibiting High Orientation to Literacy (HOL), delineating those children who receive a 3 or 4 on the rating scale, meaning the children were actively engaged and appeared interested in the story book. Children who appear unmotivated and uninterested are considered to have Low Orientation to Literacy (LOL) and receive a 1 or 2 on the rating scale. For a full description of this measure, please see Chapter 10.

Assessments Conclusion

Adults vary widely in the manner in which they share storybooks with young children. Some are naturally responsive and entertaining while they read, while at the same time taking the opportunity to focus on concepts and skills, such as vocabulary, phonological awareness, and print features. With guidance, training, and feedback, parents and educators may become skilled storybook readers, employing the positive behaviors and strategies described in the measures we have discussed. As a result, adults will not only offer children the fundamental building blocks for emergent literacy acquisition, but will also demonstrate that storybooks are fun, interactive, and worthy of attention.

Special Considerations: Assessing Quality in Difficult Storybook Reading Interactions

We have discussed the quality of shared storybook reading in the classroom for the typically developing preschool child. It is also important to discuss how to involve children who are difficult to engage in storybook reading. Children may be difficult to engage in reading interactions due to individual characteristics, such as poor motivation and socio-emotional behavioral problems. These individual differences are often problematic because they interfere with a child's ability to become actively engaged during group readings in the classroom and/or one-on-one reading sessions.

Child Level Factors That Influence Their Engagement

Children's Motivation

Some children may be hard to engage in book-reading sessions because they are not motivated to learn how to read. In general, positive shared-reading interactions nurture children's interest in and motivation to read (see Baker, Scher, & Mackler, 1997), and children with more positive attitudes toward reading read more (Greaney & Hegarty, 1987). However, some children are not motivated to read. Motivation is important given that children's self-reported motivation for reading predicts their reading skill over and above their language abilities (Frijters, Barron, & Brunello, 2000) and children with more positive attitudes toward reading (Greaney & Hegarty, 1987) and higher self-reported motivation for reading will have better reading skills (Frijters et al., 2000).

Young children's motivation for reading can be assessed using the Interest in Literacy Task (Frijters et al., 2000). For this task, children are presented with two pictures of the same child engaging in a literacy activity (e.g., reading or writing); in one picture the child is depicted with a happy face and in the other picture the child is depicted with a sad face. The examiner presents the child with pictures that match the child's sex and then says to the child, "This girl/boy likes to look at books by herself/himself [points to the happy face]. This girl/boy does not like to look at books by herself [points to the sad face]. Which girl/boy is most like you?" (Frijters et al., 2000, p. 468). The four questions used are presented in Table 5–8.

After the child chooses between whether he or she likes to engage in the reading activity, the child is then asked to indicate the degree to which he or she enjoys the task by pointing to a big circle ["a lot"] or little circle ["a little"] under each literacy picture.

Table 5–8. Interest in Literacy Task

Positive Response *(Happy Face)*	*Negative Response* *(Sad Face)*
This girl/boy likes to look at books by herself/himself.	This girl/boy doesn't like to look at books by herself/himself.
This girl/boy likes to get books for presents.	This girl/boy doesn't like to get books for presents.
This girl/boy likes to go to the library.	This girl/boy doesn't like to go the library.
This girl/boy likes to read.	This girl/boy doesn't like to read.

Source: Fritjers et al. (2000).

Scores are based on a combination of the child's dichotomous choice and their degree rating. For example, 4 = smiling face, big circle; 3 = smiling face, little circle; 2 = sad face, large circle; 1 = sad face, small circle. Scores range from 1 to 4 for each item, resulting in a maximum of 16 points. The split-half reliability for this item is comparable to other similar scales used with preschoolers ($r = 0.67$), and children's scores on this measure are related to children's literacy skills even after controlling for powerful factors, such as phonological awareness, oral language, and frequency of home literacy practices (Frijters et al., 2000).

For the unmotivated child, several strategies can be used to encourage interest in reading. For example, Justice and Ezell (2000, 2004) suggest allowing the child to choose the book and to hold it and turn the pages. They also suggest that mothers allow the child to "read" to them. Children as young as toddlers and preschoolers can pretend to read, an activity referred to as *emergent reading* (Sulzby, 1985). Children may have favorite storybooks that they like to read over and over again. They may even memorize certain books. Encouraging children to read favorite storybooks or books about topics that interest them will facilitate children's motivation in book reading.

Socio-Emotional and Behavioral Problems

Another reason children may be hard to engage during book reading is due to poor socio-emotional skills or behavior issues. Examples of pro-social behavior and self-regulation, such as cooperation, attentive listening, inhibitory control, and turn taking, are important components of shared storybook reading. Children who have difficulty with these skills may become frustrated when they want to talk while their parent is reading or impatient when they want to turn the page before the teacher has finished reading it. Further, these children's problems with emotion regulation and behavior may be interpreted negatively by their teachers and classmates. Although researchers failed to show that poor literacy skills in kindergarten are associated with aggressive behavior (Miles & Stipek, 2005), others have found an association between low reading achievement and children's antisocial behavior during elementary school (Trzesniewski, Moffitt, Caspi, Taylor, & Maughan, 2006). Similarly, Bennett, Brown, Boyle, Racine, and Offord (2003) found that children who were poor readers at school entry were more likely to have conduct problems 2 years later.

Miles and Stipek (2005) suggest that having difficulty with reading produces "acting-out" behavior in the classroom during third and fifth grade. They speculate that perhaps researchers have failed to see the link between literacy and negative social skills in young children (i.e., preschoolers and kindergartners) because during those grades, children are exposed to literacy but not necessarily expected to demonstrate their literacy competence. On the contrary, by the time children enter first grade, teachers' expectations increase and children are pressured to display their abilities by reading aloud and writing. Miles and Stipek warn that by increasing teachers' expectations of preschoolers' literacy, such as with standardized testing of preliteracy skills which require children to display their competencies, children may begin to feel pressured and hence begin to show their frustration sooner.

There are several strategies teachers can use to help children manage their frustration and negative behavior during group reading interactions. Pellitteri, Dealy, Fasano, and Kugler (2006) suggest that emotionally intelligent interventions can be used to help children who have difficulties with reading. The goal of emotionally intelligent interventions is to improve the socio-emotional functioning of students, which will indirectly have an effect on their behavior. One specific technique that can be used is to *match* children who are known to have socio-emotional behavior issues with teachers who are skilled at addressing these issues. Both parents and school counselors can advocate that these children with special needs be matched with the appropriate teachers. Another technique that can be used to help young children is to *facilitate emotional awareness* within the classroom environment by making teachers aware of how they are responding to children's misbehavior during the group reading session. Researchers have found that there is a bidirectional relationship between teachers' negative perceptions of children and children's misbehavior in the classroom (Stuhlman & Pianta, 2002).

Hence, the strategies that are most effective in managing difficult storybook readings that are the result of socio-emotional or behavior problems are best addressed via better teacher training and education because positive social and emotional reading interactions indirectly enhance children's reading skills. Some strategies teachers can use for promoting positive socio-emotional group interactions include being responsive to children's questions before, during, and after reading the story, holding the book so that all children can see it, and providing positive feedback to children via praise when they respond appropriately to a question or when they are attentive and cooperative during the interaction.

How to Encourage Children's Engagement

Children show greater gains in language and literacy development when they are given opportunities to become active participants in storybook readings (Reese & Cox, 1999; Whitehurst et al.,1999). Whitehurst and colleagues developed a specific technique called **dialogic reading** to teach adults how to prompt the child with questions, expand the child's verbalizations, and praise the child's efforts to tell the story and label objects within the book (Arnold & Whitehurst, 1994). Whitehurst and colleagues (Whitehurst, Arnold et al., 1994, Whitehurst, Epstein et al., 1994; 1999) trained Head Start parents to use dialogic reading techniques and demonstrated the positive impact on children's emergent literacy outcomes. Children were randomly assigned to either an intervention condition (dialogic reading program at home and in the classroom) or a control condition (regular Head Start curriculum). The degree to which parents complied with the dialogic reading techniques at home was related to children's scores on the language factor, which included the Peabody Picture Vocabulary Test-Revised (PPVT-R; Dunn & Dunn, 1981).

The acronyms CROWD and PEER were developed to help adults remember these techniques. The acronym CROWD represents the five types of questions asked by adults when engaging in dialogic reading: (1) *Completion prompts:* Fill-in-the blank questions; (2) *Recall prompts:* Questions that require the child to remember aspects of the book; (3) *Open-ended prompts:* Statements that encourage the child to respond to the book in his or her own words; (4) *Wh-prompts:* What, where, and why questions; and (5) *Distancing prompts:* Questions that require the child to relate the content of the book to aspects of life outside the book (Zevenbergen & Whitehurst, 2003, p. 180). Dialogic reading for children aged 4 to 5 uses different techniques from those used with children ages 2 to 3. The types of questions asked of older children are more challenging.

The PEER strategy was designed to remind adults to "*prompt* the child to label objects in the book and talk about the story, *evaluate* the child's responses, *expand* the child's verbalization by repeating what the child has said and adding information to it, and encourage the child to *repeat* the expanded utterances" (Zevenbergen & Whitehurst, 2003, p. 180). Regarding the "evaluate" component, adults are expected to praise the child's correct responses and offer alternative answers or labels for clearly incorrect responses. Adults are taught to focus on asking the child specific types of questions, evaluating the child's responses, expanding those responses, and having the child repeat the expanded utterances (Whitehurst et al., 1994a).

Another strategy for engaging children in storybook reading includes **distancing strategies**, which involve encouraging children to use decontextualized discourse. Decontextualized discourse is talk outside the immediate context; it is talk about objects and events in the past or future (Curenton & Justice, 2004), and distancing refers to imposing a cognitive demand on the child to separate him/herself mentally from what is happening in the present (Sigel, Stinson, & Flaugher, 1991).

Sigel (1982) developed a discourse model of cognitive distancing based on three types of distancing strategies: high-level, medium-level, and low-level distancing. High-level strategies included questions, evaluations, cause-effect inferences, generalizations, planning, suggesting proper alternatives, and drawing conclusions. Medium-level strategies included sequencing, reproduction, inference of similarity, asking for clarification, declaratives, and management (defined as redirecting attention and verbal modeling). Low-level demand strategies included providing labels, observing (e.g., "Watch me"), describing, and demonstrating (e.g., "I'm reading this now") (Pellegrini, Perlmutter, Galda, & Brody, 1990).

Heath (1982) is another researcher who suggested three types of decontextualized talk, or distancing strategies, during book reading. The first type of talk is called *what-explanations*. This strategy entails asking basic comprehension questions about what has already occurred in the text (e.g., helping children order story events, pick out main ideas, and remember the title). The second type of talk described by Heath (1982) is called *reason-explanations*. This strategy entails encouraging a child to think about a character's motives and/or understand why certain events happened. Further, this type of request helps children understand cause-effect relations and forces them to make explicit many of the implicit connections in a story. The third type of talk described by Heath (1982) is called *affective commentary*. This strategy entails asking not only why something happened, but also whether the action was good or bad, admirable, or immoral. Therefore, it helps children to understand motives and consequences of actions.

These strategies to promote children's involvement can even be used on children who have communication disorders. Pellegrini, Brody, and Sigel (1985) examined the cognitive demands imposed on children by mothers and fathers during book reading. Participants included 120 families of preschoolers between the ages of 3 to 5 years of age. Half of the children had been previously diagnosed with a language impairment or communication disorder, and the other half were typically developing children. Parents read two different stories and were instructed to go through the book in the same manner they would at home. Pellegrini and colleagues (1985) hypothesized that parents would use more cognitively demanding strategies with more competent children. The investigators found that parents of children with communication disorders were more likely to use low demand strategies such as labeling pictures. Parents, educators, and clinicians of children with communication disorders should engage children in book reading not only by asking children to label pictures, but also by asking children *what-explanation* prompts, such as "What do you think will happen next?," and affective commentary ("Which part of the story did you like the best?").

The distancing strategies adults use typically vary according to the type of book the adult is reading. Pellegrini and colleagues (1990) examined the effects of book genre in a study involving 13 African American Head Start mothers and their children. Mothers' book-reading strategies were classified according to the level of cognitive demand they imposed on children. They found that mothers use more high-level strategies when reading expository books as compared to narrative books, and children talk more when mothers read expository books than when they read narrative books (Pellegrini et al., 1990).

Potter and Haynes (2000) also examined the distancing strategies low-income mothers used during joint book reading with toddlers. Mothers were asked to read four different books, including two narrative and two expository books. Results revealed that, while reading expository texts, mothers used significantly more labels, asked for more what-explanations, and provided more positive and negative feedback compared to the use of these strategies while reading the narrative books. However, mothers were significantly more likely to provide descriptions while reading narrative books compared to expository books. Children demonstrated a higher frequency of imitative verbalizations and incorrect verbal responses to mothers' questions while reading the expository books compared to the narrative books. Children gave more correct nonverbal responses to mothers' questions while reading the narrative books compared to expository books (Potter & Haynes, 2000). These results suggest that reading expository texts with children promotes conversation.

Summary

To summarize, there is a body of research that highlights how some children may have difficulty engaging in storybook readings due to individual differences in motivation and socio-emotional and behavioral problems. This research has important implications for practice and for the implementation of interventions. For instance, when educators or clinicians encounter a child who is difficult to engage during storybook reading, it is important to first assess the child's motivation for reading. It could be that this child is simply not interested in literacy-related activities. If that is the case, the intervention needs to focus on enhancing the child's motivation for reading, which can be done by using distancing strategies when reading to the child. See Chapter 10 (this volume) for a thorough discussion of assessing children's motivation toward literacy activities.

The second factor to consider when a child is difficult to engage is the child's socio-emotional or behavioral skills. If the child has issues in this area, then the teacher or clinician needs to focus on techniques to help the child manage his behavior and concentration. This can be done by ensuring the child is placed in the proper classroom environment with an experienced and emotionally aware teacher who understands how to work with children with these special needs. Once children are better able to self-regulate and manage their behavior, then the distancing strategies can be incorporated into the reading session to help them maintain their concentration and keep them involved in the interaction.

References

Arnold, D. S., & Whitehurst, G. J. (1994). Accelerating language development through picture book reading. In D. Dickinson (Ed.), *Bridges to literacy: Approaches to supporting child and family literacy*. Cambridge, MA: Blackwell.

Baker, L. Scher, D., & Mackler, K. (1997). Home and family influences on motivations for reading. *Educational Psychologist, 32*, 69–82.

Baker, L., Somenschein, S., & Gilat, M. (1996). Mothers' sensitivity to the competencies of their preschoolers on a concept-learning task. *Early Childhood Research Quarterly, 11*, 405–424.

Beals, D. E., & DeTemple, J. M. (1992). Home contributions to early language and literacy development. *National Reading Conference, 42*, 207–215

Beals, D. E., DeTemple, J. M., & Dickinson, D. K. (1994). Talking and listening that support Early literacy development of children from low-income families. In D. K. Dickinson (Ed.), *Bridges to literacy: Children, families and schools* (pp. 19–40), Cambridge, MA: Blackwell.

Bennett, K. J., Brown, K. S., Boyle, M. Racine, Y., & Offord, D. (2003). Does low reading achievement at school entry cause conduct problems? *Social Science and Medicine*, 56, 2443–2448.

Bus, A. G., van IJzendoorn, M. H., & Pellegrini, A. D. (1995b). Mothers reading to their three-year-olds: The role of mother-child attachment security in becoming literate. *Reading Research Quarterly, 40*, 998–1015.

Bus, A. G., van IJzendoorn, M. H., & Pelligrini, A. D. (1995a). Joint book reading makes for success in learning to read. A meta-analysis on intergenerational transmission of literacy. *Review of Educational Research, 65*(1), 1–21.

Bus, A. G., Belsky, J., van IJzendoorn, M. H., & Crnic, K. (1997). Attachment and bookreading patterns: A study of mothers, fathers, and their toddlers. *Early Childhood Research Quarterly, 12*(1), 81–98.

Crain-Thoreson, C., & Dale, P. S. (1992). Do early talkers become early readers? Linguistic precocity, preschool language, and emergent literacy. *Developmental Psychology, 28*(3), 421–429.

Curenton, S. M., & Justice, L. M. (2004). African american and caucasian preschooler's use of decontextualized language. *Language, Speech and Hearing Services in School, 35*, 240–253.

DeBaryshe, B. D. (1993). Joint picture-book reading correlates of early oral language skill. *Journal of Child Language, 20*, 455–461

DeBruin-Parecki, A. (2006). *The Adult/Child Interactive Reading Inventory (ACIRI)*. Baltimore: Paul H. Brookes.

Dickinson, D. K., DeTemple, J. M., Hirschler, J., & Smith, M. W. (1992). Book reading with preschoolers: Co-construction of text at home and at school. *Early Childhood Research Quarterly*, 7, 323–346.

Dickinson, D. K., & Smith, M. W. (1994). Long-term effects of preschool teachers' book readings on low-income children's vocabulary and story comprehension. *Reading Research Quarterly*, 29(2), 104–122.

Dickinson, D. K., & Snow, C. (1987). Interrelationships among pre-reading and oral language skills in kindergarten from two social classes. *Early Childhood Research Quarterly*, 2, 1–25.

Dunn, L. M., & Dunn, L. M. (1981). *Peabody Picture Vocabulary Test-Revised*. Circle Pines, MN: American Guidance Service.

Elley, W. B. (1989). Vocabulary acquisition from listening to stories. *Reading Research Quarterly*, 24, 174–187

Ezell, H., & Justice, L. (2005). *Shared storybook reading: Building young children's language and emergent literacy skills*. Baltimore: Paul H. Brookes.

Flood, J. E. (1977). Parental styles in reading episodes with young children. *The Reading Teacher*, 30, 864–867.

Frijters, J. C., Barron, R. W., & Brunello, M. (2000). Direct and mediated influences of home literacy and literacy interest on prereaders' oral vocabulary and early written language skill. *Child Development*, 92, 466–477.

Girolametto, L., & Weitzman, E. (2002). Responsiveness of child care providers in interactions with toddlers and preschoolers. *Language, Speech and Hearing Services in Schools*, 33, 268–281.

Goodson, B. D., Layzer, C. J., Smith, W. C., & Rimdzius, T. (2006). *Observation Measures of Language and Literacy Instruction (OMLIT)*. Cambridge, MA: ABT Associates.

Greaney, V., & Hegarty, M. (1987). Correlates of leisure time. *Journal of Research in Reading*, 10, 30.

Haden, C. A., Reese, E., & Fivush, R. (1996). Mothers' extratextual comments during storybook reading: Stylistic differences over time and across texts. *Discourse Processes*, 21, 135–169.

Hart, B. H., & Risley, T. R. (1995). *Meaningful differences in the everyday experience of young American children*. Baltimore: Paul H. Brookes.

Heath, S. B. (1982). What no bedtime story means: Narrative skills at home and school. *Language in Society*, 11, 49–76.

Hoffman, J. V., Roser, N. L., & Battle, J. (1993). Reading aloud in classrooms: From the modal toward the "model." *The Reading Teacher*, 46, 496–503.

Justice, L., & Ezell, H. (2000). Enhancing children's print and word awareness through home based parent intervention. *American Journal of Speech-Language Pathology*, 9, 257–269.

Justice, L., & Ezell, H. (2002). Use of storybook reading to increase print awareness in at-risk children. *American Journal of Speech-Language Pathology, 11*, 17–29.

Justice, L., & Ezell, H. (2004). Print referencing: An emergent literacy enhancement strategy. *Language, Speech, and Hearing Services in the Schools, 35*, 185–193.

Justice, L., & Kaderavek, J. N. (2000) Topic control during shared story-book reading: Mothers and their children with language impairments. *Topics in Early Childhood Special Education, 23*(3), 137–150.

Justice, L.M., Sofka, A. E., Lucas, T. D., & Sutton, M.M., (2006). *Calling attention to print: An implementation manual.* University of Virginia Center for Advanced Study of Teaching and Learning, Preschool Language and Literacy Lab. Unpublished manuscript.

Justice, L.M, Sutton, M.M, Sofka, A. E., McGinty, A.S., & Pianta, R. C., (2006). *The Book Reading Assessment Scoring System.* Charlottesville, VA: Preschool Language and Literacy Lab, University of Virginia.

Kaderavek, J. N., & Justice, L. M. (2000). The effect of book genre in the repeated readings of mothers and their children with language impairment. *Child Language, Teaching, and Therapy, 21*(1), 75–92.

Kaderavek, J., & Justice, L. (2002). Shared storybook reading as an intervention context: Practices and potential pitfalls. *American Journal of Speech-Language Pathology, 11*, 395–406.

Kaderavek, J. N., & Sulzby, E. (2000). Narrative production by children with and without specific language impairment: Oral narratives and emergent readings. *Journal of Speech, Language, and Hearing Research, 436*, 34–49.

Kaderavek, J., & Sulzby, E. (1998). Parent child book reading: An observational protocol for young children. *American Journal of Speech and Language Pathology, 7*, 33–47.

Karweit, N. (1989). The effects of a story-reading program on the vocabulary and story comprehension skills of disadvantaged prekindergarten and kindergarten students. *Early Education and Development, 1*, 105–114.

Mason, J. M., Stewart, J., Peterman, C., & Dunning, D. B. (1992). *Toward an integrated model of early reading development* (Technical Report No. 566). Champaign: University of Illinois.

Miles, S. B., & Stipek, D. (2005). Contemporaneous and longitudinal associations between social behavior and literacy achievement in a sample of low-income elementary school children. *Child Development, 77*, 103–117.

Ninio, A. (1983). Joint book-reading as a multiple vocabulary acquisition device. *Developmental Psychology, 9*, 445–451.

Pellegrini, A. D., Brody, G. H., & Sigel, I. E. (1985). Parents' book-reading habits with their children. *Journal of Educational Psychology*, 77, 332–340.

Pellegrini, A. D., Perlmutter, J. C., Galda, L., & Brody, G. H. (1990). Joint reading between black Head Start children and their mothers. *Child Development*, 61, 443–453.

Pelliteri, J., Dealy, M., Fasano, C., & Kugler, J. (2006). Emotionally intelligent interventions for students with reading disabilities. *Reading and Writing Quarterly: Overcoming Learning Difficulties*, 22, 155–171.

Pianta, R. C., La Paro, K. M., & Hamre, B. K. (2006). *Classroom Assessment Scoring System Pre-K Manual.* Charlottesville: University of Virginia National Center for Early Development and Learning.

Potter, C. A., & Haynes, W. O. (2000). The effects of genre on mother-toddler interaction during joint book reading. *Infant-Toddler Intervention*, 10, 97–105.

Reese E. (1995). Predicting children's literacy from mother child conversations. *Cognitive Development*, 10(3), 381–405

Reese, E., & Cox, A. (1999). Quality of adult book reading affects children's emergent literacy. *Developmental Psychology*, 35, 20–28.

Scarborough, H. H., & Dobrich, W. (1994). On the efficacy of reading to preschoolers. *Developmental Review*, 14, 245–302.

Sénéchal, M., Thomas, B., & Monker, J. (1995). Individual differences in four-year-old children's acquisition of vocabulary during storybook reading. *Journal of Educational Psychology*, 87, 218–229.

Sigel, I. E. (1982). The relationship between parental distancing strategies and the child's cognitive behavior. In L. M. Laosa & I. E. Sigel (Eds.), *Families as learning environments for children* (pp. 47–86). New York: Plenum.

Sigel, I. E., Stinson, E. T., & Flaugher, J. (1991). Socialization of representational competence in the family: The distancing paradigm. In R. J. Sternberg & L. Okagaki (Eds.), *Directors of development: Influences on the development of children's thinking* (pp. 121–144). Hillsdale, NJ: Lawrence Erlbaum.

Silvern, S. (1985). Parent involvement and reading achievement: A review of research and implications for practice. *Childhood Education*, 62(1), 46–50.

Snow, C. (1983). Literacy and language: Relationships during the preschool years. *Harvard Educational Review*, 53, 165–189.

Snow, C. (Ed.). (1994). *Beginning from baby talk: Twenty years of research on input in interaction.* Cambridge, England: Cambridge University Press.

Stuhlman, M. W., & Pianta, R. C. (2002). Teachers narratives about their relationships with children: Associations with behavior in classrooms. *School Psychology Review*, 31, 148–163.

Sulzby, E. (1985). Children's emergent reading of favorite storybooks: A developmental study. *Reading Research Quarterly, 20*(4), 458–481.

Teale, W. H. (1983). Parents reading to their children: What we know and need to know. *Language Arts, 58,* 902–911.

Teale., W. H., & Sulzby, E. (1987). Literacy acquisition in early childhood: The roles of access and mediation in storybook reading. In D. A. Wagner (Ed.), *The future of literacy in a changing world* (pp. 111–130). New York: Pergamon Press.

Trzesniewski, K. H., Moffitt, T. E., Caspi, A., Taylor, A., & Maughan, B. (2006). Revisiting the association between reading achievement and antisocial behavior: New evidence of an environmental explanation from a twin study. *Child Development, 77,* 72–88.

van Kleeck, A., Stahl, S. A., & Bauer, E. B. (2002). *On reading books to children: Parents and teachers.* Mahwah, NJ: Lawrence Erlbaum.

van Kleeck, A., Vander Woude, J.V., Hammett, L. (2006). Fostering literal and inferential language skills in Head Start preschoolers with language impairment using scripted book-sharing discussions. *American Journal of Speech and Language Pathology, 15,* 85–95.

Wasik, B. A., & Bond, M. A. (2001). Beyond the pages of a book: Interactive book reading and language development in preschool classrooms. *Journal of Educational Psychology, 93*(2), 243–250.

Wells, G. (1985). Preschool literacy-related activities and success in school. In D. R. Olsen, N. Torrance, & A. Hildyard (Eds.), *Language, literacy and learning*. New York: Cambridge University Press.

Westby, C. (1991). Assessing and remediating text comprehension problems. In A. G. Kahmi & H. Catts (Eds.), *Reading disabilities: A developmental language perspective* (pp. 199–260.). Needham Heights, MA: Allyn & Bacon.

Whitehurst, G. J., Arnold, D. H., Epstein, J. N., Angell, A. L., Smith, M., & Fischel, J. E. (1994). A picture book reading intervention in daycare and home for children from low-income families. *Developmental Psychology, 30,* 679–689.

Whitehurst, G. J., Epstein, J. N., Angell, A. L., Payne, A. C., Crone, D. A., & Fischel, J. (1994). Outcomes of an emergent literacy intervention in Head Start. *Journal of Educational Psychology, 86,* 542–555.

Whitehurst, G. J., Falco, F. L., Lonigan, C. J., Fischel, J. E., DeBaryshe, B. D., Valdez-Menchaca, M. C., & Caufield, M. (1988). Accelerating language development through picture book reading. *Developmental Psychology, 24,* 552–559.

Whitehurst, G. J., & Lonigan, C. J. (1998). Child development and emergent literacy *Child Development, 69,* 848–872.

Whitehurst, G. J., Zevenbergen, A. A., Crone, D. A., Schultz, M. D., Velting, O. N., & Fischel, J. E. (1999). Outcomes of an emergent literacy intervention from Head Start through second grade. *Journal of Educational Psychology, 91*, 261-272.

Wood, C., & Middleton, D. (1975). A study of assisted problem-solving. *British Journal of Psychology, 66*(2), 181-191.

Yoder, P. J., Warren, S. F., McCarthern, R., & Leew, S. (Eds.). (1998). *Does adult responsivity to child behavior facilitate communication development?* (Vol. 7). Baltimore: Paul H. Brookes.

Zevenbergen, A. A., & Whitehurst, G. J. (2003). Dialogic reading: A shared picture book reading intervention for preschoolers. In A. van Kleeck, S. A. Stahl, & E. B. Bauer (Eds.), *On reading books to children: Parents and teachers*. Mahwah, NJ: Lawrence Erlbaum Associates.

APPENDIX 5-A

Exhibit 6.2
Sample Scoring of Quality Indicators on the *RAP*

Quality Indicators for Read-Aloud

RAP #1

1. Story-related vocabulary Code as "1" if no A5, B5, or C3 is circled Code item as "1" if *no new* vocabulary introduced.	☐ 1 = Minimal	☐ 2	☑ 3 = Moderate	☐ 4	☐ 5 = High
	Some story-related vocabulary words are introduced/discussed, but the definition of one or more of the words is misleading or wrong.		**One** story-related vocabulary word is introduced or discussed and the definition is accurate AND At least one of the following comprehension supports is given for the word: • A picture, gesture, or other concrete visual aid is used; • The word is linked to a rich network of related words or concepts.		**At least 2** story-related vocabulary words are introduced or discussed and the definition of each vocabulary word is accurate AND Both of the following comprehension supports are given for each word: • A picture, gesture, or other concrete visual aid is used; and • Each word is linked to a rich network of related words or concepts.

266

	☐ 1 = Minimal	☑ 2	☐ 3 = Moderate	☐ 4	☐ 5 = High
2. Adult use of open-ended questions *Code item as "1" if no open-ended questions (no A10, B11, B12, C8 or C9 circled)*	Adult poses only **one** open-ended question and does not provide opportunity for children to respond to question (child not given time to respond, or adult moves on after child has responded).		Adult poses **two** open-ended questions and provides opportunity for children to respond to **one but not both** of the questions.		Adult poses **at least four** open-ended questions and consistently shows interest in/actively encourages children's responses (e.g., pausing for children, restating question, calling on particular children, acknowledging children's response).

	☐ 1 = Minimal	☑ 2	☐ 3 = Moderate	☐ 4	☐ 5 = High
3. Depth of Post-Reading *Code item as "1" if no C1-C10 is circled*	No post-reading extension or activities. (Post-reading coded as **C11**)	Relates to the book but lasts **LESS** than 5 minutes	Discussion and/or activity that • Relates to the book but does not extend its meaning or comprehension **AND** • Lasts at least 5 minutes.	Extends comprehension but lasts **LESS** than 10 minutes	Discussion and/or activity that • Extends the meaning of the text and reinforces comprehension of the book **AND** • Lasts at least 10 minutes.

Source: From Observation *Measures of Language and Literacy Instruction-Read Aloud Profile* by B. Dillon Goodson, C.J. Layzer, W.C. Smith nd T. Rimdeius. Exhibit 6.2 from Tranining Manual. Measure developed under contract ED-01-CO-0120, as administered by Institute of Sciences, U.S. Dept of Education. Reprinted with permission.

Adult–Child Interacti

ADULT BEHAVIOR	OBSERVATION
I. Enhancing Attention to Text	
1. Adult attempts to promote and maintain physi... ...y with the child.	
2. Adult sus...ins i... ...an... ...ention through ...f ch... ...usted language, p... ...e affe... ...d reinforcement.	
3. Adult gives the ch... an opportunity to hold the book and turn pages.	
4. Adult shares the book with the ... (displays sense of audience in b... handling when reading).	
II. Promoting Interactive Reading and Supporting Comprehension	
1. Adult poses and solicits questions about the book's content.	
2. Adult points to pictures and words to assist the child in identification and understanding.	
3. Adult relates the book's content and the child's responses to personal experiences.	
4. Adult pauses to answer questions that the child poses.	
III. Using Literacy Strategies	
1. Adult identifies visual cues related to story reading (e.g., pictures, repetitive words).	
2. Adult solicits predictions.	
3. Adult asks the child to recall information from the story.	
4. Adult elaborates on the child's ideas.	

...ding Inventory (ACIRI)

CHILD BEHAVIOR	OBSERVATION
Enhancing Attention to Text	
Child seeks and maintains physical proximity.	
Child pays attention and sustains interest.	
Child holds the book and turns the pages on his or her own or when asked.	
Child initiates or responds to book sharing that takes his or her presence into account.	
Promoting Interactive Reading and Supporting Comprehension	
Child responds to questions about the book.	
Child res_____ to adult cues or identifies pi_____ords on his or her own.	
Chi_____ts to_____ the book's c_____periences.	
Child poses questions about the___ and related topics.	
Using Literacy Strategies	
Child responds to the adult___ identifies visual cues related to t___ story him- or herself.	
Child is able to guess what will happen next based on picture cues.	
Child is able to recall information from the story.	
Child spontaneously offers ideas about the story.	

Adult–Child Interactive Rea

ADULT BEHA

I. Enhancin

Date of observation _____

Program _____

Teacher/Observer _____

II. Promotin
and Supp

Adult name/Case ___ er _____

Age _____

Date of birth _____

Child name/Case number _____

III. Usin

Age _____

Date of birth _____

Title of book _____

Author _____

CHILD BEHA

I. Enhancin

Notes:

II. Promotin
and Supp

SCORE (0–3)	Pre
3 = most of the time (4 or more times)	☐
2 = some of the time (2–3 times)	
1 = infrequently (1 time)	Post
0 = no evidence	☐

III. Using Lit

...ventory (ACIRI) Scoring Sheet

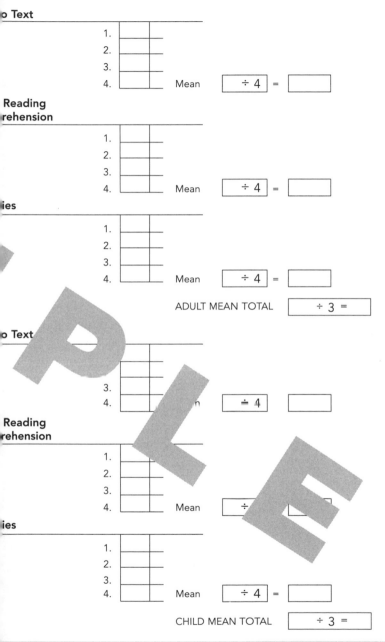

...o Text

1.		
2.		
3.		
4.		

Mean $\div 4$ = [ ]

Reading ...rehension

1.		
2.		
3.		
4.		

Mean $\div 4$ = [ ]

...ies

1.		
2.		
3.		
4.		

Mean $\div 4$ = [ ]

ADULT MEAN TOTAL $\div 3$ = [ ]

...o Text

3.		
4.		

...n $\div 4$ [ ]

Reading ...rehension

1.		
2.		
3.		
4.		

Mean $\div$ ...

...ies

1.		
2.		
3.		
4.		

Mean $\div 4$ = [ ]

CHILD MEAN TOTAL $\div 3$ = [ ]

Section II

Assessing Children's Growth and Development

Chapter Six

Assessing Phonological Awareness

C. Melanie Schuele
Lori E. Skibbe
Prema K.S. Rao

The Importance of Phonological Awareness to Emergent Literacy

Phonological Awareness and Reading

Phonological awareness refers to the ability to analyze the sound structure of spoken language. It requires nonlexical processing; that is, one has to look beyond the meaning of a word to focus on the sound structure of the word. Children who have phonological awareness can, for example, rhyme words, say the beginning sound of a word, or say each sound in a word. Phonological awareness is one aspect of metalinguistic awareness, the ability to focus on language structure separately from language meaning. For young children, the emergence of phonological awareness is no small accomplishment. Making the shift from using language to communicate (i.e., sharing meaning by talking) to also being aware of the structure of language (i.e., metalinguistic awareness) is a substantial cognitive-linguistic achievement, one that develops over a number of years.

The acquisition of phonological awareness is important to a child's early reading abilities (Catts, Fey, Zhang, & Tomblin, 2001; Cunningham & Stanovich, 1993; Scarborough, 1998; Storch &

Whitehurst, 2002). Children with good phonological awareness tend to be better readers whereas children with poor phonological awareness tend to be struggling readers (Byrne & Fielding-Barnsley, 1995; Torgesen & Mathes, 2000). A foundation of phonological awareness helps children to learn letter sounds (Burgess & Lonigan, 1998) and to decode words (Torgesen, 1999; Wagner et al., 1997). Phonological awareness, particularly phonemic awareness, is believed to have a causal role in early reading acquisition (Blachman, 1994). Phonemic awareness, a subset of phonological awareness, involves awareness specifically at the level of individual sounds. Asking a child to tell you all the sounds in *cat*, for example, requires phonemic awareness. Young children who do not have an adequate foundation of phonological awareness, and specifically phonemic awareness, are likely to be confused by sound/letter instruction and decoding instruction in kindergarten and first grade. Not fully appreciating that words are composed of individual sounds or phonemes makes it difficult to explore how letters can be used to represent those sounds.

It is important to recognize that phonological awareness relates to awareness of the sounds in speech and is distinct from print decoding knowledge (e.g., alphabetic principle, letter sounds, phonics). Phonological awareness activities require a child to focus on the sounds of words whereas decoding activities require a child to consider how the sounds of words can be represented in print. Success on decoding activities requires that a child has some phonological awareness.

Development of Phonological Awareness

Phonological awareness encompasses many different skills, but all of these skills develop from the same underlying ability (Anthony & Lonigan, 2004; Schatschneider, Francis, Foorman, Fletcher, & Mehta, 1999). Early emerging phonological awareness skills require only surface level awareness, a general appreciation of the sound structure of language. In contrast, later emerging skills, more complex in nature, require a much deeper level of awareness. Across children, phonological awareness skills are learned in the same order. Figure 6–1 illustrates the sequence of development of phonological awareness skills. At the beginning of this sequence of development,

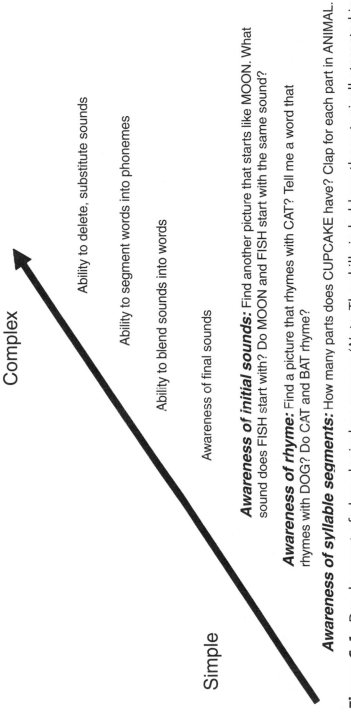

Complex

Simple

Ability to delete, substitute sounds

Ability to segment words into phonemes

Ability to blend sounds into words

Awareness of final sounds

Awareness of initial sounds: Find another picture that starts like MOON. What sound does FISH start with? Do MOON and FISH start with the same sound?

Awareness of rhyme: Find a picture that rhymes with CAT? Tell me a word that rhymes with DOG? Do CAT and BAT rhyme?

Awareness of syllable segments: How many parts does CUPCAKE have? Clap for each part in ANIMAL.

Figure 6–1. Development of phonological awareness (*Note:* The skills in bold are those typically targeted in preschool instruction).

children show an awareness of the syllable structure of language and slowly, begin to show an awareness of the individual sounds of language. Although the sequence of development is similar across children, there is much variability in the level of phonological awareness skill among groups of preschool children of the same age. The amount and nature of experiences at home as well as at preschool influence a child's phonological awareness proficiency. Individual child characteristics likely play a role as well. Some children simply seem to be more interested in playing with the sounds of language than others.

As early as 2 years of age, some children begin to show an ability to focus on the sounds of language. van Kleeck and Schuele (1987) provided many examples of spontaneous phonological awareness behaviors in young preschoolers, all recorded by parents in diary studies. Awareness of rhyme is an early emerging phonological awareness skill, something at which many 3- and 4-year-olds are quite proficient (Lonigan, Burgess, Anthony, & Barker, 1998). Breaking words into syllables is another early emerging phonological awareness skill (Fox & Routh, 1975). Older preschool children also might be proficient at focusing on the initial sounds of words, noticing when two words share the same beginning sound, for example. The ability to analyze the initial sounds of words typically emerges later than syllable awareness and rhyme (Lonigan et al., 1998). Analyzing initial sounds of words requires a child to break apart syllables into individual sounds. It is clear that children more easily understand that words can share the same beginning sound, called alliteration (e.g., *hat, hippo, hungry*), than they understand that words can share the same ending sound (e.g., *read, bed, food*). When isolating or segmenting individual speech sounds, children initially seem to be able to break the initial sound of a word (rime) from the rest of the word (onset), for example *c – at*.

Although children follow the same developmental trajectory, they do not necessarily master an earlier phonological awareness skill before they begin to work on a more difficult one. Anthony, Lonigan, Driscoll, Phillips, and Burgess (2003) suggested that children learn phonological awareness in "overlapping stages," indicating that children begin to learn more difficult concepts even before they become proficient at easier ones. They used the term "quasi-parallel progression" to describe this process. Although many programs teach phonological awareness in a developmental sequence (to follow the order whereby children learn these skills), the findings of Anthony et al. suggest that simultaneously targeting a few steps in the developmental sequence may also be a good way to teach children phonological awareness. Once a child begins to show some ability in one skill, parents and teachers can add in another skill that is just a little more difficult. Likewise, their findings suggest that educators should assess young children's phonological awareness at several different levels of complexity (e.g., different levels of complexity within an area, for example, rhyme; different levels of complexity across the developmental progression, for example, rhyme and initial sounds).

The acquisition process from emergence to mastery of phonological awareness is protracted. Although some 2- and 3-year-old children show emergence of phonological awareness, their skills are limited. Their proficiency on a particular type of task can vary greatly from day to day, and indeed from moment to moment. Although some children seem to develop a lot of phonological awareness skill without much direct teaching, for most children the acquisition of phonological awareness is highly dependent on experience and instruction. Importantly, proficiency on the more complex phonological awareness skills (e.g., phonemic awareness) is highly reliant on explicit instruction for nearly all children. For teachers, this relation between instruction-experience and learning provides three guiding principles. First, teachers should assess the phonological awareness skills that children have been given the opportunity to learn. Without instructional experiences, we would not expect most children to do well on measures of phonological awareness. Second, children will increase their phonological awareness as a function of the instructional experiences provided to them, whether these experiences are at home or at school (e.g., Byrne & Fielding-Barnsley, 1991; van Kleeck, Gillam, & McFadden, 1998). Maturation or time alone, in the absence of experience, won't bring an appreciable improvement in a child's phonological awareness, particularly for at risk children (e.g., low income children, children with language impairment). Third, proficiency on phonological awareness tasks will proceed from simple tasks to more complex tasks over the preschool and early school years.

A complete review of phonological awareness development is beyond the scope of this chapter, but there are many resources that provide excellent reviews (Gillon, 2004; Justice & Schuele, 2004; Schuele & Boudreau, 2006; Torgesen & Mathes, 2000).

Measures of Phonological Awareness

As the importance of phonological awareness to later literacy acquisition has become widely recognized, many measures to assess phonological awareness have become available. Most of the commercially available instruments have been published in the last 10 to 15 years. A number of experimental tasks that have been published in the research literature are valuable assessment tools as well. Some instruments tap several different aspects of phonological awareness, typically in separate subtests, whereas others are limited to one or two aspects of phonological awareness. A few instruments measure several levels of phonological awareness within one subtest (e.g., Lonigan, Wagner, Torgesen, & Rashotte, in press). When choosing an instrument or instruments, the educator or clinician will want to consider carefully the purpose for assessment and choose an instrument that best fits that purpose.

Many of the commercially available instruments are norm-referenced with standard scores and percentile ranks derived from chronological age comparisons. Norm-referenced comparisons of phonological awareness skills with preschool and kindergarten children, using population-based norms, are a challenge. As noted previously, a child's level of phonological awareness will be highly influenced by experiences, both at home and at school, that facilitate phonological awareness. We would expect a child who has had many experiences to have developed much more phonological awareness than a child who has had few experiences. Because a norm-referenced comparison is essentially a comparison of an individual child to the average of all children his or her age, the comparison may not be particularly informative. If a teacher finds that a large proportion of children in her classroom fall in the low ability range, this finding may reflect a lack of instructional opportunity rather than limited abilities per se on the part of children. It is unlikely that age is a fair benchmark for assuming similar experiences across children when it comes to phonological awareness. What is far more likely to be informative is a comparison of children within a local group who share a common set of experiences (e.g., a classroom of children, all children in a particular Head Start center). In these comparisons, we might test children after a period of instruction. Thus, the question asked is whether children have benefited adequately from instructional experiences. The child who scores lower than most peers clearly has not benefited from instructional experiences to the same extent as his or her peers. One more challenge with norm-referenced instruments may be that the number of items on any particular subtest is insufficient to provide an indication of the child's skill level, or strengths and weaknesses. Experimental measures or criterion-referenced measures may be more informative for these purposes.

Preschool and early school age measures of phonological awareness encompass a wide range of phonological awareness skills. Schatschneider and colleagues (1999) noted that the most informative assessment tasks will be those that tap into children's emerging skills. Testing children on skills that are far beyond their current abilities will simply indicate a lack of ability because the child will be unable to do the task. Thus, with preschool children, assessment should begin at a simple level, with developmentally appropriate phonological awareness skills. If a child is proficient or somewhat skilled on a particular task, then it will be informative to measure performance on a task slightly more complex, proceeding with gradually more complex tasks until the child becomes unsuccessful. In this chapter, we have chosen to describe phonological awareness measures that tap into the phonological awareness skills that we would expect preschool children to learn successfully, rhyme and initial sounds. We also include a section on measures of blending and segmenting because kindergartners are expected to gain skill at this level. Within each skill area, we describe several measures and present those measures in alphabetical order. See Table 6–1 for a complete list of all measures cited in this chapter.

Measuring Rhyme Judgment

Measures of rhyme judgment are designed to investigate whether children are aware that some words sound the same (e.g., *fat, cat*). Rhyme words differ in onset but share a rime. Thus, *cat* and *fat*, begin with different sounds (onset), but the rime of the word, *at*, is the same. Measures of rhyme judgment require children to demonstrate an understanding of rhyme without having to produce any rhymes. Rhyme is one of the earliest emerging phonological awareness

Table 6–1. Summary of Phonological Awareness Measures for Preschool and Kindergarten

Measure (date)	Ages	Time*	Administration	Relevant Subtests	Scores	Language	Uses
Abecedarian Reading Assessment (2002)	Kindergarten and first grade	5–20 min.	Individual	Rhyming Perception Rhyming Production Phoneme Awareness Phoneme Production First Sounds Last Sounds Segmentation	Raw Scores	English	Screening; Progress Monitoring
DIBELS (2002)	Kindergarten	Less than 5 min.	Individual	Initial Sounds Fluency Phoneme Segmentation	Raw Scores; Risk Status; Benchmark Comparison	English	Screening; Progress Monitoring; Outcomes
Get It, Got It, Go (1998; 2000)	Preschoolers	10–15 min.	Individual	Rhyme Alliteration	Raw Scores	English	Screening; Progress Monitoring; Outcomes
Get Ready to Read! Screening Tool (2001)	Year prior to Kindergarten entry	9 min.	Individual, up to three times per year	No subtests. 20 items; 7 items assess phonological awareness.	Raw Scores	English Spanish	Screening; Progress Monitoring

Measure (date)	Ages	Time*	Adminis- tration	Relevant Subtests	Scores	Language	Uses
PALS-K (2002)	Kindergarten	30 min.	Group and Individual	Rhyme Awareness Beginning Sound Awareness Spelling	Raw Scores	English	Screening; Outcomes
PALS-PreK (2004)	Preschool	20–25 min.	Individual	Beginning Sound Awareness Rhyme Awareness Nursery Rhyme Awareness	Raw Scores; Benchmark Comparison	English	Screening; Progress Monitoring; Outcomes
PAYC: Assessing Phonological Awareness (1998)	Kindergarten	30 min.	Small group	Detecting Rhyme Counting Syllables Matching Initial Sounds Counting Phonemes	Raw Scores	English	Screening; Progress Monitoring; Outcomes
PIPA (2003)	4;0 to 6;11	30 min.	Individual	Rhyme Awareness Syllable Segmentation Alliteration Awareness Sound Isolation Sound Segmentation	Raw Scores; Percentile Ranges	English	Norm- referenced comparison

continues

283

Table 6–1. *continued*

Measure (date)	Ages	Time*	Adminis-tration	Relevant Subtests	Scores	Language	Uses
PAT (1997)	5 to 9; Kindergarten to second grade	30–45 min.	Individual	Rhyming Segmentation Isolation Blending	Raw Scores; Percentile Ranks; Standard Scores	English	Norm-referenced comparison; Diagnostic
TOPA-2+ (2004), Kindergarten Version	Kindergarten	30–45 min.	Individual, small group, or classroom group	Initial Sounds	Raw Scores; Percentile Ranks; Standard Scores	English	Identify children in the latter half of kindergarten who have insufficient phonological awareness and need specialized intervention (e.g., Tier 2 in an RTI model)
TOPEL (in press)	3;0 to 5;11 Preschool	30 min.	Individual	Phonological Awareness (elision and blending)	Raw Scores; Percentile Ranks; Standard Scores	English	Screening; Progress Monitoring; Outcomes

*Time indicated is total administration unless otherwise noted.

Note: Experimental measures published in the research literature were not included in this table; they are discussed only in the text.

skills and, as such, will be a commonly measured skill in preschool. Several formats are used to measure children's ability to judge rhymes, for example, indicating whether two words rhyme, matching rhymes, or choosing the nonrhyming item from a group of words or pictures.

The Abecedarian Reading Assessment: Rhyme Perception

The Abecedarian Reading Assessment (Wren & Watts, 2002), a criterion-referenced measure, provides information about children's literacy skills to individualize instruction for children within classrooms. This measure, along with the scoring sheets, may be downloaded in its entirety from the World Wide Web (www.balanced reading.com). Although standard scores and percentile ranks are not provided as part of this measure, the authors provide general guidelines concerning the skills that children should have entering kindergarten and first grade. This measure is available in English and is designed to be administered individually by teachers. Each subtest has two lists of stimuli which allow for repeated assessment. Subtests are arranged in order of increasing difficulty and each child should be given only subtests deemed appropriate for his or her individual level. Thus, testing time for individual children will vary. Some of the subtests appear problematic; therefore, we have only included some of the subtests in our discussion.

For the Rhyming Perception subtest, three practice items, administered with feedback from the examiner, orient the child to the task. There are 10 test items. For each item, children are asked whether two words rhyme (e.g., *Does PILL rhyme with HILL?*) All words included in this subtest are monosyllabic and most of the words should be words that preschoolers have heard in the past, although some words may not be known by all children (e.g., *grain, west*). No picture support is provided. Children are considered to have passed this measure if they are able to answer 8 of the 10 items correctly. This subtest should take less than 5 minutes to administer. A concern with this subtest is the nature of half of the test items (numbers 6–10). On these test items, words differ only in their medial sound (e.g., *fear–far; bike–bake)* and thus, the rhyme judgment required may be particularly complex. Children who fail these items may nevertheless have sufficient rhyme knowledge.

Get It! Got It! Go!: Rhyming

Get It! Got It! Go! (Early Childhood Research Institute on Measuring Growth and Development, 1998, 2000) is a preschool screening and monitoring tool described by the authors as a "general outcome measure." It allows assessment of a child's current abilities and rate of development, because the measure can be administered repeatedly over short periods of time. The measure, individually administered, includes two phonological awareness tasks, Rhyming and Alliteration; it is available on the World Wide Web (http://ggg.umn.edu) free of charge. Get It! Got It! Go! was designed to identify 3- to 5-year-old children who are at risk and to monitor the effectiveness of intervention. This measure can be administered by teachers, paraprofessionals, and those trained in child development, including volunteers. Raw scores indicate the number of correct responses on each subtest. If one registers on the main Web site noted above, it is possible to create online graphs from local scores by collecting data from 30 to 50 children in a suitable comparison group. Educators type demographic and assessment information into a form provided on the Web page. This information can be used to create individual or group graphs. Although no specific benchmarks are provided for this test, these charts can be used to monitor children's progress over time. Each of the phonological awareness assessment tasks can be administered in 5 minutes or less.

On the Rhyming task, for each test item, a card is presented with a target picture at the top and three additional pictures in a row on the bottom. The examiner names the pictures and asks the child to point to the picture at the bottom that rhymes with the target picture. There are 2 sample items that orient the child to the task and 54 test items. The child is taught the task with six items. The examiner demonstrates the task with sample items 1 and 2. Four additional items (presented as items 3 through 6), selected randomly from the tests items, are presented and a child response is elicited. For items 3 and 4, feedback is provided to the child regarding response accuracy. No feedback is provided for items 5 and 6. If the child passes two items in items 3 through 6, the remainder of the test is administered. Up to 50 test items are presented in 2 minutes. The raw score is a sum of any of items 3 through 6 answered correctly as well as the number of correct responses provided in the 2 minutes.

Rhyme Awareness Subtest of the Phonological Awareness Literacy Screening—PreKindergarten

The Phonological Awareness and Literacy Screening—PreKindergarten (PALS-PreK; Invernizzi, Sullivan, Meier, & Swank, 2004) was designed to identify children who have inadequate early literacy skills and to inform the nature of instruction that occurs within the classroom. It is appropriate for preschoolers and for children who may begin kindergarten with very minimal phonological awareness skills. The PALS-PreK can be administered by classroom teachers as well as other professionals, such as speech-language pathologists. Administration of the entire PALS-PreK takes 20 to 25 minutes. The test is available in English.

The Rhyme Awareness subtest includes 10 test items. For each item, children are shown four pictures, a target picture and three additional pictures (e.g., *cat*, followed by *hat, whale, ring*). The examiner names the pictures and asks the child to identify which of the three additional pictures rhymes with the target picture. One point is awarded for each correct response. The authors provide a benchmark to interpret 4-year-old children's performance. In the spring of a 4-year-old class, the benchmark is 5 to 7 points. Raw scores can be converted into age-equivalent scores.

The Phonological Awareness Literacy Screening—Kindergarten (PALS-K; Invernizzi, Juel, Swank, & Meier, 2005) was created both to inform classroom practice and to identify kindergarten children whose early literacy development is deficient as compared to same-grade peers. This measure can be administered by classroom teachers as well as other professionals. Two subtests, Rhyme Awareness and Beginning Sound Awareness, allow for either group administration or individual administration. The remaining subtests are administered individually. Three subtests tap children's phonological awareness: Rhyme Awareness, Beginning Sound Awareness, and Spelling. This test, available in English, is untimed; administration time is approximately 20 minutes per child.

The Rhyme Awareness subtest follows the same format as the Rhyme Awareness subtest on the PALS-PreK. The total possible raw score is 10 points. The authors provide fall and spring benchmarks to interpret children's performance. The fall benchmark is 5 points and the spring benchmark is 9 points. Thus, task mastery is expected by the end of kindergarten.

Rhyme Awareness Subtest of the Pre-Reading Inventory of Phonological Assessment

The Pre-Reading Inventory of Phonological Awareness (PIPA; Dodd, Crosbie, McIntosh, Teitzel, & Ozanne, 2003) is described by the authors as "a research-based, individually administered, norm-referenced diagnostic test " (p. 1). Although the primary use of this instrument is diagnostic, the authors suggest it can be used as an "outcomes-based measure" (p. 1). The PIPA, available only in English, has normative data on children 4 years, 0 months through 6 years, 11 months. It can be administered by trained professionals (e.g., speech-language pathologists, teachers) or paraprofessionals under appropriate supervision. There are six subtests, five of which tap phonological awareness knowledge. One can choose to administer all or only some of the subtests. If a child does not respond or responds incorrectly to the trial items for a particular subtest, that subtest should not be administered. There are ceilings for each subtest as well. Administration of each subtest is estimated at 4 to 5 minutes and administration of the entire test at 25 to 30 minutes.

There is no composite score for the PIPA. Rather, for each subtest, to compare an individual's performance to same age peers, the raw score is assigned a *percentile range* (e.g., 40–44th percentile). There is no use of standard scores. The use of percentile ranges is unique to this instrument; the authors do not explain the use of percentile range rather than rank but likely it is an artifact of the statistical analysis of the normative data.

The authors of the PIPA designate percentile ranges to three categories of achievement: *emerging/below basic* (0 to 30th percentile range), *basic* (30th to 70th percentile range), and *proficient* (70th to 100th percentile range). They suggest that all children scoring below the 40th percentile should receive "targeted instructional intervention." Users of this instrument are cautioned about the authors' nontraditional interpretation of percentile performance—the interpretation is more akin to a criterion-referenced test than a norm-referenced test—as well as floor and ceiling effects for some subtests and ages.

The PIPA includes one subtest of rhyme judgment, Rhyme Awareness. For each of the 12 items, the child is shown 4 pictures that are named by the examiner and the child is asked to point to or name the nonrhyming word. The subtest word stimuli are likely to be familiar to preschool children.

Detecting Thymes Subtest of the Phonemic Awareness in Young Children: A Classroom Curriculum: Assessment Test

Phonemic Awareness in Young Children: A Classroom Curriculum (PAYC; Adams, Foorman, Lundberg, & Beeler, 1998) includes a criterion-referenced assessment of the phonological awareness skills targeted in this kindergarten curriculum. The criterion-referenced measure includes six subtests, each with five items, which can be used to assess performance at the outset of instruction and to monitor children's response to instruction (e.g., every 2 months). Because the instrument is a paper-pencil measure, it can be administered to small groups of about six kindergarten children. Only raw scores can be obtained (i.e., no percentile ranks or standard scores). There is no reported information on the psychometric properties of this measure; thus, the measure should be conceptualized as informal.

One subtest evaluates children's rhyme judgment abilities, Detecting Rhymes. In presenting the demonstration items, the examiner provides some explanation about rhymes and examples to orient the child to the task. For the test items, each child has a page with 10 pictures. They are instructed to match each picture in the column on the left to a rhyming picture, by drawing a line between pictures. Before the children begin the task, the examiner names all the pictures. In total, children can identify five rhyming pairs, with one point awarded for each correct response (maximum of 5 points).

Rhyming-Discrimination Subtest of the Phonological Awareness Test

The Phonological Awareness Test (PAT; Robertson & Salter, 1997) is an individually administered, norm-referenced adaptation of an earlier published criterion-referenced instrument by the same authors, The Phonological Awareness Profile (Robertson & Salter, 1995). The PAT, available only in English, includes subtests that evaluate phonological awareness as well as subtests that measure phoneme-grapheme correspondence. Although the primary purpose of the PAT is diagnostic, it may have some use as a screening tool or for measuring outcomes. This measure, administered individually by a trained professional (e.g., speech-language pathologist or special educator), is designed for children ages 5 to 9 (kindergarten through second grade). It is not appropriate for preschool children.

In total there are eight subtests and each subtest consists of two or more tasks. Each task is administered in its entirety. An age-equivalent score, percentile rank, and standard score can be derived from the raw score for each task, each subtest, and for the total test. The composite score for the total test involves children's phonological awareness and sound-symbol knowledge; there is no composite score for just the phonological awareness subtests. Administration time for the entire instrument is 40 minutes. Computerized scoring is available. It appears that selected subtests can be administered, although validity and reliability of individual subtests do not appear to have been clearly established (cf. Turkstra, 1999). For the youngest age groups (5;0–5;5 and 5;6–5;11), there are some concerns with floor effects.

Rhyme judgment is evaluated in one task on the Rhyming subtest, Rhyming Discrimination. For each of the 10 items, the examiner says two words aloud and the child is asked to indicate if the two words rhyme. There is no picture support to the task. There is one trial item to orient the child to the task.

Rhyme Judgment Task

Ball (1993) provided a rhyme judgment task adapted from Lenel and Cantor's research (1981) with 4- to 6-year-old children. For each item, children are shown three pictures that are named by the examiner and asked to indicate which two words rhyme. There are two demonstration items that orient the child to the task. The unique aspect of this experimental measure is that the 27 items are divided into 5 stimulus categories that presumably relate to task complexity: no common phonemes, initial common phoneme, medial common phoneme, final common phoneme, and two common phonemes. By differentiating type of stimuli, this measure could yield detailed information on the level of rhyme knowledge for an individual child.

Measuring Rhyme Production

Although still only a simple phonological awareness task, rhyme production measures require more phonological awareness than rhyme judgment measures. Typically the child is given a word and asked to generate one or more words that rhyme with the target word. In rhyme judgment tasks, chance performance is involved (i.e., a child can just guess correctly). In contrast, in a rhyme production task, it is unlikely a child will be consistently successful without clear knowledge of rhyme. Children may produce real words or nonsense words as rhymes.

The Abecedarian Reading Assessment: Rhyming Production

General information about the Abecedarian can be found in the rhyme judgment section. Similar to the rhyme awareness measure, three practice items orient the child to the task. The test items include 10 words. For each of the 10 test items, the examiner says a word (e.g., hall) and the child is asked to provide two additional words that rhyme with the target word. Credit is given for nonsense word rhymes (e.g., *nall, zall*) and real word rhymes (e.g., *ball, fall*). Passing criteria is set at eight correct items. Testing should be discontinued if a child does not correctly answer at least half of the initial five test items. If a child is not able to pass this measure, then an easier subtest on the measure, Rhyme Perception, can be administered.

PALS-PREK: Nursery Rhyme Awareness

General information about the PALS-PreK can be found in the rhyme judgment section. Rhyme production is measured on the Nursery Rhyme Awareness subtest. Teachers read aloud common nursery rhymes (e.g., *Twinkle Twinkle Little Star, Baa Baa Black Sheep*) and the child is asked to say the last word of the nursery rhyme (e.g., *Three four. Shut the _____*). There are 10 items on this subtest. The designated spring benchmark for a 4-year-old classroom is 6 or more points (maximum of 10 points). This subtest involves memory for nursery rhymes and, as such, may not be a clear indication of the more advanced rhyme skill of rhyme production.

PAT: Rhyming-Production

General information about the PAT can be found in the rhyme judgment section. In the Rhyming subtest, the Production task requires a child to generate a rhyme word for 10 target words provided by the examiner. Real word or nonsense word rhymes are acceptable answers.

Segmentation of Words Into Syllables

Awareness of syllable boundaries in words emerges early in the sequence of phonological awareness development, perhaps concurrently with the emergence of rhyme. The early emergence of awareness of syllable boundaries relates to the clarity and reality of syllable boundaries; the same is not true for phonemes. That is, phonemes are not discrete units within a syllable, rather the production of phonemes within a syllable overlaps. One sound influences how another sound in the syllable is produced. For example, in *tan* the vowel sound has a nasal quality, influenced by the syllable final nasal sound /n/, whereas the same vowel in *bat* does not have that nasal quality. The important point is that syllables are discrete, easily separated units of speech, phonemes are not.

When we measure children's ability to segment words into syllables, we are measuring whether children are aware and can take advantage of the natural break or divisions between syllables. Some tests include a measure of segmenting sentences into words (Robertson & Salter, 1997), but this task differs from segmenting words into syllables and requires word awareness as well as some phonological awareness (van Kleeck & Schuele, 1987). The two tasks would be comparable only if all the words in the sentence were monosyllabic words. Syllable segmentation is a simple phonological awareness task, tapping into surface level phonological awareness abilities.

PAT: Segmentation–Syllables

General information about the PAT can be found in the rhyme judgment section. The Syllables task on the Segmentation Subtest of the PAT includes 1 trial item that orients the child to the task and

10 test items. The examiner says a word and the child is asked to clap one time for each syllable in the word. Test items are one to four syllables in length.

PAYC Assessment Test: Counting Syllables

General information about the PAYC Assessment Test can be found in the rhyme awareness section. On the Counting Syllables measure, prior to administration of the demonstration and test items, the teacher or examiner demonstrates segmentation of one (e.g., *cat*), two (e.g., *bas-ket*), and three syllable words (e.g., *bas-ket-ball*) by clapping the number of syllables while saying the word. Two demonstration items orient the child to the task, which includes five test items. One point is awarded for each correct answer (possible 5 points). The task requires that the child look at a picture named by the examiner, figure out the number of syllables, and make one slash mark for each syllable. As noted above, this measure was designed for kindergarten children, and likely, the format would be difficult for a preschool child.

PIPA: Syllable Segmentation

General information about the PIPA can be found in rhyme judgment section. The PIPA includes one subtest, Syllable Segmentation, that evaluates a child's ability to segment words into syllables. Test items are two to five syllables in length. Test words are presented verbally by the examiner; no picture support is provided. Of the 4 trial words and 12 test words, it is unlikely that more than a few of these words will be in a child's lexicon. A substantial memory component is involved in this subtest. If a child cannot remember the word, which may be difficult when the word is unfamiliar to the child, then clearly the child cannot segment the word into syllables. This challenge is of substantial concern in that children who are likely to be at risk for reading disability are also likely to have poor phonological memory (Wagner, Torgesen, & Rashotte, 1994). If a child performs poorly on this subtest, it may not be immediately apparent whether the child is lacking phonological awareness or whether the child has poor phonological memory. Thus, we suspect that this subtest will *not* be very informative as to a child's phonological awareness.

Initial Sound Awareness and Segmentation

Awareness and segmentation of initial sounds in words is typically the first step in a child's ability to access subsyllabic units (i.e., phonemes). Some researchers have argued that awareness of the onset-rime boundary is easily acquired by children. Initial sound awareness tasks, requiring surface level phonological awareness, tap into a child's ability to compare and judge initial sounds of words. For example, a child might be asked to match words with the same beginning sound, judge whether two words begin with the same sound, or choose which of three words does not begin with the same sound. In contrast, initial sound segmentation tasks require more complex skills because they tap into a child's ability to explicitly isolate or segment the first sound in a word, for example, *Tell me the first sound in FISH*. A phoneme response is required.

To measure preschool and kindergarten children's awareness or segmentation of initial sounds, word stimuli should begin with single consonants (e.g., *top, sun*) rather than consonant blends (e.g., *stop, plum*). Analysis of the individual sounds in a blend is typically just emerging at the end of kindergarten. In all initial sound tasks, children will be more successful on words that begin with continuing sounds (e.g., *sun, van, foot*; continuing sounds can be produced by holding out or elongating the production of the sound, *sssssun*) as compared to stop sounds (e.g., *top, goat*). In addition, initial sound awareness or segmentation will be easier with monosyllabic word stimuli than multisyllablic words (e.g., *sun* will be easier than *Sunday*; Treiman & Weatherston, 1992). Also, words that begin with vowels may be more difficult for children than words that begin with consonants. Words that begin with vowels have no onset, just a rime (i.e., there are no sounds before the vowel). Isolating the onset seems to be easier than breaking apart the rime.

In this section, we describe measures that assess a child's awareness of initial sounds or their segmentation of initial sounds. Note that measures of initial sound *awareness* tap a less complex, earlier emerging skill than *segmentation* of initial sounds.

Categorization

Swank and Catts (1994) present an experimental task adapted from Bradley and Bryant's (1983) research with preschool children. Children are presented with four spoken words, three with the same initial sound, and asked to indicate the word that does not belong (e.g., *mouse, moon, door, mop*). This format is often referred to as an odd-one-out task. Concern has often been expressed about the memory component of this task if picture support is not provided. Bradley and Bryant as well as others have found this task to differentiate between preschool children with more or less phonological awareness. The format of this task has also been used to measure awareness of rhymes and awareness of final sounds. On the Swank and Catts version of this odd-one-out task, a raw score is summed from all correct responses.

Dynamic Indicators of Basic Early Literacy Skills: Initial Sounds Fluency

The Dynamic Indicators of Basic Early Literacy Skills (DIBELS; Good & Kaminski, 2002) is a criterion-referenced instrument in English that is available online at http://dibels.uoregon.edu/. A Spanish version is underway. DIBELS is widely used with school-age children. It is an individually administered measure, with each subtest timed. The DIBELS subtests can be used for diagnostic, progress monitoring, and outcomes measurement. Two subtests measure phonological awareness at the kindergarten level, Initial Sounds Fluency and Phonemic Segmentation Fluency. Each subtest takes only a few minutes to administer by a trained examiner. For each subtest, a child's raw score can be compared to grade level benchmarks (beginning, mid, end of year) to interpret performance and determine the need for intervention. Performance across all subtests is used to assign a child to an instructional need level: intensive, strategic, benchmark. There are multiple forms of each subtest, which allow repeated testing for progress monitoring (e.g., every few weeks).

The Initial Sound Fluency task on DIBELS measures a child's awareness of initial sounds. There are two types of items: (a) choosing one of four pictures that begins with a sound given by the examiner and (b) saying the beginning sound for a word spoken by the examiner. The examiner administers as many test items as the child can respond to in one minute. The raw score is the total number of correct items. Benchmarks are established for the beginning and middle of kindergarten; mastery of the task is expected by mid kindergarten.

Get It! Got It! Go!: Alliteration

General information about Get It! Got it! Go! can be found in the rhyme awareness section. The Alliteration measure on Get It! Got It! Go! evaluates preschool children's awareness of initial sounds of words. Similar in format to the Get It! Got It! Go! Rhyming task, for each alliteration test item, the child is presented with a card with one picture at the top and three additional pictures in a row at the bottom. The examiner names the first picture, and then names the remaining pictures, asking the child to point to the picture that "starts with the same sound as [says name of first picture]." There are 2 sample items that orient the child to the task and 44 test items. The child is taught the task with 6 items. The examiner demonstrates the task with sample items 1 and 2. Four additional items (presented as items 3 through 6), selected randomly from the tests items, are presented and a child response is elicited. For items 3 and 4, feedback is provided to the child regarding his or her response accuracy. No feedback is provided for items 5 and 6. If the child passes two items in items 3 through 6, testing proceeds. In 2 minutes, the child is presented with the remaining test items (up to 40). The raw score is a sum of any of items 3 through 6 answered correctly as well as the number of correct responses provided in the 2 minutes. The words used in this measure are highly likely to be in the lexicon of preschool children.

PALS-PreK: Beginning Sound Awareness

General information about the PALS-PreK is provided in the rhyme judgment section. The Beginning Sound Awareness subtest on the PALS-PreK assesses preschoolers' ability to segment the initial sound of words. Four practice items are used to orient the child to the task. These practice items can be repeated until the child has learned the task. There are 10 test items. The examiner shows a picture to the child, names the picture emphasizing the beginning sound, and asks the child to say the initial sound of the word. Corrective feedback is given for the practice items and also for all test items as indicated. In addition, examiners are encouraged to help children group items according to their beginning sounds (e.g., *man* and *mop*), although no additional points are given for these groupings. The raw score, total number correct, is interpreted relative to the benchmark; for a 4-year-old classroom, the spring benchmark is 5 to 8 points.

PALS-K: Beginning Sound Awareness

General information on the PALS-K is provided in the rhyme awareness section. The PALS-K includes a subtest of initial sound awareness, Beginning Sound Awareness. In this 10-item task, the examiner lays out 4 header pictures, and asks the child to match 10 additional pictures, based on the initial sound, to 1 of the 4 header pictures. The child is not required to segment the initial sound of the words, only to match words based on initial sound. When presenting the header pictures, the examiner names the pictures, emphasizing the initial sound of each word. For each test word, the adult names the picture and the child repeats the name of the picture before matching the picture. Child responses are scored as correct or incorrect and the total number correct is tallied. Chance (25%) does factor into a child's score on this task. We have observed some children, who have little awareness of initial sounds, respond by matching the pictures sequentially to the header pictures. The subtest raw score is interpreted relative to the established benchmark of 5 points at the beginning and 9 points at the end of kindergarten. Thus, young kindergartners are expected to show some skill, whereas at the end of kindergarten mastery of this task is expected.

Test of Phonological Awareness—2+: Initial Sounds, Kindergarten Version

The Test of Phonological Awareness—Second edition: Plus (TOPA-2+; Torgesen & Bryant, 2004) is a measure of phonological awareness that includes two versions, Kindergarten and Early Elementary. This paper-pencil measure, available only in English, can be administered individually, to small groups of children, or to classroom groups, in about 30 to 45 minutes. We summarize only the Kindergarten version. The authors recommend that only trained professionals administer the TOPA-2+. According to the authors, the TOPA-2+ "is an economical means of identifying children who are relatively delayed in their development of phonological awareness" (p. 1) and "who are in need of special or supplemental training or support to accelerate their growth in phonemic awareness" (p. 4). The authors also suggest that the instrument may have use in research. The TOPA-2+, Kindergarten version has two subtests, Initial Sounds and Letter Sounds. Each subtest is scored separately and no composite score can be derived. We discuss only the Initial Sounds subtest.

The Initial Sounds subtest includes 20 items. In the first 10 test items, which are preceded by 3 trial items to orient the child to the task, children are asked to identify pictured words with the same initial sound. Each child has a response booklet that he or she marks. For each item, the child views a row of four pictures. The examiner labels the first picture in the row, and then the remaining pictures. The examiner asks the children to "Mark the one picture that begins with the same sound as [name of first picture]." Feedback is provided only on the three trial items. In the final 10 test items (which are also preceded by three trial items), children are asked to identify which of four pictured words begins with a different sound. The format of testing is identical to the first 10 items, but the examiner asks the child to "Mark the one that has a different first sound than the other three" (p. 11). The raw score is the total number of correct on the 20 items of the test.

The TOPA-2+, Kindergarten version, is recommended for use in the second half of kindergarten, presumably after children have received some school-based instruction in phonological awareness. Norm-referenced, age-based comparisons can be made for children between the ages of 5;0 and 6;11, in four 6-month age intervals. From the raw score, one can assign a percentile rank and several types of standard scores. Educators and clinicians will be most familiar with typical standard scores, called an "ability score." An examination of the normative data raises one concern. Because the comparisons are made in 6-month intervals (e.g., 5;0 to 5;5 and 5;6 to 5;11), there are substantial shifts in performance between age intervals, particularly in the first three intervals, 5;0 to 5;5, 5;6 to 5;11, and 6;0 to 6;5. For example, for a child at 5 years, 5 months, a raw score of 8 would yield a percentile rank of 35 (Ability Score = 90), but for a child at 5 years, 6 months, the same raw score of 8 would yield a percentile rank of 14 (Ability Score = 84). The child of 5;5 would be judged as performing within the expected range, whereas a child of 5;6 would be judged as outside the expected range.

In the design of this instrument, the authors paid careful attention to the word stimuli used. They note that the test words are highly likely to be in the lexicon of kindergarten children and that the phonemes in the test words would be mastered in the speech production or articulation of nearly all kindergarten age children. Only monosyllabic words are included in this instrument. This deliberate attention to test stimuli addressed in the TOPA:2 is not addressed in most other measures or instruments, unfortunately.

PAT: Isolation—Initial Sounds

General information about the PAT can be found in the rhyme awareness section. The Isolation subtest of the PAT includes three tasks, one of which is isolation of initial sounds. There are 10 test items on this task. In addition, one demonstration item orients the child to the task. For each item, the examiner says a word and asks the child "to tell me the beginning or first sound in the word." The test items include monosyllabic and polysyllabic stimuli that are likely to be in the lexicon of kindergarten children.

PIPA: Sound Isolation

General information about the PIPA can be found in the rhyme judgment section. The PIPA subtest, Sound Isolation, evaluates a child's ability to segment the initial sounds of words. Two trial items orient the child to the task (e.g., *apple, ball*). For each of the 12 test items, the examiner verbally presents a word and asks the child to indicate the first sound in the word. There is no picture support for test items, although the training items include picture support. Testing is discontinued if a child misses four consecutive items.

This measure may underestimate a young child's phonological awareness because of the nature of the task, the characteristics of the stimuli, and the ordering of the stimuli. For children with poor verbal/phonological memory, the lack of picture support may indicate that memory limitations are a factor in poor performance. Of the 12 test items, 4 are multisyllabic words, 2 items begin with vowels, 3 items begin with consonant blends, and 3 test items begin with later developing speech sounds (e.g., /l/). The subtest stimuli do not appear to be ordered by complexity.

PAYC Assessment Test: Matching Initial Sounds

General information on the PAYC Assessment Test is given in the rhyme judgment section. The Matching Initial Sounds subtest is similar in format to the Detecting Rhymes subtest. Along with the demonstration items that orient the child to the task, the examiner provides an explanation of initial word sounds. In this paper-pencil task, children are asked to match picture pairs that begin with the same sound. The total possible points is five (five initial sound pairs) and the task can be completed in 5 minutes. As noted previously, this measure was designed for kindergarten children and the format may be difficult for preschool children.

Segmentation and Blending of Sounds in Words

The ability to segment words into sounds and blend sounds into words is a critical phonological awareness skill associated with early word decoding and spelling achievement. Children who do not understand that words are composed of sounds are more likely to have difficulty learning how speech sounds can be represented with print symbols (i.e., phonics, decoding). Both blending and segmenting sounds in words require skill at the level of phonemic awareness. Children are required to isolate individual speech sounds. A child who can segment words into sounds can produce all of the individual phonemes in the words. Thus for *ship*, the child would produce sh – i – p with a pause between each speech sound. A child who can blends sounds into words would produce "ship" in response to *Put these sounds together, sh – i – p. What word do you get?*

From a developmental perspective, the ability to blend sounds into words seems to be somewhat easier for children than segmenting (Torgesen, Morgan, & Davis, 1992), but these skills often are taught as reciprocal skills. Typically, children successfully segment and blend words that have continuing consonant sounds, such as *fish* or *sun,* before words that have stop consonant sounds, such as *cat* or *beep.* Segmenting and blending words with consonant blends (e.g., *skip, fast*) requires more advanced skill than segmenting CVC (C = consonant, V = vowel) or CV or VC words. We would not expect preschool children to be able to segment or blend words with consonant blends. At the end of kindergarten, some children may show beginning success at this advanced level of segmentation and blending. Although we typically think of segmentation and blending as a skill that cuts across speech sounds, a few speech sounds appear to be more difficult due to the nature of the sounds (see Ladefoged, 2005; Moats, 2000). For example, vowels may be more difficult to segment than consonants because consonants provide more articulatory feedback (e.g., specific place where the tongue is placed). The consonant sounds of /l/ and /r/ may be difficult for children to segment and blend because the sounds are later developing speech sounds, but more importantly, because /l/ and /r/ are not true consonants when they occur at the end of a syllable (e.g., *car, ball*) or in a syllable final blend (e.g., *old*). We would like to see assessment and instructional materials not include word stimuli with /l/ and /r/.

Phoneme segmentation and blending are complex phonological awareness skills that require a deep level of phonological awareness. Typically, we would not expect preschool curricula to include phoneme segmentation and blending to the extent that mastery is expected. However, preschool curricula or intervention programs (e.g., van Kleeck et al., 1998) might introduce these activities to begin to stimulate emergence of segmenting and blending phonemes (cf. Ukrainetz, 2006; Ukrainetz, Cooney, Dyer, Kysar, & Harris, 2000). Preschool children may not be ready for these activities, particularly those at risk for reading disabilities (e.g., low SES children, children with language impairments). In contrast, kindergarten curricula will include substantial focus on phoneme segmentation and blending. Also, kindergarten children who struggle to acquire these skills may be engaged in intensive small group interventions (e.g., Blachman, Ball, Black, & Tangel, 2000; Schuele & Dayton, 2000). Thus, assessment of blending and segmenting will be unlikely with preschool children but common with kindergarten children.

DIBELS: Phoneme Segmentation Fluency

General information about DIBELS can be found in the initial sound awareness and segmentation section. The Phonemic Segmentation Fluency (PSF) subtest measures a child's ability to segment words into phonemes. All test stimuli are monosyllables. For each item, the examiner says the test word aloud and the child breaks the word into sounds. Credit is given for any subsyllabic unit provided by the child, thus allowing the awarding of partial credit for individual words. For example, if *cat* is broken into three sounds, then three points are awarded. But if *cat* is broken into two parts, /c/ and /at/, two points are awarded. The test is administered for 1 minute and the child responds to as many test items as possible in that 1 minute. The raw score is the sum of points awarded for each word.

PALS-K: Spelling

General information on the PALS-K can be found in the rhyme judgment section. On the PALS-K there is not a measure of sound segmentation that is purely a measure of phonemic awareness. Rather the PALS-K includes a spelling measure that taps children's phoneme segmentation abilities and their ability to represent phonemes with print symbols (letters). Stahl and Murray (1994) argued that measures of developmental spelling or invented spelling are good measures of phonemic awareness because they make fewer demands on children's memory than a purely spoken phoneme segmentation task. Nevertheless, it is important to recognize that a spelling measure taps phonological awareness as well as letter-sound knowledge.

On the PALS-K, children are asked to spell five CVC words (e.g., *top*). Their responses are scored for logical representation of speech sounds (15 points) and an additional point is awarded for a correct spelling (5 points) for a total of 20 points. So, for example, a child who spells *van* as *vn* would get two points. The test authors provide benchmarks for fall (2 points) and spring (12 points) of kindergarten. Thus, little skill is expected in the fall but the spring benchmark suggests that children should have advanced segmentation skills, albeit still developing.

PIPA: *Sound Segmentation and Blending*

General information about the PIPA can be found in the rhyme judgment section. One subtest on the PIPA, Sound Segmentation, evaluates a child's ability to segment words into sounds. Because the child is required to isolate and produce individual phonemes in words, the task taps a child's phonemic awareness. There are 4 training items that orient the child to the task and 12 test items. The training items include a CV, two CVC and one CVCV word. Recall that if a child is not successful on the training items then the subtest should not be administered. For each test item, the examiner says the word aloud and asks the child to say the individual phonemes in the word. Although picture support is provided for the training items, the test items do not have picture support. Target words, however, are likely to be known by most 4-year-olds. The response for each word is scored for complete accuracy; thus to receive credit, the child must correctly segment the words into all of its phonemes as no partial credit is given. This manner of scoring could underestimate a child's skill, particularly when the ability to segment is just emerging. On this subtest of the PIPA, if the child has four consecutive errors, the subtest is discontinued (i.e., ceiling).

There are some concerns with the word stimuli on this subtest. First, two items include final /r/ and one includes initial /r/. Words with /r/ or /ə/ (*father*) or /ɜ/ (*her*) will be difficult for many children to segment, particularly preschool children. These phonemes are later developing and many children in preschool and kindergarten will have developmental articulation errors on /r/. Moreover, the features of these phonemes make them difficult to segment (Ladefoged, 2005; Moats, 2000). Second, the 12 test words do not appear to be arranged developmentally and the technical manual provides no explanation for the sequence of test items. A developmental arrangement of test stimuli would include initial test items that include continuing phonemes (e.g., *fan, mice*); CV (*me*), VC (*up*), and CVC (*bat*) words should appear before words with consonant clusters or blends (*stop, jump*). Third, the percentile range assignments, for raw scores indicates that for children between 4:0 and 5;11, floor effects are an issue. That is, children will obtain a percentile score within an acceptable range if their raw score is 0, 1, or 2 points. Thus, for identifying which children are poor in phoneme segmentation, the test will be most informative when children have reached 6 years, 0 months of age or older.

Phonological Awareness Subtest of the Test of Preschool Early Literacy

The Test of Preschool Early Literacy (TOPEL; Lonigan et al., in press) is a soon to be published instrument; extensive work and years of research have contributed to the development of this test. Because it is not yet published, limited information is available. We include the TOPEL as it is likely to garner much attention when published. The TOPEL will be available in English and takes approximately 30 minutes to conduct in its entirety. It is appropriate for children from 3;0 to 5;11. The TOPEL is designed to identify preschoolers with underdeveloped emergent literacy, to monitor preschoolers' literacy achievement over time, and can be used as an outcome measure in research projects. It can be individually administered by teachers, psychologists, parents, and paraprofessionals. The TOPEL is norm-referenced; thus, raw scores will yield standard scores and percentile ranks.

The phonological awareness subtest measures children's segmentation and blending skills in one subtest, Phonological Awareness. Phoneme segmentation abilities are measured in an elision task, for example, *Say cat. Now say cat without the /k/.* Many researchers have employed elision tasks to measure segmentation abilities in young children (e.g., Catts et al., 2002), presumably because a high degree of reliability across examiners can be achieved (cf. Wagner, Torgesen, & Rashotte, 1999).

PAYC Assessment Measure: Counting Phonemes

General information on the PAYC measure can be found in the rhyme awareness section. The Counting Phonemes task on the PAYC follows a format similar to the Counting Syllables task. The task is introduced by the examiner with two demonstration items and accompanying explanation. The examiner administers the five items by naming each picture and asking the children to indicate the number of sounds in each word with slash marks. The two demonstration items include a CV and CVC word, and the five test words include a CV, two CVC, and two words with blends (CCVC, CVCC).

PAT: *Segmentation and Blending*

General information on the PAT can be found in the rhyme judgment section. There is a phoneme segmentation task in the Segmentation subtest, Phonemes, as well as a Phonemes task on the Blending subtest. In the Segmentation—Phonemes task, the examiner says a word and asks the child to produce the individual sounds in each word. Test stimuli include monosyllabic and polysyllabic words. The initial four items are simple words (CV, VC, CVC) and the remainder are multisyllabic or include blends.

Dynamic Assessment Measures of Phonological Awareness

Because phonological awareness is a developing skill in preschool and kindergarten, static measures, such as those described thus far, may provide a limited view of a child's abilities. Consider that two children who receive the same low raw score on a static measure may have very different underlying abilities. One child may indeed have little skill whereas the other child may have some skill that is not accessed in a static measure. A dynamic assessment measure, thus, may provide more information about a child's ability, particularly instructionally relevant information (see Feuerstein, Rand, & Hoffman, 1979; Lidz, 1987; Lidz & Pena, 1996; Schneider & Watkins, 1996). In a dynamic assessment measure, interest is not simply in the child's independent responses. Rather, the examiner provides varying degrees of support to explore how the child's performance can be improved beyond the child's independent response level. Children who show responsiveness to support are considered to have greater ability than children who are not responsive to support.

Spector (1992) described a dynamic assessment task to explore children's phoneme segmentation skills. Although this task is not appropriate for preschool children, we briefly describe the format to provide educators with insight into how they might design a dynamic assessment task for other phonological awareness skills. Briefly, in Spector's measure, the child is initially prompted to segment a word into sounds with no support. If the child is not successful, the examiner moves through six levels of increasing support until the child achieves success. There are a total of 12 test items. The child's responses indicate (a) the level of support he or she needed to be successful and (b) the extent to which the child seems to "catch on" to the task, as evidenced by success on individual items with less support testing proceeds.

Instruments That Measure Multiple Aspects of Phonological Awareness

In the preceding sections, we described a number of tools that assess various aspects of phonological awareness within particular tasks or within subtests of an omnibus measure. In some instances, the measure is exclusively or primarily focused on phonological awareness; in other cases, the instrument taps phonological awareness as well as other aspects of emergent literacy. A few instruments are available that do not employ a subtest format or that assess several aspects of phonological awareness within one subtest. Because these instruments are well designed, easily available, and/or commonly used, we include them here.

Get Ready to Read! Screening Tool

The Get Ready to Read! Screening Tool (GRTR; Whitehurst & Lonigan, 2001) was developed to screen preschool children's early literacy skills in the year prior to kindergarten. The screening tool can be administered up to three times per year. It is administered online with an adult and child seated at the computer. The instrument (and supporting materials) can be found at http://www.getready toread.org/. GRTR initially was developed in English but a Spanish translation is available online as well. The child's responses are scored automatically and the examiner receives an immediate report on the child's performance. This screening tool can be administered in approximately 10 minutes and has 20 items that sample children's print knowledge, emergent writing knowledge, and phonological awareness. All items must be administered and the child points to one of four picture plates that matches a question or statement read by the examiner. Across the test, there are seven items that involve phonological awareness, including two initial sound items, one rhyme item, three blending items, and one deletion item. Based on the results of the screening tool, the Web site offers appropriate emergent literacy activities that are matched to a child's developmental level. The ease of access to this instrument is one of its greatest advantages and parents or teachers can easily administer the GRTR screening to children.

Special Considerations for Assessing Phonological Awareness

Educators must address the assessment needs of a diverse population of preschool children. Special consideration must be given to the needs of children who are English second language learners, children who are bilingual or multilingual, and children with developmental disabilities. In addition, in other countries, educators may wish to assess the phonological awareness skills of young children who speak languages other than English. In this section, we first address considerations for assessing children who are learning English as a second language or who are multilingual or bilingual, and then we consider the assessment of phonological awareness in nonalphabetic script languages. Lastly, we make assessment considerations for children with developmental disabilities (e.g., speech-language impairments, mental retardation, cerebral palsy).

Special Considerations for Linguistic Diversity

Given the diverse population of children in early childhood education, preschool teachers and speech-language pathologists frequently encounter situations where they need to assess and foster phonological awareness in children whose first language is not

English. Sometimes these children are instructed in their own language as well as English; in other instances, children may encounter only English instruction in school. Teachers of preschool children in non-English-speaking countries seek to foster children's phonological awareness as well. Although the majority of phonological awareness research has focused on children who speak English, there is increasing information on children who speak languages other than English. The development of phonological awareness for linguistically diverse children is likely influenced by the characteristics of the speech sounds in a given language. In addition, learning more than one language may influence the development of metalinguistic skills, including phonological awareness.

Development of Phonological Awareness in Bilingual or Multilingual Children

Children who are bilingual (two languages) or multilingual (more than two languages) learn to communicate in more than one linguistic system. Children can be equally proficient in more than one language, or more typically, their proficiency in one language may be superior to the other language(s) being learned.

Overall, it seems that young children who are learning more than one language have an advantage over monolingual children on measures of phonological awareness (Bialystok, McBride-Chang & Luk, 2005; Mumtaz & Humphreys, 2001; Stewart, 2004; Yelland, Pollard & Mercuri, 1993). Learning different languages appears to enhance young children's ability to focus on the structure of language separately from focusing on the meaning of language. Thus, educators should not regard bilingualism or multilingualism as a disadvantage in the acquisition of phonological awareness (Goswami & Martin, 2000). However, the advantage bilingualism confers for early phonological awareness development seems to disappear by early grade school when explicit instructional experiences have had a strong influence on all children's phonological awareness (Chen, Anderson, Li, Hao, Wu & Shu, 2004). Of interest is the extent to which a child's phonological awareness in one language transfers to phonological awareness in another language. If the child's two languages are similar in nature, then it seems reasonable to expect transfer across languages (Cho & McBride-Chang, 2005). The transfer may be less evident if the child's languages are dissimilar (Bialystok et al., 2003; Shanbal & Rao, in press; Stuart-Smith & Martin, 1997).

Phonological Awareness Assessment Considerations for Bilingual or Multilingual Children

Teachers of preschoolers are likely to wonder in which language a child's phonological awareness should be assessed. Should the child's phonological awareness be assessed only in English, especially if that is the language of instruction? Or should assessment include only the child's first language? Or should assessment be in both (all) languages? Do the answers to these questions differ for children who are struggling to acquire early literacy skills? Unfortunately, the extant literature does not provide definitive answers to any of these questions. However, it does point to a need to assess phonological awareness across languages (Karanth, 1992; Stuart-Smith & Martin, 1999; Whitehurst & Lonigan, 2001). However, few instruments are available to assess phonological awareness across languages. If educators have an understanding of the developmental sequence of phonological awareness and the various languages children speak, they may be able to formulate criterion referenced instruments that parallel published English criterion-referenced instruments. There have been recent attempts to develop measures of phonological awareness to suit bilingual populations (Invernizzi & Ford, in press; Stuart-Smith & Martin, 1999; Whitehurst & Lonigan, 2001).

When assessing phonological awareness in English, several considerations for linguistically diverse children can be made. First, directions to tasks can be given in the child's native language, to ensure that lack of task understanding is not the basis of a child's poor performance. Second, it may be helpful to provide trial items in the child's native language along with English trial items. A few test items in the child's native language may assure the examiner that the child understands the task, prior to the actual assessment. Third, as noted above, language-specific criterion-referenced instruments may be devised to parallel English tasks. Fourth, careful consideration of performance across children may help teachers and clinicians to understand the influence of language features and child characteristics. Fifth, meeting children's needs will be enhanced through careful collaboration between bilingual educators and monolingual educators.

Considerations for Assessing Phonological Awareness in Languages With Nonalphabetic Scripts

Phonological awareness is critical to understanding how speech maps to print in an alphabetic orthography such as English. The alphabetic symbols are used to represent the speech sounds, or phonemes, of English, although it is important to recognize that the morphology of words influences print representation as well (see Moats, 2000). In contrast, in languages with nonalphabetic scripts, phonological awareness may be less important to early reading success. If the orthography does not code at the level of speech sounds (e.g., logographic, syllabaries, semisyllabaries), the ability to analyze the sound structure of the language, particularly at the phoneme level, may not play such a large role in early reading success. Thus, it is important to consider the demands on phonological awareness that a particular writing system involves (Coulmas, 1989). Structural characteristics of different writing systems influence the relation between orthography, phonology, morphology, and meaning in processing written language.

Writing systems can be based primarily on morphemes (e.g., Chinese), syllables (e.g., Japanese and majority of the Indian languages), or phonemes (e.g., English). The specific relation between the oral language and the notational system requires different levels of phonological awareness in each of these systems to acquire decoding skills. Whereas Chinese character acquisition depends heavily on morpheme awareness, English word recognition depends primarily on phonological awareness, and the Indian letters, the semisyllabaries, require a combination of both syllables and phonemes. Different orthographies have different rules for mapping letters onto sounds and the consistency of such mappings in a given language is a major factor in how easily a child can learn to read and write.

This perspective has led to a significant increase in cross-linguistic research on children's reading (Goulandris, 2003). Research in the past two decades on nonalphabetic orthographies[1] has raised

---

[1] For example, see Mann, 1986 (Japanese); Cossu, Shankweiler, Liberman, and Katz., 1988 (Italian); Caravolas and Bruck, 1993 (Czech); Huang and Hanley, 1994 (Chinese: Mandarin and Cantonese); Prakash, Rekha, Nigam, and Karanth, 1993 (Indian language such as Hindu); Prema and Karanth, 2003 (Kannada).

many issues for examination, prominent among them being the significance of phonological awareness in learning to read different scripts. The majority of these studies have considered how children learn to read in two languages that are based on different writing systems. Studies on nonalphabetic orthographies such as Chinese, Japanese, and Indian languages have suggested that the phonological awareness that is so crucial for acquisition of reading in alphabetic orthographies is not so essential for nonalphabetic orthographies. On the contrary, it is reported that some phonological skills develop as a consequence of exposure to the alphabetic scripts in the course of learning to read English (and/or any other alphabetic script) in schools.

Recent studies comparing reading acquisition in different orthographic systems pointed out that factors such as the level of orthographic transparency of the alphabet of the language and the characteristics of the spoken language influence the acquisition of phonological awareness as well as literacy. Alphabetic orthographies, such as English, in which the correspondence between the grapheme and the phoneme is quite inconsistent and unpredictable, are treated as an opaque orthography whereas, in Spanish, the grapheme–phoneme correspondence rules are highly consistent and, hence, treated as having a shallow or transparent orthography (similarly the Italian, German, Serbo-Croatian, Portuguese, and majority of Indian languages).

Studies to examine the levels of phonological awareness in preliterate and literate Spanish-speaking preschoolers, kindergarteners, and first-grade children are reported by Goikoetxea (2005). He reported that the preliterate children found ending units easier than beginning units, syllables easier than onset–rime units, and onset–rime units easier than phoneme units. However, literate children were best at initial linguistic units, particularly initial syllables. Results support that the phonological awareness development is sensitive to degree of transparency of the orthographic units used by children from the time they begin to read.

The degree of transparency of orthography influences the degree of predictability of grapheme–phoneme correspondence rules, which in turn influences reading acquisition. Development of reading in transparent orthographies is generally faster as measured by nonword reading (Seymour, Aro, & Erskine, 2003) whereas the beginning readers of opaque orthography take a protracted period of time to acquire and automatize orthography-phonology mappings (Trieman, Mullennix, Bijeljac-Babic, & Richmond-Welty, 1995). Acquisition of reading in a shallow orthography (such as Dutch) is based on a single (alphabetic) process, whereas the acquisition of reading in deep orthography (such as English) requires the formation of a dual (alphabetic + logographic) foundation. Thus "learning under conditions where attention and processing resources are divided between two functions will occur more slowly than learning under conditions where all resources are focused on a single function" (Seymour et al., 2003, p. 168). Because the mappings between orthography and phonology in regular transparent orthographies are highly consistent, resources necessary are also minimal; hence, children learn to decode quickly in these languages. Karanth, Mathew, and Kurien (2004) suggest considering orthography-specific variables in understanding reading. Considering this evidence, it is advisable to employ alternate measures (such as automaticity, reading speed, rapid automatized naming) for assessment of reading in nonalphabetic scripts as phonological awareness may have less significance as a measure by itself.

Further, the levels of phonological awareness necessary for word recognition have been examined for a clearer picture of its associations with different languages that differ in scripts (Cho & McBride-Chang, 2005). Although it is expected theoretically that learning two languages facilitates the development of sensitivity to the structures of these languages, the reports suggest that only sustained and systematic instruction in first and second languages (English language learners) leads to conscious access to the formal characteristics. Taken together, the results underscore the importance of different levels of phonological awareness for understanding reading across scripts and that sensitivity to both orthography and phonology of English is essential to learning to read and spell English words and that neither construct by itself is sufficient.

Phonological awareness is an essential construct in literacy learning irrespective of the nature of scripts. However, the type and the levels of phonological awareness may vary depending on the nature of scripts. Studies in languages differing in their orthographic structures are broadly consistent with the view that the level of phonological awareness required for learning to read a particular orthography varies dependent on the specific features of the language and script. The majority of the studies also emphasize that not all types of phonological awareness skills are necessary for reading development in transparent languages as is the case of opaque languages. Further, there are very distinct patterns in the reading strategies such as automaticity, speed, and accuracy of reading; hence, certain measures are not applicable equally well as a measure of phonological awareness across all the scripts. Because reading builds on fundamentally different cognitive skills in different languages, the cognitive resources required for reading acquisition differ depending on the complexity of the phonological and orthographic structures of a language in question.

Special Considerations for Assessing Phonological Awareness in Children With Developmental Disabilities

It has been convincingly said over and over again that phonological awareness is an important skill for the acquisition of literacy skills. In the previous sections, influence of bilingualism and orthographic features on the acquisition of phonological awareness was discussed. Given the intricate relationship between oral language skills and phonological awareness, it is quite plausible that children with communication disorders (children with special needs) who generally lag behind same-age peers in their oral communication skills show deficits in phonological awareness, as a consequence of which they are likely to show deficits in the acquisition of literacy as well.

Considerations for Children With Speech and/or Language Impairments

Preschool children with language impairments, some of whom have concomitant speech disorders, are at high risk for reading disabilities (for a review, see Schuele, 2004). They are six to eight times more likely to have a reading disability than a child without language impairment (Catts, Fey, Tomblin, & Zhang, 2002). Children with language impairments show deficits in phonological awareness beginning in preschool (Boudreau & Hedberg, 1999; Kamhi, Lee, & Nelson, 1985). Assessment of phonological awareness in these children can be challenging because of their low skill level.

Additionally, task characteristics may unduly influence the perform-ance of children with speech-language impairments. Receptive rather than productive tasks may be more valid, particularly for children whose speech is difficult to understand. Likewise tasks with fewer extraneous demands (e.g., low memory demands, mono-syllabic words rather than multisyllabic, inclusion of picture sup-port) may be more valid. It may be particularly important to have task stimuli that include familiar words. And it may be important for task stimuli to include only speech sounds that are in the child's speech repertoire (Foy & Mann, 2001).

Considerations for Children With Mental Retardation, Including Children With Down Syndrome

Children with mental retardation are a diverse group of children. For some children, mental retardation is associated with an identified syndrome, such as Down syndrome; for other children, typically children with mild mental retardation, there is no known cause of the cognitive impairment. Patterns of cognitive functioning vary across children with mental retardation, with some syndromes having very distinct profiles of deficit.

For all children with mental retardation, depressed function-ing across developmental domains influences educational achieve-ment. Although we expect literacy development to be slowed in children with mental retardation, most children with mental retar-dation will develop some level of literacy skill. Researchers have suggested that the skills we know to be important for literacy acquisition in children with typical cognitive skills will also be important for children with cognitive deficits. Thus, in preschool and kindergarten, we are likely to assess the phonological aware-ness skills of children with mental retardation in the same way as their typical peers.

If the development of phonological awareness relates to over-all language achievement, we can expect the phonological aware-ness skills of preschool and kindergarten children with mental retardation to be depressed relative to their typical peers. Further, other skills closely related to phonological awareness (e.g., phono-logical memory) may be particularly problematic for children with cognitive deficits (Conners, Rosenquist, & Sligh, 2001). The goal of assessment likely will be to determine whether phonological awareness skills are emerging for these children (rather than mastery). As such, measures that are sensitive to emerging skills (i.e., simple tasks) and that are sensitive to subtle changes in ability will be most informative.

For children with Down syndrome, assessment of phonological awareness may be particularly challenging because their oral language skills are more deficient than would be predicted by their overall cognitive deficits. Their language deficits may present particular challenges to assessment and to understanding their performance on phonological awareness tasks. Some authors (Cossu, Rossini, & Marshall, 1993) have argued that phonological awareness may be less important to early reading acquisition for children with Down syndrome, but this is not a universally held view (Cupples & Iacono, 2000; Gombert, 2002). Some phonological awareness measures may be less sensitive for children with Down syndrome (Cupples & Iacono, 2000).

In summary, for preschool and kindergarten children with cognitive impairments, teachers will want to choose measures that tap early developing skills and are sensitive to small changes in ability. Task demands, particularly memory tasks demands, may be very important to consider. Additionally, given the intellectual and linguistic deficits of these children, teachers may want to be cautious in using tasks that are too complicated, for which the instructions are complex, or for which repetition is not allowed. Finally, demonstration items that clearly illustrate the task may be particularly important for children with cognitive impairments.

Special Considerations for Children With Cerebral Palsy

Assessment of children with motor impairments, for example, children with cerebral palsy, can be quite challenging. Preschool children with cerebral palsy, depending on severity, may have limited speech output, may rely on augmentative communication devices, and/or may have cognitive impairments. Although the development of literacy in this population is not well understood (e.g., Sandberg & Hjelmquist, 1997; Vandervelden & Siegel, 1999), there is agreement that it is essential to measure the underpinnings of literacy in these children if we are to advance their literacy skills. Below we consider the assessment of children with cerebral palsy who do not appear to have substantial cognitive impairment and for whom we might expect literacy to develop to more advanced levels.

One of the greatest challenges in assessing children with motor impairments is the design of tasks to which children can reliably respond. For many children with cerebral palsy, spoken responses are not possible and alternate modes of responding (e.g., pointing, yes/no response, eye gaze) are necessary. Communication devices may need to be programmed for response to specific assessment tasks. Also, the time taken for assessment should be considered. For example, if the child shows proficiency on a few items at a particular level, it may be best to proceed to a more complex task to gain additional information before the child fatigues. Designing valid and reliable measures for this special population will require that professionals pay careful attention to the range of sensory, motor, linguistic, and cognitive abilities of these children.

Special Considerations for Children With Hearing Loss

Proficient reading and writing skills have not been characteristic of children with hearing loss who wear hearing aids. However, with the technology of cochlear implants, literacy outcomes for children with hearing loss appear to be improving. Thus, increasingly, we may begin to expect preschool and kindergarten children with hearing loss or with cochlear implants (who do not have cognitive limitations) to have developing phonological awareness skills (Dillon & Pisoni, 2004; Dodd et al., 2003; Sterne & Goswami, 2000). Nevertheless, it is important to consider the nature and severity of the hearing loss. When assessing preschool children with hearing loss, begin with simple tasks and move to more complex tasks as proficiency is demonstrated. Be sure that hearing is optimized in the testing environment (e.g., minimize noise) and that the child's amplification system is working properly. In addition, one will need to consider the child's spoken language abilities, as well as the educational approach used with the child in order to get an accurate assessment of the child's phonological awareness abilities.

Interpreting the Results of Assessments of Phonological Awareness With Preschool and Kindergarten Children

The authors of each of the measures we have described provide some guidelines on the interpretation of children's performance. For the norm-referenced instruments, the primary interpretation of the results will be the child's performance relative to peers of the same age. Psychometricians caution about going beyond this level of interpretation with norm-referenced instruments as the design of the instrument is not intended for such interpretations. Regardless, as we noted previously in the initial section of this chapter, one substantial challenge with preschool norm-referenced phonological awareness instruments is simply using a nationally derived group mean as a source of comparison. Thus, when a child obtains a score below expectations, rather than assuming the child has a deficit per se and is impaired, professionals will first want to consider the nature and quantity of learning experiences that have been available to the child. What is a reasonable expectation for child performance, based on that experience?

With preschool and kindergarten children, the criterion-referenced instruments described may be more informative with respect to planning instruction and evaluating individual child progress. Criterion-referenced instruments with benchmarks associated with them help teachers understand where their children should perform after the provision of instructional experiences. For example, when using the PALS-K in a kindergarten phonological awareness project, the children who failed to make sufficient progress were clearly outliers. That is, their performance at the end of the year was very clearly deficient relative to the majority of their classroom peers (Schuele & Justice, 2004).

Recall that on a norm-referenced test, by definition some children will always fall below any identified "deficiency" cutoff. Thus, children who score low could in theory not be deficient but rather just lower in skill than their peers. They may nevertheless have a sufficient level of the skill of interest. On a criterion-referenced instrument, this issue is not a problem. The instrument has not been set up so that a portion of children will always score below the benchmark.

Criterion-referenced instruments that do not have benchmarks (or interpretation guidelines) can be challenging for educators to interpret. At what level should teachers expect their children to perform at various points of the year? At the beginning of the academic year, these measures inform teachers as to the skill level of children, without reference to the instructional experiences provided. That is, teachers do not have first-hand knowledge of the learning opportunities a child has had. As the year progresses, the measures inform as to which children are benefiting from instruction. If all children continue to score low on a measure, two considerations should be made. First, the instructional experiences may not be adequate. Maybe the children need more instruction. Maybe the learning activities are too complex. Maybe the teacher's instruction is not sufficiently supportive (Ukrainetz, 2006). Second, perhaps the measure chosen is not adequately capturing the change in children's knowledge and skills. We illustrate this important point in the next paragraph.

Let us assume that a teacher chose a phoneme segmentation measure for her 4-year-old classroom. There are 10 items and children must segment the whole word into sounds to obtain a point for each test item. At the outset of the year, nearly all children obtained 0 points. This did not surprise the teacher as she expected their phonological awareness skills to be low. Over the course of the school year, the teacher provides instruction targeted at rhyme and segmenting initial sounds. As a group, the children are becoming better at the instructional tasks. Midyear testing on the assessment instrument, however, reveals that few children have made any change in performance. Most children still score 0 on the measure. Unfortunately, in this case, the instrument the teacher chose to use is not sensitive to capturing the emerging phonological awareness skills of her 4-year olds. Measures of rhyme and initial sound awareness likely would have provided a much different picture of student progress. It is important for teachers to choose measures that are age and developmentally appropriate and relevant to the classroom instruction.

In conclusion, in this chapter, we have described a variety of instruments that can evaluate the phonological awareness skills of preschool and kindergarten children. As educators choose instruments to evaluate the emerging phonological awareness skills of children, it is essential to link the choice of instrument to the purpose of assessment. Norm-referenced instruments, in particular, may have limited value in informing the instruction of preschool and kindergarten children.

References

Adams, M., Foorman, B., Lundberg, I., & Beeler, T. (1998). *Phonemic awareness in young children: A classroom curriculum.* Baltimore: Paul H. Brookes.

Anthony, J., & Lonigan, C. (2004). The nature of phonological awareness: Converging evidence from four studies of preschool and early grade school children. *Journal of Educational Psychology, 96,* 43-55.

Anthony, J., Lonigan, C., Driscoll, K., Phillips, B., & Burgess, S. (2003). Phonological sensitivity: A quasi-parallel progression of word structure units and cognitive operation. *Reading Research Quarterly, 38,* 470-487.

Ball, E. (1993). Assessing phoneme awareness. *Language, Speech, and Hearing Services in Schools, 24,* 130-139.

Bialystok, E., Majumder, S. & Martin, M. M. (2003). Developing phonological awareness: Is there a bilingual advantage? *Applied Psycholinguistics, 24,* 27-44.

Bialystock, E., McBride-Chang, C., & Luk, G. (2005). Bilingualism, language proficiency, and learning to read in two writing systems, *Journal of Educational Psychology, 9,* 580-590.

Blachman, B. (1994). What we have learned from longitudinal studies of phonological processing and reading *and* some unanswered question: A response to Torgesen, Wagner, and Rashotte. *Journal of Learning Disabilities, 27,* 287-291.

Blachman, B., Ball, E., Black, R., & Tangel, D. (2000). *Road to the code: A phonological awareness program for young children.* Baltimore: Paul H. Brookes.

Boudreau, D., & Hedberg, N. (1999). A comparison of early literacy skills in children with specific language impairment and their typically developing peers. *American Journal of Speech-Language Pathology, 8,* 249-260.

Bradley, L., & Bryant, P. (1983). Categorizing sounds and learning to read—a causal connection. *Nature, 301*(3), 419-421.

Burgess, S. R., & Lonigan, C. J. (1998). Bidirectional relations of phonological sensitivity and prereading abilities: Evidence from a preschool sample. *Journal of Experimental Child Psychology, 70,* 117-141.

Byrne, B., & Fielding-Barnsley, R. (1991). Evaluation of a program to teach phonemic awareness to young children. *Journal of Educational Psychology*, *83*, 451-455.

Byrne, B., & Fielding-Barnsley, R. (1995). Evaluation of a program to teach phonemic awareness to young children: A 2- and 3-year follow-up and a new preschool trial. *Journal of Educational Psychology*, *87*, 488-503.

Caravolas, M., & Bruck, M. (1993). The effect of oral and written language input on children's phonological awareness: A cross-linguistic study. *Journal of Experimental Child Psychology*, *55*, 1-30.

Catts, H., Fey, M., Tomblin, J. B., & Zhang, X. (2002). A longitudinal investigation of reading outcomes in children with language impairments. *Journal of Speech, Language, and Hearing Research*, *45*, 1142-1157.

Catts, H., Fey, M., Zhang, X., & Tomblin, J. B. (2001). Estimating the risk of future reading difficulties in kindergarten children: A research-based model and its clinical implementation. *Language, Speech, and Hearing Services in Schools*, *32*, 38-50.

Chen, X., Anderson, R. C., Li, W., Hao, M., Wu, X., & Shu, H. (2004). Phonological awareness of bilingual and monolingual Chinese children. *Journal of Educational Psychology*, *96*, 142-151.

Cho, J.R., & McBride-Chang, C. (2005). Correlates of Korean Hangul acquisition among kindergarteners and second graders. *Scientific Studies of Reading*, *9*, 3-16.

Conners, F., Rosenquist, J., & Sligh, A. (2001). Abilities underlying decoding differences in children with intellectual abilities. *Journal of Intellectual Disability Research*, *45*, 292-299.

Cossu, G., Rossini, F., & Marshall, J. (1993). When reading is acquired but phonemic awareness is not: A study of literacy in Down syndrome. *Cognition*, *46*, 129-138.

Cossu, G., Shankweiler, D., Liberman, I. Y., & Katz, L. (1988). Awareness of phonological segments and reading ability in Italian children. *Applied Psycholinguistics*, *9*, 1-16.

Coulmas, F. (1989). *The writing system of the world*. Oxford, England: Blackwell.

Cunningham, A. E., & Stanovich, K. E. (1993). Children's literacy environments and early word recognition subskills. *Reading and Writing: An Interdisciplinary Journal*, *5*, 193-204.

Cupples, L., & Iacono, T. (2000). Phonological awareness and oral reading skill in children with Down syndrome. *Journal of Speech, Language, and Hearing Research*, *43*, 595-608.

Dillon, C., & Pisoni, D. (2004). Nonword repetition and reading in deaf children with cochlear implants. *International Congress Services*, *1273*, 304-307.

Dodd, B., Crosbie, S., McIntosh, B., Teitzel, T., & Ozanne, A. (2003). *The Pre-Reading Inventory of Phonological Awareness*. San Antonio, TX: The Psychological Corporation.

Early Childhood Research Institute on Measuring Growth and Development. (1998; 2000). *Individual growth and development indicators for pre-school children: Picturing naming/expressing meaning, rhyming/early literacy, alliteration/early literacy, picture naming in Spanish/expressive meaning*. Minneapolis, MN: Center for Early Education and Development, University of Minnesota. (Available online at www.get gotg.net).

Feuerstein, R., Rand, Y., & Hoffman, M. (1979). *The dynamic assessment of retarded performers*. Baltimore: University Park Press.

Fox, B., & Routh, D. (1975). Analyzing spoken language into words, syllables, and phonemes: A developmental study. *Journal of Psycholinguistic Research*, *4*, 331–342.

Foy, J., & Mann, V. (2001). Does strength of phonological representations predict phonological awareness in preschool children? *Applied Psycholinguistics*, *22*, 301–325.

Gillon, G. (2004). *Phonological awareness: From research to practice*. New York: Guilford Press.

Goikoetxea, E. (2005). Levels of phonological awareness in preliterate and literate Spanish-speaking children. *Reading and Writing*, *18*, 51–79.

Gombert, J. (2002). Children with Down syndrome use phonological knowledge in reading. *Reading and Writing: An Interdisciplinary Journal*, *15*, 455–469.

Good, R., & Kaminski, R. (Eds.). (2002). *Dynamic indicators of Basic Early Literacy Skills* (6th ed.). Eugene, OR: Institute for the Development of Educational Achievement. Available online from: http://dibels.uoregon.edu/

Goswami, U., & Martin, E. (2000). Rhyme and analogy in beginning reading: Conceptual and methodological issues. *Applied Psycholinguistics*, *21*, 63–93.

Goulandris, N. (2003). *Dyslexia in different languages: Cross-linguistic comparisons*. London: Whurr.

Hanson, V. (1989). Phonology and reading: Evidence from profoundly deaf readers. In D. Shankweiler & I. Liberman (Eds.), *Phonology and reading disability: Solving the reading puzzle* (pp. 68–89). Ann Arbor: University of Michigan Press.

Huang, H. S., & Hanley, R. (1994). Phonological awareness and visual skills in learning to read Chinese and English, *Cognition*, *54*, 73–98.

Invernizzi, M., & Ford, K. (in press). *Phonological Awareness Literacy Screening: Español*. Charlottesville: University of Virginia.

Invernizzi, M. Juel, C., Swank, L., & Meier, J. (2005). *Phonological Awareness Literacy Screening- Kindergarten.* Charlottesville: University of Virginia.

Invernizzi, M., Sullivan, A., Meier, J., & Swank, L. (2004). *Phonological Awareness Literacy Screening-PreKindergarten.* Charlottesville: University of Virginia.

Justice, L., & Schuele, C. M. (2004). Phonological awareness: Description, assessment, and intervention. In J. Bernthal & N. Bankson (Eds.), *Articulation and phonological disorders* (5th ed., pp. 376–405). Boston: Allyn & Bacon.

Kamhi, A., Lee, R., & Nelson, L. (1985). Word, syllable, and sound awareness in language-disordered children. *Journal of Speech and Hearing Disorders, 50,* 207–212.

Karanth, P. (1992). Developmental dyslexia in bilingual-biliterates. *Reading and Writing: An Interdisciplinary Journal, 4,* 297–306.

Karanth, P., Mathew, A., & Kurien, P. (2004). Orthography and reading speed: Data from native readers of Kannada. *Reading and Writing: An Interdisciplinary Journal, 17,* 101–120.

Ladefoged, P. (2005). *Vowels and consonants: An introduction to the sounds of languages.* Malden, MA: Blackwell.

Lenel, J., & Cantor, J. (1981). Rhyme recognition and phonemic perception in young children. *Journal of Psycholinguistic Research, 10,* 57–67.

Lidz, C. (Ed.). (1987). *Dynamic assessment: An interactional approach to evaluating learning potential.* New York: Guilford Press.

Lidz, C., & Pena, E. (1996). Dynamic assessment: The model, its relevance as a nonbiased approach, and its application to Latino American preschool children. *Language, Speech, and Hearing Services in Schools, 27,* 367–372.

Lonigan, C., Burgess, S., Anthony, J., & Barker, T. (1998). Development of phonological sensitivity in two- to five-year-old children. *Journal of Educational Psychology, 90,* 294–311.

Lonigan, C., Wagner, R., Torgesen, J., & Rashotte, C. (in press). *Test of Preschool Early Literacy.* Austin, TX: Pro-Ed.

Mann, V. A. (1986). Phonological awareness: The role of reading experience. *Cognition, 24,* 65–92.

Moats, L. (2000). *Speech to print: Language essentials for teachers.* Baltimore: Paul H. Brookes.

Mumtaz, S. & Humphreys, G. W. (2001). The effects of bilingualism on learning to read English: Evidence from the contrast between Urdu-English bilingual and English monolingual children. *Journal of Research on Reading, 24,* 113–134.

Prakash, P., Rekha, D., Nigam, R., & Karanth, P. (1993). Phonological awareness, orthography and literacy. In R. J. Scholes (Ed.), *Literacy and language analysis* (pp. 55–70). Hillsdale, NJ: Lawrence Erlbaum.

Prema, K. S., & Karanth, P. (2003). Assessment of learning disability: Language-based tests. In P. Karanth & J. Rozario (Eds.), *Learning disabilities in India, willing the mind to learn* (pp. 138-149). New Delhi: Sage.

Robertson, C., & Salter, W. (1995). *The Phonological Awareness Profile*. East Moline, IL: Linguisystems.

Robertson, C., & Salter, W. (1997). *The Phonological Awareness Test*. East Moline, IL: Linguisystems.

Sandberg, A. D., & Hjelmquist, E. (1997). Language and literacy in nonvocal children with cerebral palsy. *Reading and Writing: An Interdisciplinary Journal, 9*, 107-133.

Scarborough, H. S. (1998). Predicting the future achievement of second graders with reading disabilities: Contributions of phonemic awareness, verbal memory, rapid naming and IQ. *Annals of Dyslexia, 48*, 115-136.

Schatschneider, C., Francis, D., Foorman, B., Fletcher, J., & Mehta, P. (1999). The dimensionality of phonological awareness: An application of response theory. *Journal of Educational Psychology, 91*, 439-449.

Schneider, P., & Watkins, R. (1996). Applying Vygotskian developmental theory to language intervention. *Language, Speech, and Hearing Services in Schools, 27*, 157-170.

Schuele, C. M. (2004). The impact of developmental speech and language impairments on the acquisition of literacy skills. *Mental Retardation and Developmental Disabilities Research Reviews, 10*, 176-183.

Schuele, C. M., & Boudreau, D. (2006). *Phonological awareness: Beyond the basics*. Manuscript submitted for publication.

Schuele, C. M., & Dayton, N. D. (2000). *Intensive Phonological Awareness Program*. Nashville, TN: Authors.

Schuele, C. M., & Justice, L. (2004, June). *Promoting kindergarten phonological awareness: Evaluating a two-tiered intervention.* Paper presented at the Poster session presented at Headstart's 7th National Research Conference, Washington, DC.

Seymour, P. H. K., Aro, M., & Erskine, J. M. (2003). Foundation literacy acquisition in European orthographies. *British Journal of Psychology, 94*, 143-174.

Shanbal, J. C., & Rao, P. (in press). Cross-language transfer in bilingual children—Effect on literacy in a second language? *International Journal of Dravidian Linguistics.*

Spector, J. (1992). Predicting progress in beginning reading: Dynamic assessment of phonemic awareness. *Journal of Educational Psychology, 84*, 353-363.

Stahl, S., & Murray, B. (1994). Defining phonological awareness and its relationship to early reading. *Journal of Educational Psychology, 86*, 221-234.

Sterne, A., & Goswami, U. (2000). Phonological awareness of syllables, rhymes and phonemes in deaf children. *Journal of Child Psychology and Psychiatry, 41*, 609–625.

Stewart, M. R. (2004). Phonological awareness and bilingual preschoolers: Should we teach it and, if so, how? *Early Childhood Education Journal, 32*(1), 31–37.

Storch, S. A., & Whitehurst, G. J. (2002). Oral language and code-related precursors to reading: Evidence from a longitudinal structural model. *Developmental Psychology, 38*, 934–947.

Stuart-Smith, J., & Martin, D. (1997). Investigating literacy and pre-literacy skills in Panjabi/English school children. *Educational Review, 49*, 181–197.

Stuart-Smith, J., & Martin, D. (1999). Developing assessment procedures for phonological awareness for use with Punjabi-English bilingual children. *International Journal of Bilingualism, 3*, 55–80.

Swank, L., & Catts, H. (1994). Phonological awareness and written word decoding. *Language, Speech, and Hearing Services in Schools, 25*, 9–14.

Torgesen, J. (1999). Assessment and instruction for phonemic awareness and word recognition skills. In H. Catts & A. Kamhi (Eds.), *Language and reading disabilities* (pp. 128–153). Boston: Allyn & Bacon.

Torgesen, J., & Bryant, B. (2004). *Test of Phonological Awareness— Second Edition: Plus*. Austin, TX: Pro-Ed.

Torgesen, J., & Mathes, P. (2000). *A basic guide to understanding, assessing, and teaching phonological awareness*. Austin, TX: Pro-Ed.

Torgesen, J., Morgan, S., & Davis, C. (1992). Effects of two types of phonological awareness training on word learning in kindergarten children. *Journal of Educational Psychology, 84*, 364–370.

Trieman, R., Mullennix, J., Bijeljac-Babic, R. & Richmond-Welty, E. D. (1995). The special role of rimes in the description, use, and acquisition of English orthography. *Journal of Experimental Psychology, 124*, 107–136.

Treiman, R., & Weatherston, S. (1992). Effects of linguistic structure on children's ability to isolate initial consonants. *Journal of Educational Psychology, 84*, 174–181.

Turkstra, L. (1999). Language testing in adolescents with brain injury: A consideration of the CELF-3. *Language, Speech, and Hearing Services in Schools, 30*, 132–140.

Ukrainetz, T. (2006). Scaffolding young students into phonemic awareness. In T. Ukrainetz (Ed.), *Contextualized language intervention: Scaffolding PreK-12: Literacy achievement* (pp. 429–467). Eau Claire, WI: Thinking Publications.

Ukrainetz, T., Cooney, M., Dyer, S., Kysar, A., & Harris, T. (2000). An investigation into teaching phonemic awareness through shared reading and writing. *Early Childhood Research Quarterly, 15*, 331–355.

van Kleeck, A., Gillam, R., & McFadden, T. (1998). A study of classroom-based phonological awareness training for preschoolers with speech and/or language disorders. *American Journal of Speech-Language Pathology*, 7(3), 65-76.

van Kleeck, A., & Schuele, C. M. (1987). Precursors to literacy: Normal development. *Topics in Language Disorders*, 7(2), 13-31.

Vandervelden, M., & Siegel, L. S. (1999). Phonological processing and literacy in AAC users and students with motor speech impairments. *Augmentative and Alternative Communication*, 15, 191-209.

Wagner, R., Torgesen, J., & Rashotte, C. (1994). Development of reading-related phonological processing abilities: New evidence of bidirectional causality from a latent variable longitudinal study. *Developmental Psychology*, 30, 73-87.

Wagner, R., Torgesen, J., & Rashotte, C. (1999). *Comprehensive Test of Phonological Processing*. Austin, TX: Pro-Ed.

Wagner, R., Torgesen, J., Rashotte, C., Hecht, S., Barker, T., Burgess, S., et al. (1997). Changing relations between phonological processing abilities and word-level reading as children develop from beginning to skilled readers: A 5-year longitudinal study. *Developmental Psychology*, 33, 468-479.

Whitehurst, G., & Lonigan, C. (2001). *Get Ready to Read!* Available online from: www.getrteadytoread.org

Wren, S., & Watts, J. (2002). *The Abecedarian Reading Assessment*. Austin, TX: Balanced Reading. Available online from: www.balancedreading.com

Yelland, G. W., Pollard, J., & Mercuri, A. (1993). The metalinguistic benefits of limited contact with a second language. *Applied Psycholinguistics*, 14, 423-444.

Chapter Seven

Assessing Print Knowledge

Sonia Q. Cabell
Anita S. McGinty
Laura M. Justice

Print Knowledge and Emergent Literacy Development

Emergent literacy theories identify *print knowledge* as a key area of preschool literacy development (Whitehurst & Lonigan, 1998). This knowledge encompasses children's early understandings about the forms, features, and functions of print. Simply stated, print knowledge refers to what young children know about print—what it is and how it works—prior to formal reading instruction. In this chapter, we have organized discussion of print knowledge into three separate, albeit interrelated, areas of development: print concepts, alphabet and letter-sound knowledge, and emergent writing.

Print concepts is a term used to describe children's understandings about print conventions and print units. Knowledge of print concepts reflects children's growing awareness that print is systematic, following its own rule system, and is different from other visual patterns, such as pictures (Adams, 1990). Generally, this area of development includes children's knowledge of how to handle books, such as holding a book upright, finding a book title, opening a book from left to right, and turning pages within books. It also includes knowledge of conventions regarding how print is organized within a book, such as knowing that print is read from the top to bottom and from left to right (Hiebert, 1981; Justice & Ezell, 2001a; Lomax & McGee, 1987; Mason, 1980). This knowledge extends print across various print genre—not only books but signs, menus, lists, and logos.

Print concepts also include children's understanding of different print units and how each serves different purposes. At the most basic level, children must differentiate letters from words. Later, they develop an awareness of more sophisticated types of print units, such as exclamation points, question marks, and commas. During the preschool years, one of the most sophisticated developments concerning knowledge of print units is the child's understanding of words as basic units of print, called *concept of word in text* (or, alternatively, *concept of word in print*). Some children acquire this understanding between the ages of 3 and 5 years, whereas others develop this concept during formal reading instruction in kindergarten and beyond. Experts view concept of word in text to be a fundamental understanding that children must grasp to progress as readers (Bear, Invernizzi, Templeton, & Johnston, 2004; Morris, Bloodgood, Lomax, & Perney, 2003). To develop a concept of word in text, children must first recognize that words are made up of and quite different from letters (Justice & Ezell, 2004; Morris, 1981). Beyond being able to parse words as printed units, concept of word in text also involves the phonological skill of parsing the oral speech stream into word segments and recognizing that there are spaces between words. In addition, concept of word requires letter-sound knowledge, at least at the level of beginning consonants in words, to accurately match speech to print. Research suggests that a stable concept of word in text facilitates children's ability to segment a word into its individual sounds (Morris et al., 2003).

Alphabet and letter-sound knowledge is a second area of development that characterizes children's achievements in print knowledge. Important to children's development in literacy is moving from broad discoveries of print, such as the organization of print within a book or the fact that print holds meaning, to more specific *code-related* insights. Alphabet knowledge is an example of children's increasing sophistication of print knowledge, as their focus moves from understanding broad organizational properties of print (i.e., print concepts) to learning about the specific units of print within a word. Alphabet knowledge (or letter knowledge) describes children's knowledge of individual letter names, including both the upper- and lowercase forms. Children must associate these letter names with their written symbols, and an ingrained knowledge of this connection is viewed as a critical index of early literacy development. However, learning the alphabet letters is simply a means to an end, as the end goal of alphabet knowledge is to acquire the sounds associated with the symbols, termed letter-sound knowledge. Each letter has one (or, in some cases, several) sounds associated with it, and children must learn these systematic pairings. Alphabet knowledge is considered to be causally related to later reading achievement through its facilitation of letter-sound knowledge (McBride-Chang, 1999; Treiman & Broderick, 1998). In short, a child must realize that a letter not only has a name, but also that it represents a speech sound. This, indeed, is the essence of the alphabetic principle.

Emergent writing, children's creation and expression of language using print, describes the meaningful scribbles and marks of young children and is the third area of development reflective of children's growing print knowledge. Long before they are writing in a conventional sense, children are scribbling, drawing, using letter-like forms, and writing random letters (Bear et al., 2004). Importantly, even as preschoolers, children's early writing performance (as unconventional as it may appear) is significantly associated with knowledge in other literacy domains, including knowledge of the alphabet and phonological awareness (Welsch, Sullivan, & Justice, 2003). Indeed, children's early writing attempts are anything but trivial: when a 3-year-old child scribbles next to a self-portrait and identifies that scribble as his name, he possesses the early understanding that print is distinct from a drawing. If the child scribbled from left to right, he would be exhibiting the print concept of directionality as well.

Recent federal policy initiatives, such as Early Reading First, have placed a premium on ensuring that all children develop a body of knowledge about print prior to entering kindergarten, which includes print concepts, alphabet and letter-sound knowledge, and emergent writing abilities. These areas tend to be underdeveloped at school entry for children with disabilities, children learning English as a second language, and children reared in households characterized by poverty. The National Research Council, in a federally commissioned report (Snow, Burns, & Griffin, 1998), suggested that children who lack these foundational understandings will likely be at an increased risk for developing reading difficulties. As a result, numerous public policy initiatives emphasize the importance of ensuring a strong knowledge base concerning print for all young children and the need for early educators to systematically monitor children's achievements in these areas to guide scientifically based emergent literacy interventions.

At least in part, these initiatives promoting emergent literacy are based on research demonstrating that measures of print knowledge are significant predictors of later reading success. For preschool and kindergarten children, measures of print concepts, alphabet and letter-sound knowledge, and emergent writing are consistently shown to be among the better predictors of later reading success, particularly in the area of decoding (Badian, 2000; Hammill, 2004; Scarborough, 1998). A meta-analysis of 234 studies involving longitudinal study of children from preschool through the elementary grades conducted by the National Early Literacy Panel (2004) also confirmed that measures of print knowledge provide useful and positive predictors of later literacy success. For instance, the panel found the average correlation between preschool measures of print concepts and later decoding skill to be 0.46, characterizing a strong, positive relationship between early print-concept development and later reading success. Similarly, measures of preschoolers' alphabet knowledge and name writing ability, respectively, had average correlations of 0.45 and 0.5 with later decoding. As a benchmark for comparison, measures of phonological awareness have an average correlation of 0.44 with later decoding skills. As these data show, knowledge about a child's performance on measures of print knowledge can be extremely useful in identifying children who may be at risk for later problems in reading, particularly decoding.

Assessing young children's knowledge of print is also important for guiding effective early instruction focused on facilitating print knowledge. Children served in the early education and early intervention system vary widely in their understanding of how print works, and educators must be vigilant in identifying children who require additional opportunities or supports to develop this body of knowledge. To illustrate, one recent study showed that preschoolers from low-income homes scored more than one standard deviation lower than preschoolers from middle-income homes on a measure of print-concept knowledge. Similarly, preschoolers with language impairments also scored more than one standard deviation lower than preschoolers with typical language skills (Justice, Bowles, & Skibbe, 2006). As this and other studies show, early childhood educators and other professionals can use measures of print knowledge not only to identify children struggling with these foundational skills but also to design print-focused interventions. A recent review of promising emergent literacy interventions indicated that print knowledge can be readily improved through targeted interventions delivered at home and in preschool classrooms (Justice & Pullen, 2003).

This chapter describes assessment tools that professionals may use to examine print knowledge in young children from preschool through kindergarten, corresponding roughly to the ages of 3 to 6 years. Following from our discussion earlier in this chapter about how one might organize children's myriad accomplishments in print knowledge, we have organized description of these tools using these categories: (a) print concepts, (b) alphabet and letter-sound knowledge, and (c) emergent writing. It is important to note that this chapter addresses primarily measures of print knowledge appropriate for children who are not yet reading, which may include typically developing children into kindergarten and children with disabilities beyond this period. Because of our focus on prereaders, we do not include measures of decoding that can be used only with children who are beginning to read at least some words.

Measures for Assessing Print Knowledge

Measuring Print Concepts

Measures that examine children's knowledge of print concepts attempt to estimate what children know about print organization and print meaning across different contexts. These measures study children's understanding of how books work (e.g., whether a child can differentiate the front and back of a book), the way print is organized in books and other media (e.g., the directionality of print), and the functions of print as a communication device. Assessing children's knowledge of print concepts provides the professional with insight into the child's experience with print (Lonigan, Burgess, & Anthony, 2000) and his or her conceptual understanding of print and print materials (Adams, 1990; Goodman, 1984). Table 7–1 provides an overview of measures related to print concepts.

Table 7-1. Overview of Print Concepts Measures

Measure	Skills Assessed	Approximate Administration Time	Scoring
Developing Skills Checklist: Print Concepts (CTB/ McGraw-Hill, 1990)	Book conventions, differentiating print from pictures, identifying print units (letters, words, sentences, punctuation)	5–10 minutes	Norm-referenced
Early Reading Diagnostic Assessment-Revised: Concept of Print Observation Checklist (The Psychological Corporation, 2002)	Identifying letters in name, print directionality, matching speech to print, pausing between sentences	NA	Qualitative
Emerging Literacy Screening: Print Awareness Section (Paulson et al., 2001)	Book conventions, written name identification, emergent writing	10 minutes	Criterion-referenced
Fox in a Box: Concepts of Print (CTB/McGraw-Hill, 1998)	Book conventions, concept of word in text	15 minutes	Criterion-referenced
An Observational Survey of Early Literacy Achievement: Concepts About Print (Clay, 2005)	Book organization, print directionality, punctuation, concepts of letter and word, relationship between letters and words	10 minutes	Norm-referenced

Measure	Skills Assessed	Approximate Administration Time	Scoring
Phonological Awareness Literacy Screening for Preschool: Print and Word Awareness (Invernizzi, Sullivan, et al., 2004)	Concepts of letter and word, book and print organization, directionality	5 minutes	Criterion-referenced
Phonological Awareness Literacy Screening for Kindergarten: Concept of Word (Invernizzi, Juel et al., 2004)	Concept of word in text	5 minutes	Criterion-referenced
Preschool Word and Print Awareness (Justice et al., 2006)	Book and print organization, concept of letter, print meaning	10 minutes	Criterion-referenced
Test of Early Reading Ability-3: Conventions (Reid et al., 2001)	Book and print organization, identifying punctuation marks, print forms, print meaning	5–10 minutes	Norm-referenced

Developing Skills Checklist (DSC)
(CTB/McGraw-Hill, 1990)

The Developing Skills Checklist (DSC) is a commercially available, norm-referenced assessment designed to measure a wide range of skills in preschool and kindergarten children. The primary purpose of the DSC is to assist teachers in instructional planning, but the measure also may be used for program evaluation and federal reporting. The individually administered, standardized tool includes subtests related to prereading, math, social/emotional development, fine/gross motor development, print concepts, and early writing. In terms of reading, the DSC measures the precursor skills necessary for successful transition into formal reading instruction, namely, print concepts, alphabet knowledge, and writing. Norms are available for ages 4 to 6 years, as well as for the spring of preschool and three testing points in kindergarten. Psychometric properties (i.e., reliability and validity) are detailed in the technical reference.

DSC: Print Concepts (CTB/McGraw-Hill, 1990). The Print Concepts subtest of the DSC measures young children's early understandings of how print works. Using the book *A Day at School*, the examiner asks the child a series of questions designed to tap into children's knowledge of book conventions and print units. First, the examiner begins the assessment by placing the book face up and asking the child to look through it to find a specific picture. As the child completes this task, the examiner assesses the child's ability to hold a book upright and turn pages appropriately. Second, the examiner shows the child a picture from the book that depicts children engaged in a variety of activities. The child identifies people in the picture who are reading. Third, the examiner displays a page containing both pictures and print, and asks the child to identify letters, words, and numbers. As the child responds, the examiner records whether the child can differentiate between these print units. Finally, the examiner displays a page with a drawing and printed story written by a character in the book. The child identifies where to begin reading, and points to print units, including letters, words, sentences, and punctuation marks. Responses are scored as "observed" or "unobserved" behaviors. Normative data are available in the technical reference. Total administration time for the subtest is approximately 5 to 10 minutes.

Early Reading Diagnostic Assessment—Revised (ERDA-R) (The Psychological Corporation, 2002)

The Early Reading Diagnostic Assessment—Revised (ERDA-R) is a commercially available, norm-referenced screening and diagnostic tool designed to measure children's early reading skills in kindergarten through grade 3. One main purpose of the standardized ERDA-R is to identify children at risk for not meeting grade-level expectations in reading without intervention. Another purpose is to provide teachers with a tool to assist in planning instruction. This teacher-friendly measure is individually administered and targets the following areas: concepts of print, phonological awareness, phonics, fluency, vocabulary, and text comprehension. Each grade level administration involves three groups of subtests: the Screener, the Diagnostic, and the Optional subtests. The Screener subtests are administered first, and depending on the results, the Diagnostic subtests are administered to obtain more information regarding children's specific areas of need. Total administration time is approximately 45 minutes. Normative data allow professionals to compare students' progress with that of their peers. The administration manual provides detailed information regarding standardized administration, scoring, interpretation, and instructional planning. Psychometric properties for the ERDA-R are available in the technical manual.

ERDA-R: Concept of Print Observation Checklist (The Psychological Corporation, 2002). Concept of Print Observation Checklist, Part A of the ERDA-R, is woven into the administration of the Letter Recognition subtest. For an explanation of the Letter Recognition subtest, see the description of the measure under the Alphabet and Letter-Sound Knowledge section of this chapter. To assess print concepts, the examiner displays a page of approximately nine letters and asks a child to pick a letter that is in his or her name. The child's response is scored as "yes" or "no" on the Concept of Print Observation Checklist, Part A. Two other items on Part A ask whether the child reads the letters from left to right and from top to bottom. Part B of the checklist follows the Reading Comprehension subtest, and addresses whether the child reads with left-to-right directionality, tries to match speech to print when reading, and pauses between sentences while reading. The test manual docs not provide normative data for this checklist. Rather, the examiner simply records the qualitative information from the checklist on the student record form to assist in planning instruction.

Emerging Literacy Screening (Paulson, Noble, Jepson, & van den Pol, 2001)

The Emerging Literacy Screening is part of a commercially available activity resource book, *Building Early Literacy Language Skills* (Paulson et al., 2001), that probes 3- to 6-year-old children's skills in print concepts and emergent writing (called print awareness), as well as oral communication (i.e., print relevant vocabulary, expressive sentence structure, speech intelligibility, prosody), and phonological awareness (i.e., rhyming, blending syllables, blending sounds, segmenting sounds). Items within each section are developmentally sequenced to proceed from easier to more complex skills. The measure provides a profile of emergent literacy skills and assists in goal setting or instructional planning.

The entire assessment typically is completed in 10 to 20 minutes and should be individually administered. The resource book provides specific administration and scoring guidelines for each test item, as well as a list of needed materials (Paulson et al., 2001). Some minimal preparation is required, including cutting out picture cards (provided in the resource book), creating index cards with children's names, and identifying a familiar book.

The Emerging Literacy Screening is criterion-referenced and the resource book provides a conversion of raw score points to percentage correct to assist in identifying areas of relative strength and weakness, as well as areas of concern for children who are at risk for or identified with disabilities. For children with disabilities, specific Individual Education Plan (IEP) goals are outlined in the resource book and can assist special educators or speech-language pathologists in IEP development. This measure can also be used to chart progress in response to instruction or intervention. The test developers assert that the skills targeted in this screening measure reflect a set of abilities expected to be in place by the end of kindergarten (Paulson et al., 2001). No psychometric properties are available.

Emerging Literacy Screening: Print Awareness Section (Paulson et al., 2001). The print awareness section of the Emerging Literacy Screening takes approximately 10 minutes to administer and includes tasks examining children's print concepts (primarily book awareness), written name identification, and print development. Although we discuss measures related to print concepts in this section, we will also describe the aspects of this subtest related to emergent writing (written name identification task). The print concepts (i.e., book awareness) task assesses children's ability to turn a book right side up, flip pages one at a time, identify print versus pictures, recognize the left-to-right directionality of print, and track a line of print. This screening tool does not require that the examiner read the book in its entirety, rather the book is used as a familiar prop to provide a global rating of children's book and print knowledge. Although the examiner can use any book familiar to the children, the authors of this tool recommend *Brown Bear, Brown Bear, What Do You See?* (Martin & Carle, 1992).

The written name identification task measures children's ability to identify their first names and the individual letters within their names. The examiner asks the child to point to his name from three choices on cards: the child's name (e.g., Mark), another name that begins with the same letter (e.g., Mindy), and a third name as a distractor (e.g., Kelly). Next, the examiner asks the child to identify the first letter of his name, the last letter, and finally, any other letters.

The print development task measures children's emergent writing ability. The examiner can score an existing writing sample or ask the child to produce a new sample. If the examiner chooses to elicit a writing sample, the child draws a self-portrait and writes a sentence or story about the picture. The child is encouraged to use child-friendly writing. Scoring is based on whether the child is using scribbles, letter-like forms, random letters, or semiphonetic spelling. Based on children's performance in each task within the print awareness section of the Emerging Literacy Screening, the examiner assigns ratings based on a developmental scale of 0 to 3.

Fox in a Box (CTB/McGraw-Hill, 1998)

Fox in a Box is a commercially available, criterion-referenced assessment designed to measure early literacy skills in children from kindergarten through grade 2. It includes tasks in the following literacy areas: phonemic awareness, phonics, reading and oral expression, and listening and writing. Created primarily to help teachers in planning classroom instruction, each task is easy to administer and interpret. A fox puppet is used during some of the tasks to help children understand directions and remain engaged. Fall (October/ November) and early spring (March/ April) administrations are recommended with a total approximate administration time of 35 minutes for individual tasks and 80 minutes for group tasks. The end-of-semester minimum benchmarks found in the teacher's guide are designed to reflect the literacy guidelines in *Preventing Reading Difficulties in Young Children* (Snow et al., 1998).

Fox in a Box: Concepts of Print (CTB/McGraw-Hill, 1998). The Concepts of Print task of Fox in a Box is a 5-item checklist which examines young children's knowledge of book conventions and concept of word in text. The task is administered within the context of a shared storybook reading of a book entitled *Monday*. The examiner asks the child to point to the front and back of the book. The child is then asked to open the book to the page on which the story begins. Next, the child points to a picture and identifies where to begin reading, demonstrating that he knows the difference between pictures and print. After reading the first page, the examiner asks the child where to read next. The final item documents the child's concept of word boundaries, as he or she tracks the print while the examiner reads. Total administration time is approximately 15 minutes.

An Observational Survey of Early Literacy Achievement (Clay, 2005)

Clay's Observational Survey is likely the most well-known commercially available set of standardized observation protocols designed to measure early literacy skills in 5- to 7-year-old children. It has been adopted by the Reading Recovery program to study the progress of children struggling with early reading (Clay, 1993). The measure evaluates children's skills in the following areas: letter identification, print concepts, word encoding from dictation, sight word reading, vocabulary word writing from memory, and oral reading at the text level. The measure is designed to provide information about children's performance in the context of their everyday learning environments, to guide instructional planning, and to monitor improvements during instruction. Normative data also allow professionals to identify children who are substantially behind their peers in these early literacy skills. The test manual provides details regarding psychometric properties.

An Observational Survey of Early Literacy Achievement: Concepts About Print (Clay, 2005). The Concepts About Print task is a 24-item measure of the standardized, norm-referenced Observational Survey of Early Literacy Achievement. It examines 5- to 7-year-old children's knowledge of print concepts, including book and print organization, concept of letter, and concept of word. Book and print organization questions comprise 11 of the 24 task items and ask children to: identify the front of the book, identify where reading begins, demonstrate left-to-right directionality, demonstrate top to bottom orientation when reading, recognize when print is upside-down, recognize reading text from top to bottom, and identify left-to-right page order in a book. Concept of letter questions comprise 7 of the task items and ask children to identify upper- and lowercase letters, identify a letter as distinct from words, identify the first and last letter of a word, and demonstrate knowledge that letters make up words. Concept of word questions comprise 4 of the task items and ask children to identify a word in text, demonstrate knowledge that words are different from letters, demonstrate knowledge of word order in text, and point to each word the examiner reads.

Administered in approximately 10 minutes, assessors give this subtest in the context of a shared one-on-one storybook reading using one of four books designed specifically for this task: *Sand* (Clay, 1972), *Stones* (Clay, 1979), *Follow Me, Moon* (Clay, 2000a), or *No Shoes* (Clay, 2000b). The assessor reads the book in its entirety, embedding a series of print-related questions (usually one or two per page) into the reading interaction to assess the child's knowledge of different print concepts. Children's raw scores are summed and can be converted to a stanine score, based on normative data from either a 5- to 7-year-old New Zealand sample or a stratified national random sample of first-grade students in the United States. These normative data are available to interpret children's performance against same-age peers. Also, item-level data from this subtest can be used informally to assist in instructional planning and to monitor children's progress in reading-related skill development over the course of an intervention or school year.

Phonological Awareness Literacy Screening for PreKindergarten (PALS-PreK) (Invernizzi, Sullivan, Meier, & Swank, 2004)

The Phonological Awareness Literacy Screening for Preschool (PALS-PreK) is a commercially available, standardized assessment designed to measure emergent literacy skills in 4-year-old children. It was developed at the University of Virginia as part of an initiative funded by the Virginia Department of Education to provide educators with a tool for measuring the emergent literacy skills of children during the preschool years. The PALS-PreK comprises six tasks that provide a profile of children's strengths and weaknesses in emergent literacy skills and assist in developing goals in instructional planning. The six tasks include name writing, alphabet knowledge, beginning sound awareness, print and word awareness, rhyme awareness, and nursery rhyme awareness. Total administration time is approximately 20 to 25 minutes.

Scoring of each task is independent of the other tasks. The measure is criterion-referenced and uses simple raw scores on individual tasks to compare against typical developmental ranges for 4-year-old children in the spring of the preschool year. These provide a frame of reference to help determine children's gaps or relative weaknesses. The PALS-PreK Teacher's Manual provides details regarding psychometric properties.

PALS-PreK: Print and Word Awareness (Invernizzi, Sullivan, et al. 2004). The Print and Word Awareness task of the PALS-PreK examines children's knowledge of print concepts, including concepts of letter and word, as well as book and print organization. In administering this task, the examiner reads a short booklet (*Hey Diddle, Diddle*) with the child and embeds 10 questions into the reading. One question examines the child's ability to identify a letter. Six questions address concept of word in text, asking the child to point to individual words in the text and to demonstrate word-by-word pointing. Three questions address knowledge of book and print organization and include asking the child to point to the title of the booklet, identify where on a page reading should begin, and track the left-to-right directionality of a line of print. Total administration time is approximately 5 minutes. A raw score is calculated by summing the points for each of the 10 questions and is compared against a spring developmental range.

Phonological Awareness Literacy Screening for Kindergarten (PALS-K) (Invernizzi, Juel, Swank, & Meier, 2004)

The Phonological Awareness Literacy Screening for Kindergarten (PALS-K) is a commercially available standardized assessment designed as a screening tool to identify kindergarten students at risk for later reading difficulty. PALS-K also provides teachers with diagnostic information for instruction. The tasks measured by PALS-K include rhyme awareness, beginning sound awareness, lowercase alphabet recognition, letter sounds, spelling, concept of word in text, and word recognition in isolation (optional). The majority of the tasks are individually administered by the child's teacher with a few small group tasks. Children's scores are interpreted in a criterion-referenced manner against benchmarks for minimal competencies established for fall and spring assessment points. The authors recommend that children who score below benchmark at either assessment point receive additional instruction. It is important to note that these benchmarks represent minimal competencies and should not be confused with grade-level expectations. Psychometric properties are detailed in the PALS-K Technical Reference, which is available at no charge online (see http://pals.virginia.edu).

An administration feature of the PALS-PreK and PALS-K warrants additional consideration. The entire battery, including the letter recognition and letter sounds tasks, can be scored directly on the computer using the Online Assessment Wizard instead of traditional pencil-and-paper scoring. Teachers who use this feature have access to item-level reports that provide class profiles of children's knowledge.

PALS-K: Concept of Word (Invernizzi, Juel et al., 2004)
The PALS-K Concept of Word task measures children's ability to match spoken words to written words using one-to-one correspondence and takes approximately 5 minutes to administer. Before administration of the task, children are helped to memorize a short 4- or 5-line poem using picture prompts. Once the poem has been memorized, a printed version is presented in a small booklet. Next,

the examiner models the task of fingerpointing to each word in the poem as the poem is recited. The child then joins the examiner to chorally read the poem and observe the fingerpointing a second time. Finally, the examiner asks the child to recite the poem alone while touching each word in the booklet. A point is awarded for each line a child tracks correctly with word-by-word pointing on his or her own. After the word-pointing task is completed, the examiner asks the child to identify two words on each page of the booklet by pointing to the word and asking, "What word is this?" This is followed by asking the child to read, in isolation, a list of 10 words from the poem. A total concept of word in text score is determined by adding the pointing, word identification, and word list scores.

Preschool Word and Print Awareness (PWPA) (Justice et al., 2006)

The Preschool Word and Print Awareness is a 12-item standardized, criterion-referenced measure designed to assess print-concept knowledge in children between the ages of 3 to 5 years. Although not commercially sold, the test is available in the appendix of research articles (see Justice & Ezell, 2001b; Justice et al., 2006) and is also reprinted in Appendix 7. The PWPA assesses children's print knowledge in areas such as book and print organization, concept of letter, and print meaning. Eight items are specifically related to book and print organization and ask children to identify the front of the book, identify and explain the meaning of the title of a book, indicate where reading begins, and demonstrate knowledge of print directionality (i.e., left to right of a line, left to right of pages, top to bottom on a page). These questions cover a range of difficulty levels, with questions about the title and front of the book being easier and questions about print directionality providing more challenge. Three items are related to print functionality and ask children to explain the meaning of print in pictures and recognize a speech bubble as representing a character's speech. Three items are related to the concept of letter and ask children to identify a letter in print, identify a capital letter, and identify a lowercase letter. The measure is designed to provide a criterion-referenced profile of children's strengths and weaknesses for guiding instructional planning, monitoring children's progress, and gauging the efficacy of intervention efforts conducted in the classroom or in a clinical environment (Justice & Ezell, 2001b). Mean scores (i.e., "trait estimates") for children in different risk groups, including children in lower income homes and children with language impairment, are available in Justice et al. (2006).

The test takes approximately 10 minutes to administer and is given in the context of a one-on-one book reading session using the commercial storybook *Nine Ducks Nine* (Hayes, 1990). Administration is standardized, with the test protocol providing language for introducing the task and embedding specific questions at various points in the book; performance feedback or prompting are not allowed when giving the test. For the majority of test items, children can answer questions nonverbally through pointing, although for two questions children are required to provide a verbal answer or explanation about an aspect of print. Children's performance is summed and raw scores can be used for descriptive comparison against data for typically developing 4-year-olds (Justice & Ezell, 2001b) or can be converted to standard scores and interpreted against normative references based on age (Justice et al., 2006).

Test of Early Reading Ability-3 (TERA-3) (Reid, Hresko, & Hammill, 2001)

The Test of Early Reading Ability-3 (TERA-3) is a commercially available, norm-referenced test designed to assess emergent literacy skills of children ages 3 to 8 years. The measure includes three subtests: conventions of print (i.e., the rules governing print), alphabet knowledge, and meaning. It is designed to identify children who are showing delayed or deviant early literacy development, provide a profile of children's early literacy skills across a range of abilities, and measure progress or growth in early literacy skills as a result of intervention. Although the information gleaned from the assessment may be helpful in lesson planning, the authors state that it is not designed to inform instruction and is not sufficiently detailed, contextualized, or individualized to guide instruction on its own.

Examiners using this measure should have experience with diagnostic testing or be supervised by someone with the appropriate background and training. The test record booklet provides standardized instructions, stimulus questions, prompts, and feedback.

To reduce the time of testing, each subtest has an age-equivalent start point and allows testing to be discontinued when a child misses three items in a row. Administration occurs in a quiet setting on an individual basis, with total administration time ranging from 15 to 45 minutes. The assessor can convert the raw score of each subtest into several derived scores, including a standardized score, percentile rank, age equivalent and grade equivalent score, as well as obtain an overall Reading Quotient standard score and percentile rank. To assist in data interpretation, the record form provides a space to plot each subtest standard score as a visual representation of a child's relative strengths and weaknesses and to plot a Reading Quotient against aptitude tests or other standardized, norm-referenced tests. The test manual includes information on the psychometric properties of the test and subtests disaggregated by gender, ethnicity or race, linguistic, or disability status.

TERA-3: Conventions (Reid et al., 2001). The 21-item Conventions subtest comprises one of three parts of the standardized, norm-referenced TERA-3. This subtest evaluates children's knowledge of print concepts using a broad range of tasks and includes questions at difficulty levels appropriate for emergent readers through early readers. In the area of print concepts, this subtest assesses children's knowledge of book handling, parts of a book, print organization on a page, punctuation marks, print meaning, concept of word, sight word reading, spelling, and sentence completion. For example, items include identifying which two pictures of a book (out of six pictures) show the book as "right side up," identifying the top of the book in a picture of a book cover, and identifying the label on a picture of an orange juice carton. Items also ask children to distinguish between letters and numbers. All tasks are administered using test plates rather than authentic stimuli (e.g., real storybooks).

Administration is standardized and total administration time is approximately 5 to 10 minutes. Although the test provides only a standardized score, percentile rank, age-equivalent and grade-equivalent for the subtest as a whole, the majority of items for younger children assess their understanding of book and print organization. Therefore, children between the ages of 3 and 6 years scoring within the normal range or above the normal range have likely obtained an adequate amount of book and print convention knowledge. Children scoring below the normal range may need additional help or services; however, this test does not guide instructional or intervention goals and further testing or probing may be required to develop an understanding of a child's individual strengths and weaknesses in this area.

Measuring Alphabet and Letter-Sound Knowledge

Measures of alphabet knowledge and letter-sound knowledge seek to identify what children know about the alphabet, including how specific sounds correspond with specific letters. These measures typically ask children to identify letters as they are named (receptive alphabet knowledge), say or write the names of individual letters (expressive alphabet knowledge), and identify the sounds that match specific letters. Measures will vary in the number of letters sampled, with some measures including all letters as stimuli and others sampling only a few letters, and whether the format is timed or untimed. Many researchers have constructed their own measures to evaluate children's alphabet and letter-sound knowledge, although more formal procedures are also available. The advantage of formal procedures is that stimuli are controlled when tracking children's progress over time and, at least for some available measures, scores can be interpreted against normative references. Alphabet tasks involving children's writing of letters are addressed under the Emergent Writing section of this chapter. Table 7–2 provides an overview of measures related to alphabet and letter-sound knowledge.

DSC: Memory (Naming Letters, Identifying Sounds and Letters) (CTB/McGraw-Hill, 1990)

The Memory subtest of the DSC measures young children's ability to recall visual and auditory information. Although the subtest includes measures of short-term memory and blending consonant-vowel-consonant (CVC) words, we describe only the tasks relevant to assessing print knowledge: Naming Letters and Identifying Sounds and Letters. During administration of the Naming Letters task, the examiner shows the child a "base wheel," which displays one letter at a time. The base wheel includes a sample of six uppercase and six lowercase letters. The examiner records

Table 7-2. Overview of Alphabet and Letter-Sound Knowledge Measures

Measure	Skills Assessed	Approximate Administration Time	Scoring
Developing Skills Checklist: Memory (CTB/ McGraw-Hill, 1990)	Upper- and lowercase letter recognition, letter-sound knowledge	10 minutes	Norm-referenced
Dynamic Indicators of Basic Early Literacy Skills: Letter Naming Fluency (Kaminski & Good, 2002)	Fluency of upper- and lowercase alphabet recognition	1 minute	N/A
Early Reading Diagnostic Assessment-Revised: Letter Recognition (The Psychological Corporation, 2002)	Letter matching, lowercase letter recognition	3–5 minutes	Norm-referenced
Fox in a Box: Uppercase Names, Lowercase Names, and Letter Sounds (CTB/McGraw-Hill, 1998)	Uppercase alphabet recognition, lowercase alphabet recognition, letter-sound knowledge measured with lowercase letters	5 minutes	Criterion-referenced
An Observational Survey of Early Literacy Achievement: Letter Identification (Clay, 2005)	Uppercase alphabet recognition, lowercase alphabet recognition, letter-sound knowledge	3–5 minutes	Norm-referenced

Measure	Skills Assessed	Approximate Administration Time	Scoring
Phonological Awareness Literacy Screening for PreKindergarten: Upper-Case and Lower-Case Alphabet Recognition (Invernizzi, Sullivanet al., 2004)	Uppercase alphabet recognition, lowercase alphabet recognition	3–5 minutes	Criterion-referenced
Phonological Awareness Literacy Screening for PreKindergarten and Kindergarten: Letter Sounds (Invernizzi, Juel et al., 2004; Invernizzi, Sullivan et al., 2004)	Letter-sound knowledge using upper-case letters, digraphs (ch, th, sh)	3–5 minutes	Criterion-referenced
Pre-Reading Inventory of Phonological Awareness (Dodd et al., 2000)	Letter-sound knowledge, including consonants, digraphs (ch, th), consonant blends (st, fl), vowels	3–5 minutes	Norm-referenced
Test of Early Reading Ability-3: Alphabet (Reid et al., 2001)	Recognition of upper- and lowercase alphabet, digraphs, long vowel patterns	10 minutes	Norm-referenced
Woodcock Johnson III- Tests of Achievement: Letter-Word Identification (Woodcock et al., 2001)	Letter matching, alphabet recognition	5–10 minutes	Norm-referenced

347

whether the child named each letter correctly. The Identifying Sounds and Letters task requires that the child look at a picture (e.g., drawing of a sun), say its beginning sound (e.g., /s/), and tell the letter that the picture starts with (e.g., *s*). Scoring is based on the entire Memory subtest and normative data are available in the technical reference. Total administration time for the subtest is approximately 10 minutes. (For an overview of the DSC, see the description of the measure in the Print Concepts section of this chapter.)

Dynamic Indicators of Basic Early Literacy Skills (DIBELS) (Kaminski & Good, 2002)

The Dynamic Indicators of Basic Early Literacy Skills (DIBELS) is a standardized tool available online at no charge that is designed to measure children's prereading and reading skills in kindergarten through grade 6. The assessment tool comprises seven individually administered 1-minute subtests measuring phonological awareness, the alphabetic principle, and oral reading fluency. Per the recommendations of the National Reading Panel Report (2000) and *Preventing Reading Difficulties in Young Children* (Snow et al., 1998), DIBELS is designed specifically to monitor the progress of early reading skills within the context of reading instruction and to identify students at risk for later reading difficulties. The administration and scoring guide provides benchmarks for most of the subtests at three testing points in the school year. Psychometric information is available online in a downloadable technical report (http://dibels.uoregon.edu/).

DIBELS: Letter Naming Fluency (Good & Kaminski, 2002).

Comprising one of seven subtests of DIBELS, the Letter Naming Fluency (LNF) subtest is an individually administered, timed measure of children's ability to name letters quickly. The test administrator uses a standardized script to introduce the task to the child: "Here are some letters. Tell me the names of as many letters as you can. When I say 'begin,' start here, and go across the page. Point to each letter and tell me the name of that letter. If you come to a letter you don't know I'll tell it to you. Put your finger on the first letter. Ready, begin" (Good & Kaminski, 2002). Upper- and lowercase letters are then presented to students in a random order, with approximately 110 letters (both upper- and lowercase) provided on a single printed sheet. Children name as many letters as possible in 1 minute, and one point is awarded for each letter named correctly. It is important to note that this task is not designed to provide information regarding children's knowledge of specific letter names but rather to identify children at risk in literacy development.

Although Letter Naming Fluency is recommended for children in kindergarten (beginning, middle, and end) through the beginning of first grade, benchmarks are not provided for this task because the authors maintain that knowledge of letter names is not sufficiently linked to later reading outcomes. Nevertheless, the authors recommend that schools use this measure to compare individual student outcomes with established local district norms to identify those at risk. The DIBELS administration and scoring guide provides a description of the psychometric properties for the Letter Naming Fluency subtest.

ERDA-R: Letter Recognition (The Psychological Corporation, 2002)

The Letter Recognition subtest of the standardized, norm-referenced ERDA-R is individually administered and measures children's ability to match and name letters. For the first three items, the examiner shows a lowercase letter (e.g., *c*) in a stimulus flip-book, asking the child to "look carefully at this letter." After 1 second, the examiner turns the page and displays an array of three letters (e.g., *c, e, a*), asking the child to say or point to the letter that is the same as the previous letter. The remaining items require children to name the 26 lowercase letters of the alphabet, with approximately nine letters on a page in random order.

Although the subtest is untimed, the examiner allows approximately 3 seconds of response time per item and total administration time is approximately 3 to 5 minutes. After seven consecutive errors, the subtest is discontinued. One point is awarded for each correct response, and raw scores can be converted to percentile ranges for both fall and spring kindergarten assessment points. The Concept of Print Observation Checklist, Part A is administered in tandem with the Letter Recognition subtest; for a description of the checklist and an overview of the ERDA-R, readers should refer to the Print Concepts section of this chapter.

Fox in a Box: Alphabet Recognition (CTB/McGraw-Hill, 1998)

The Alphabet Recognition section of the criterion-referenced Fox in a Box is divided into three tasks: Uppercase Names, Lowercase Names, and Letter Sounds. Together, administration time for these tasks is approximately 5 minutes. The Uppercase Names task measures children's ability to name the uppercase letters of the alphabet. The 26 uppercase letters are presented in a random order on a single page. Using a "window" card, the examiner displays one line at a time, each providing a view of approximately five letters. One point is awarded for each uppercase letter named correctly, with fall and spring kindergarten benchmarks detailed in the teacher's guide for interpreting performance.

The Lowercase Names and Letter Sounds tasks are administered simultaneously. The 26 lowercase letters of the alphabet are presented in a random order on a single page. The examiner asks children to name the lowercase letter and give its sound. One point is awarded for each letter named correctly and for each correct sound, with kindergarten benchmarks detailed in the teacher's guide. It is important to note that both the soft and hard consonant sounds for letters (such as *g* or *c*) and both short and long vowel sounds are acceptable. (For an overview of Fox in a Box, see the description of the measure in the Print Concepts section of this chapter.)

An Observational Survey of Early Literacy Achievement: Letter Identification (Clay, 2005)

The Letter Identification task of the Observational Survey requires children to identify each of the upper- and lowercase alphabet letters by saying the letter name, sound of the letter, or a word that begins with the target letter. Administration is standardized and requires approximately 3 to 5 minutes. The examiner presents a single printed sheet of letters in a large font and then orients the child to the task by asking, "What do you call these?" Then, she points to each letter and asks, "What is this one?" The examiner records the child's response verbatim on a score sheet and separately tallies the number of letters named, the number of letters whose sound was named, and the number of letters for which a correct word was given in order to assist in instructional decision-making, although the total raw score for this subtest does not distinguish these subcategories of responses. Information from this task can be used to guide instruction by identifying letters that are unfamiliar to children. (For an overview of An Observational Survey of Early Literacy Achievement, see the description of the measure in the Print Concepts section of this chapter.)

PALS-PreK: Uppercase and Lowercase Alphabet Recognition (Invernizzi, Sullivan et al., 2004)

The Uppercase and Lowercase Alphabet Recognition tasks represent two additional standardized, criterion-referenced tasks of the PALS-PreK, an instrument discussed previously in this chapter. These two tasks examine 4-year-old children's knowledge of all 26 upper- and lowercase alphabet letter names. The authors of the measure recommend that the Lowercase Alphabet Recognition subtest be administered only to children who receive a raw score of 16 or higher on the Uppercase Alphabet Recognition task.

Administration is standardized and each subtest can be given in approximately 3 to 5 minutes. Both use the same procedures, in which children are asked to name each of the 26 individual letters that are presented in random order of presentation on a single printed sheet. Examiners may assist children in tracking the letters or may reduce distractions by showing children only one letter at a time, but cannot provide assistance or feedback on the accuracy of the children's performance. The examiner scores children's responses to each item on a score sheet and a raw score is calculated representing the total number of letters accurately named. Raw scores can be interpreted against spring developmental ranges for 4-year-olds and may also be used to inform classroom teaching practices and provide a profile of individual children's progress in alphabet knowledge. It is important to note that the Lowercase Alphabet Recognition task on PALS-K is identical to its analog in the PreK version, but the scores on the PALS-K are compared against fall and spring kindergarten minimum benchmarks. (For an overview of PALS-PreK, see the description of the measure in the Print Concepts section of this chapter.)

PALS-PreK and PALS-K: Letter Sounds (Invernizzi, Juel et al., 2004)

The Letter Sounds task is identical in both the PALS-PreK and PALS-K versions. This standardized task is administered in approximately 3 to 5 minutes. Twenty-three uppercase letters are displayed on a single printed sheet as well as three digraphs (sh, th, ch). The examiner asks the child to point to each letter and tell what sound the letter makes. Each item is scored as correct or incorrect, and children receive a raw score ranging from 0 to 26. The authors recommend that the measure only be used with preschool children who know nine or more lowercase letters, but can be used with all kindergarten children in the fall and spring of the year.

Scores on these measures are interpreted against developmental ranges (PALS-PreK) and minimal competency benchmarks (PALS-K) provided in the administration and scoring guide; these ranges are primarily based on data collected on Virginia's public school children.

Pre-Reading Inventory of Phonological Awareness (PIPA) (Dodd, Crosbie, McIntosh, Teitzel, & Ozanne, 2000)

The Pre-Reading Inventory of Phonological Awareness (PIPA) is a commercially available, standardized assessment designed to measure phonological awareness and letter-sound knowledge in 3- to 6-year-old children. It is designed to identify children at risk for literacy difficulties as a result of poor phonological skills. The tasks measured by the PIPA include rhyme awareness, syllable segmentation, alliteration awareness, sound isolation, sound segmentation, and letter-sound knowledge.

Administration of the PIPA is standardized and requires approximately 25 to 30 minutes per child. Raw scores can be converted to a percentile score, allowing for a determination of whether children's achievement falls into the Emerging/Below Basic, Basic, or Proficient range. The PIPA manual also provides details regarding psychometric properties (i.e., reliability and validity).

PIPA: Letter-Sound Knowledge (Dodd et al., 2000).

The Letter-Sound Knowledge task of the PIPA investigates children's ability to generate the sound that corresponds to a given letter. The examiner shows the child two pages of letters and asks the child to name each individual letter sound. Stimuli includes single consonant letters, digraphs (e.g., ch, th), blends (e.g., st, fl), and vowels. If a child responds incorrectly to 10 consecutive letters on a page, the examiner asks whether the child knows any letters on the page, scores any answers given, and presents the next page of letters. A total raw score is obtained by summing the number of correct letter-sounds produced by the child. This score can be converted to a percentile rank and performance range (i.e., Emerging/Below Basic, Basic, or Proficient). Additionally, an item analysis can be performed to determine whether a child's difficulty is limited to consonants, vowels, diagraphs, or clusters.

TERA-3: Alphabet (Reid et al., 2001)

The Alphabet subtest of the standardized, norm-referenced TERA-3 is a 29-item test that investigates children's knowledge of letter names, letter sounds, and syllables; it also includes word recognition and sentence reading. The items assess children's understanding of these concepts using both upper- and lowercase letters, different font types (e.g., bubble letters with shadow), spelling patterns with short and long vowels and digraphs, as well as real words and nonsense words. One point is awarded for each correct item, with points summed for a raw score, which can be converted into standard scores, percentiles, and age/grade equivalents. (For an overview of the TERA-3, see the description of the measure in the Print Concepts section of this chapter.)

Woodcock-Johnson III—Tests of Achievement (WJ-III) (Woodcock, McGrew, & Mather, 2001)

The Woodcock-Johnson III- Tests of Achievement (WJ-III) is a widely used, commercially available standardized assessment designed to measure performance in the areas of reading, oral language, mathematics, written language and academic knowledge in individuals 2 to 90 years of age. The standard battery consists of 12 tasks, which cluster into these academic areas and include both timed and untimed tasks. The test is designed to be a comprehensive diagnostic measure of academic strengths and weaknesses for one or more of the following purposes: diagnosing specific disabilities, developing educational programming, developing individual goals (as in an IEP), assessing growth, and/or determining effectiveness of educational programs (Mather & Woodcock, 2001).

Examiners using this measure should have knowledge of the standardized administration and scoring procedures and experience with diagnostic testing. Administration occurs in a quiet setting on an individual basis and an experienced administrator requires approximately 60 to 70 minutes to give the standard battery of tasks. To reduce testing time, each subtest has a suggested starting point based on age, and testing is discontinued according to each subtest's testing rules. The majority of tasks are scored by giving the participant one point for a correct answer and no points for an incorrect answer; however, exceptions exist and the manual provides procedures for calculating raw scores for these tasks. Additionally, the manual provides guidance in scoring answers that require examiner judgment in determining if an answer is correct or incorrect. Age- and grade-equivalent scores, standard scores, and percentile ranks can be obtained for subtests and at a summary level as a total achievement score. Interpretation of results for diagnostic decision-making is typically made by someone with graduate level training in educational assessment or a related professional area. Psychometric properties are available in the technical reference.

WJ-III: Letter-Word Identification (Woodcock et al., 2001).

The 71-item Letter-Word Identification task comprises one of the tests of the reading cluster of the standardized, norm-referenced WJ-III measure. It assesses children's ability to identify and name letters as well as to identify written words. For questions specific to alphabet knowledge, children select the letter that matches a target letter, point to the correct letter when given its name, and name letters indicated by the examiner. Although the test is not timed, the examiner scores the item as incorrect and presents the next question if no response is given within 5 seconds. Administration time is approximately 5 to 10 minutes. Each correctly answered item is given one point and points are summed for a subtest raw score, which is then converted to a standard score and percentile rank.

Measuring Emergent Writing

Measures that examine emergent writing can provide professionals with a valuable insight into young children's understanding of how print works. Writing tends to develop in synchrony with children's reading behaviors (Bear et al., 2004), and name writing is often a child's first attempt to communicate meaning through print and is closely correlated with other emergent literacy skills (Bloodgood, 1999; Welsch et al., 2003). Measures of writing not only include name writing tasks but also alphabet production, writing sample analysis, copying, word writing (dictation), and spelling. There are few commercial writing measures for preschool children, who are typically writing with no letter-sound correspondences. In kindergarten, children typically make the transition from emergent writing to early writing, and begin to represent speech sounds and word boundaries in their writing. Both emergent and early writing tasks are included in this chapter. Table 7-3 provides an overview of measures related to emergent and early writing.

DSC: Writing and Drawing Concepts (CTB/McGraw-Hill, 1990)

The Writing and Drawing Concepts subtest of the norm referenced DSC measures young children's emergent writing abilities. To administer this task, the examiner first gives the child a blank sheet of paper and a pencil and asks the child to write his or her name at the top of the page. The child then draws a self-portrait. Next, the examiner prompts the child to write a message to a person or to write about the self-portrait, encouraging the child to pretend to write (if necessary). The name writing task is scored on a 4-point scale representing a continuum from letter-like forms to conventional name writing. The 7-point scoring scale for the drawing a person task involves comparing the child's drawing with existing categories of children's drawings, with more points awarded for facial expressions and representation of movement in the picture. Children's written messages are scored based on two scales: mechanics and quality. The 4-point mechanics scale awards points for scribbling, letter-like forms, recognizable letters, and a readable message with invented spelling. The 6-point quality scale takes into

Table 7–3. Overview of Emergent and Early Writing Measures

Measure	Skills Assessed	Approximate Administration Time	Scoring
Developing Skills Checklist: Writing and Drawing Concepts (CTB/McGraw-Hill, 1990)	Name writing, drawing a person, message mechanics and quality	10 minutes	Norm-referenced
Fox in a Box: Alphabet Writing (CTB/McGraw-Hill, 1998)	Writing uppercase and lowercase forms of 10 alphabet letters	5 minutes	Criterion-referenced
Fox in a Box: Spelling (CTB/ McGraw-Hill, 1998)	Writing initial, medial, and final sounds of CVC words	10 minutes	Criterion-referenced
An Observational Survey of Early Literacy Achievement: Writing Samples (Clay, 2005)	Linguistic organization, message quality, and directional principles	N/A	Criterion-referenced
An Observational Survey of Early Literacy Achievement: Writing Vocabulary (Clay, 2005)	Writing words from memory	10 minutes	Norm-referenced

Measure	Skills Assessed	Approximate Administration Time	Scoring
Oral and Written Language Scales: Written Expression Scale (Carrow-Woolfolk, 1996)	Name writing, word copying, writing dictated letters and sounds, labeling pictures, writing a question	10 minutes	Norm-referenced
Phonological Awareness Literacy Screening for PreKindergarten: Name Writing (Invernizzi, Sullivan et al., 2004)	Name writing, distinguishing name from drawing	5–10 minutes	Criterion-referenced
Phonological Awareness Literacy Screening for Kindergarten: Spelling (Invernizzi, Juel et al., 2004)	Spelling of CVC words using conventional letters or phonetically acceptable substitutions	5–10 minutes	Criterion-referenced
Woodcock Johnson III—Tests of Achievement: Spelling (Woodcock et al., 2001)	Prewriting skills, writing upper- and lowercase letters, spelling words increasing in orthographic difficulty	5–10 minutes	Norm-referenced

account the length of the message and spacing between letters and words. Normative data are available on name writing, drawing a person, and message quality. The Writing and Drawing Concepts subtest takes approximately 10 minutes and can be group administered. (For an overview of the DSC, see the description of the measure in the Print Concepts section of this chapter.)

Fox in a Box: Alphabet Writing (CTB/McGraw-Hill, 1998)

The Alphabet Writing task of Fox in a Box measures young children's ability to write dictated upper- and lowercase letters. Children write their name at the top of a piece of paper. After modeling the writing of one alphabet letter (in both upper- and lowercase forms), the examiner dictates 10 letters for children to write on their own. The examiner has some flexibility in choosing which letters to dictate, although different letters are chosen for the fall and spring kindergarten administrations and some letters are excluded (e.g., *V v, Y y,* and *Z z*). One point is awarded for each upper- or lowercase letter written correctly, with reversals (i.e., mirror images) noted but not counted as errors. Minimum benchmarks are available for fall and spring testing points, and total administration time is approximately 5 minutes. (For an overview of Fox in a Box, see the description of the measure in the Print Concepts section of this chapter.)

Fox in a Box: Spelling (CTB/McGraw-Hill, 1998)

The Spelling task of Fox in a Box measures children's spellings of initial consonants, final consonants, and medial vowels in simple words following the consonant-vowel-consonant (CVC) pattern. It is recommended that this task be administered only after children have demonstrated the ability to write letters. Children are given incomplete spellings, with one letter missing per word. In the fall of kindergarten, two lists are administered, each containing five words. In the first list, children write the missing initial consonant sounds (e.g., _ip). In the second list, children write the missing final consonant sounds (e.g., ba_). In the spring of kindergarten, children repeat these lists and also receive a third list with words missing the medial vowel sounds (e.g., p_t). One point is awarded for each sounds missing letter filled in correctly. (Note that this task does not allow for phonetically acceptable substitutions.) Total administration time is approximately 10 minutes (5 minutes over 2 days).

An Observational Survey of Early Literacy Achievement: Writing Samples (Clay, 2005)

Clay (2005) recommends assessing young children's attempts to write stories by evaluating three writing samples taken over the course of a few days or weeks. For these samples, a child should write on a blank page (i.e., a page with no lines) and the examiner should not focus on a child's handwriting as young children vary in their level of fine motor control. The writing samples are evaluated using three rating scales (ranging in scores from 1 to 6): language level, message quality, and directional principles. The language level refers to the child's "linguistic organization," with scoring as follows: 1—letters only, 2—any words, 3—a two-word phrase, 4—a simple sentence, 5—a punctuated story with two or more sentences, or 6—a two-themed paragraphed story. To evaluate the quality of a child's message, the examiner uses the following scoring rubric: 1—a "concept of signs" (i.e., uses letter-like forms, letters, punctuation), 2—writing that conveys a message, 3—a copied message, 4—repeating sentence patterns (e.g., I like . . .), 5—records own ideas, and 6—a well-composed writing. The third rating scale involves the evaluation of a child's knowledge of directionality: 1—no directionality, 2—partial directionality, 3—reversed directionality (i.e., right to left), 4—correct directionality, 5—correct directionality with spaces between words, and 6—elaborate text with directionality and spacing. Scoring is interpreted for each rating scale using two categories: "probably satisfactory" or "not yet satisfactory." (For an overview of An Observational Survey of Early Literacy Achievement, see the description of the measure in the Print Concepts section of this chapter.)

An Observational Survey of Early Literacy Achievement: Writing Vocabulary (Clay, 2005)

The Writing Vocabulary task of the Observational Survey of Early Literacy Achievement measures the number of words children can write in 10 minutes. Children begin by writing their name and then proceed to write any words that come to mind. If a child is resistant to writing his or her name, the child is asked to write simple words, such as *I* or *is*. When children come to a stopping point, the examiner can repeatedly provide prompts by suggesting words that they may know. Dictation of a list of words should be avoided. Each correctly spelled word is awarded one point. Stanines are available for interpretation of performance, beginning with age 5 years.

Oral and Written Language Scales (OWLS) (Carrow-Woolfolk, 1996)

The Oral and Written Language Scales (OWLS) is a commercially available, norm-referenced tool designed to measure oral and written language in children and young adults. Three scales may be administered individually or in small groups: Listening Comprehension, Oral Expression, and Written Expression. The scales measure vocabulary, grammar, and function in the use of oral and written language. OWLS is designed to assist professionals (e.g., speech-language pathologists, early childhood specialists) in identifying children with difficulties, planning appropriate instruction, and monitoring progress over time. The ideal examiner is trained at the graduate level in the use and interpretation of standardized measures.

The administration manual provides information for professionals who wish to compare a child's results across scales. Psychometric properties are also available in the administration manual.

OWLS: Written Expression Scale (Carrow-Woolfolk, 1996). The Written Expression Scale of the OWLS measures children's ability to use conventions (e.g., letter formation, spelling, punctuation), to use linguistic forms (e.g., phrases, sentences, verb forms), and to communicate adequately (e.g., content, details, word choice). Test items are grouped into age-appropriate sets of approximately 16 items per set. The first set, for 5- to 7-year-old children, includes items requiring children to write their first and last names; copy words; write dictated letters, letter sounds, and sentences; label pictures; combine two sentences; write a question; and retell a story. Detailed scoring guidelines are available in the administration manual, taking into account handwriting and phonetic spelling. Normative data are provided for the Written Expression Scale, beginning with age 5 years. Total administration time is 10 minutes for 5- to 7-year-old children.

PALS-PreK: Name Writing (Invernizzi, Sullivan et al., 2004)

The Name Writing task of the PALS-PreK measures preschool children's familiarity with writing with a focus specifically on children's own names. The task takes approximately 5 to 10 minutes but is variable in length because it involves asking children to draw a self-portrait and then to write their name. (Some children take longer than others on this task.) If a child is unwilling to write his or her name, the examiner prompts the child to "pretend" to write his or her name. If this does not work, an informal writing sample can be analyzed (e.g., artwork from a class activity; Invernizzi, Sullivan et al., 2004).

Scoring for the Name Writing task is based on a developmental continuum of young children's early development in writing, ranging from scribbles to a more conventional representation of one's name. Scores range from 0 to 7, with higher scores representing more sophisticated representations. For example, 1 point is awarded if a child's scribbled name is intertwined with a picture, and 7 points are awarded if the name is written correctly. The 7-point Name Writing scoring guide is presented in Figure 7–1. Scores are interpreted against 4-year-old developmental ranges provided in the Teacher's Manual. (For an overview of PALS-PreK, see the description of the measure in the Print Concepts section of this chapter.)

PALS-K: Spelling (Invernizzi, Juel, et al., 2004)

The PALS-K Spelling task measures kindergartners' phonetic spelling as applied to simple three-phoneme words following the consonant-vowel-consonant pattern (e.g., *sad*). Administration time is approximately 5 to 10 minutes, and the task may be administered individually or to small groups of children. As a sample item,

0 points	Name is a scribble and the picture represents both child's picture and written name.	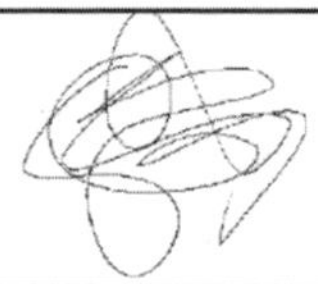 Janelle
1 point	Name is a scribble intertwined with picture. The child identifies the picture or part of the picture as his/her written name.	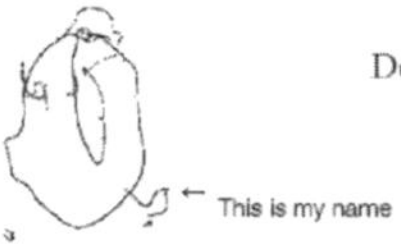 Deja This is my name
2 points	Name is an unrecognizable scribble but name is separate from picture.	 Taylor
3 points	Name consists of random letters and symbols. Name is separate from picture.	 Chiu
4 points	Name consists of some correct letters and possibly some filler letters or symbols. The name is separate from picture.	 Adam
5 points	Name consists of many correct letters with no filler letters or symbols. The name is separate from picture.	 Michayla
6 points	Name is generally correct and is separate from picture. Some letters may be written backwards or name may be completely written in a mirror image.	 Raj
7 points	Name is correct with no backwards letters or mirror image writing. The name is separate from picture.	 Cierra

Figure 7–1. PALS-PreK Name Writing Scoring Samples (From *Phonological Awareness Literacy Screening: Preschool*, by M. A. Invernizzi, A. Sullivan, J. D. Meier, & L. Swank, 2004, p. 14. Copyright 2004 University of Virginia. Reprinted with permission of the publisher).

the examiner first spells the word *mat* for the children, stretching out each sound and writing the corresponding letters. Afterwards, five items are dictated and children are asked to spell each one. Children may use an alphabet strip provided on the PALS-K Spelling sheet for reference. When scoring the children's spelling, one point is awarded for each phoneme represented within a word, and a bonus point is awarded for an entire word spelled correctly, for a possible total of 20 points for the entire task. It is important to note that scoring for this task is based on phonetically acceptable letter-sound matches and children receive credit for acceptable substitutions. For example, if a child writes *cad* for the word *sad,* he or she receives a point for the *c,* but is not eligible for the bonus point. Static reversals (i.e., mirror images) but kinetic are reversals (e.g., *net* for *ten*) are not counted as errors, but kinetic reversals are ineligible for the bonus point. The administration and scoring guide provides further details regarding scoring. Children's performance is interpreted against minimal kindergarten benchmarks for representing phonemes in kindergarten. (For an overview of the PALS-K, see the description of the measure in the Print Concepts section of this chapter.)

WJ-III: Spelling (Woodcock et al., 2001)

The 59-item Spelling task comprises one of the tests of the written language cluster of the standardized, norm-referenced WJ-III measure. It assesses children's ability to spell dictated words as well as prewriting skills. Items 1 through 3 address the ability to copy a vertical mark, a scribble, and a straight line connecting two dots. Items 4 through 7 address the ability to trace and/or copy uppercase letters. For items 8 through 12, the examiner asks the child to write a specific letter, with either an uppercase or lowercase response acceptable. Items 13 and 14 require the child to write specific lowercase letters of the alphabet. The remainder of the test items require spellings of words, increasing in difficulty. Each correctly answered item is given one point and points are summed for a subtest raw score, which is then converted to standard scores and percentile ranks. Total administration time is approximately 5 to 10 minutes. (For an overview of the WJ-III, see the description of the measure in the Alphabet and Letter-Sound Knowledge section of this chapter.)

Special Considerations for Assessing Print Knowledge

Children's emergent literacy development, including their attainment of print knowledge, is influenced by a range of developmental and environmental influences. For instance, children who are reared in lower income homes and children whose parents exhibit limited literacy may have little exposure to books and other print-related activities (Justice & Ezell, 2001a). Consequently, these children may have less knowledge about print compared to more advantaged children. Likewise, children who are learning English as a second language may have little familiarity with the English orthography, and children who exhibit developmental disabilities, such as language or cognitive impairment, may show slower development of print knowledge compared to their typically developing peers (Justice et al., 2006). Use of measures to estimate print-knowledge development and to guide design of effective instruction and intervention is particularly important for these young children, given the integrative relationships between early print knowledge and later achievement of skilled reading (e.g., Storch & Whitehurst, 2002).

When using print-knowledge assessments for children who have little knowledge about print due to environmental and/or developmental factors, it may be necessary to make adjustments to the measures employed, including (1) designing forerunner tasks, (2) modifying administration, and (3) developing dynamic tasks. Forerunner tasks are tasks that look at precursors to print knowledge, such as children's ability to distinguish between two graphically similar letters of the alphabet (e.g., *B* and *P*). Presumably, children need to realize that each of the 26 alphabet letters has a distinct shaping prior to being able to map the names of letters onto the letters themselves. For children who have no knowledge of the alphabet, simply looking at whether they can distinguish among letters in terms of visual characteristics may be a useful forerunner task. Other examples of forerunner tasks include asking children to identify features of very familiar books (e.g., the title of the book, the front of the book, a word in the book) rather than the more decontextualized and unfamiliar books and materials used in standardized assessment tasks. Similarly, another example is determining if children can identify words they commonly see in their own learning environments, like the names of peers on cubbies in their preschool classrooms.

At times, it also may be important to modify the administration of measures. Children with processing difficulties may require additional time or prompts to perform structured assessment tasks. Children who speak a language other than English may need materials translated for them. For this latter group of children, versions in other languages are available for some of the measures presented in this chapter; however, it is very important that such measures are carefully studied to determine how the measure was developed. For instance, straight translation of items from English to another language is considered an inappropriate test-development method. Of course, whenever a standardized measure is modified, it affects the validity of findings. Thus, any modifications to standardized measures should be carefully noted on administration records, and results should be interpreted cautiously. Nonetheless, modified administration may, in fact, provide more useful information than standardized administration for children who exhibit special learning challenges. For example, a child with severe speech intelligibility issues may not be able to name the individual letters of the alphabet but may be able to point to all of them correctly, which would be a more valid approach for identifying his level of alphabet knowledge.

A final consideration is the potential for using dynamic assessment with children who exhibit very little knowledge of print. Dynamic assessment is a way to examine whether a child's knowledge or ability is in the process of maturing by looking at performance within adult-mediated activities (see Spector, 1992). It provides an important alternative to traditional assessments that look not at maturing abilities but only those that are fully formed and independent. Consider, for instance, the case of Tahim, a 4-year-old child who has severe language impairment. A speech-language pathologist (SLP) administers the Preschool Word and Print Awareness Assessment (PWPA; Justice & Ezell, 2001b) to estimate his knowledge of print concepts. Tahim receives a score of 0 given traditional administration. The savvy SLP wonders, however, if Tahim may have some knowledge of print concepts that is not yet fully formed but rather is in the process of maturation. She decides to use dynamic assessment, particularly a test-teach-retest approach, to determine if this might be the case. The SLP rereads to Tahim the book used with the PWPA and models each of the print concepts tested on this measure. For example, for the cover of the book, she says, "This is the cover of the book. This is the title of the book. Show me the title of the book." After reading the book this second time, the SLP then readministers the PWPA to Tahim, and finds that he can identify five of the print concepts that he could not previously. The SLP interprets this to show that these five concepts are in the process of maturing, whereas the other five concepts (none of which he is still able to identify) are relatively immature by comparison. Importantly, the clinician's use of dynamic assessment has shown that Tahim has some understanding of print concepts, rather than none at all.

Interpreting the Results of Assessments of Print Knowledge

Essentially, measures of print knowledge can be used for three purposes: (1) screening, (2) diagnosis, and (3) monitoring progress. Screening tools and diagnostic tools typically are used to identify children whose scores are significantly below those of their peers and who may need special assistance to improve their abilities in key areas. Some screening tools are designed to identify children's relative strengths and weaknesses in print knowledge, and can be used for more criterion-referenced purposes. Some of these tools are used for "high-stakes" purposes, such as identifying whether a child qualifies for a special supplemental literacy intervention or whether a child qualifies for special education services; thus, ensuring the psychometric quality of such tools is important. Most of the measures discussed in this chapter were designed to serve as screening and/or diagnostic tools. Progress monitoring tools typically are designed to provide ongoing measures of progress over time, as is needed to document progress in print knowledge during classroom-based instruction or more specialized intervention programs. Tools used for frequent progress monitoring must be (a) sensitive to changes in the domain being assessed, and (b) amenable to repeated use and resistant to practice effects. Few of the tools discussed in this chapter have been studied for these features; thus their use for progress monitoring purposes should occur with caution.

For many professionals, measures of print knowledge are used primarily to (a) identify children's level of print knowledge across different areas (e.g., alphabet knowledge, print concepts, emergent writing) to determine if intervention is warranted, (b) select targets for instruction and/or intervention, and (c) document effects of intervention. It is unlikely that one measure will serve all of these purposes, and professionals likely will want to utilize a portfolio of tools to serve different purposes. For the first purpose, both screening tools and diagnostic tools can be used. For the second purpose, measures that are most amenable are those that include a sufficient number of task items to guide target selection, which some persons refer to as "instructional transparency." For example, if an SLP wants to select specific alphabet letters to work on with a specific child, a measure that only samples a few letters (e.g., the Alphabet subtest of the TERA-3) would not be particularly useful; rather, a measure that documents performance on all 26 letters would be most helpful (e.g, Alphabet Recognition task of the PALS-PreK). For the third purpose, one wants to be sure that the measure is adequately stable for repeated administration and that the scores are interpretable to show performance gains over time.

When selecting targets for intervention, as identified through use of print-knowledge measures, professionals typically follow one of two approaches to selecting specific objectives within a developmental domain: vertical structuring and horizontal structuring (Fey, 1986). With vertical structuring, an objective is targeted to mastery, at which point a new objective is selected for targeting. For example, with alphabet knowledge, a professional might select the letter *s* to work on and target this intensively until the child masters it before moving onto another letter. With horizontal structuring, a variety of objectives are targeted simultaneously, often through a cycles approach (Hodson, 1989). For example, a teacher might choose to work on four letters for several weeks and then cycle to four different letters without regard to whether the child has mastered the first four. There is little evidence to suggest whether vertical or horizontal structuring is more appropriate for promoting print knowledge, but research from other areas of intervention suggest that horizontal approaches are more efficient in the long run (e.g., Klein, 1996).

Professionals need to consider whether they will use vertical or horizontal structuring when targeting print-knowledge objectives across domains within intervention sessions. In other words, in a given session, does the professional work only on objectives in one domain (e.g., print concepts) or in several domains simultaneously (e.g., print concepts, alphabet and letter-sound knowledge, and emergent writing)? Research considering the effectiveness of print-knowledge interventions for typical and at-risk preschoolers shows that multiple domains can be addressed simultaneously within a single session and even within a single activity; for instance, when reading a book with a child, a teacher can target skills in print concepts, alphabet knowledge, and letter-sound knowledge simultaneously, building skills across all domains (Justice & Ezell, 2000, 2002). Given the importance of early print-related skills to later reading outcomes, professionals may want to utilize approaches affording the greatest efficiency in outcomes. Accordingly, we recommend utilizing horizontal structuring in both goal selection and goal targeting to promote the greatest amount of developmental change in the shortest amount of time.

References

Adams, M. J. (1990). *Learning to read: Thinking and learning about print.* Cambridge, MA: MIT Press.

Badian, N. A. (2000). Do preschool orthographic skills contribute to prediction of reading? In N. Badian (Ed.), *Prediction and prevention of reading failure.* Timonium, MD: York Press.

Bear, D. R., Invernizzi, M., Templeton, S., & Johnston, F. (2004). *Words their way: Word study for phonics, vocabulary, and spelling instruction* (3rd ed.). Upper Saddle River, NJ: Pearson Education.

Bloodgood, J. (1999). What's in a name? Children's name writing and literacy acquisition. *Reading Research Quarterly, 34,* 342–367.

Carrow-Woolfolk, E. (1996). *Oral and written language scales: Written expression scale manual.* Circle Pines, MN: AGS.

Chaney, C. (1994). Language development, metalinguistic awareness, and emergent literacy skills of 3-year-old children in relation to social class. *Applied Psycholinguistics, 15,* 371–394.

Clay, M. M. (1972). *Sand—The concepts about print test.* Auckland, New Zealand: Heinemann.

Clay, M. M. (1979). *Stones—The concept about print test.* Auckland, New Zealand: Heinemann.

Clay, M. M. (1993). *Reading recovery: A guidebook for teachers in training.* Auckland, New Zealand: Heinemann.

Clay, M. M. (2000a). *Follow me, moon.* Auckland, New Zealand: Heinemann.

Clay, M. M. (2000b). *No shoes.* Auckland, New Zealand: Heinemann.

Clay, M. M. (2005). *An observation survey of early literacy achievement,* (2nd ed.) Auckland, New Zealand: Heinemann.

CTB/McGraw-Hill. (1990). *Developing skills checklist.* Monterey, CA: Author.

CTB/McGraw-Hill. (1998). *Fox in a box: An adventure in literacy.* Monterey, CA: Author.

Dodd, B., Crosbie, S., McIntosh, B., Teitzel, T., & Ozanne, A. (2000). *Prereading inventory of phonological awareness.* San Antonio, TX: Harcourt Assessment.

Fey, M. (1986). *Language intervention with young children.* San Diego, CA: College-Hill Press.

Good, R. H., & Kaminski, R. A. (Eds.). (2002). *Dynamic indicators of basic early literacy skills* (6th ed). Eugene, OR: Institute for the Development of Educational Achievement. Retrieved from: http://dibels.uor regon.edu/

Goodman, Y. (1984). The development of initial literacy. In A. Oberg, H. Goelman, & F. Smith (Eds.), *Awakening to literacy. The University of Victoria Symposium on Children's Response to a Literate Environment: Literacy Before Schooling.* Exeter, NH: Heinemann Educational Books.

Hammill, D. D. (2004). What do we know about the correlates of reading? *Exceptional Children, 70,* 453–469.

Hayes, S. (1990). *Nine ducks nine.* Cambridge, MA: Candlewick Press.

Hiebert, E. H. (1981). Developmental patterns and interrelationships of preschool children's print awareness. *Reading Research Quarterly, 16,* 236–260.

Hodson, B. (1989). Phonological remediation: A cycles approach. In N. A. Creaghead, P. W. Newman, & W. A Secord (Eds.), *Assessment and remediation of articulatory and phonological disorders* (2nd ed., pp. 323–334). Boston: College-Hill Press.

Invernizzi, M., Juel, C., Swank, L., & Meier, J. (2004). *Phonological awareness literacy screening: Kindergarten.* Charlottesville: University of Virginia.

Invernizzi, M. A., Sullivan, A., Meier, J. D., & Swank, L. (2004). *Phonological awareness literacy screening: PreKindergarten*. Charlottesville: University of Virginia.

Justice, L. M., Bowles, & Skibbe, L. (2006). Measuring preschool attainment of print concepts: A study of typical and at-risk 3- to 5-year-old children. *Language, Speech, and Hearing Services in Schools, 37,* 1–12.

Justice, L. M., & Ezell, H. K. (2000). Stimulating children's print and word awareness through home-based parent intervention. *American Journal of Speech-Language Pathology, 9,* 257–269.

Justice, L. M., & Ezell, H. K. (2001a). Written language awareness in preschool children from low-income households: A descriptive analysis. *Communication Disorders Quarterly, 22,* 123–134.

Justice, L. M., & Ezell, H. K. (2001b). Word and print awareness in 4-year-old children. *Child Language Teaching and Therapy, 17,* 207–225.

Justice, L.M., & Ezell, H.K. (2002). Use of storybook reading to increase print awareness in at-risk children. *American Journal of Speech-Language Pathology, 11,* 17–29.

Justice, L. M., & Ezell, H. K. (2004). Print referencing: An emergent literacy enhancement strategy and its clinical applications. *Language, Speech, and Hearing Services in Schools, 35,* 185–193.

Justice, L. M., & Pullen, P. (2003). Early literacy intervention strategies: A review of promising findings. *Topics in Early Childhood Special Education, 23,* 99–113.

Kaminski, R. A., & Good, R. H. (2002). Letter Naming Fluency. In R. H. Good & R. A. Kaminski (Eds.), *Dynamic indicators of basic early literacy skills* (6th ed.). Eugene, OR: Institute for the Development of Educational Achievement. Retrieved from: http://dibels.uoregon.edu/

Klein, E. S. (1996). Phonological/traditional approaches to articulation therapy: A retrospective group comparison. *Language, Speech, and Hearing Services in Schools, 27,* 314–323.

Lomax, R. G., & McGee, L. M. (1987). Young children's concepts about print and reading: Toward a model of word reading acquisition. *Reading Research Quarterly, 22,* 237–256.

Lonigan, C. J., Burgess, S. R., & Anthony, J. L. (2000). Development of emergent literacy and early reading skills in preschool children: Evidence from a latent-variable longitudinal study. *Developmental Psychology, 36,* 596–613.

Martin, B. Jr. & Carle, E. (1992). *Brown bear, brown bear, what do you see?* New York: Henry Holt.

Mason, J. M. (1980). When do children begin to read: An exploration of four year old children's letter and word reading competencies. *Reading Research Quarterly, 15,* 203–227.

Mather, N., & Woodcock, R. W. (2001). *Examiner's manual: Woodcock-Johnson III tests of achievement.* Itasca: IL: Riverside.

McBride-Chang, C. (1999). The ABCs of the ABCs: The development of letter-name and letter-sound knowledge. *Merrill-Palmer Quarterly, 45,* 285–307.

Morris, D. (1981). Concept of word: A developmental phenomenon in the beginning reading and writing process. *Language Arts, 58,* 659–668.

Morris, D., Bloodgood, J. W., Lomax, R. G., & Perney, J. (2003). Developmental steps in learning to read: A longitudinal study in kindergarten and first grade. *Reading Research Quarterly, 38,* 302–328.

National Early Literacy Panel. (2004, November). *The National Early Literacy Panel: A research synthesis on early literacy development.* Presentation to the National Association of Early Childhood Specialists, Anaheim, CA.

National Reading Panel. (2000). *Report of the National Reading Panel: Teaching children to read.* Washington, DC: National Institute of Child Health and Human Development.

Paulson, L. H., Noble, L. A., Jepson, S., & van den Pol, R. (2001). *Building early literacy and language skills.* Longmont, CO: Sopris West.

Psychological Corporation. (2002). *Early reading diagnostic assessment—revised.* San Antonio, TX: Author.

Reid, D. K., Hresko, W. P., & Hammill, D. D. (2001). *Test of early reading ability—Third edition.* Austin, TX: Pro-Ed.

Scarborough, H. S. (1998). Early identification of children at risk for reading difficulties: Phonological awareness and some other promising predictors. In B. K. Shapiro, P. J. Accardo, & A. J. Capute (Eds.), *Specific reading disability: A view of the spectrum* (pp. 75–199). Timonium, MD: York Press.

Snow, C. E., Burns, M. S., & Griffin, P. (Eds.). (1998). *Preventing reading difficulties in young children.* Washington, DC: National Academy Press.

Spector, J. (1992). Predicting progress in beginning reading: Dynamic assessment of phonemic awareness. *Journal of Educational Psychology, 84,* 353–363.

Storch, S. A., & Whitehurst, G. J. (2002). Oral language and code-related precursors to reading: Evidence from a longitudinal structural model. *Developmental Psychology, 38,* 934–947.

Treiman, R., & Broderick, V. (1998). What's in a name: Children's knowledge about the letters in their own names. *Journal of Experimental Psychology, 70,* 97–116.

Welsch, J. G., Sullivan, A., & Justice, L. M. (2003). That's my letter!: What preschoolers' name writing representations tell us about emergent literacy knowledge. *Journal of Literacy Research, 35,* 757–776.

Whitehurst, G. J., & Lonigan, C. J. (1998). Child development and early literacy. *Child Development, 69,* 848–872.

Woodcock, R.W., McGrew, K.S., & Mather, N. (2001). *Woodcock-Johnson Tests of Achievement—III.* Itasca, IL: Riverside.

APPENDIX 7*

Preschool Word and Print Awareness (PWPA) Assessment Tool

Laura M. Justice and Helen K. Ezell

DIRECTIONS: Present the following tasks in the order depicted below. Use the book *Nine Ducks Nine* (Hayes, 1990). Read the text presented on the page and then administer the task. Each item may be repeated one time. Do not prompt, reinforce, or provide feedback to the child in any way. Score 0 for items to which the child does not respond or provides an answer that does not meet scoring criteria.

SAY: *We're going to read this book together, and I need you to help me read.*

Score/Item	Page: *Examiner Script*	Scoring Criteria
___ 1. Front of book	***Before administering task:*** Give book to child with spine facing child. **Cover: *Show me the front of the book.***	1 pt: turns book to front or points to front
___ 2. Title of book	**Cover: *Show me the name of the book.***	1 pt: points to one or more words in title
___ 3. Role of title	**Cover: *What do you think it says?***	1 pt: says 1 or more words in title or relevant title
___ 4. Print vs pictures	**Pages 1–2: *Where do I begin to read?*** ***After administering task:*** Put finger on first word in top line and say: ***I begin to read here.***	2 pts: points to first word, top line 1 pt: points to any part of narrative text
___ 5. Directionality	**Pages 1–2: *Then which way do I read?***	2 pts: sweeps left to right 1 pt: sweeps top to bottom

continues

APPENDIX 7–A. *continued*

Score/Item	Page: *Examiner Script*	Scoring Criteria
____ 6. Contextualized print	**Pages 3–4: *Show me where one of the ducks is talking.***	1 pt: points to print in pictures
____ 7. Directionality (left/right)	**Pages 5–6: *Do I read this page (point to left page) or this page (point to right page) first?***	1 pt: points to left page
____ 8. Directionality (top/bottom)	**Pages 7–8: *There's four lines on this page (point to each). Which one do I read first?*** *After administering task:* Put finger on first line and say: ***I read this one first.***	1 pt: points to top line
____ 9. Directionality (top/bottom)	**Pages 7–8: *Which one do I read last?***	1 pt: points to bottom line
____10. Print function	**Pages 9–10:** *Point to the words spoken by the ducks in the water, and say:* ***Why are there all these words in the water?***	1 pt: tells that words are what ducks say or similar (e.g., *"because they are talking"*)
____11a. Letter concept	**Pages 11–12: *Show me just one letter on this page.***	1 pt: points to one letter
____11b. First letter	**Pages 11–12: *Show me the first letter on this page.***	1 pt: points to first letter
____11c. Capital letter	**Pages 11–12: *Now show me a capital letter.***	1 pt: points to capital letter
____12. Print function	**Pages 23–24: *And the fox says "stupid ducks." Where does it say that?***	2 pts: points to fox's words 1 pt: points to other print on page

OBSERVATIONS	SCORING INSTRUCTIONS
___ Difficulty attending	**Total Raw Score:** _____
___ Asked for repetition	Add the numbers to the left of each item in the Item column.
___ Timid or reticent	**Print-Concept**
___ Difficult to understand	**Knowledge Estimate:** _____
Other:	Use the scale provided below to convert total raw scores to PCK Estimates

Raw Score	PCK Estimate	Raw Score	PCK Estimate	Raw Score	PCK Estimate
0	46	6	97	12	118
1	63	7	100	13	123
2	74	8	104	14	128
3	82	9	107	15	134
4	88	10	111	16	145
5	92	11	115	17	161

*From "Word and Print Awareness in 4-Year-Old Children," by L. M. Justice & H. K. Ezell, 2001, *Child Language Teaching and Therapy, 17*, pp. 207–226. Copyright 2001 by Sage Publishers. Reprinted with permission of the publisher.

Chapter Eight

Assessing Young Children's Oral Narrative Skills

The Story Pyramid Framework

Stephanie M. Curenton
Tamika D. Lucas

Importance of Narrative Assessment

The purpose of this chapter is to describe the materials and techniques educators and professionals can use to assess children's narrative skills. Narrative skills can be considered the *"gateway to reading and writing"* (Hirsh-Pasek, Kochanoff, Newcombe, & de Villiers, 2005, p. 6) because creating a narrative requires a child to produce a *decontextualized* description of events. The descriptions are decontextualized because they focus on objects that are not immediately present or on events removed from the current context. The use of decontextualized language sets the foundation for literacy (Crais & Lorch, 1994; Dickinson & McCabe, 1991; Gillam & Johnston, 1992; Heath, 1982; Reese, 1995), and narratives provide children with ample opportunity to use this type of language.

Researchers agree it is important and necessary to assess young children's narratives because a wealth of information about oral language and emergent literacy can be gathered from narratives (Chaney, 1998; Paris & Hoffman, 2004; Paris & Paris, 2003). Children who have good narrative skills have better emergent literacy skills and better reading abilities then those who do not (Bishop & Edmundson, 1987; Griffin, Hemphill, Camp, & Wolf, 2004; Miles & Chapman, 2002).

Determining What a Narrative Is

Narratives are language tools used to describe ideas, emotions, history, and heritage. An *oral narrative* consists of a child's spoken description of real or fictional events experienced in the past, the present, or the future. According to Labov's (1972) classic definition, a narrative must contain a minimum of two sequential independent clauses that focus on the same event or experience. Clauses in a narrative are confined to the same *time*, *space,* or *theme*, such as when a child says, "In art class today we made bunnies. Robbie ripped his up." On the contrary, two unrelated comments, such as "In art class today we made bunnies. I want to watch TV now," would not be considered a narrative because the two clauses are not about events or ideas that are related.

Narratives are therefore descriptions of events or ideas that are logically related because they fall within the same *time* period, which is usually indicated by verb tense. For example, in the narrative above about art class, both clauses contained past tense verbs. Events in narratives can be logically related because they take place in the same *space* (or setting), such as art class in our prior example. Events in a narrative can also be logically connected because the clauses are about the same theme or topic (e.g., what happened in art class). Sometimes it is difficult to determine the theme of longer narratives because the narrative may contain a *meta-theme*, meaning a larger overarching theme that houses several smaller, related themes (*subthemes*). For example, the story about art class could have been subsumed under a larger theme about what happened at school and the child might have said, "In art class today we made bunnies. Robbie ripped his up. And at lunch Robbie spilled his milk." In this example, the meta-theme is about what happened at school, but the two subthemes are what happened in art class and the difficulties Robbie encountered that day. Notice, however, that these subthemes are still confined by space (i.e., school) and time (i.e., past tense verb).

Story Pyramid Framework for Assessing Narratives

Narratives are typically assessed at two structural levels—the macrolevel and the microlevel. The *macrolevel* consists of the general organization and structure of the narrative, whereas the *microlevel* consists of grammatical and semantic features of the narrative. Combined, these two levels capture important multiple features of narratives that traditionally have been assessed in the field, including the analysis of story grammar (a macrolevel feature) and grammatical cohesion (a microlevel feature), and both levels have a solid history of research in the language and education fields. Nevertheless, approaching narrative assessment from this two-pronged (or layered) format sometimes results in other important features of narratives, such as psychological causation, being overlooked.

Rather than approaching narrative assessment from the macro- and microstructure framework, we propose approaching it from a framework that will elevate all features to an equal level of prominence during the assessment. Although we are proposing a new framework for approaching narrative assessment, we are by no means suggesting that the traditional features of narratives be discarded. On the contrary, we argue that these traditional measures maintain their level of importance, but suggest that other features of narratives be elevated to a similar level of importance to facilitate a denser, more sophisticated and culturally-sensitive assessment of narrative. Hence, we propose a **story pyramid** framework for assessing young children's narrative skills, which is presented in Figure 8–1.

The story pyramid framework has several strengths over the traditional two-pronged approach that contains only the macro- and microlevel elements. First, the story pyramid approach allows for a richer analysis of children's stories by considering a broader range of narrative features, such as *language structure, story structure*, and *psychological structure*. Each of these features of the story pyramid are discussed in the upcoming sections. Second, the framework builds on an interdisciplinary literature base by combining literature from fields like psychology and education that have conducted research on cultural traditions of narrating and psychological causation in narratives. Third, this framework is a more culturally sensitive approach to narrative assessment because it permits clinicians and educators to consider cultural traditions of narratives in conjunction with the other traditional measures. It is important to consider these cultural traditions along with other features of narratives because cultural traditions in narrating style have implications for how a child organizes his or her story, uses grammar within the story, and develops the characters. Thus, we

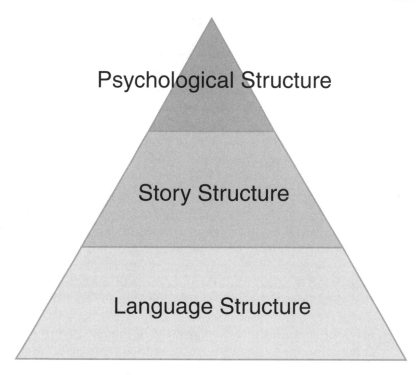

Figure 8–1. Story pyramid.

believe that approaching narrative assessment from this framework will enhance the current body of knowledge in the research field and promote more valid assessments of all children's narrative skills.

The story pyramid conceptual framework can be used by educators and clinicians to ensure they are evaluating a child's narrative as a holistic unit in which the child may be strong in one feature but weak in another. An assessment would entail a detailed description of the particular feature in which the child was weak along with a description of the other features in which he or she was strong. Using this framework would allow for the design and implementation of narrative interventions specifically tailored to children's particular strengths and weaknesses, which ultimately will make the intervention more successful at enhancing the child's narrative abilities.

Collecting a Narrative Sample

The first step in narrative assessment is collecting the narrative sample. For other aspects of emergent literacy, such as vocabulary, alphabet knowledge, or phonological awareness, children typically have to respond to a set of questions or tasks that the examiner puts forth. For narrative assessment, children do not display their skills simply by responding to standard, external stimuli; instead, children display their skills by creating (or *generating*) a corpus of data, which then will be analyzed. Therefore, serious thought has to be given as to how educators and clinicians should proceed to inspire children to produce narratives that accurately represent their abilities.

Narrative Genre

First, it is necessary to determine what *narrative genre* one wants to capture, (i.e., the *type of narrative* you want to collect). Young children are able to produce a wide variety of narrative genres (Miller, Hengst, Alexander, & Sperry, 2000). Children first begin to create *autobiographical narratives* about their personal past experiences as early as age 2 (McCabe, 1997b), such as "Yesterday when we went to the store, daddy bought me a doll. I thought the doll was so pretty!" The purpose of autobiographical narratives is to allow the child to share a personal experience from his or her past, and these narratives are typically told using the past tense. To get children to produce an autobiographical narrative, a clinician might ask them to talk about a time when they felt a particular emotion (Curenton & Wilson, 2003) or ask them to talk about a time when something significant happened to them (e.g., Have you ever broken your arm? Tell me about it? McCabe, 1997b). Of all of the narrative genres, autobiographical narratives are the ones most subject to cultural influences because these narratives are about children's actual experiences, and all personal experiences take place in a cultural context.

Another type of narrative is a nonfiction *scripted narrative,* which describes generalized routine events. These narratives usually are told in the present tense. These types of narratives are intended to examine the child's ability to describe a sequence of actions in a temporal and logical order. For instance, a clinician might ask a child to describe what happens when visiting the doctor or shopping at the grocery store. The child's task is to describe these routine events in a sequential manner. Script narratives also can be elicited by asking child to describe how to make (or do) something (e.g., "How do you build a tower of blocks?"). Because some children might produce too little or too much information about a scripted routine, Hughes, McGillivray, and Schmidek (1997) suggest that clinicians specifically ask children to tell them four or five things that happen when acting out the scripted event. Another option is to ask children to create scripted narratives within a pretend scenario, such as "Pretend you are talking to a child who has never gone to see a doctor before. Tell her five things that happen when you go to the doctor."

A third type is a *fictional narrative*, which typically follows the format of a storybook, fairy tale, myth, or fable. This type of narrative typically is used by clinicians and educators to assess children's narrative skills because it is similar to the storytelling format that children hear in storybooks. Children's ability to tell a fictional narrative is based on whether they can efficiently weave together a plot that is based on events that are psychologically relevant to the characters in the story.

Narrative Elicitation Techniques

Typically, children are asked to produce a narrative via two types of narrative elicitation techniques, story retelling and story generation. In *story retelling*, the examiner shares a story with a child and then asks the child to repeat the story. A story retelling task allows one to examine children's story comprehension, memory, and sense of story structure (Gambrell, Koskinen, & Kapinus, 1991; Morrow, 1985). *The Bus Story* (Renfrew, 1969) is a common assessment used to measure children's story retelling. For this assessment, the examiner first tells the child a story using a wordless picture book, and then the child is asked to look through the pictures again and retell the story.

Care must be taken during the administration of a story retelling task so that children understand they are to repeat the story as it was told to them. In some cultural traditions of storytelling, such as the African American tradition, storytellers are expected to embellish and add to any story they have heard. As a result, African American children have been scored lower than European Americans on story retelling tasks because they added extra details and events to the story to make the story more interesting (see Vernon-Feagans, Hammer, Miccio, & Manlove, 2002). Therefore, the expectations for the tasks must be made explicit to children, especially those children who come from certain storytelling traditions.

The second type of narrative elicitation task is *story generation*, which is the act of asking children to generate a story on their own. Story generation might be a better technique to use when trying to assess the macrolevel of children's stories because it allows children to impose their own structure onto the story (Hughes et al., 1997). However, it must be noted that when children are asked to generate autobiographical narratives, they are less likely to produce stories that adhere to a linear format. Specifically, Champion (1998) found that African American elementary schoolchildren were more likely to produce linear stories when they were asked to retell a story than when they were asked to produce an autobiographical narrative. Such a finding is logical given that all experiences happen within a cultural framework, and therefore, the "reliving" of these events in the form of an autobiographical narrative should be more susceptible to cultural storytelling traditions. These findings indicate that cultural narrating traditions can be evoked by certain tasks more so than others.

Narrative Props

Several stimuli, or narrative props, can be used to help children during the story retelling or story generation tasks. Suggestions for stimuli include verbal prompts (e.g., "Tell me a story about . . . "), dolls/puppets, and wordless pictures/books. These stimuli may be used individually or in combination with each other. For example, an examiner may use dolls or puppets to act out a verbal prompt and then allow the child to create a story using the same dolls or puppets. Practitioners must carefully consider which type of stimuli they want to employ because children have various levels of success with different stimuli (Ripich & Griffith, 1988).

Verbal Prompts

McCabe (1997b) suggests using a *conversational map* to elicit children's narratives. A conversational map is a brief narrative about something that happened to the interviewer or clinician (e.g., "One time I got stung by a bee") followed by an open-ended request for the child to talk about a similar experience (i.e., "Have you ever been stung by a bee?"). Champion (1998) provides a conversational map about a trip to the hospital: "When I was younger, my brother and I were down South visiting my aunt. My brother climbed a tree in the backyard and fell out of the tree onto a wagon. He hurt his leg and had to go to the hospital to get stitches. Did something like that ever happen to you or someone you know?" (p. 257). Although conversational maps make for lively stories, they typically are based on negative situations that unavoidably result in children describing negative emotional experiences. Another limitation of the conversational maps is that not all children may have experience with a particular situation (e.g., if a child had not ever been stung by a bee then she would have no story to tell).

If children have difficulty creating stories based on the conversational maps, the examiner may consider using an *emotional prompt* (see Curenton & Wilson, 2003) as a catalyst for children's storytelling. The advantage of presenting children with an emotional prompt in lieu of or in addition to a conversational map (see Champion, 1998) is that all children are assured to have experienced the emotion, thus, increasing the number of stories children can create. Emotional prompts and conversational maps are typically used to elicit children's autobiographical narratives, but other types of verbal prompts can be used to effectively elicit children's script narratives as well.

When using a verbal prompt to elicit a script narrative, it is important that the verbal prompt cannot be interpreted as a request to tell an autobiographical narrative. For example, we suggest that examiners avoid prompts like, "Have you ever been to McDonald's? What exactly do you do? What do you do first when you walk in the door?" (see Hughes et al., 1997). A child can easily interpret this as a request to talk about what happens to *her* when she goes to McDonald's. As a result the child might mention characters who typically accompany her when she goes to McDonald's (such as her brother or father), and her story may move from a general description of what happens when someone goes to McDonalds' to a story about something that happened when she went to McDonald's. Thus, the child might view such a prompt as a polite request by this stranger to make conversation and become acquainted with her, which might prompt her to tell an autobiographical narrative.

Dolls and Puppets

Another popular method used to elicit young children's stories are dolls and puppets. The MacArthur Story Stem Battery (MSSB; Bretherton, Oppenheim, Buschsbaum, Emde, & the MacArthur Narrative Group, 1990) is a popular method used to elicit narratives from children, especially children who have been mistreated. The MSSB contains 11 brief story stems that tap into children's schemas about their family life and experiences. The examiner uses the dolls to act out an emotionally charged story, then the child is allowed to take the dolls and is told, "Show me and tell me what happens next" (for administration details see Oppenheim, Emde, & Wamboldt, 1996; Oppenheim, Emde, & Warren, 1997). An example of a story stem is given below (Oppenheim et al., 1996, 1997):

Hot Gravy

Mother: "I am making some dinner now but it is not ready yet. Don't get too close to the stove!"

Child: "Mmm, that looks good, I don't want to wait, I'd like some right now!" (reaches over and spills the hot pot).

Child: "Ow, I cut my finger, I need a [B]andaid!"

Similar techniques with doll play have been used with ethnically and socioeconomically diverse groups of children (Craig, Washington, & Thompson-Porter, 1998; Murray, Woolgar, Briers, & Hipwell, 1999; Robinson, Herot, Haynes, & Mantz-Simmons, 2000).

Wordless Picture Books

Wordless picture books are the narrative prompts most widely used to elicit fictional stories from children. In fact, several authors have published work on children's narrative abilities using a series of books by Mercer Mayer, a children's illustrator who publishes books of drawings about a boy and his pets and family (see Bamberg, 1997). These books have been used widely because they depict a character who encounters a problem, engages in goal-based actions to solve the problem, and resolves the conflict. Preschoolers are able to generate complex stories when asked to tell a make-believe story when shown problem-based pictures rather than simple action or event-based pictures (Shapiro & Hudson, 1991). When preschoolers are prompted by materials that provide a story structure, they can create stories that are rich in plot, themes, and internal states (Benson, 1997). Although research suggests that children perform poorly when they are asked to tell a story about only one problem-based picture (Pearce, 2003), researchers have found that children produce longer and more complex narratives when they are allowed to tell a story about a picture they drew (Spinillo & Pinto, 1994). Therefore, wordless picture books and drawings are a valid way to elicit narratives from young children.

Transcribing Narratives

Narratives should always be audio- or videotaped and then later transcribed verbatim. There are two popular computer programs that can be used for the transcription and analysis of narratives. One is the Systematic Analysis of Language Transcripts (SALT; Miller & Chapman, 1983), and the other is the Child Language Analysis (CLAN; McWhinney, 1995). Some researchers would suggest that narratives be transcribed to include the examiner's comments as well as the child's because the experimenter's comments might lead a child to respond in a certain way. It is important to transcribe examiner comments if one is interested in how the child responds to a particular question or if the narrative takes place during a dialogue between the child and examiner. An example of a 3-year-old, European American boy's narrative in which it would be important to include the experimenter comments is given below:

*EXP: tell me about a time when you felt scared.

*EXP: hmm?

*Jake: xxx any more.

*EXP: tell me about a time when you felt scared.

*Jake: xxx scared.

*EXP: what do you do when you're scared?

*Jake: my sister beat me up and I bit her with my mouth.

*EXP: your sister beat you up and you bit her with your mouth?

*EXP: ok.

To facilitate the child's ability to create a story, the examiner modified the original verbal prompt that asked the child to talk about a specific incident (i.e., "Tell me about a time you felt scared") to a prompt that asked him to describe what he usually does when he is afraid (i.e., "What do you do when you're scared"). This modified prompt was easier for the child to respond to; however, it caused the child to respond with an explanation that is focused on his actions. Therefore, it provides an example of how the wording of the prompt might skew a child's responses.

It is acceptable to transcribe only children's comments during a story when the examiner is trained to respond to the child in a nonleading and consistent manner. For instance, McCabe (1997b) suggests that examiners respond to children only by saying, "Tell me more," or "Uh-huh," or "Then what happened?" (p. 141). By responding in this neutral manner, children perceive that the adult is interested, but they are not swayed by the adult's questions or responses. When examiners systematically respond in this neutral manner with all children they are interviewing, then any examiner comments can be deleted from the transcript.

Researchers may wish to delete other statements from the transcript as well. For instance, they may be interested in deleting any remarks the child makes that are not relevant to the story. Although it is acceptable to delete superfluous comments, the deletion process must follow a defined procedure. Deleting unnecessary comments ultimately will aid in the segmentation process. Curenton and Justice (2004) followed the deletion procedures described in Appendix 8-A before segmenting their sample of narratives generated by low-income children.

Language Structure

The manner in which children use language in their narratives provides the basic level of their pyramid. This level of the pyramid addresses children's ability to coherently weave together grammatical features and to use a precise and diverse lexicon. The two features of language structure discussed in this chapter are: (a) grammatical complexity and (b) vocabulary.

Grammatical Complexity

Segmenting Communication Units

After a narrative has been transcribed, it must be segmented into meaningful language units. When listening to a recording of a child's narrative, it is often difficult to determine how to break the stream of speech into meaningful units. *Communication units* (C-units) are a segmentation method that allows a clinician to segment the narrative into grammatical units (Crais & Lorch, 1994; Loban, 1976). Hughes et al. (1997) report that segmenting narratives into C-units has become conventional because C-units were specifically designed for oral narrative analyses. In addition, it is useful to segment using these procedures because there are comparative data on both language-impaired and typically developing children using this procedure (Greenhalgh & Strong, 2001), and because there is a significant correlation between average C-unit length and age (Craig et al., 1998).

C-units are grammatical units that are based on a clausal structure (i.e., a subject-predicate clause). In a clause the subject is usually the noun, and it is the topic of the clause (i.e., what the clause is about). The predicate is the verb phrase part of the clause, and it describes the action of the clause (i.e., what is being done). A C-unit consists of either (a) an independent clause or (b) an independent clause along with its dependent clause(s). An independent clause expresses a main idea, whereas a dependent clause expresses an idea that supplements the main idea. One example of a C-unit would be "Shelby feels sad," which is a single independent clause. Yet another example would be, "Shelby feels sad (independent clause) because she lost her new doll (dependent clause)." The statement,

"Shelby feels sad" is an independent clause, and the statement "because she lost her new doll" is a dependent clause because it supplements (or *modifies*) the idea of the main clause by providing additional information about why Shelby is sad. The dependent clause cannot function alone grammatically, which is why it is considered dependent (or *subordinate*).

Appendix 8–B outlines specific guidelines for segmenting a narrative into C-units compiled and adapted from various sources (Curenton & Justice, 2004; Hughes et al., 1997; Strong & Shaver, 1991). Typically, C-units are parsed at coordinating conjunctions (e.g., and, or, but, so) if they are preceded and followed by a subject-verb clause. For example the comment "The reindeer picked him up, and it threw him in the water" is counted as two C-units: (1) "The reindeer picked him up" <u>and</u> (2) "And it threw him in the water."

C-units are also parsed at conjunctive adverbs when they are preceded and followed by an independent clause; for example, "The little boy ran as fast as he could so that he could win the race" consists of two C-units: (1) "The little boy ran as fast as he could" and (2) "so that he could win the race." Dependent clauses are preceded by subordinating conjunctions (e.g., because, if, when) or conjunctive adverbs (e.g., then, that). Dependent clauses are not counted as separate C-units because they modify independent clauses.

When segmenting narratives into C-units, even statements that do not adhere to a clausal structure can still be considered in the analysis if they are responses to a question (Craig et al., 1998) or a part of dialogue. Given that dialogue is an important and sophisticated component of narratives, special considerations must be made regarding its inclusion and how it should be counted. For example, "The boy said, 'I want my frog back. I miss him. Frog, oh, frog!'" could be counted as three C-units. One C-unit is "The boy said, 'I want my frog back.'" the second is "I miss him," and the third is "Frog, oh, frog!" By making such allowances in the traditional definition, the integrity of the dialogue will be preserved.

Defining Grammatical Complexity

Grammatical complexity weaves the story together and makes the ideas/events vivid and clear. Measures of grammatical complexity can be assessed by the *number of C-units* a child uses in his or her narrative and by the average number of words per C-unit, the *mean length of C-unit (MLCU)*. The number of C-units is a measure of how many subject-predicate clauses the child uses, and this can be determined by counting the number of C-units. A narrative with more C-units indicates the child has a greater command of the clausal structure. On the other hand, the MLCU must be calculated by dividing the total number of words per C-unit by the total number of C-units in the child's story. The MLCU provides an index of how well a child has modified the clauses. For instance, a C-unit consisting of "the boy sits" is less complex than the C-unit "the angry boy sits in the corner alone."

After determining these quantitative indicators of grammatical complexity, it is important to examine *how* the clause is modified, meaning what type of grammatical features are used to modify the clause. Assessing *literate language features* (LLF) is one method for investigating the types of grammatical devices children use. The four grammatical devices most commonly associated with literate language are *elaborated noun phrases, adverbs, conjunctions,* and *mental/linguistic verbs* (Curenton & Justice, 2004; Greenhalgh & Strong, 2001; Pellegrini, 1985; Westby, Van Dongen, & Maggart, 1989). The usage rate of children's LLF can be calculated by dividing the number of each feature by the total number of C-units. Appendix 8–C provides a detailed list of literate language features.

Grammatical Complexity in Children Who Speak African American English

Some researchers calculate the number of grammatically correct C-units. If this procedure is used, then it is important to consider the child's dialect use. Many dialects are spoken in the United States. Dialects may occur based on the speaker's geographical location or ethnicity, and may include individuals from all levels of the socioeconomic strata (Heath, 1982; Rickford, 1999, Wolfram & Fasold, 1974). Increasingly, studies inclusive of dialect, specifically children's use of African American English (AAE), have been undertaken (Jackson & Roberts, 2001; Seymour, Bland-Stewart, & Green, 1998; Smith, Lee, & McDade, 2001). Based on these studies, linguists, researchers and speech-language pathologists know that

AAE is a systematic, rule-governed dialect of American English. For a comprehensive explanation of this dialect, see Rickford (1999), Washington and Craig (1994), Washington and Craig (1998), and Craig et al. (2003).

Because clinicians must measure language abilities in multi-cultural and multilingual populations, the guidelines for counting and segmenting C-units must be inclusive of nonstandard forms of English to ensure an unbiased narrative assessment. C-units have been found to serve as an unbiased assessment measure for cultur-ally and/or linguistically diverse children's language abilities (Craig et al., 1998, 2003; Jackson & Roberts, 2001; Smith, et al. 2001). For example, Craig et al. (1998) found that the relationship between MLCU and grammatical complexity is the same for AAE as it is for Standard American English; specifically, they found that African American children who used longer C-units demonstrated greater grammatical complexity in their speech and oral narratives than those who used shorter C-units.

Below is an example of a narrative by Eric, an African Ameri-can boy who speaks AAE throughout his story:

Eric: the frog wasn't in the jar.

Eric: the frog gone.

Eric: the frog was in the hole.

Eric: the frog!

Eric: the mole pinch him on his nose.

Eric: take it off!

Eric: who is that?

Eric: the dog trying to look for the frog.

Eric: the owl done knocked him down.

Eric: is he going to fell off the rock.

Eric: he went.

Eric: he was fell off the rock.

Eric: he fall.

The first feature of AAE Eric uses in his story is the *Zero copula* or *Auxiliary* feature (see Washington & Craig, 1998), which indicates that "to be" verbs or auxiliary verbs may be nonobligatory; for example, Eric says "The dog trying to look for the frog," in which he has omitted the auxiliary verb form "*is*." Another feature Eric uses is the *Completive "done"* when he remarks, "The owl *done* knocked him down.*"* In this example, he uses the morpho-syntactic rule (see Craig et al., 2003) governing the use of *done* to describe an action that was recently completed. Other examples of AAE in his story are the statements "He fall" and "The mole pinch him on his nose." In these statements he uses the *Zero Past Tense* (see Craig et al., 2003) rule in which past tense markers of verbs are variably used (e.g., *pinch* instead of *pinched*) and/or the present tense forms of irregular verbs are used (e.g., *fall* instead of *fell*). These previous three examples are instances when the child demonstrates that he can use AAE correctly. However, there are statements in his story where Eric makes grammatical errors that are not characteristic of the features of AAE, such as "he was *fell* off the rock." The construction of this statement does not adhere to any of the features of AAE, and thus could be accurately classified as a grammatical error. If the rules of AAE had not been used to judge the grammatical complexity of Eric's narrative, then he would have been assessed as having six grammatical errors, but the accurate assessment is only two errors.

All grammatical systems, including Standard American English and AAE, are based on morpho-syntactic rules that have evolved over time based on the needs of particular language communities. The ultimate goal in assessing grammatical complexity is to ensure that children can systematically apply these arbitrary rules to structure their language because failure to systematically apply morpho-syntactic rules puts children at risk for communication difficulties. It was once assumed that African American children's use of AAE was a language *disorder*; however, evidence from linguists and speech-language pathologists makes it very clear that AAE is a rule-governed system; thus, clinicians are now able to understand the use of AAE is a language *difference*.

Lexical Diversity

Lexical diversity is another key feature of the language structure of children's narratives. It is a measure of expressive vocabulary size

(Klee, 1992; Miller, 1991; Watkins, Kelly, Harbers, & Hollis, 1995) and includes indicators of vocabulary that children use in their narratives. Lexical diversity has been found to be influenced by the presence of language impairment (Goffman & Leonard, 2000), elicitation procedures (Gazella & Stockman, 2003), and a child's age (Miller, 1991).

The most common measure of lexical diversity is the *type-token ratio* (TTR; Miller, 1981, Templin, 1957; Wachal & Spreen, 1973; Watkins, Rice, & Moltz, 1993). TTR is calculated by creating a ratio based on the total number of different words versus the total number of words in the narrative. Yet, the use of TTR has been criticized for its inability to differentiate typically developing children from those with language impairment. Furthermore, TTR was found to be an insensitive measure of the language abilities of culturally and linguistically diverse children. For example, the use of TTR reduced the validity of findings for children who speak AAE (Oetting & McDonald, 2002). Therefore, additional measures of lexical diversity have been studied.

Other assessments of lexical diversity include calculating the total *number of different words* (NDW; Miller, 1991; Watkins et al., 1995) and calculating verb usage (Blake, Myszczyszyn, & Jokel, 2004; Rice & Bode, 1993). Scott and Windsor (2000) posit that the NDW is better for assessing narratives than TTR. NDW is calculated by dividing the number of single occurring words by the total number of words in the narrative (Craig & Washington 2002; Gazella & Stockman, 2003; Watkins, Kelly, Harbers, & Hollis, 1995). Watkins et al. (1995) found that when controlling for utterance length within the narrative, the NDW can reliably differentiate typically developing preschool children and children with language impairment, whereas TTR cannot. However, counting the NDW words in a child's narrative has been criticized by researchers because it is influenced by narrative length (Klee, Stokes, Wong, Fletcher, & Gavin, 2004; McKee, Malvern & Richards, 2000; Owen & Leonard, 2002; Richards & Malvern, 1997). Therefore, Owen and Leonard (2002) view NDW as a measure of verbosity rather than a true measure of lexical diversity.

Owen and Leonard (2002) developed a measure of lexical diversity that is less sensitive to narrative length. The measure is *D*, a mathematical formula designed to account for variability in the language output of children during assessment. *D* is calculated through repeated measures of TTR to estimate how TTR changes based on narrative length (see Duran, Malvern, Richards, Chipere, 2004; Klee et al., 2004; MacWhinney, 2000; McKee, Malvern & Richards, 2000; Owen & Leonard, 2002; Richards & Malvern, 1997).

The prior measures of lexical diversity consist of calculations that simply assess the size of a child's vocabulary. However, there are additional measures that assess *how* children use words in their narratives. One measure is the calculation of verb usage (Blake et al., 2004; Rice & Bode, 1993). Verb usage has been studied to understand the skills that differentiate typically developing children from children with language impairment. For example, Blake et al. (2004) found that children with language impairment had difficulty producing the correct irregular past tense forms (fell, blew, etc.) when compared to their typically developing peers. Another measure that assesses how children use words is the proportion of rare words in a child's narrative. Rare words include those that are unusual for a preschooler to have been exposed to in the past (Beals 1997; Beals & Tabors, 1995; Hall, Nagey, & Linn, 1984). Beals (1997) posits that the presence of rare words in the language output of children results from direct exposure. Thus, studies of rare words arise from researchers studying adult-child book readings (Ninio, 1983; Whitehurst et al., 1988) and adult-child conversations (Beals, 1997; Beals & Tabors, 1995). Additional studies of the proportion of rare words in a child's vocabulary are necessary to determine the extent to which uncommon words serve as a reliable indicator of lexical diversity in children's narratives.

Story Structure

Assessing the story structure of a narrative is important because it is this level of the pyramid that assists the listener in comprehending the story (see Griffin et al., 2004) by presenting the events in a temporal, spatial, and causal manner. Presently, several systems are available for analyzing a child's story structure. All of these systems provide categorical approaches that span a continuum of poorly developed narratives to sophisticated narratives. Although each system captures a particular aspect of narrative ability, all are relatively comparable and can be used individually or in combination. In the following sections, we provide a brief description of the various organizational structures.

Applebee's Narrative Levels

A popular structural analysis of children's fictional and autobiographical stories is Applebee's Narrative Levels (Applebee, 1978). This level of analysis includes a *centering strategy* (i.e., the central theme of the story) and a *chaining strategy* (i.e., how the events of the story are linked). Applebee proposed six narrative levels. The most complex level is called a *true narrative* because the story has a theme/moral with a central character and events that revolve around a core idea or event. *Focused chains* have a main central character who experiences events that are related, but no true theme is indicated. On the other hand, *unfocused chains*, which are rare, have main characters who experience related events, but these stories may drift off topic. *Primitive narratives* have a concrete core that is surrounded by events that amplify or clarify it, and the events are linked by a shared situation. *Sequences* have ideas/events that are related temporally but not causally. Finally, *heaps*, the lowest level of narratives, consist of ideas or events that are not linked temporally or causally; instead, the organization is based on perception.

Story Grammar

Another method for categorizing stories into various levels is story grammar, which is the most widely used measure of the story organization. Story grammar is ideal for analyzing fictional stories in which the protagonist exhibits goal-directed behavior. Table 8-1 describes the elements of story grammar that can be used to assign a story to a story structure level (Stein & Glenn, 1980). Some researchers have suggested that the analysis of story grammar features is more appropriate for use with school-age children than preschoolers because young children's stories often do not

Table 8–1. Story Grammar Elements

Story Grammar	Description
Setting (S)	References to the plot, including specific mention of time, place, and character
Initiating Event (IE)/Problem (P)	A complicating event that sets the story in motion is introduced, including a problem that needs resolving, and shows that the character wants to achieve a goal
Internal Response (IR)	Statements about how the character feels in response to the initiating event. It usually includes some reference to the mental states of the characters, even though these goals may not be explicitly stated; they serve as the motivation for the character
Internal Plan (IP)	A statement that might fix the problem (sometimes this may be part of the IR)
Attempt (A)	Actions taken by the character to solve the problem; there may be several attempts
Consequences (C)	The consequences of the attempted actions to solve the problem
Resolution/ Reaction (R)	The final situation that is triggered by the initiating event; it does not lead to further attempts to solve the problem
Ending (E)	A statement that clearly indicates the story is over

Source: Stein & Glenn, 1979

incorporate all of the elements (Hedberg & Westby, 1993). Nonetheless, the story structure levels can still be used to categorize young children's narratives because more complex features of story grammar are not included at all levels (see Hedberg & Westby, 1993; Peterson & McCabe, 1983; Stein & Glenn, 1980). For example, preschool-age children are able to produce *descriptive sequences* that describe the character(s) and settings but contain no causal or temporal links. *Action sequences* list actions that are chronologically but not causally linked. Finally, *reactive sequences* describe a series of actions that are chronically and causally linked, but there is no mention of the character's goal-directed behavior.

High Point Analysis

High point analysis, originally described by Labov (1972), is commonly applied to autobiographical narratives. High point analysis examines a narrative for six features. First, it assess the use of an *Introducer*, which occurs at the beginning of the narrative and is used to provide a summary statement of what the narrative is about (e.g., "One time I was sad when a kid almost stole my bike"). Next, it examines the use of an *Orientation,* which is used to provide setting information (e.g., "It was a bright sunny day."). Third is the *Complicating Action*, which describes the actions that lead up to the high point (e.g., "And Rob, the neighborhood bully, saw me riding my new bike. And he came over and took it from me.") followed by the *Evaluation* of the action (e.g., "I was so mad!"). The *Resolution* explains how the action is resolved (e.g., "But my big brother saw him and yelled for him to stop"). Finally, the narrator ends the story with a *Coda,* which closes the story and bridges the story back to the present (e.g., "My big brother has always been there for me to help me when I need him.").

McCabe and her colleagues (McCabe, 1997; McCabe & Peterson, 1990) extended Labov's (1972) work on high point analysis to include structural patterns by which young children's narratives could be classified. She describes the most complex narrative as *classic* because the story builds to a climax, evaluates the climax, and then resolves it. An *end-at-high-point* narrative is not as complex as a classic narrative because it builds up to and then ends at an unresolved climax. The *leapfrog* narrative jumps from one related event to the other, leaving out major events. In a *chronological* narrative, a child is simply describing a sequence of events that are related temporally but not spatially. Research with preschoolers and school-age children (Champion, 1998; McCabe, 1990) indicates that the aforementioned patterns can be used to classify most children's narratives. However, there is a small percentage of narratives that might be described by the following patterns. A *two-event* narrative is a story that consists of too few events for a climax to be reached, and in these stories the narrator reiterates and reevaluates these same two events. A *disoriented* narrative is confusing and difficult to comprehend. Any narrative that does not fit into McCabe's (1990, McCabe & Peterson, 1997) categories would be classified as *miscellaneous*.

Analysis of Scripted Narratives

Analysis of scripted narratives is different from autobiographical or fictional narratives because scripts are used to assess children's ability to logically describe the sequence of a repeated, generalized event. Unlike the goal of autobiographical or fictional narratives, which typically is to entertain, the goal of a scripted narrative is to instruct. When analyzing a script it is important to assess three aspects: *temporal order* (Hughes et al., 1997), *key routine events* (Hughes et al., 1997), and *level of detail*. To analyze for temporal order, one could examine the narrative for use of connectives (e.g., and, then, first, next). To analyze for routine, one could make sure that key events of the routine are mentioned. For example, if the routine is going to the grocery store, then key routine events could include getting a cart, paying for the groceries, carrying the bags to the car. The final feature we suggest analyzing is the level of detail. Hughes et al. (1997) suggest that level of detail is a distinguishing feature between language-impaired and typical children and between talkative and nontalkative children. Therefore, the level of detail, such as the number of key routine events, would be important to consider.

Psychological Structure

One feature of narratives that is often overlooked by clinicians and researchers is the social-cognitive component of a narrative. This level of analysis is important because it demonstrates children's understanding of the character's goals, thoughts, and feelings. Being able to tell a story that includes the psychological structure of the characters is important because adults rate stories with internal state information and goal-directed behavior by the protagonists more highly than stories that do not have such information (Schneider & Windship, 2002).

Internal State Terms

One technique to assess the social-cognitive component of a narrative is to calculate the number of *internal state terms* used in the narrative. Children's internal state talk in their narratives is correlated with their narrative structure and format (Charman & Shmueli-Goetz, 1998; Curenton, 2004). Internal state terms can include words or phrases that relate to beliefs, desires, emotions, intentions, or motives (see Bartsch & Wellman, 1995; Churchland, 1994; Hall, 1981). The frequency and rate of children's use of internal state words can be analyzed using CLAN or SALT. However, when using these statistical programs to assess internal state talk the evaluator must be sure that children only receive credit for genuine mention of internal states. Therefore, responses such as "You know what?" or "I don't know" should not be counted as a use of internal state terms.

Internal state information is typically missing from very young stories, but researchers report a higher rate of internal state talk in children's narratives as they mature (Bamberg & Damran-Frye, 1991; Benson, 1997; Curenton & Justice, 2004; Morrow, 1985). The absence of age-appropriate use of internal state language may be an indicator of a developmental delay because children who have language impairment, learning disabilities, or autism do not frequently include these references in their narratives (Baron-Cohen, Leslie, & Frith, 1986; Hughes et al., 1997; Roth & Spekman, 1986; Stein & Glenn, 1987).

Assessing internal state language in narratives is difficult because the rate of children's internal state talk during storytelling typically is low (Clarke-Stewart & Beck, 1999; Curenton & Justice, 2004; Tager-Flushberg & Sullivan, 1995). However, the *frequency* with which children use internal state terms increases with age as does the *manner* in which they use these terms. For instance, work by Bamberg and Damrad-Frye (1993) suggests that children's internal state references increase as the children get older and that children use causal explanations to explain the character's internal states (e.g., "the dog was scared 'cause all the bees were coming to get the dog").

Story Landscapes

Because the use of internal state terms is limited in young children's narratives, a supplemental method can be used to assess how children use psychological causation in a story. According to Bruner (1986), all stories contain two landscapes, the *Action Landscape* and the *Consciousness Landscape*. The Action Landscape consists of information about the plot, the setting, and events in the story, and the Consciousness Landscape consists of information about the character's psychological states (e.g., her goals, feelings, and thoughts). Hence, the Action Landscape describes what is happening in the story, whereas the Consciousness Landscape represents the character's interpretation of why events are happening in the story; and it also explains why a character is motivated to engage in certain actions. Sophisticated stories successfully weave together the two landscapes (Astington, 1990; Bruner, 1986). However, younger preschoolers may find the Consciousness Landscape challenging to articulate because they have difficulty explaining a character's emotional responses, desires, and thoughts (Curenton, 2004; John, Lui, & Tannock, 2003). Curenton (2004) developed a coding scheme based on *Frog, Where Are You?* (Meyer, 1969), in which low-income 3- to 5-year-olds' oral stories were classified according to Bruner's theoretical landscapes. In order for stories to be considered as having addressed the Consciousness Landscape, the child must have mentioned both the plot and the character's motives and internal states. She found a developmental trend for which children used these landscapes: Only 5% of the 3-year-olds produced a story that addressed the character's consciousness, compared to 56% of the 4-year-olds and 67% of the 5-year-olds.

Special Considerations for Assessing Narratives

Cultural Narrating Styles

By the time children enter school, their cultural norms of storytelling (i.e., *cultural narrating styles*) are well developed (for a review, see McCabe, 1997b). Cultural narrating styles are acquired through children's social interactions; therefore, these narrating styles represent culturally laden values and beliefs about *what* stories should be about and *how* stories should be told (Gee, 1989; Wiley, Rose, Burger, & Miller, 1998). Therefore, children's oral narrative styles will be different based on their social, cultural, and socioeconomic background (for a review see Curenton, 2006).

Often, teachers' and clinicians' judgments of the quality of a story are based on a European cultural narrating tradition (McCabe, 1997a). Children from other cultural narrating traditions are more likely to have their stories rated poorly by clinicians and teachers. It is important for clinicians and educators not to erroneously assess children's narrative skills because they do not understand the different cultural narrating traditions. Below we provide a brief description of a few cultural narrating styles.

European Cultural Narrating Styles

The European cultural narrating tradition dates as far back as Aristotle (see McCabe, 1997a). This tradition dictates that stories should have a clear beginning, middle, and end and should revolve around a single episodic event that follows a linear temporal sequence. In addition, oral stories in this tradition are most commonly *monologues* or uninterrupted streams of talk. In monologue narratives, the individual is wholly responsible for communicating the story, and the storyteller's perception is considered paramount.

African Cultural Styles

Stories from the African cultural narrating traditions are usually based around a theme, and several episodes or events illustrate this theme (McCabe, 1997a). Instead of a linear temporal pattern, narratives in this tradition might follow a circular temporal pattern that might weave together events from the past, present, and future in the same narrative (Ani, 1990; Champion, 1998).

One narrating tradition that is common in the African American culture is the use of joint-storytelling. *Joint-storytelling* is the involvement of multiple speakers in cocreating a narrative. According to this tradition, it is common for multiple speakers to chime in if they have information to add to the story. This information can be confirmatory (e.g., "He sure did. And then he . . . ") or contradictory (e.g., "No that is not what he said. He told you . . . "). The audience is expected to collaborate in the construction of the narrative by asking and answering questions (Bliss, Covington, & McCabe,

1999). Joint-storytelling is especially common when children and adult African Americans share autobiographical narratives, and Vernon-Feagans (1996) has also found that African American children in North Carolina engage in joint-storytelling during pretend play.

Another feature in the African American cultural narrating tradition is how the listener is expected to respond during the storytelling. African Americans engage in a tradition called *call and response* (Smitherman, 1977), in which the audience of the story is expected to provide evaluative feedback about the story while the narrator is creating it. If an adult fails to provide this feedback, then the child may misinterpret the adult's silence to mean that he or she is not interested in the story, which may result in the child cutting his or her story short or becoming disinterested in the task.

Asian Cultural Narrating Styles

In the Asian cultural narrating tradition, stories are typically concise because there is a cultural value of brevity and a taboo against verbosity (Minami & McCabe, 1991). Minami and McCabe (1991) explain that as a result of these cultural values, Japanese communication relies heavily on implicit, nonverbal, and intuitive communication rather than verbal information. Children are not encouraged to narrate elaborate or detailed descriptions in their stories because it is the listener's responsibility to infer these details and to make sense of the message. These cultural differences in narrating style may be especially salient when children are asked to create autobiographical narratives. Han, Leichtman, and Wang (1998) found that Chinese and Korean children talked about their past experiences in less detail than European American children did, and the Asian children used fewer internal state terms and more descriptions of activities with others in their narratives than the European American children used. Also, because of cultural values supporting the hierarchy of adults and children (see Han et al., 1998), Asian children may tend to be less talkative around adults in general, which might further be a cause for a very brief, concise narrative.

Latino Cultural Narrating Styles

The Latino cultural narrating tradition differs from other traditions because of the number of characters that are involved in the story.

Specifically, stories from the Latino tradition tend to revolve around multiple characters. Also, like the African tradition, stories from the Latino tradition are not confined to a linear temporal sequence but instead are linked by an overall theme (Melzi, 2000; Perez & Tager-Flushberg, 1998). These narratives are also characterized by many evaluative comments (see Perez & Tager-Flushberg, 1998) and internal state talk about the characters' emotions (Eisenberg, 1999).

Interpreting the Results of Narrative Assessments

After assessing young children's narratives, the collected data can be utilized to inform clinical interventions and educational practices. Narratives are good tools for identifying children who have typical and atypical language development (Paul, Hernandez, Taylor, & Johnson, 1996; Paul & Smith, 1993). Typical language development is characterized by successfully meeting age-appropriate developmental milestones, whereas atypical development is characterized by language impairment or delay. Hadley (1998) found that evaluating children's narratives is a better method for demonstrating language vulnerabilities than one-on-one conversations with children. In fact, researchers have found that narrative ability is a strong predictor of children's later language skills (Bishop & Edmundson, 1987) and school achievement (Paul & Smith, 1993).

Narratives allow for closer inspection of linguistic richness that may not be captured when utilizing standardized assessments, and this is particularly important for culturally, socioeconomically, and linguistically diverse children. Researchers have found that standardized tests may not capture low-income and ethnic minority children's language skills (Campbell, Dollaghan, Needleman, & Janosky, 1997; Washington & Craig, 1992). Unlike standardized tests, narratives are not subject to socioeconomic bias. In general, research examining narrative production and comprehension in low-income samples tends to find that low-income children are able to perform well using these methods (Benson, 1997; Craig & Washington, 1994; Murray et al., 1999; Snow, Tabor, Nicholson, &

Kurkland, 1995). Narrative assessments place fewer constraints on the child's language than the structured, question-answer format of standardized tests. Therefore, children are given more of an opportunity to freely demonstrate their abilities.

Bliss et al. (1999) describe two major deficits that should be examined for when assessing the quality of all children's narratives. The first is a deficiency at the "linguistic processing" level (Bliss et al., 1999, p. 161), which is at the language structure level of our pyramid. Such a deficit typically would be evident in the child's (a) inability to produce C-units; (b) use of simplistic, repetitive vocabulary; or (c) lack of LLF use. A second deficit is the child's inability to produce a coherent narrative, which is at the story structure level of the pyramid. Deficiency at this level would consist of the child's failure to link the ideas and events in her narrative via time or space. According to our framework, a child may demonstrate another deficit in narrative ability, specifically the inability to create a narrative that contains a psychological structure. Deficits at this level would be the child's inability to describe the character's motives, goals, or internal states, and such a deficit would be characteristic of children who might have pervasive developmental delays, such as autism (Baron-Cohen et al., 1986).

In the remainder of this section, we provide examples of children's stories and explain how the Story Pyramid can be used to interpret these narratives. We propose three types of pyramids with various levels of complexity. In Table 8–2 we provide a description of the pyramid and a list of how our classification system overlaps with the theoretical frameworks of other researchers. In each section, we provide a description of the level and examples of preschooler's stories elicited by the wordless picture book, *Frog, Where Are You?* (Mayer, 1969). After the example is presented, we offer suggestions for clinical, classroom, and home-based interventions. Holistic interventions for students with language impairments as well as for students who are at risk for language and/or literacy problems involve teachers, parents, and SLPs working together (Prelock, 2000; Prelock, Miller, & Reed, 1995). Speech-language pathologists' (SLP) collaboration with educators and parents provides opportunities for joint intervention to solve children's oral language problems (Borsch & Oaks, 1992; Sanger, Hux, & Griess, 1995).

Table 8–2. Levels of Story Pyramids

Story Pyramid Level	Similarity to Other Researchers and Theorists	Examples
No Foundation The child is unable to demonstrate his or her grammatical skills because the narrative is not based on C-units. The ideas/events in the story are one-word descriptions of objects or activities that are unrelated temporally, spatially, or in terms of psychological causation. The child fails to demonstrate that he or she has a concept of a story.	**High Point Analysis (McCabe, 1997)** Impoverished Narratives	Tommy: house. Tommy: tree. Tommy: trees. Tommy: tree. Tommy: tree. Tommy: a snake. Tommy: a snake again. Tommy: a boy.
Basic Pyramid The child demonstrates his/her grammatical skills by creating a narrative that is based on grammatical units (C-units), but the ideas/events in the story are not linked temporally or spatially. The story is a description of unrelated events/ideas without any mention of the characters' motives, goals, or internal states.	**Applebee's Narrative Levels (1978)** Heaps **High Point Analysis** Leapfrog **Story Structure Levels (Stein & Glenn, 1979)** Descriptive Sequence	Mathew: he look at his frog. Mathew: then the dog did. Mathew: the frog jump. Mathew: he stand up. Mathew: he sneaked out the bowl. Mathew: the doggie jumped on the bed. Mathew: he watched. Mathew: he looking for his frog. Mathew: he jumped. Mathew: and his dog went in the thing. Mathew: and his room is all messy. Mathew: he looking in the glass.

continues

405

Table 8–2. *continued*

Story Pyramid Level	Similarity to Other Researchers and Theorists	Examples
		Mathew: the doggie climbing down.
		Mathew: and he looking.
		Mathew: he watching the dog.
		Mathew: and this window he come down and come out.
		Mathew: looking for his frog.
		Mathew: they lost.
	Applebee's Narrative Levels Sequences Focused Chains Primitive Narratives	Rose: I think xxx with this dog. Rose: I don't get no frog. Rose: he looking for his froggie. Rose: he got a thing on his head. Rose: that's my doggy.
	High Point Analysis Chronological End-at-High-Point	Rose: that looks like number one. Rose: that's my puppy. Rose: and that's my little brother. Rose: he's trying to catch a bunch of bees. Rose: he looking for an owl.
	Story Structure Levels Action Sequence Reactive Sequence Abbreviated Sequence Action Landscape	Rose: my puppy is running from the bees [*child makes a buzzing sound*]. Rose: he's flying a kangaroo. Rose: it looks like an owl. Rose: oh now he upset. Rose: look what he doing. Rose: he in the water.
Intermediate Pyramid The child demonstrates his or her grammatical skills by creating a narrative that is based on grammatical units (C-units). The ideas and events in the story are linked temporally and/or spatially, but these ideas/events are still not framed in context of the characters' motives, goals, and internal states. The child clearly articulates *what* is happening in the story, but he or she provides no insight into why these events are happening.		

406

Story Pyramid Level	Similarity to Other Researchers and Theorists	Examples
		Rose: now they get out of the water.
		Rose: the little boy found his frog.
		Rose: that's his.
		Rose: [child laughs] he's little.
	Applebee's Narrative Levels	Sara: the dog is looking in the jar for food.
	True Narrative	
		Sara: he's asleep.
	High Point Analysis	Sara: but the frog is going to get out and put on his slippers.
	Classic Narrative	
		Sara: the frog is xxx.
	Story Structure Levels	Sara: he don't know where the frog is.
	Complete Episode	Sara: dog xxx can't find food.
	Consciousness Landscape	Sara: he doesn't know where the frog is.
		Sara: he doesn't know where.
		Sara: he's looking for the.
		Sara: the dog is trying to find the frog his food.
		Sara: he doesn't know where the frog is.
		Sara: he can't find the frog.
		Sara: he doesn't know where the frog is.
Complex Pyramid		Sara: they're looking for him.
The child demonstrates his or her grammatical skills by creating a narrative that is based on C-units. The ideas/events in the story are linked temporally and/or spatially, and they are also linked in terms of psychological causation (i.e., there is mention of the characters' motives, goals, and internal states). There is a clear connect between *what* is happening in the story, *why* it is happening, and (perhaps) even *how* the character feels about what is happening.		Sara: maybe he in that tree.

continues

Table 8–2. *continued*

Story Pyramid Level	Similarity to Other Researchers and Theorists	Examples
These narratives end with a resolution of the problem, moral lesson, or evaluation of the story.		Sara: then he can't know where the frog gone.
		Sara: um, there's bees.
		Sara: he can't know where . . .
		Sara: there are bees trying to sting the dog.
		Sara: there's a owl.
		Sara: owl live in that hole.
		Sara: trying to kill the boy.
		Sara: there's a moose.
		Sara: the moose is running.
		Sara: oh, they're falling into the water.
		Sara: he's saying "help!"
		Sara: they're getting out.
		Sara: there's a log.
		Sara: so he can step out.
		Sara: he saying "ssh."
		Sara: they're climbing over the log.
		Sara: they're out the water.
		Sara: there's the frogs.
		Sara: he's going bye.

Assessing Children's Narratives:

Examples for A Narrative With No Foundation

Unfortunately, there are some instances where children fail to demonstrate adequate narrative abilities. Inadequate narratives are those in which the child does not use any C-units; therefore, the child does not demonstrate his or her grammatical skills. Also, the vocabulary in these narratives is repetitive and oversimplified; the stories consist of one-word descriptions of objects or activities that are unrelated temporally, spatially, or in terms of psychological causation. In these instances, the child fails to demonstrate that he or she has a concept of story. The following example by Tommy illustrates a narrative with no foundation:

Tommy: house.

Tommy: tree.

Tommy: trees.

Tommy: tree.

Tommy: tree.

Tommy: a snake.

Tommy: a snake again.

Tommy: a boy.

Based on his oral story, a clinician would be concerned about Tommy's limited grammatical skills. Tommy provides no evidence that he can create a subject-predicate clause because he uses no C-units. Therefore, the number of C-units for his story would equal zero, and a MLCU could not be calculated. Furthermore, Tommy's story demonstrates limited *language structure* because the vocabulary used in his story consists of only very basic nouns (house, tree[s], snake, boy). Tommy only uses two LLFs in his narrative ("a"), which is a simple article, and the adverb (again), which is used incorrectly because it does not modify on adjective, adverb, or verb. Because Tommy's story represents so many problems with the language structure of the pyramid, more sophisticated aspects of the pyramid, such as the story structure and psychological structure, are completely absent.

Narratives such as Tommy's might be characteristic of typically developing toddlers or preschoolers who have a severe language delay. The first step in the clinical intervention process should be for the clinician to build a stronger rapport with Tommy because children respond better when they feel comfortable with the examiner. After the clinician has established a trusting relationship with Tommy, she should retest him using standardized assessments for other areas of oral language (e.g., vocabulary, pragmatics, syntax). Additional testing of basic cognitive skills would need to be assessed by other trained professionals serving on an interdisciplinary team. The clinician should also talk with Tommy's teacher to find out how Tommy uses language when he is in class; for instance, she needs to know whether Tommy can communicate effectively with his classmates and whether he is engaged during story reading in the classroom. The clinician should also contact his parents to understand Tommy's language use at home. Based on the results of these standardized assessments and consultation with the parents and teacher, the clinician can begin a clinical intervention specifically designed to meet his needs. In addition, she should work with Tommy's parents on a home-based intervention that would incorporate more language interactions into the family's routine. Finally, after the intervention phase, the clinician should retest his narrative skills using various other elicitation techniques, such as puppets/dolls, wordless picture books, and verbal prompts, in order to develop a corpus of data about the growth and development of Tommy's narrative skills.

Basic Pyramids

The Basic Pyramid is characterized by children's use of utterances that can be segmented into C-units. However, the ideas/events in the story are not linked temporally or spatially (i.e., they are not linked by time or place). The story is merely a description of events without any mention of the characters' motives, goals, or internal states (i.e., psychological causation). In the following example, Emily tells a story that can be classified as a Basic Pyramid:

Emily: it looks like a animal.

Emily: it looks like a frog.

Emily: it is a frog!

Emily: and here's a little . . .

Emily: and the dog looking in the water.

Emily: him playing in the sand.

Emily: the dog's playing in the sand.

Emily: look at the reindeer.

Emily: it's done.

Emily: look.

Emily: this page's the dog's on the man's shoulder.

Emily: and the dog's running around like the man.

Emily's story is grammatically structured into 12 C-units with an average of 5 words per C-unit (MLCU = 4.92). Emily uses a few rare words in her story (reindeer, sand, shoulder), but there are several places where she repeats nonspecific nouns (it) or where she repeats her verbs (look, playing). The events in her story are not linked in terms of time or space, and she is not providing any information about the character's internal states or goals/motives. Emily is simply describing the pictures in the book, and furthermore, she is only focusing on one aspect of the picture when she presents her descriptions.

Mathew's story is another example of a Basic Pyramid:

Mathew: he look at his frog.

Mathew: then the dog did.

Mathew: the frog jump.

Mathew: he stand up.

Mathew: he sneaked out the bowl.

Mathew: the doggie jumped on the bed.

Mathew: he watched.

Mathew: he looking for his frog.

Mathew: he jumped.

Mathew: and his dog went in the thing.

Mathew: and his room is all messy.

Mathew: he looking in the glass.

Mathew: the doggie climbing down.

Mathew: and he looking.

Mathew: he watching the dog.

Mathew: and this window he come down and come out.

Mathew: looking for his frog.

Mathew: they lost.

Mathew's story has an MLCU of 4.5 across 18 C-units. In terms of vocabulary, Mathew uses a variety of verbs (jump, stand, sneaked, watched, looking, climbing, lost) to describe the actions of his characters. In terms of LLF, he uses interesting adjectives (messy) and adverbs (down, out). Although Mathew's story is rich in language structure, his story structure level is basic because he is not providing any indication of how the events are linked in terms of space or time. Mathew's story, like Emily's, is simply a sequence of events about what is happening in the story, yet Mathew does provide one statement in his narrative that shows he is beginning to grasp the concept of what is happening in the story ("they lost"). However, Mathew still provides no information about why the character is lost and how the characters feel about being lost.

Stories like Mathew's and Emily's are characteristic of 3-year-olds because they are merely descriptions of events or pictures. At this level, children are able to demonstrate that they can describe a sequence of pictures. There is no concept of a plot or setting for the story. Clinical interventions with these children should focus on boosting children's understanding of how stories are organized by a sequence of related events that lead up to a climax, and that all stories contain a setting and a plot. In addition, Emily might benefit from an intervention designed to increase her vocabulary. These interventions could be conducted through story reading sessions with the clinician or parent using storybooks that present a clear sequence of actions and one simple plot and setting. These story reading interventions might feature adult prompts that ask the child questions, such as "Where is this story taking place? What was the first thing he did? Why did he do that first? What was the last thing he did? and Why did he do that last?"

Intermediate Pyramids

Next, there is the Intermediate Pyramid. In these narratives the child demonstrates his or her grammatical skills by creating a narrative that is based on grammatical units (C-units). At this level, the ideas and events in the story are linked temporally and/or spatially, but these ideas/events are still not framed in context of psychological causation (e.g., the characters' motives, goals, and internal states). In other words, the child clearly articulates *what* is happening in the story, but provides no insight into *why* these events are happening. The majority of typically developing 4-year-olds' narratives will be classified as Intermediate Pyramids because at this age most children have a clear concept that a story is based around a series of related events. However, 4-year-olds still have difficulty understanding the psychological motivations of protagonists. James' story is an example of a child who can create a story with a plot but one that is still lacking in terms of psychological causation.

James: a frog getting out.

James: he's gone.

James: he holding the dog.

James: and he jumped out the window.

James: the dog's sticking his head out.

James: then the boy's [*child makes a howling sound to signify dialogue*].

James: they're playing together.

James: and he's mad.

James: and the dog is [*child makes a barking sound to signify dialogue*].

James: dog's all by himself.

James: he's up in the tree.

James: a owl knocked the boy down.

James: the reindeer knocked him off.

James: he knocked him off his body.

James: he knocked him in the water.

James: and the dog watching the frogs.

James: the dog and the frog and the dog sliding together.

His story has 17 C-units with an MLCU of 4.88. In terms of lexical diversity, his vocabulary has a variety of verbs (holding, jumped, sticking, playing, knocked, watching, sliding), and he uses some LLFs, including the adverbial phrase "playing together." The events in James' story are also sequenced temporally, such as when he opens his story by saying that the frog is "getting out" and then next says "he's gone." The events in his story are also sequenced spatially when he implies that the owl knocked the boy out of the tree ("He's up in the tree. A owl knocked the boy down"). When listening to James' story, the clinician should have a clear idea of what events are happening in the story and in what order these events happened. James also illustrates that he has a concept of a story by creative use of dialogue (i.e., making a howling sound for the boy and a barking sound for the dog to signify a dialogue). However, the listener would have limited information about the psychological structure of the story because James does not provide any details about the characters' goals or motives. Although he does use an internal state term (mad), James' story still does not fully address the psychological structure of a narrative because the listener has no idea *why* James is mad.

Another example of an Intermediate Pyramid is a story by Rose:

Rose: I think . . . with this dog.

Rose: I don't get no frog.

Rose: he looking for his froggie.

Rose: he got a thing on his head.

Rose: that's my doggy.

Rose: that looks like number one.

Rose: that's my puppy.

Rose: and that's my little brother.

Rose: he's trying to catch a bunch of bees.

Rose: he looking for an owl.

Rose: my puppy is running from the bees [*child makes a buzzing sound*].

Rose: he's flying a kangaroo.

Rose: it looks like an owl.

Rose: oh now he upset.

Rose: look what he doing.

Rose: he in the water.

Rose: now they get out of the water.

Rose: the little boy found his frog.

Rose: that's his.

Rose: [*child laughs*] he's little.

This story has 20 C-units with an average of 5 words per C-unit (MLCU = 4.80). In Rose's example, she provides some additional commentary on the book's content by saying things like "that looks like number one," and by personalizing the characters, such as when she says "that's my puppy" and "and that's my little brother." These side comments are unique features of Rose's narrating style and should not be deleted from the transcript because they are still relevant to the story.

Interventions with children who create Intermediate Pyramids should focus on conversations about why something has happened in the story and should focus more on talk about the character's internal states, goals/plans, and motives.

Complex Pyramids

Finally, there is a Complex Pyramid, which has all the features of a sophisticated story. This narrative is grammatically organized into C-units. The ideas/events in the story are linked temporally and/or spatially, and they are also linked in terms of psychological causation (i.e., there is mention of the characters' motives, goals, and internal states). There is a clear connection between *what* is happening in the story, *why* it is happening, and perhaps even *how* the character feels about what is happening. Furthermore, these narratives are ended with a resolution of the problem, moral lesson, or evaluation of the story. Children who produce this level of story are typically older preschoolers and kindergartners (ages 5–6).

Mark's story is an example of a Complex Pyramid:

Mark: once upon a time there was a boy who had a dog and a frog.

Mark: he was showing it.

Mark: and the dog was looking at it.

Mark: and he went asleep.

Mark: and the frog came out.

Mark: and he wake up.

Mark: and there no frog in there.

Mark: he wasn't there.

Mark: he drop it.

Mark: and he got mad.

Mark: he said, "Bumpy, Bumpy, where are you?"

Mark: he probably up in the bee hive.

Mark: but he's not.

Mark: he's probably up.

Mark: but he dropped . . . they really drop the bee hive.

Mark: and they gonna fix the steamed dog.

Mark: he's looking there.

Mark: and there's a owl that's chasing after dog bees.

Mark: and he called, "Willy, where are you?"

Mark: and "Where did you go?"

Mark: there was a moose.

Mark: and he knocked him down in the pond.

Mark: and where is froggy?

Mark: he's probably there.

Mark: he look.

Mark: he said, Ssh!

Mark: and he found them, my babies!

Mark: and "Come everybody let's go home."

Mark: the end.

Mark's example includes an average of 5 words per C-unit (MLCU = 5.14) across 29 C-units. His story includes conventional features of Story Grammar (Stein & Glenn, 1979), such as openings like "Once upon a time . . . " and closings like "The end." This child also uses dialogue sophisticatedly. He presents a clear resolution at the end of his story (i.e., "And he found them, "My babies! Come everybody. Let's go home."). Mark uses novel internal state words, such as when he describes the dog as being "steamed" rather than angry.

Sara's example is another story that would be classified as a Complex Pyramid:

Sara: the dog is looking in the jar for food.

Sara: he's asleep.

Sara: but the frog is going to get out and put on his slippers.

Sara: the frog is xxx.

Sara: he don't know where the frog is.

Sara: dog can't find food.

Sara: he doesn't know where the frog is.

Sara: he doesn't know where.

Sara: he's looking for the . . .

Sara: the dog is trying to find the frog his food.

Sara: he doesn't know where the frog is.

Sara: he can't find the frog.

Sara: he doesn't know where the frog is.

Sara: they're looking for him.

Sara: maybe he in that tree.

Sara: then he can't know where the frog gone.

Sara: um, there's bees.

Sara: he can't know where

Sara: there are bees trying to sting the dog.

Sara: there's a owl.

Sara: owl live in that hole.

Sara: trying to kill the boy.

Sara: there's a moose.

Sara: the moose is running.

Sara: oh, they're falling into the water.

Sara: he's saying "Help!"

Sara: they're getting out.

Sara: there's a log.

Sara: so he can step out.

Sara: he saying "Ssh."

Sara: they're climbing over the log.

Sara: they're out the water.

Sara: there's the frogs.

Sara: he's going bye.

Sara's story has 33 C-units with an MLCU of 5.09. Sara's story does not include the traditional story openings and closings, but she still provides a resolution at the end: "He's going bye."

Children who create Complex Pyramid narratives are not in need of one-on-one clinical interventions, but these children can still benefit from more advanced story interactions in the classroom and at home that continue to facilitate children's social-perspective taking ability and social skills via stories. These children can create stories that allow them to reason about characters' internal states and motives, and they can understand the causes and consequences of a character's actions. Therefore, storytelling may be an effective method for instilling in these children an understanding of morals and social skills (see Kilpatrick, 1993; Lamme, Krogh, & Yachmetz, 1992). Many preschoolers' storybooks talk about the characters' internal states (Dyer, Shatz, & Wellman, 2000), and educators and parents can select these books to read to children. Also, educators and parents can continue to scaffold children's understanding by prompting children to reason about how the events in a story are similar to or different from their own lives or by prompting them to talk about times when they felt the way a protagonist felt.

Acknowledgments. We would like to thank Michelle J. Craig at Florida State University for her assistance with editing this chapter.

References

Ani, M. (1990). The implications of African-American Spirituality. In M. K. Asante & K. W. Asante (Eds.), *African culture: The rhythms of African unity*. Trenton, NJ: Africa World Press.

Applebee, A. (1978). *The child's concept of story*. Chicago, IL: University of Chicago Press.

Astington, J. W. (1990). Narrative and the child's theory of mind. In B. K. Britton & A. D. Pellegrini (Eds.), *Narrative thought and narrative language* (pp. 151–171). Hillsdale, NJ: Lawrence Erlbaum.

Bamberg, M. (1997). *Narrative development: Six approaches*. Mahwah, NJ: Lawrence Erlbaum.

Bamberg, M., & Damrad-Frye, R. (1991). On the ability to provide evaluative comments: Further explorations of children's narrative competencies. *Journal of Child Language, 18*, 689–710.

Baron-Cohen, S., Leslie, A. M., & Frith, U. (1986). Mechanical, behavioral, and intentional understanding of picture stories in autistic children. *British Journal of Developmental Psychology, 4,* 113–125.

Bartsch, K., & Wellman, H. (1995). *Children talk about the mind.* New York: Oxford University Press.

Beals, D. E. (1997). Sources of support for learning words in conversation: Evidence from mealtimes. *Journal of Child Language, 24,* 673–694.

Beals, D. E., & Tabors, P. O. (1995). Arboretum, bureaucratic, and carbohydrates: preschoolers' exposure to rare vocabulary at home. *First Language, 15,* 57–76.

Benson, M. S. (1997). Psychological causation and goal-based episodes: Low-income children'semerging narrative skills. *Early Childhood Research Quarterly, 12,* 439–457.

Bishop, D. V., & Edmundson, A. (1987). Language-impaired 4-year-olds: Distinguishing transient from persistent impairment. *Journal of Speech and Hearing Disorders, 52,* 156–173.

Blake, J., Myszczyszyn, D., & Jokel, A. (2004). Spontaneous measures of morphosyntax in children with specific language impairment. *Applied Psycholinguistics, 25,* 29–41.

Bliss, L. S., Covington, Z., & McCabe A. (1999). Assessing the narratives of African American children. *Contemporary Issues in Communication Sciences and Disorders, 26,* 160–167.

Borsch, J. C., & Oaks, R. (1992). Implementing collaborative consultation collaboration effective collaboration at Central Elementary School [commentary]. *Language, Speech, and Hearing Service in Schools, 23,* 367–368.

Bretherton, I., Oppenheim, D., Buchsbaum, H., Emde, R. N., & The MacArthur Narrative Group. (1990). *MacArthur Story-Stem Battery.* Unpublished manual.

Bruner, J. S. (1986). *Actual minds, possible worlds.* Cambridge, MA: Harvard University Press.

Campbell, T., Dollaghan, C., Needleman, H., & Janosky, J. (1997). Reducing bias in language assessment: Processing-dependent measures. *Journal of Speech, Language, and Hearing Research, 40,* 519–525.

Champion, T. B. (1998). "Tell me something good": A description of narrative structures among African American children. *Linguistics in Education, 9,* 251–286.

Chaney, C. (1998). Preschool language and metalingusitc skills are linked to reading success. *Applied Psycholinguistics, 19,* 433–446.

Charman, T., & Shmueli-Goetz, Y. (1998). The relationship between theory of mind, language, and narrative discourse: An experimental study. *Current Psychology of Cognition, 17,* 245–271.

Churchland, P. S. (1994). "Can neurobiology teach us anything about consciousness?" Presidential Address to the American Philosophical Association, Pacific Division. In: *Proceedings and Addresses of the American Philosophical Association*. Lancaster, PA: Lancaster Press.

Clarke-Stewart, K. A., & Beck, R. J. (1999). Maternal scaffolding and children's narrative retelling of a movie story: The influence of joint encoding on later recall by young children. *Early Childhood Research Quarterly, 14*, 409–434.

Craig, H. K., Connor, C. M., & Washington, J. A. (2003). Early positive predictors of later reading comprehension for African American students: A preliminary investigation. *Language, Speech, and Hearing Services in Schools, 34*, 31–43.

Craig, H. K., & Washington, J. A. (1994). The complex syntax skills of poor, urban, African American preschoolers at school entry. *Language, Speech, and Hearing Services in Schools, 25*, 181–190.

Craig, H. K., & Washington, J. A. (2002). Oral language expectations of African American preschoolers and kindergartners. *American Journal of Speech Language Pathology, 11*, 59–70.

Craig, H., Washington, J., & Thompson-Porter, C. (1998). Average C-unit lengths in the discourse of African American children from low-income, urban homes. *Journal of Speech, Language, and Hearing Research, 41*, 433–444.

Crais, E. R., & Lorch, N. (1994). Oral narratives in school-age children. *Topics in Language Disorders, 14*, 13–28.

Curenton, S. M. (2004). The association between narratives and false belief in low-income preschoolers. *Early Education and Development, 15*, 121–145.

Curenton, S. M. (2006). Oral storytelling: A cultural art that promotes school readiness. *Young Children, 61*, 78–89.

Curenton, S. M., & Justice, L. (2004). African American and Caucasian preschoolers' use of decontextualized language: Use of literate language features in oral narratives. *Language, Speech, and Hearing Services in the Schools, 35*, 240–253.

Curenton, S. M., & Wilson, M. N. (2003). "I'm happy with my mommy:" Low-income preschoolers' causal attributions for emotions. *Early Education and Development, 14*, 199–213.

Dickinson, D. K., & McCabe, A. (1991). The acquisition and development of language: A social interactionist account of language and literacy development. In J. F. Kavanagh (Ed.), *The language continuum from infancy to literacy* (pp. 1–40). Parkton, MD: York Press.

Dyer, J. R., Shatz, M., & Wellman, H. M. (2000). Young children's storybooks as a source of mental state information. *Cognitive Development, 15*, 17–37.

Eisenberg, A. R. (1999). Emotion talk among Mexican American and Anglo American and children from two social classes. *Merrill-Palmer Quarterly, 45*, 267–284.

Gambrell, L., Koskinen, P. S., Kapinus, B. A. (1991). Retelling and the reading comprehension of proficient and less-proficient readers. *Journal of Educational Research*, *84*, 356–362.

Gazella, J. & Stockman, I. (2003). Children's story retellelling under different modality and task conditions: Implications for standardizing language sampling procedures. *American Journal of Speech-Language Pathology*, *12*, 61–72.

Gee, J. P. (1989). Literacy, discourse and linguistics. *Journal of Education*, *171*(1), 75–96.

Gillam, R. B., & Johnston, J. R. (1992). Spoken and written language relationships in language/learning impaired and normally achieving school-age children. *Journal of Speech and Hearing Research*, *35*, 1303–1315.

Goffman, L., & Leonard, J. (2000). Growth of language skills in preschool children with specific language impairment: Implications for assessment and intervention. *American Journal of Speech-Language Pathology*, *9*, 151–161.

Greenhalgh, K. S., & Strong, C. J. (2001). Literate language features in spoken narratives of children with typical language and children with language impairments. *Language, Speech, and Hearing Services in Schools*, *32*, 114–125.

Griffin, T. M., Hemphill, L., Camp, L., & Wolf, D. P. (2004). Oral discourse in the preschool years and later literacy skills. *First Language*, *24*, 123–147.

Hadley, P. A. (1998). Language-sampling protocols for eliciting text-level discourse. *Language, Speech, and Hearing Services in Schools*, *29*, 132–147.

Hall, E. T. (1981). *Beyond culture.* Garden City, NY: Andor Books.

Hall, W., Nagy, W. & Linn, R. (1984). *Spoken words: Effects of situation and social group on word usage and frequency.* Hillsdale, NJ: Lawrence Erlbaum.

Han, J. J., Leichtman, M. D., & Wang, Q. (1998). Autobiographical memory in Korean, Chinese, and American children. *Developmental Psychology*, *34*, 701–713.

Heath, S. B. (1982). What no bedtime story means: narrative skills at home and at school. *Language in Society 11*, 49–76.

Hedberg, N. L., & Westby, C. E. (1993). *Analyzing story skills: Theory to practice.* Tucson, AZ: Communication Skills Builders.

Hirsh-Pasek, K. , Kochanoff, A., Newcombe, N., & deVilliers, J. (2005). Using scientific knowledge to inform preschoolers: Making the case for "Empirical validity." *SRCD Social Policy Report*, *14*(1), 3–19.

Hughes, D., McGillivray, L., & Schmidek, M. (1997). *Guide to narrative language: Procedures for assessment.* Eau Claire, WI: Thinking Publications.

Jackson, S. C., & Roberts, J. E. (2001). Complex syntax production of African American preschoolers. *Journal of Speech, Language, and Hearing Research, 44*, 1083–1096.

John, S. F., Lui, M., & Tannock, R. (2003). Children's story retelling and comprehension using a new narrative resource. *Canadian Journal of School Psychology, 18*, 91–113.

Kilpatrick, W. (1993, Summer). The moral power of good stories. *American Educator*, 24–35.

Klee, T., Stokes, S. F., Wong, A. M-Y., Fletcher, P., & Gavin, W. J. (2004). Utterance length and lexical diversity in Cantonese speaking children with and without specific language impairment. *Journal of Speech, Language, and Hearing Research, 47*, 1396–1410.

Labov, W. (1972). *Sociolinguistic patterns*. Oxford: Blackwell.

Lamme, L. L., Krogh, S. L., & Yachmetz, K. A. (1992). *Literature based on moral education: Children's books and activities for teaching values, responsibility and good judgment in the elementary school*. Phoeniz, AZ: Oryx Press.

Loban, W. (1976). *Language development kindergarten through age twelve*. Urbana, IL: National Council of Teachers of English.

Mayer, M. (1969). *Frog Where Are You?* New York: Dial Books for Young Readers.

McCabe, A. (1997a) Cultural background and storytelling: A review and implications for schooling. *The Elementary School Journal, 97*, 453–473

McCabe, A. (1997b). Developmental and cross-cultural aspects of children's narration. In M. Bamberg (Ed.), *Narrative development* (pp. 137–174). London: Lawrence Erlbaum.

McCabe, A., & Peterson, C. (1990). What makes a narrative memorable? *Applied Psychololinguistics, 11*, 73–82.

McKee, G., Malvern, D., & Richards, B. (2000). Measuring vocabulary diversity using dedicated software. *Literacy and Linguistic Computing, 15*, 323–337.

McWhinney, B. (1995). *The CHILDES project: Tools for analyzing talk* (2nd ed.). Hillsdale, NJ: Lawrence Erlbaum.

Melzi, G. (2000). Cultural variations in the construction of personal narratives: Central American and European American mothers' elicitation styles. *Discourse Processes, 30*, 153–177.

Miles, S., & Chapman, R. S., (2002). Narrative content as described by individuals with Down syndrome and typically developing children. *Journal of Speech, Language, and Hearing Research, 45*, 175–189.

Miller, J. F. (1981). *Assessing language production in children*. Baltimore: University Park Press.

Miller, J. F. (1991). *Research on child language disorders: A decade of progress*. Austin, TX. Pro-Ed.

Miller, J. F., & Chapman, R. S. (1993). *SALT: Systematic analysis of language transcripts.* Madison, WI: Waisman Center.

Miller, P. J., Hengst, J., Alexander, K., & Sperry, L. L. (2000). Versions of personal storytelling/versions of experience: Genres as tools for creating alternate realities. In K. Rosengren, C. Johnson, & P. Harris (Eds.), *Imagining the impossible: The development of magical, scientific, and religious thinking in contemporary society* (pp. 212–246). New York: Cambridge University Press.

Minami, M., & McCabe, A. (1991). Haiku as a discourse regulation device: A stanza analysis of Japanese children's personal narratives. *Language in Society, 20,* 577–599.

Morrow, L. M. (1985). Retelling stories: A strategy for improving children's comprehension, concept of story structure and oral language complexity. *The Elementary School Journal, 85,* 647–661.

Murray, L., Woolgar, M., Briers, S., & Hipwell, A. (1999). Children's social representations in dolls' house play and theory of mind tasks, and their relation to family adversity and child disturbance. *Social Development, 8,* 179–200.

Ninio, A. (1983). Joint book reading as a multiple vocabulary acquisition device. *Developmental Psychology, 19,* 445–451.

Oetting, J. B., & McDonald, J. L. (2002). Methods for characterizing participants' Nonmainstream dialect use in child language research. *Journal of Speech, Language, and Hearing Research, 45,* 505–518.

Oppenheim, D., Emde, R. N., & Wambolt, F. S. (1996). Associations between 3-year-olds' narrative co-constructions with mothers and fathers and their story completions about affective themes. *Early Development and Parenting, 5,* 149–160.

Oppenheim, D., Emde, R. N., & Warren, S. (1997). Children's narrative representations of mothers: Their development and associations with child and mother adaptation. *Child Development, 68,* 127–138.

Owen, A. J., & Leonard, L. B. (2002). Lexical diversity in the spontaneous speech of children with speech language impairment: Application of D. *Journal of Speech, Language, and Hearing Research, 45,* 927–937.

Paris, A. H., & Paris, S. G. (2003). Assessing narrative comprehension in young children. *Reading Research Quarterly, 38,* 36–76.

Paris, S. G., & Hoffman, J. V. (2004). Reading assessments in kindergarten through third grade: Findings from the Center of Early Reading Achievement. *Elementary School Journal, 105,* 199–217.

Paul, R., Hernandez, R., Taylor, L., & Johnson, K. (1996). Narrative development in late talkers: Early school age. *Journal of Speech and Hearing Research, 39,* 1295–1303.

Paul, R., & Smith, R. L. (1993). Narrative skills in 4-year-olds with normal, impaired, and late developing language. *Journal of Speech and Hearing Research, 36,* 592–598.

Pearce, W. M. (2003). Does the choice of stimulus affect the complexity of children's oral narratives? *Advances in Speech Language Pathology, 5,* 95–103.

Pellegrini, A. D. (1985). Relations between preschool children's symbolic play and literate language behavior. In L. Galda & A. D. Pellegrini (Eds.), *Play, language, and stories* (pp. 79–97). Norwood, NJ: Ablex.

Perez, C., & Tager-Flusberg, H. (1998). Clinicians' perceptions of children's oral personal narratives. *Narrative Inquiry, 8,* 181–201.

Peterson, C., & McCabe A. (1983). *Developmental psycholinguistics: Three ways of looking at a child's narrative.* New York: Plenum.

Prelock, P. A. (2000). An intervention focus for inclusionary practice. *Language, Speech, and Hearing Service in Schools, 31,* 296–298.

Prelock, P. A., Miller, B. L., & Reed, N. L. (1995). Collaborative partnerships in a language in the classroom program. *Language, Speech, and Hearing Services in Schools, 26,* 286–292.

Reese, E. (1995). Predicting children's literacy from mother-child conversations. *Cognitive Development, 10,* 381–405.

Renfrew, C. (1969). *The bus story: A test of continuous speech.* North Place, Old Headington, Oxford.

Rice, M. L., & Bode, J. V. (1993). GAPS in the verb lexicons of children with specific language impairment. *First Language, 13,* 113–131.

Richards, B., & Malvern, D. (1997). *Quantifying lexical diversity in the study of language development.* The New Bulmershe Papers. Reading, UK: University of Reading.

Rickford, J. (1999). *African American vernacular English.* Malda, MA: Blackwell.

Ripich, D., & Griffith, P. (1988). Narrative abilities of children with learning disabilities and nondisabled children: Story structure, cohesion, and propositions. *Journal of Learning Disabilities, 21,* 165–173.

Robinson, J., Herot, C., Haynes, P., & Mantz-Simmons (2000). Children's story stem responses: A measure of program impact on developmental risks associated with dysfunctional parenting. *Child Abuse and Neglect, 24,* 99–110.

Roth, F. P., & Spekman, N. (1986). Narrative discourse: Spontaneously generated stories of learning-disabled and normally achieving students. *Journal of Speech and Hearing Disorders, 51,* 8–23.

Sanger, D. D., Hux, K., & Griess, K. (1995). Educators' opinions about speech-language pathology services in schools. *Language, Speech, and Hearing Services in Schools, 26,* 75–86.

Schneider, P., & Winship, S (2002). Adults' judgments of fictional story quality. *Journal of Speech, Language, and Hearing Research*, *45*, 372–383.

Scott, C. (1988). Spoken and written syntax. In M. Nippold (Ed.), *Later language development* (pp. 49–95). San Diego, CA: College-Hill Press.

Scott, C. M., & Windsor, J. (2000). General language performance measures in spoken and written narrative and expository discourse of school-age children with language learning disabilities. *Journal of Speech, Language, and Hearing Research*, *43*, 324–329.

Seymour, H. N., Bland-Stewart, L., & Green, L. J. (1998). Difference versus deficit in child African American English. *Language, Speech, and Hearing Services in Schools*, *29*, 96–108.

Shapiro, L. R., & Hudson, J. A. (1991). Tell me a make-believe story: Coherence and cohesion in young children's picture-elicited narratives. *Developmental Psychology*, *27*, 960–974.

Shaughnessy, A. Sanger, D., Matteucci, C., & Ritzman, M. (2004, Feb. 3). Early childhood language and literacy: Survey explores kindergarten teacher's perceptions. *ASHA Leader*, pp. 2–18

Smith, T. T., Lee, E., & McDade, H. L. (2001). An investigation of T-units in African American English-speaking and Standard American English-speaking fourth-grade children. *Communication Disorders Quarterly*, *22*, 148–157.

Smitherman, G. (1977). *Talkin' and testifyin': The language of Black America*. Boston: Houghton Mifflin.

Snow, C. E., Tabors, P. O., Nicholson, P. A., & Kurkland, B. F. (1995). SHELL: Oral language and early literacy skills in kindergarten and first-grade children. *Journal of Research in Childhood Education*, *10*, 37–48.

Spinillo, A. G., & Pinto, G. (1994). Children's narrative under different conditions: A comparative study. *British Journal of Developmental Psychology*, *12*, 177–194.

Stein, N., & Glenn, C. (1979). An analysis of story comprehension in elementary school children. In R. O. Freedle (Ed.), *Advances in discourse processing* (Vol. 2). Norwood, NJ: Ablex.

Strong, C. J., & Shaver, J. P. (1991). Stability of cohesion in the spoken narratives of language-impaired and normally developing school-aged children. *Journal of Speech and Hearing Research*, *34*, 95–111.

Tager-Flusberg, H., & Sullivan, K. (1995). Attributing mental states to story characters: A comparison of narratives produced by autistic and mentally retarded individuals. *Applied Psycholinguistics*, *16*, 241–256.

Templin, M. C. (1957). *Certain language skills in children: Their development and interrelationships*. Westport, CT: Greenwood.

Vernon-Feagans, L. (1996). *Children's talk in communities and classrooms*. Cambridge, MA: Blackwell.

Vernon-Feagans, L., Hammer, C. S., Miccio, A., & Manlove, E. (2002). Early language and literacy skills in low-income African American and Hispanic children. In S. B. Neuman & D. K. Dickinson (Eds.), *Handbook of early literacy research*. New York: Guilford Press.

Wachal, R. S., & Spreen, O. (1973). Some measures of lexical diversity of aphasic and normal language performance. *Language and Speech, 16,* 169–181.

Washington, J., & Craig, H. (1992). Performances of low-income, African American preschool and kindergarten children on the Peabody Picture Vocabulary Test—Revised. *Language, Speech, and Hearing Services in Schools, 23,* 329–333.

Washington, J., & Craig, H. (1994). Dialectal forms during discourse of urban, African American preschoolers living in poverty. *Journal of Speech and Hearing Research, 37,* 816–823.

Washington, J., & Craig, H. (1998). Socioeconomic status and gender influences on children's dialectal variations. *Journal of Speech, Language, and Hearing Research, 41,* 618–626.

Watkins, R., Kelly, D., Harbers, H., & Hollis, W. (1995). Measuring children's lexical diversity: Differentiating typical and impaired language learners. *Journal of Speech and Hearing Research,* 38, 1349–1355.

Westby, C. E., Van Dongen, R., & Maggart, Z. (1989). Assessing narrative competence. *Seminars in Speech and Language, 10,* 63–76.

Whitehurst, G., Falco, F., Lonigan, C., Fischel, J., DeBaryshe, B., Valdez-Menchaca, M. & Caulfield, M. (1988). Accelerating language development through picture book reading. *Developmental Psychology, 24,* 552–559.

Wiley, A. R., Rose, A. J., Burger, L. K., & Miller, P. J. (1998). The construction of autonomy through narrative practices: A comparative study. *Child Development, 69,* 833–847.

Wolfram, W., & Fasold, R. (1974). *The study of social dialects in American English.* Englewood Cliffs, NJ: Prentice-Hall.

APPENDIX 8–A

Deletion Procedures*

1. The transcripts were modified to include only the child statements that were directly relevant to the story. Irrelevant remarks, such as "Why is my chair black?" were deleted.

2. Experimenter statements were deleted.

3. Child statements that were responses to the experimenters questions or request for elaboration were excluded, except for those statements that were responses to the standard probes— "Tell me about this page," "What about this page?," "What happened on this page?," "Is there anything else you want to tell me about this story?"

4. Repetitions within utterances were deleted. For example,
   *CH1: and the dog running, <del><because he think> [/]</del> because he think the bird is scared.

5. Repetitions that clarified what the child had said were deleted. For example,
   *C10: I like froggy.
   <del>*EXP: hmm?</del>
   <del>*C10: I like froggy.</del>

6. Words such as "hmm," "uhhuh" and "huh" were deleted when they were the only words in the utterance.

7. False starts and retraces were deleted. For example,
   *CH1: and um <del><the little> [//]</del> the boy was happy because <del>animals [/]</del> the little bit animals was right there.

8. Uncodable utterances which stood alone were deleted. For example, *CH7: xxx.

---

*Reproduced with permission from "African American and Caucasion Preschoolers Use of Decontextualized Language: Use of Literate Language Features in Oral Narratives" by S. M. Curenton and L. M. Justice in *Language, Speech and Hearing Services in the Schools, 35*, 240–253. Copyright 2000 American Speech-Language Hearing Association.

9. Children's denials ("I don't know") and refusals to read were deleted. For example,

   *EXP: ~~go ahead tell me a story.~~

   *CH4: ~~I don't know.~~

10. Talk about the book or reading were deleted. Additionally, children's questions about guidance of where to begin reading were deleted. For example,

    *CH4: ~~what, here?~~

APPENDIX 8–B

C-Unit Segmenting Rules

Definition of C-units

1. A C-unit can be (a) an *independent clause* ("Joey looked in the closet"); (b) an *independent clause* <u>and</u> its *dependent clause* ("Joey looked in the close because he thought his shoes where in there).

2. A C-unit can be grammatically correct according to Standard American English and/or African American English

3. Statements that do not adhere to a subject-verb clausal structure can be defined as a C-unit if (a) it is part of *dialogue* (e.g., "My shoes!"); (b) it is a *response* to a question

4. *Infinitives* (Joey wanted <u>to find</u> his shoes), *gerunds* (Joey remembered <u>seeing</u> them in the closet), or *participles* (Joey saw his brother <u>wearing</u> them yesterday) are **not** counted as separate C-units.

Segmenting C-Units

1. C-units are segmented at coordinating conjunctions

2. C-units are segmented at conjunctive adverbs (*also, besides, however, rather, so that, then*)

3. C-units in dialogue are segmented as follows:
   a. first independent clause and dependent clause is one C-unit
   b. any subsequent independent and dependent clauses are counted as separate C-units (James said, <u>I don't like what you're doing</u> [1 C-unit], and <u>I want my mom</u> [1 C-unit]).

APPENDIX 8–C

Descriptions and Examples of Literate Language Features*

1. **Conjunctions:** Conjunctions are used in discourse to organize information and clarify relationships among elements. They can be categorized as either coordinating or subordinating. Coordinating conjunctions include <u>and</u>, <u>for</u>, <u>or</u>, <u>yet</u>, <u>but</u>, <u>nor</u>, and <u>so</u>. Subordinating conjunctions are more numerous, and include the following examples: <u>after</u>, <u>although</u>, <u>as</u>, <u>because</u>, <u>for</u>, <u>if</u>, <u>how</u>, <u>since</u>, <u>still</u>, <u>that</u>, <u>though</u>, <u>unless</u>, <u>when</u>, <u>where</u>, <u>while</u>, and <u>why</u>.

2. **Elaborated Noun Phrases:** An elaborated noun phrase is a group of words comprising a noun at its head and one or more modifiers providing additional information about the noun. Modifiers may include articles (e.g., <u>a</u>, <u>an</u>, <u>the</u>), possessives (e.g., <u>my</u>, <u>his</u>, <u>their</u>), demonstratives (e.g., <u>this</u>, <u>that</u>, <u>those</u>), quantifiers (e.g., <u>every</u>, <u>each</u>, <u>some</u>), wh-words (e.g., <u>what</u>, <u>which</u>, <u>whichever</u>), and true adjectives (e.g., <u>tall</u>, <u>long</u>, <u>ugly</u>). Examples of elaborated noun phrases include <u>my dog</u> (possessive + noun), <u>the big tree</u> (article + adjective + noun), and <u>some mean boys</u> (quantifier + adjective + noun).

   a. **Simple elaborated noun phrase:** Simple phrases consist of a single modifier and a noun. Examples include *big doggy* (adjective + noun), *that girl* (determiner + noun), and *those ones* (demonstrative + noun).

   b. **Complex elaborated noun phrase:** Complex phrases consist of two or more modifiers and a noun. Examples include *big red house* (adjective + adjective + noun), *a tall tree* (article + adjective + noun), and *some mean boys* (quantifier + adjective + noun).

---

*Reproduced with permission from "African American and Caucasion Preschoolers Use of Decontextualized Language: Use of Literate Language Features in Oral Narratives" by S. M. Curenton and L. M. Justice in *Language, Speech and Hearing Services in the Schools, 35*, 240–253. Copyright 2000 American Speech-Language Hearing Association.

3. **Mental and Linguistic Verbs:** This relatively small group of verbs refer to various acts of thinking and speaking. Mental verbs include think, know, believe, imagine, feel, consider, suppose, decide, forget, and remember. Linguistic verbs include say, tell, speak, shout, answer, call, reply, and yell.

4. **Adverbs:** Adverbs are a particular syntactic form that are used to modify verbs. These modifiers increase the explicitness of action and event descriptions. Adverbs provide additional information about time (e.g., suddenly, again, now), manner (e.g., somehow, well, slowly), degree (e.g., almost, barely, much), place (here, outside, above), reason (therefore, since, so), and affirmation or negation (e.g., definitely, really, never).

Chapter 9

Assessing Vocabulary Knowledge

Khara L. Pence
Kathryn E. Bojczyk
Rihana S. Williams

The Importance of Vocabulary Knowledge to Emergent Literacy

Vocabulary, or a language user's knowledge base of words, is a salient component of an emergent reader's repertoire, given the integral role of vocabulary to early and later reading and academic success. Although vocabulary knowledge is only moderately related with decoding achievement—the primary focus of beginning reading instruction—it is critical for the application of decoding skills to reading for meaning, a later acquired reading ability (de Jong & van der Leij, 2002; National Reading Panel, 2000; Torgesen, Wagner, Rashotte, Burgess, & Hecht, 1997). Put another way, as children progress through elementary school and arrive at critical transitions in reading development, their ability to "read to learn" (Chall, 1996) depends not only on having "learned to read," but also on having sufficient vocabulary to *comprehend* what they read in order to build novel concepts on known concepts.

If children are to be successful readers beyond the third grade, they must possess both fluent word-recognition skills and adequate vocabulary knowledge. Although the presence of these two abilities does not guarantee strong reading comprehension, the lack of either word recognition or vocabulary knowledge almost surely guarantees poor reading comprehension (Biemiller, 2006). Early vocabulary delays are one manifestation of risk for later reading disabilities (e.g., Scarborough, 1990) and children who enter school with fewer words are at a greater risk for developing reading difficulties than children who enter school with more words. Stanovich (1986) explained this phenomenon in terms of a Matthew effect, whereby children who are poorly equipped to acquire reading skills are unlikely to catch up to their peers who are aptly equipped to acquire reading skills. Of particular import to vocabulary knowledge is research demonstrating that school contexts have a relatively minor impact on children's vocabulary acquisition; home context (including the total number of words used in the home and the number of different words) is a much larger predictor of a child's vocabulary knowledge at the end of second grade than instruction that takes place in the school setting (Christian, Morrison, Frazier, & Massetti, 2000; Hart & Risley, 1995). Because children acquire the majority of words that will become the foundation for later reading comprehension in the years prior to formal schooling, it is important for early literacy professionals to assess children's vocabulary as soon as possible upon entry to preschool or kindergarten to determine whether children's vocabulary knowledge is developing in a typical fashion.

Today, when educational policies emphasize equalizing disparities among learners in reading achievement as well as precursors to reading achievement as early as possible, it is important to establish clear expectations for what children should know and how early literacy professionals should assess children's knowledge in order to screen children's vocabulary knowledge, monitor their word learning progress, and diagnose deficiencies in vocabulary knowledge before formal reading instruction begins. Specifically, there are several issues that teachers, and other early literacy professionals must consider when selecting measures of vocabulary knowledge. These issues relate to the complexity in defining the construct of vocabulary, which relates primarily to the breadth and depth of a child's *word knowledge.* Some specific considerations include (a) establishing goals for the number of words children should attain and (b) identifying the depth or level of knowledge for each of these words. Solutions to these considerations cannot be formulated easily, however, because of the discrepancies surrounding foundational questions such as: What is a word? How many words do children need to know and at what rate does their word knowledge naturally grow? What level or depth of word knowledge is appropriate for children to attain? What assessment formats are most appropriate for measuring word knowledge?

What Is a Word?

Words are lexical representations of objects, events, and concepts in the world. When children learn words, they essentially map an object, event, or concept onto its phonological (sound) or orthographic (spelling) representation. What it means to know a word varies depending on the definition one adopts. Baumann and Kame'enui (1991) summarize three major positions on word knowledge that vary along semantic, graphic, psychological, sociological, historical, and philosophical dimensions. The first position is that of Vygotsky (1962), who defines words as *units of verbal thought,* whose meanings are *dynamic rather than static* (Baumann & Kame'enui, 1991, p. 605). The second position is that of Serra (1953), who contends that words have agreed-on meanings and agreed-on sounds, which are represented by agreed-on sequences of letters. The third position is that of Nagy and Anderson (1984), whose operational definition of a word includes reference to semantic relatedness (i.e., the relative ease with which one who knows the meaning of one word can reliably infer the meaning of a related word when encountering it in context). In this chapter, we take the definition that a word is a lexical representation for an entity in the world that can have agreed-on meanings and agreed-on phonological and orthographical representations.

How Many Words Do Children Need to Know and at What Rate Does Their Word Knowledge Naturally Grow?

There is large variation in the number of words children are reported to know. Estimates range from 2,500 to 5,000 words for first-grade students (Beck & McKeown, 1991). Previous estimates have included even greater variability, ranging from 2,562 to 26,000 words, as

Graves (1986) reports on studies of vocabulary size conducted prior to 1960. Much of the variation can be attributed to how word knowledge is defined and how children's development of knowledge about a particular word is measured. Similar discrepancies exist with respect to reports of children's rate of vocabulary growth. Nagy and Herman's (1987) estimate of 3,000 new words per year, or 7 new words per day, is widely cited. Previous estimates have ranged between an annual growth rate of 644 words (Dupuy, 1974) and an annual growth rate of 2,389 words (Smith, 1941). Importantly, although such estimates provide accounts of the average number of words children acquire over a particular period of time, it is also relevant that studies show significant variability in the rate of acquisition for particular subgroups of children. For example, children with language impairment (LI) learn new words more slowly than their typically developing peers (Nash & Donaldson, 2005); likewise, children reared in homes in which verbal interactions are relatively infrequent also develop their vocabulary at slower rates than their more advantaged peers (Hart & Risley, 1995).Thus, although evidence is available to estimate the rate of vocabulary growth for children in general, it is also necessary to recognize that there is great variability across children in their rate of vocabulary growth.

What Depth of Word Knowledge Is Appropriate for Children to Attain?

Knowing the meaning of a word is not an all-or-nothing phenomenon. Many researchers view word learning as a gradual process in which word representations progressively develop from immature, incomplete representations to mature, accurate, and precise representations. Children are able to acquire a general representation of a new word with as little as a single exposure through *fast mapping* (Carey, 1978). After fast mapping occurs, children engage in the process of *slow mapping*, during which representations are gradually refined over time with multiple exposures to the word in varying contexts. Children may have as many as 1,600 words at any time for which they are refining meanings (Carey, 1978). Dale (1965) presented word knowledge development as a four-stage process, with Stage 1 describing no knowledge of a word ("I never saw it before"), Stage 2 reflecting emergent knowledge ("I've heard of it, but I don't know what it means"), Stage 3 describing contextual knowledge ("I recognize it in context—it has something to do with . . . "), and Stage 4 referencing full knowledge ("I know it") (p. 43). Curtis (1987) has argued that Stage 3 and Stage 4 knowledge can be determined only by examining the quality of children's definitions of particular words, a task that reveals the maturity and precision of children's knowledge of a given word.

Baumann and Kame'enui (1991) propose a three-level model to define depth of word understanding. The first level, which enables a person to link a new word with a specific definition or a particular context, is called *verbal association knowledge.* The second level, *partial concept knowledge*, allows a person to use a word in a limited number of ways, but difficulty may still exist in discriminating a word's meaning from meanings of other similar words (see also Shore & Durso, 1990). The third level, *full concept knowledge*, enables a person to use a word in novel circumstances. When a person possesses full concept knowledge of a word, he or she additionally knows multiple meanings of multiple-meaning words and is able to discriminate a word's meaning from other similar words.

What Assessment Formats Are Most Appropriate for Measuring Word Knowledge?

Two major types of vocabulary assessment formats exist: standardized measures and experimenter-generated or study-specific measures. The National Reading Panel (2000) suggests that early literacy professionals might use standardized measures of vocabulary as screening instruments to identify children who may be in need of intervention and include an experimenter- or teacher-generated measure of vocabulary as at least one component of evaluating an intervention. As an example of the latter, Justice, Meier, and Walpole (2005) used an experimenter-generated word-knowledge tool to characterize kindergartners' development of vocabulary within the context of a 10-week book-reading intervention. These researchers developed their assessment to identify children's progress toward knowledge of a corpus of 60 words that occurred in the storybooks used during the intervention.

Measures for Assessing Vocabulary Knowledge

Three major constructs typically measured by assessments of vocabulary knowledge are receptive vocabulary, expressive vocabulary, and word learning abilities/potential. This section of the chapter explores each of these three constructs in detail and describes both commercial and noncommercial measures of vocabulary knowledge pertaining to each construct. Whenever available, we provide the following details about each measure: the time required to administer the measure, the ages for which the measure is appropriate, how the measure is administered (e.g., individually, in small groups), the names of the subtests that assess the vocabulary construct under consideration, languages permitted for administration, possible score types (e.g., raw scores, standard scores, percentile ranks, age equivalent scores), qualifications required for administration, and specific uses of the measure (e.g., used for progress monitoring, for identifying risk) as well as ways in which outcomes of the measure are interpreted and used for various purposes.

The measures reviewed in this chapter were selected to meet the psychometric criteria proposed by McCauley and Swisher (1984). These measures are widely used to assess vocabulary in children who are between 3 and 6 years of age, and who are typically developing or who may have language impairment. We included assessments that are a unique measure of receptive vocabulary or expressive vocabulary as well as assessments that include subtests to measure both areas. However, an assessment was *not* included if it did not uniquely tap the domain of vocabulary knowledge, even if the measure was cited as having *sufficient* evidence for the purpose of assessing vocabulary in our targeted age range. Further, if a measure includes multiple subtests, we describe in detail only the subtests relevant to receptive or expressive vocabulary and not those that assess other language abilities such as syntax, pragmatics, morphology, or phonology.

Measuring Receptive Vocabulary

Receptive vocabulary describes the words that an individual understands (either in spoken or written form). Similar to other aspects of receptive language (e.g., syntax, morphology, pragmatics), children's receptive vocabulary development usually outpaces their expressive vocabulary development. There are a few explanations for why language comprehension precedes language production (Golinkoff & Hirsh-Pasek, 1999). One reason is that language comprehension requires only that we retrieve words from our *lexicon*, or mental dictionary, whereas language production requires that we retrieve words and apply proper pronunciation as we utter them. Another reason that language comprehension outpaces language production is that with language comprehension, the speaker, not the listener, bears the responsibility for organizing sentences with lexical items and a syntactic structure. Language production, however, requires that we search for words in our lexicon and organize them into sentences.

The discrepancy between children's receptive and expressive vocabulary becomes evident in infancy, when children first begin to learn words, and continues through adulthood. The norming study for the MacArthur Communicative Development Inventory (CDI; Fenson et al., 1993) (now called the MacArthur-Bates Communicative Development Inventory) provides evidence of this discrepancy in infancy. Figure 9-1 illustrates vocabulary comprehension data (along the horizontal axis) and vocabulary production data (along the vertical axis) for 673 children between 8 and 16 months of age who participated in the norming study for the CDI Infant Form (see the section in this chapter on Measuring Expressive Vocabulary for more information on the CDI). It is noteworthy that the majority of infants in the sample understand more words than they produce. Even more striking is that infants performing at −1.28 SD below the mean who produce no words may understand up to 200 words (as indicated by the series of connected circles). See Table 9-1 for a summary of the measures of receptive vocabulary included in this chapter.

Oral and Written Language Scales (OWLS; Carrow-Woolfolk, 1995)

The OWLS is an individually administered assessment of receptive and expressive language for children and young adults between 3 and 21 years of age. The OWLS can be used for a variety of purposes, including identification, intervention, monitoring growth, and research. For identification purposes, OWLS may be used to determine the extent to which a student exhibits a language impair-

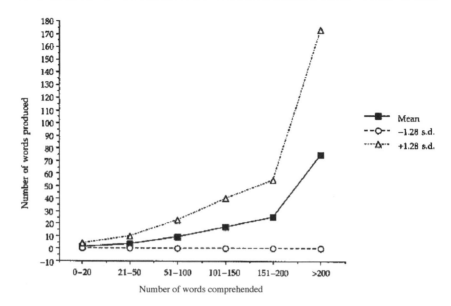

Figure 9–1. Comprehension versus production as measured by a parent-report instrument (From "Individual Differences and Their Implications for Theories of Language Development," by E. Bates, P. S. Dale, & D. Thal, 1995. In P. Fletcher, & B. MacWhinney, Eds., *The Handbook of Child Language*, p. 112. Copyright 1995 Blackwell Publishers. Reproduced with permission).

ment. For intervention purposes, the OWLS can be used to assess potential areas of language difficulties for students. For progress monitoring purposes, the OWLS can be used to provide a record of students' language growth across a year or from early childhood through adolescence, using the same instrument. Several applications to research also exist. For example, researchers can use the OWLS to investigate the language abilities of certain populations of children or to investigate the relation between language abilities and reading development. The OWLS is a norm-referenced assessment, meaning that children's performance on this assessment can be compared to that of their same-age peers. Three co-normed scales form the OWLS: the Listening Comprehension Scale, the Oral Expression Scale, and the Written Expression Scale. The Listening Comprehension Scale and the Oral Expression Scale are both oral language scales and are appropriate for assessing emergent readers.

Table 9–1. Summary of Receptive Vocabulary Measures

Measure	Time (in min.)	Adminis-tration	Relevant Subtests	Languages	Scores	Uses	Ages
OWLS	8	Individual	Listening Comprehension Scale	English	1. Raw score 2. Four deviation-type normative scores 3. Developmental-type normative score	1. Identification 2. Progress monitoring 3. Research	3–21
PLS-4	25–45	Individual	Auditory Comprehension	English	1. Raw score 2. Standard score 3. Percentile rank 4. Age equivalent	1. Identification	Birth–6;11
PPVT-III and PPVT-4	11–12	Individual	NA	English	1. Raw score 2. Four deviation-type normative scores 3. Developmental-type normative score *Note.* The PPVT-4 additionally provides a grade equivalent score and growth scale values (GSVs)	1. Achievement test of Standard English receptive vocabulary 2. Screening test of verbal ability	2.5–90

continues

441

Table 9–1. *continued*

Measure	Time (in min.)	Adminis- tration	Relevant Subtests	Languages	Scores	Uses	Ages
ROWPVT	10–15	Individual	NA	English	1. Raw score 2. Six deviation-type normative scores 3. One developmental-type normative score	1. Assessing cognitive ability 2. Diagnosing reading difficulties 3. Screening 4. Monitoring growth 5. Evaluating program effectiveness	2.0–18;11
TOLD-P:3	30–60 for six Core subtests	Individual	Picture Vocabulary	English	1. Raw score for each subtest 2. Age equivalents for each subtest 3. Percentile scores for each subtest 4. Standard scores for each subtest 5. Composite quotients for combinations of subtests	1. Identification 2. Progress monitoring 3. Research	4.0–8;11

442

Together, the Listening Comprehension Scale and the Oral Expression Scale of the OWLS measure four areas of language meaning or *semantics:* lexical semantics, syntactic semantics, pragmatic semantics, and supralinguistic semantics (see Table 9–2). We discuss the Oral Expression Scale in the section of the chapter on measuring expressive vocabulary.

The Listening Comprehension Scale of the OWLS measures receptive vocabulary, which is the construct of interest for this section of the chapter. During administration, the examiner reads the item aloud (word, phrase, or sentence) and the child must point to the corresponding picture on a page containing four black-and-white pictures (the child can also say the number corresponding to the appropriate picture). The Listening Comprehension Scale of the OWLS takes between 3 and 15 minutes to administer to children between the ages of 3 and 5; average administration time is 8 minutes. Possible score types include raw scores, standard scores and confidence intervals, percentile ranks, normal curve equivalents, stanines, and test-age equivalents. The OWLS was normed with native speakers of English and should be administered only in English. To administer the OWLS, the examiner should have graduate level training in the use of individually administered assessment instruments. Potential examiners include speech-language pathologists, psychologists, reading specialists, literacy coaches, and others in related fields.

Preschool Language Scale, Fourth Edition (PLS-4; Zimmerman, Steiner, & Pond, 2002)

The PLS-4 is designed to measure receptive and expressive language in children from birth through 6 years, 11 months of age and can be used to assist professionals in identifying children who have a language impairment. The PLS-4 contains two subscales, Auditory Comprehension and Expressive Communication. The Auditory Comprehension scale, which evaluates the language a child understands, includes several items that target receptive vocabulary. For preschool-age children and kindergartners, items target vocabulary relating to colors; categories of objects; concepts such as more, most, tall, long, short, shapes, spatial concepts, quantity, body parts; and time and sequence concepts, among others. The PLS-4 contains a color picture manual, a record form for each individual being

Table 9–2. Four Categories of Semantics Measured by the OWLS

Semantics Category	Description	OWLS Subtest/s That Measure Category
Lexical	▪ Meanings of single words and word combinations ▪ Includes nouns, verbs, adjectives, and adverbs as well as idioms and words with multiple meanings	▪ Listening comprehension ▪ Oral expression
Syntactic	▪ Meaning derived from adding, subtracting, or reordering language structures ▪ Examples include: word order (Doesn't she enjoy running? →She doesn't enjoy running), grammatical morphemes (shoe→shoes), tense marker (paint→painted)	▪ Listening comprehension ▪ Oral expression
Pragmatic	▪ Meaning derived from the context within which specific linguistic structures are used ▪ Examples include social variables (setting, age, roles, relationship, and number of participants), linguistic variables (type of discourse such as conversation or narrative), and the intention, motivation, and style of the sender	▪ Oral expression
Supralinguistic	▪ Meaning that requires an additional level of processing ▪ Examples include interpretation of nonliteral and indirect language, sarcasm, and humor	▪ Listening comprehension ▪ Oral expression

Source: Carrow-Woolfolk (1995). *Oral and Written Language Scales (OWLS) Manual: Listening Comprehension and Oral Expression* (pp. 9–10). Circle Pines, MN: American Guidance Service, Inc.

assessed, and a box of manipulatives (e.g., blocks, cups, spoons). Administration time for both subscales of the PLS-4 is reported to range from 25 to 45 minutes for children age 4 years and older. Score types include age-based standard scores, percentile ranks, and age-equivalent scores. Individuals qualified to administer the PLS-4 include speech-language pathologists, early childhood specialists, psychologists, educational diagnosticians, and other professionals with appropriate training in early childhood assessment. Even though paraprofessionals may be trained to administer the PLS-4 by *recording* children's responses, only clinicians with experience in diagnostic assessment should be permitted to *score* children's responses and interpret their scores. Modifications are suggested for children who have severe developmental delays to provide criterion-referenced information about a child's language abilities; however, the PLS-4 Examiner's Manual cautions that raw scores cannot be translated into standard scores or percentile ranks when modifications to the directions are made.

Peabody Picture Vocabulary Test, Third Edition (PPVT-III; Dunn & Dunn, 1997a)

The PPVT-III is a measure of receptive vocabulary that requires examinees to select a picture that best depicts the verbal stimulus given by the examiner (e.g., "Point to *dog*" "Point to *crying*"). Children look at four picture alternatives while the examiner reads aloud the stimulus word. Children must then choose the picture that best depicts the definition of the stimulus word. All items are presented in black and white. Stimulus items are presented in ascending difficulty across sets (which include 12 items each). Within a given set, the items are arranged so that the first three items are the easiest, the last three are the second easiest, and the middle six are the most difficult (Dunn & Dunn, 1997b). The PPVT-III has been deemed appropriate for ages 2.5 to 90. The PPVT-III is an untimed assessment, but children are only tested over a "critical range" of items (so that they receive items that are neither far too easy nor far too difficult), and so the average administration time is 11 to 12 minutes per child. Examiners should have experience with administering assessments individually to young children, but no formal qualifications are required.

The PPVT-III was designed to be administered in English only, and was normed on a large sample of English-speaking children and adults. The norming sample did not include persons with uncorrected hearing or vision loss or persons with limited English proficiency. The assessment yields a raw score, which can be converted to four deviation-type normative scores (standard score, percentile rank, normal curve equivalent, stanine) and one developmental-type normative score (age equivalent). The PPVT-III was designed for two specific purposes: first, as an achievement test of receptive vocabulary for Standard English, and second, as a screening test of verbal ability (e.g., as a measure of English proficiency for persons learning English as a second language.)

Peabody Picture Vocabulary Test, Fourth Edition (PPVT-4; Dunn, & Dunn, 2007)

The latest revision to the Peabody Picture Vocabulary test is scheduled to be available in 2007. Additions to this version include color pictures, updated illustrations, a larger easel, more target words (i.e., 228 stimulus words per test form), and wireless technology (Pearson Assessments, 2006). Similar to the PPVT-III, the PPVT-4 raw score can be converted to several different deviation-type normative scores (age- and grade-based standard scores, percentile rank, normal curve equivalent, stanine) and two developmental-type normative scores (age and grade equivalent scores). In addition, the PPVT-4 includes a new metric, growth scale values (GSV), which allow measurement of a student's progress over time. Conversion of an examinee's raw score into a GSV can be accomplished by utilizing values included in tables in the new Examiner's Manual. It is also possible to convert scores on the PPVT-III to scores on the PPVT-4, which makes it easier to track a child's progress across versions of the instrument.

Receptive One-Word Picture Vocabulary Test (ROWPVT; Brownell, 2000c)

This standardized measure assesses children's receptive vocabulary skills in English. A parallel version, ROWPVT: Spanish-Bilingual Edition, is used to measure the receptive vocabulary skills of children who speak both Spanish and English. To administer this assessment, the examiner names a picture and the child locates it on a picture plate containing four different pictures, all of which are presented in color. The ROWPVT has been deemed appropriate for ages 2.0 through 18 years, 11 months; the ROWPVT: Spanish-Bilingual edition has been deemed appropriate for ages 4.0 to 12 years, 11 months. Like the PPVT-III, the ROWPVT is an untimed test in which individual children are tested over a critical range of items, and the average administration time is 10 to 15 minutes per child.

Regarding the sample on which this instrument was standardized, approximately 90% of the children did not have a disability, 5.7% had a speech-language disorder, 2.4% had a learning disability, and 2% had other conditions. Although the ROWPVT was intended to be administered individually, the test was administered to a group of 289 children in third grade or above for the standardization sample. Group administration is appropriate only for children in grades 3 and above (Brownell, 2000d). The assessment yields a raw score, which can be converted to six deviation-type normative scores (standard score, percentile rank, normal curve equivalent, T-scores, scaled scores, and stanine) and one developmental-type normative score (age equivalent).

The ROWPVT was designed to measure an individual's English hearing vocabulary. According to the manual (Brownell, 2000d, pp. 14–15), there are a variety of additional uses, including assessing cognitive ability, diagnosing reading difficulties, screening preschool and kindergarten children, monitoring growth, and evaluating program effectiveness. The ROWPVT should be administered by trained professionals or by persons supervised by trained professionals. Results should only be interpreted by someone with formal psychometric training (Brownell, 2000d).

Test of Language Development-Primary-Third Edition (TOLD-P:3; Newcomer & Hammill, 1997)

The TOLD-P:3 measures children's semantics, syntax, and phonology through nine subtests. Six of the subtests (measuring semantics and syntax) are considered to be the Core subtests; the remaining three subtests measuring phonology are considered to be supplemental. The six Core subtests (in order of preferred administration) include: Picture Vocabulary, Relational Vocabulary, Oral Vocabulary, Grammatic Understanding, Sentence Imitation, and Grammatic Completion.

The TOLD-P:3 was designed for four purposes: (1) to identify children whose language proficiency is below their peers, (2) to determine children's specific language strengths and weaknesses, (3) to determine children's progress as a result of an intervention, and (4) to measure language for research purposes.

For the purposes of this section on measuring receptive vocabulary, we describe the Picture Vocabulary subtest in detail. The Picture Vocabulary subtest contains one training item and 30 assessment items. Similar to the ROWPVT, four color drawings are presented on each page and the examiner asks the child to point to the picture he or she names. Each correct answer receives one point and each incorrect answer receives no points. The examiner discontinues the assessment after five consecutive incorrect items. The assessment is untimed, but authors report that testing time for the six Core subtests is approximately 30 minutes to 1 hour. In addition to a raw score for each of the subtests, the assessment yields age equivalents for each subtest, percentile scores for each subtest, standard scores for each subtest, and composite quotients for particular combinations of subtests. Norms exist for children between 4 years and 8 years, 11 months of age. Examiners should have some formal training in assessing children.

Measuring Expressive Vocabulary

Expressive vocabulary describes the words that an individual can produce (either in spoken or written form). Expressive vocabulary knowledge is different from receptive vocabulary knowledge on several levels. To use vocabulary expressively requires that the speaker have knowledge of denotations, connotations, syntactic constraints, derivations, co-occurrence restrictions, and register (Crow, 1986). Denotation describes the most precise and specific meaning of a word. For example, the word *devour* denotes eating eagerly or greedily, whereas the word *nibble* denotes eating intermittently or gently with small bites. Connotation describes the implied or suggested meaning of a word. Connotation is important for using figurative language and words with multiple meanings. For example, if someone were to say "that woman is really cold," the listener would need to know whether the speaker was using a literal connotation

to describe the woman's physical condition, or a nonliteral connotation to describe the woman's emotional state. Syntactic constraints
involve knowing how to use a particular word correctly in sentence frames; they are also important for using vocabulary expressively. For example, a speaker must know that to use the form
enjoy + verb, the verb must be expressed in gerund form (*I enjoy
reading*, not *I enjoy to read*). Derivations allow persons using
vocabulary expressively to change a word's part of speech (read =
verb, readable = adjective). Co-occurrence restrictions are rules
that designate how words can be used in a language. For example,
the word *noise* can be described as being little or big, short or
long, but not as being tall. Finally, a speaker must have a sense of
language register, or how to use words in various social contexts.
See Table 9–3 for a summary of the measures of expressive vocabulary we describe in this chapter.

Clinical Evaluation of Language Fundamentals-Preschool 2nd Edition (CELF-P2; Wiig & Secord, 2003)

The CELF-P2 is an individually administered assessment of general language ability that is appropriate for children between 3 and 6 years of
age. This assessment can be used to identify and diagnose language
deficits in children and evaluate a child's general language ability, early
classroom and literacy fundamentals, and communication in context.
Three subtests of the CELF P-2 can be combined to produce a "core
language score": Sentence Structure, Concepts and Following Directions, and Expressive Vocabulary. For the purposes of this chapter,
we will discuss the Expressive Vocabulary subtest. The Expressive
Vocabulary subtest evaluates a child's ability to label illustrations of
people, objects, and actions (referential naming). The subtest contains
20 items, each of which can receive a score of 2 points for target
responses or semantically correct responses that take into account
cultural diversity, or 0 points for semantically incorrect responses.
Some items can receive a score of 1 point if they are somewhat
related to the target response. For example, on the item designed to
elicit the 2-point word *veterinarian* or *vet*, the child receives 1 point
for responding with *pet doctor* or *animal doctor*. The examiner
presents all 20 items unless the child receives seven consecutive
0 scores, at which point the examiner discontinues the subtest.

Table 9–3. Summary of Expressive Vocabulary Measures

Measure	Time (in min.)	Adminis-tration	Relevant Subtests	Languages	Scores	Uses	Ages
CELF-P2	5	Individual	Expressive Vocabulary	English	1. Raw Score 2. Two deviation-type normative scores 3. Developmental-type normative score	1. Identify and diagnose language deficits 2. Evaluate general language ability 3. Evaluate early classroom and literacy fundamentals 4. Evaluate communication in context	3–6
EOWPVT	10–15	Individual	NA	English	1. Raw score 2. Six deviation-type normative scores 3. One developmental-type normative score	1. Assessing cognitive ability 2. Diagnosing reading difficulties 3. Diagnosing expressive aphasia 4. Screening 5. Evaluating an English learner's vocabulary 6. Monitoring growth 7. Evaluating program effectiveness	2.0–18;11

Measure	Time (in min.)	Administration	Relevant Subtests	Languages	Scores	Uses	Ages
EVT and EVT-2	15	Individual	NA	English	1. Raw score 2. Four deviation-type normative scores 3. One developmental-type normative score *Note.* The EVT-2 additionally provides a grade-equivalent score and growth scale values (GSVs)	1. Screening 2. Progress monitoring 3. Research	2.5–90
IGDI	1	Individual	Picture Naming	English	1. Number of pictures administered 2. Number of pictures correct 3. Number of pictures incorrect	1. Evaluate risk 2. Evaluate program effectiveness	31–69 months

continues

Table 9–3. *continued*

Measure	Time (in min.)	Adminis- tration	Relevant Subtests	Languages	Scores	Uses	Ages
MacArthur-Bates CDI	Approx. 10 for short form; Approx. 60 for long form	Parent Report	Words and Sentences	English plus approxi- mately 40 additional languages	1. Raw score 2. Percentiles	1. Comparison to norms 2. Outcome measure 3. Dependent or independent variable for experimental studies 4. Tracking instrument for case studies 5. Screening for clinical purposes	16–30 months
OWLS	11	Individual	Oral Expression	English	1. Raw score 2. Four deviation-type normative scores 3. Developmental-type normative score	1. Identification 2. Progress monitoring 3. Research	3–21

Measure	Time (in min.)	Adminis-tration	Relevant Subtests	Languages	Scores	Uses	Ages
TOLD-P:3	30–60 for six Core subtests	Individual	Oral Vocabulary	English	1. Raw score for each subtest 2. Age equivalents for each subtest 3. Percentile scores for each subtest 4. Standard scores for each subtest 5. Composite quotients for combinations of subtests	1. Identification 2. Progress monitoring 3. Research	4.0–8,11
TOPEL	30	Individual	Definitional Vocabulary	English	1. Raw scores 2. Percentile ranks 3. Standard scores 4. Qualitative descriptors	1. Identifying risk for language and literacy difficulties 2. Progress monitoring 3. Research	3–5

Based on our experience, administration time for the subtest is approximately 5 minutes. A raw score for the Expressive Vocabulary subtest is created by summing the scores on all items administered. The raw score can then be converted to deviation-type normative scores, such as a scaled score, a percentile rank, or a developmental-type score, the age equivalent. Because the CELF-P2 is a downward extension of the CELF-4, the Expressive Vocabulary subtest overlaps with the Expressive Vocabulary subtest on the CELF-4. The subtests of the two versions are highly correlated ($r = 0.86$). The CELF-P2 should be administered by speech-language pathologists, school psychologists, special educators, and trained diagnosticians. Currently the CELF-P2 is not available in Spanish and should be administered in English only.

Expressive One-Word Picture Vocabulary Test (EOWPVT; Brownell, 2000a)

The EOWPVT is a standardized measure of children's expressive vocabulary skills in English. A parallel version, the EOWPVT: Spanish-Bilingual Edition, is used to measure the expressive vocabulary skills of children who speak both Spanish and English. Children view a series of pictures and are asked to name the picture (e.g., kite) or provide a word that describes a series or category of objects (e.g., flying). All items are presented in color. When presenting individual picture plates, two types of verbal instructions are employed: prompts and cues (Brownell, 2000b). A prompt such as "*What's this?*" is used for an object; "*What is he/she doing?*" is used for an action; and "*What word names all of these?*" is used for a concept. If the examinee's response reveals that the child is not attending to the appropriate features of the picture, then a cue may be used to clarify the intent of the item (Brownell, 2000b). For example, for the test item "foot," a child may respond "toe." The examiner then points to the part of the picture where the arrow is pointing and says, "*What's this?*"

If children will also be tested on a receptive vocabulary measure, such as the ROWPVT, Brownell (2000b) recommends administering the EOWPVT first because learning may occur during the administration of the receptive measure. The EOWPVT has been deemed appropriate for ages 2.0 to 18 years, 11 months; the EOW-

PVT: Spanish-Bilingual Edition has been deemed appropriate for ages 4.0 to 12 years, 11 months. The assessment is untimed, and the average administration time is 10 to 15 minutes per child. Typically only one session is necessary to complete the assessment although with very young children and with reluctant children, it may be appropriate to assess over more than one session (Brownell, 2000b). The assessment yields a raw score, which can be converted to six deviation-type normative scores (standard score, percentile rank, normal curve equivalent, T-score, scaled score, and stanine) and one developmental-type normative score (age equivalent).

The EOWPVT was designed to measure the magnitude of an individual's spoken vocabulary. According to the manual (Brownell, 2000b, pp. 14–15), there are a variety of additional uses, including assessing cognitive ability, diagnosing reading difficulties, diagnosing expressive aphasia, screening preschool and kindergarten children, evaluating an English learner's vocabulary, monitoring growth, and evaluating program effectiveness. The EOWPVT should be administered by trained professionals or persons supervised by trained professionals. Results should only be interpreted by someone with formal psychometric training (Brownell, 2000b).

Expressive Vocabulary Test (EVT; Williams, 1997)

The EVT is appropriate for screening for expressive language problems and word retrieval. It can be used as a record of growth across a broad age span, from age 2½ to age 90. It takes approximately 15 minutes to administer and can be administered in English only. In general, the EVT has been found to be a culturally fair test of expressive vocabulary (Restrepo et al., 2006; Thomas-Tate, Washington, Craig, & Packard, 2006). The authors of the assessment examined the validity of the EVT for African American preschool and kindergarten children and reported that the mean performance of African American children was not significantly different from the standardized mean. The EVT has been deemed appropriate for use by paraprofessionals working under supervision, teachers and teaching assistants, and graduate and undergraduate students in education or psychology or related helping professions. Score types include raw scores, standard scores and confidence intervals, percentile ranks, normal curve equivalents, stanines, and test-age equivalents.

Expressive Vocabulary Test-Second Edition (EVT-2; Williams, 2007)

An updated version of the EVT is scheduled to be available in 2007. This version includes two parallel test forms each with 190 items, modernized pictures and vocabulary, technology updates to expedite administration, scoring, and interpretation of results, and a larger easel The second edition also includes a new metric, growth scale values (GSVs), which allows for measuring children's progress over time.

The Individual Growth and Developmental Indicators (IGDI; Early Childhood Research Institute on Measuring Growth and Development, 1998; Missall & McConnell, 2004)

The Picture Naming subtest of IGDI is a progress monitoring measure of vocabulary that has been developed for use with children between the ages of 31 to 69 months. This subtest is individually administered by presenting children with colored pictures of objects, including animals, people, food, clothing, household objects, games, vehicles, tools, and sporting equipment. Children are required to name as many pictures as they can correctly in 1 minute. Scores include the number of pictures correctly identified, the number of pictures incorrectly identified, and the total number of pictures administered. Using this information, the percentage of correctly identified pictures may be calculated. The IGDI can be administered by psychologists, teachers, paraprofessionals, or others with advanced training. The test is appropriate to use with native English speakers.

Reliability and validity studies have been conducted with typically developing children, children enrolled in Head Start, and ELLS between the ages of 36 and 60 months. McConnell, Priest, Davis, and McEvoy. (2002) provide psychometric information from a cross-sectional (all English-speaking children without disabilities; $n = 39$) and longitudinal study (children enrolled in Head Start; $n = 14$). The relationship between children's scores and age demonstrated that the picture naming subtest measures growth. However, the relationship was weaker in the longitudinal Head Start sample ($r = 0.32$) than in the cross-sectional sample of English speaking children without disabilities ($r = 0.63$). In a study with more closely matched sample sizes, Missall and McConnell (2004) compared the performance of children enrolled in Head Start ($n = 12$), children enrolled in childcare centers ($n = 12$), and Spanish-speaking children ($n = 19$) on the picture naming subtest. Spanish-speaking children showed less growth ($B = 2.64$) than both children enrolled in Head Start ($B = 16.51$) and children enrolled in childcare centers ($B = 16.97$).

MacArthur-Bates Communicative Development Inventory (CDI; Fenson et al., 1993)

The CDI (formerly the MacArthur Communicative Development Inventory) Words and Sentences Toddler Form is a parent-report measure of expressive vocabulary designed for toddlers from 16 to 30 months of age, although it is also useful for older children with developmental delays (e.g., Thal, O'Hanlon, Clemmons, & Fralin, 1999). The authors suggest that the CDI is useful as a comparison to established norms, as an outcome measure for large-sample studies, as a dependent or independent variable for experimental studies, as a tracking instrument for case studies, and as a screening tool for clinical purposes. The long form of the instrument contains a 680-item checklist on which parents check whether or not their child produces a given word. The long form of the CDI also contains a 37-item grammatical complexity checklist. There are also two short form versions of the instrument (Form A and Form B), each containing 100 vocabulary items and a question asking parents to report whether or not their child is combining words. The CDI results in a raw score (the number of words the parent reports the child can produce), which can be converted to percentiles that are based on the norming sample of more than 1,800 infants and toddlers (Dale & Fenson, 1996). The CDI has been adapted for use in approximately 40 languages in addition to American English (e.g., Spanish; Jackson-Maldonado, Bates, & Thal, 2003) and norms exist for some of these languages as well.

Oral and Written Language Scales (OWLS; Carrow-Woolfolk, 1995a)

We introduced the OWLS in the section on measuring receptive vocabulary. In this section, we discuss The Oral Expression Scale of the OWLS. The Oral Expression Scale measures children's understanding and use of spoken language and contains 96 items arranged in order of difficulty. The Oral Expression Scale measures four categories of language: lexical, syntactic, pragmatic, and supralinguistic. The lexical category of language is relevant to expressive vocabulary and includes items that require the child to produce nouns, verbs, modifiers, personal and demonstrative pronouns, prepositions, idioms, words with double meanings, words that represent direction, quantity, and spatial relations, and so forth (Carrow-Woolfolk, 1995b). The Oral Expression Scale of the OWLS takes from 4 to 18 minutes to administer to children between the ages of 3 and 5. The average administration time for children in this age range is 11 minutes.

Test of Language Development–Primary, Third Edition (TOLD-P:3; Hammill & Newcomer, 1997)

We provided a general description of the TOLD-P:3 in the section on measuring receptive vocabulary. Here we describe the Oral Vocabulary subtest, which measures expressive vocabulary. The Oral Vocabulary subtest contains 28 items that require the child to provide a definition for words that the examiner produces. Children must provide a precise definition of a word in order to receive one point for that item, and in most cases, they may also produce two descriptive characteristics of a word to receive one point (e.g., for cow: gives milk and has hooves; Newcomer & Hammill, 1998, p. 23). For information on possible score types, time to administer, and examiner qualifications, please see the section of this chapter that describes measures of receptive vocabulary.

Test of Preschool Early Literacy Definitional Vocabulary Subtest (TOPEL; Lonigan, Wagner, Torgesen, & Rashotte, 2006)

The TOPEL is an individually administered measure that can be used to quantify oral vocabulary for 3- to 5-year-olds. The TOPEL can be used to identify children who are having problems or who are at risk for having literacy problems and to document their oral vocabulary ability. The TOPEL can also be used to measure a child's vocabulary progress in intervention programs twice per year. The Definitional Vocabulary subtest assesses two aspects of a child's knowledge about an item, labeling and function. If general responses are given by the child, the administration procedure allows for the examiner to give probes to elicit knowledge that is more precise. Administration time is approximately 30 minutes.

Administration of the TOPEL does not require formal training. However, the examiner should be knowledgeable and experienced in administration, scoring, and interpretation of norm-referenced assessments. Score types include raw scores, percentile ranks, standard scores, and qualitative descriptors based on standard scores (e.g., poor, average, above average, superior). According to the manual, the three general uses of the assessment are: (1) identifying risk for language and literacy difficulties, (2) monitoring student progress, and (3) measuring vocabulary for research purposes.

Measuring Word-Learning Abilities and Potential

In addition to measuring a child's static receptive or expressive vocabulary knowledge, it is useful to measure word-learning ability and potential to gauge the success or difficulty an individual might experience when learning new words. Measuring a child's potential for learning new words involves examining the processes by which he or she acquires the meaning of new words and takes into account factors such as the rapidity of word acquisition and the depth and breadth of one's word knowledge. There are at least two reasons that early literacy professionals should consider measuring children's word learning abilities and potential. First, understanding a child's word-learning abilities and potential can help to elucidate the source of vocabulary limitations. Some children, for example, might have limited vocabularies because, in the course of regular instruction, they do not receive the amount of repeated exposure to new words in multiple contexts that they require to fully grasp the meaning of those words. Other children might have limited vocabularies in the sense that they have only a single meaning for words that have multiple meanings. Second, understanding a child's word-learning abilities and potential can provide insight into designing vocabulary interventions for children who lag significantly behind their peers in this area. Knowing the source of a child's vocabulary limitations can assist early literacy professionals in designing specific interventions, which might be targeted, for example, toward providing a child with extra exposure to specific vocabulary words that other classmates have acquired with ease. As another example, a vocabulary intervention might be targeted toward expanding a child's semantic network in an academic area, such as science.

We discuss three different methods for assessing children's word learning abilities and potential (see Table 9–4 for a summary): (1) fast mapping, (2) quick incidental learning, and (3) measures of lexical diversity. Methods for assessing children's word learning abilities and potential differ from measures of receptive and expressive vocabulary knowledge in that no accepted standardized procedures exist in this area. For this reason and because these procedures produce information about *how* children learn new words and *how* they store words in their lexicon, these procedures probably would appeal mainly to researchers, psychologists, and those interested in how children develop.

Fast Mapping Tasks

Fast mapping (Carey & Bartlett, 1978) is the process by which children minimally acquire the partial meaning of a novel word with only brief exposure, by using linguistic or nonlinguistic cues (or some combination of linguistic and nonlinguistic cues) to infer the word's meaning. One way in which a child might fast map a novel word is by using the principle of mutual exclusivity, which states that objects have only one label (Markman, 1989; Merriman & Bowman, 1989). For example, if a preschool teacher asks a student to retrieve a *medicine dropper* from a box in the science area of the classroom containing a magnifying glass, a book, and a medicine dropper, the student would likely select the medicine dropper, even if she does not know that word, but knows that the magnifying glass is not called *medicine dropper* and that the book is not called *medicine dropper*.

Children also can use syntactic cues that provide information about a novel word's form class (e.g., noun, verb, adjective) when fast mapping. For example, a child who hears "This is a dax" is likely to interpret *dax* to be a *count noun*; a child who hears "This is Dax" is likely to interpret *Dax* to be a *proper name*; and a child who hears "This is a dax one" is likely to interpret *dax* to be an

Table 9–4. Summary of Measures of Word Learning and Potential

Measure	Time (in min.)	Adminis-tration	Relevant Subtests	Languages	Scores	Uses	Ages
Fast Mapping	Varies	Individual, group	NA	any	NA	To assess the ease with which children learn new information	any
QUIL	Varies	Individual, group	NA	any	NA	To assess the ease with which children learn new information (especially in incidental situations)	any
Lexical Diversity	Varies	Individual, group	NA	any	1. TTR 2. NDW 3. *D* 4. Proportion verbs 5. Proportion rare words	To assess one's breadth of word knowledge	any

adjective (Hall, Burns, & Pawluski, 2003). Syntactic cues such as these aid in the fast mapping process because they let children know whether novel words describe objects, persons, or attributes.

Examining a child's ability to fast map novel words provides information about his or her ability to learn new information easily (Hirsh-Pasek, Kochanoff, Newcombe, & de Villiers, 2005). Fast mapping tasks require that the examiner use a tightly controlled set of procedures to assess a child's word learning abilities. Although there is no standardized procedure for assessing fast mapping, tasks generally involve reading a storybook to the child or having the child watch a video that contains novel words interspersed with familiar words and then assessing the child's understanding of the novel words. It is recommended that examiners use pseudowords (plausible, invented words corresponding to the sound patterns of the child's native language) and novel objects, actions, or attributes to rule out the possibility that the child already knows the words being assessed.

In one study assessing children's fast mapping abilities, Heibeck and Markman (1987) had young children retrieve objects corresponding either to a novel color term, shape term, or texture term. For example, when assessing fast mapping of a novel color term, the experimenter asked "Could you bring me the bice one, not the blue one, the bice one" (p. 1023). Following this introducing event, children participated in three tasks: (1) a production task that assessed whether children could produce the new color term, (2) a hyponym task that assessed whether children had knowledge of the domain to which the novel term belonged, and (3) a comprehension task that assessed whether children could select the new color from a group of distractors. Fast mapping tasks have also been used to assess the abilities of children with specific language impairment (e.g., Alt, Plante, & Creusere, 2004; Eyer, Leonard, Bedores, McGregor, Anderson, & Viescas, 2002; Gray, 2003, 2004), and individuals with Down syndrome (Kay-Raining Bird, Chapman, & Schwartz, 2004).

Quick Incidental Learning

Quick Incidental Learning (QUIL), a phrase coined by Rice (1990), describes children's ability to acquire the partial meaning of a novel word in contexts that lack ostensive labeling by others. QUIL is consistent with the notion of fast mapping, but it makes a stronger claim for the "incidental" nature of word learning than fast mapping. In studies assessing QUIL, few controls are introduced. Children typically watch a video containing novel words that are neither isolated nor contrasted with familiar words and then participate in an assessment of the target words. There are two important assumptions regarding QUIL: First, QUIL varies as a function of learner characteristics (e.g., age, aptitude). Second, QUIL varies as a function of the type of word being mapped (e.g., noun, verb) (Oetting, Rice, & Swank, 1995).

Measures of Lexical Diversity

In addition to using fast mapping tasks and QUIL tasks, researchers might investigate lexical diversity in spontaneous or semistructured language samples to gain a deeper understanding of the breadth of a child's word knowledge. Chapter 8 in this book presents a thorough discussion of how researchers and clinicians might measure lexical diversity in children's narratives. Five methods commonly used to measure lexical diversity include (1) type-token ratio (TTR), which is calculated by dividing the number of different words in a language sample by the total number of words in that sample; (2) number of different words (NDW), which is a count of the number of different words appearing in a language sample; (3) *D*, which is a mathematical formula measuring lexical diversity that takes into account the size of the language sample being assessed; (4) the proportion of verbs children use in a language sample; and (5) the proportion of rare words children produce in a language sample.

Special Considerations for Assessing Vocabulary Knowledge

This section of the chapter addresses the assessment of culturally and linguistically diverse (CLD) children. Individual differences in vocabulary performance are strongly associated with reading comprehension (National Reading Panel, 2000) and school success (Biemiller & Slonim, 2001; Jenkins, Matlock, & Slocum, 1989). Current vocabulary assessment instruments if used alone run the risk of inappropriately identifying children from CLD backgrounds as having language impairment (Ukrainetz, Harpell, Walsh, & Coyle, 2000; Washington & Craig, 1999). Without knowing about the factors that influence the manner in which children demonstrate their knowledge, it is challenging to develop valid and reliable vocabulary assessments. The specific areas we highlight include: (1) assessment construct, (2) assessment format (3) assessment contexts, and (4) child factors.

Historical Background

The population of CLD children in the United States is growing rapidly, particularly among low-income families. For instance, the percentage of children living in the United States who are classified by their ethnicity as Hispanic is increasing, with corresponding decreases in European American (EA) children. From 2000 to 2050, the Hispanic population is predicted to increase by 188% and the African American population is projected to increase by 71% (U.S. Census Bureau, 2004). Children from these populations are likely to be typically developing with below average scores on vocabulary assessments, as suggested by the stable 30- to 40-point difference between EA and CLD children on the National Assessment of Educational Progress (NAEP) reading assessment since the 1970s (Snow, Burns, & Griffin, 1998). These differences also have major consequences for children and their school systems as a result of the current No Child Left Behind mandate. Reading readiness for young children currently is assessed on the basis of models that view oral language skills narrowly, including such abilities as vocabulary knowledge and letter name recognition, rather than a more comprehensive assessment of literacy development (National Institute of Child Health and Human Development Early Child Care Research Network, 2005). A better understanding of the problems that CLD children face is needed to improve prevention and early intervention efforts. Further investigation into the individual differences that CLD children bring to assessment situations as well as factors that might optimize their performance on various assessments is clearly warranted.

Assessment Construct

Discrepancies in estimates of children's receptive and expressive vocabulary may arise due to contextual constraints of assessments and individual differences among examinees. For example, a remarkable pattern exists whereby CLD children often have higher scores on expressive measures as compared to receptive measures. Restrepo et al. (2006) administered the third edition of the Peabody Picture Vocabulary Test (PPVT-III) and the Expressive Vocabulary Test (EVT) to preschool EA and African American children and reported that 34.8% of their sample scored significantly lower on the PPVT-III as compared to the EVT. When this discrepancy was further examined, there were more African American children with significant discrepancies between the PPVT and EVT than EA children. Moreover, African American children performed better in general on the EVT than they did on the PPVT-III. Teuber and Furlong (1985) also observed an advantage of expressive vocabulary scores over receptive vocabulary scores in Mexican American preschool- and elementary-age children. This pattern may be due to the fact that expressive measures permit a less restrictive range of acceptable responses than receptive measures. For example, many expressive measures allow examinees to draw upon their partial word knowledge whereas receptive vocabulary measures generally force examinees to select from among a set of items containing the single best answer as well as semantically or perceptually related distracter items.

A second remarkable pattern is that the correlation between measures in each domain (i.e., convergent validity) is stronger for EA children than it is for CLD children. Several studies have reported moderate to strong correlations between measures in each modality suggesting good convergent validity for EA children [$r_{receptive} = 0.52$, $r_{expressive} = 0.77$ (Gray, Plante, Vance, & Henrichsen, 1999); $r_{receptive} = 0.58$, $r_{expressive} = 0.64$ (Qi, Kaiser, Milan, Yzquierdo, & Hancock, 2003); $r_{receptive} = 0.79$, $r_{expressive} = 0.80$ (Ukrainetz & Blomquist, 2002)]. In contrast, weaker correlations are found for African American children, $r_{receptive} = 0.57$, $r_{expressive} = 0.48$ (Qi et al., 2003).

Assessment Format

Multiple Choice

A variety of assessment formats are used to measure an individual's level of vocabulary knowledge including the multiple-choice format, the interview method, and dynamic assessment. The *multiple-choice* format using a polychotomous scoring model is one of the most widely used methods (see Smith, 1987 for issues regarding validity). Read (2000) proposes certain limitations for multiple-choice tests; of which assessors working with CLD children should be aware:

1. Test construction, field testing, and refinement can be time- and labor-intensive.
2. The student may know a meaning for the target word, but not the one sought.
3. The student may choose the correct word by process of elimination.
4. Items may test a student's knowledge of distracters rather than his or her ability to identify the exact meaning of the target word (i.e., to fast map the novel term by eliminating implausible distracter items).
5. The student may miss an item for lack of knowledge of words or lack of understanding of syntax in the distracters.
6. The format permits only a very limited sampling of the student's total vocabulary (pp. 77–78).

Interview

Another widely used format is the *interview* method. This method has been adopted as the testing format for several assessments, such as the vocabulary subtest of the Wechsler Intelligence Scale for Children, Third Edition (WISC-III), the vocabulary subtest of the Stanford-Binet Intelligence Scale, the EVT, and the EOWPVT. For example, the Vocabulary subtest of the WISC-III (Wechsler, 1991) requires the child to orally define increasingly difficult stimulus words presented by the examiner. The child receives a score of 0, 1, or 2 points for each item based on the quality of the definition. A 0-point response represents a wrong or vague answer; a score of 1 indicates a minor use of the word, an example using the word, or a vague synonym; and a score of 2 indicates a major use of the word, a good synonym, or a correct definition of the word. Participants' responses can be scored in two ways: by using the standard scoring method of 0-, 1-, or 2-point responses, or by using a modified method in which a correct response receives 1 point and an incorrect response receives 0 points. The downside of assessing children's depth of word knowledge using the interview method is that the pool of items administered may not be comprehensive enough to gain a solid understanding of cross-cultural differences. Additionally, without formal training, it is difficult to notice patterns across responses that reflect partial knowledge of an item.

Dynamic Assessment

Dynamic assessment (DA) is an alternative approach to traditional standardized assessments. The use of dynamic assessment to measure cognitive abilities with young children has been evolving since the late 1970s based on a cognitive developmental model proposed by Vygotsky (1978). Vygotsky's cognitive developmental model influences the structure of the dialogue between the assessor and the student during the assessment process, for example. Vygotsky's *zone of proximal development* is defined as the difference between a child's "actual developmental level as determined by independent problem solving" and his or her level of "potential development as determined through problem solving under adult guidance or collaboration with more capable peers" (p. 86). By using DA, the examiner can assist the child by providing additional opportunities for the child to respond during the assessment process.

It has been suggested that DA may minimize the gap in performance between different subgroups of the population. DA has been shown to minimize differences between children from differing socioeconomic statuses and cultural backgrounds, as well as between typically developing children and children with mental handicaps, developmental delays, and specific learning disabilities (e.g., Peña, Iglesias, & Lidz, 2001; Tzuriel, 2001). For example, Peña, Bedore, and Rappazza (2003) found that English language learners who were provided multiple opportunities to demonstrate their knowledge during an assessment performed as well as EA children.

Assessment Context

The assessment of young children can be conducted in a variety of settings including school, the child's home, a research laboratory, or a clinic. Particular to each environment is its physical context and the type of examiner who interacts with the child. Assessment in the school provides a familiar location and often a familiar examiner for the child. Assessment in the child's home also provides a familiar and comfortable context for the child but is more susceptible to distractions (e.g., noise, siblings). In contrast, assessment in a research laboratory or clinic provides neither a familiar environment nor a familiar examiner. However, children's familiarity with the environment has not been found to strongly influence their performance on assessments (Jensen, 1980). By contrast, the match or mismatch between a child and an examiner may affect a child's attitude and engagement, which in turn may affect the child's performance (Fuchs & Fuchs, 1989; Kea, Campbell-Whatley, & Bratton, 2003; Kim, Baydar, & Greek, 2003; Nabors, Evans, & Strickland, 2000).

Issues relating to testing context may become more complex when a child is bilingual. Often not only is the examiner unfamiliar, but he or she may also not be well trained in assessing young children, particularly if the examiner's primary training is in language translation. A meta-analysis conducted by Fuchs and Fuchs (1989) shows that the performance of Hispanic children increases when the examiner is familiar to them. However, there is only anecdotal evidence to support the finding that examiner's conceptualization of testing requirements pertaining to ELL populations relates to an ELL's level of engagement during testing (Puente & Ardila, 2000).

Child Factors

Gender

Few studies have found differences in vocabulary assessment performance between CLD girls and boys. The common finding is similar to the finding in EA children, whereby girls outperform boys on measures of vocabulary knowledge (Qi, Kaiser, Milan, & Hancock, 2006).

Socioeconomic Status (SES)

The relation between SES and vocabulary performance has been well established (Hall, Nagy, & Linn, 1984; Hart & Risely, 1995; Ryan, Fauth, & Brooks-Gunn, 2006). SES is a variable that is akin to culture in the sense that the detrimental effects on performance stem from differences in exposure to language in the home environment. Over the years, the advent of better measurement tools and special programs such as Head Start, Early Reading First, and

Reading First have helped to curtail the skewed distribution of children's vocabulary performance. For example, by spring of their preschool year, children attending Head Start score very close to the normative mean of receptive vocabulary measures (Administration for Children and Families; 2006; Head Start Bureau, 2006; Williams Smith, Bojczyk, Tannenbaum, & Torgesen, 2006).

Atypical Development

Practitioners and researchers use a variety of assessments to determine atypical development. The recent trend is to use a combination of standardized vocabulary and oral language assessments along with measures derived from natural language samples (Condouris, Meyer, & Tager-Flusberg, 2003; Craig & Washington, 2000; Rhyner, Kelly, Brantley, & Krueger, 1999; Rodekohr & Haynes, 2001) Children who are not developing typically tend to score lower than typically developing children on assessments of vocabulary knowledge. Because several sources can underlie low performance (e.g., SES, culture, language status) and each standardized test has differential sensitivity and specificity in identifying language impairment (see Gray, Plante, Vance, & Henrichsen, 1999), researchers and clinicians should exercise caution when considering scores from a single measure in isolation.

Language and Cultural Status

The words in our vocabulary are the primary vehicle for transmitting and internalizing culture. The relationship between culture, language, and cognition has been debated. One view is that culture, through language, influences people's thinking (Whorf, 1956). Therefore, it is reasonable to assert that culture influences the manner in which we conceptualize words in our vocabulary.

Cross-cultural and cross-linguistic research on vocabulary knowledge has been limited by the assessments traditionally used to assess vocabulary knowledge. Knowledge-based tests such as standardized tests of vocabulary are not adequate reflections of the true language abilities of members of cultural and linguistically diverse populations (Craig & Washington, 2000, Laing & Kamhi,

2003; Restrepo et al., 2006; Stockman, 2000; Washington & Craig, 1999). Further, certain assessment formats may not be compatible with a child's home language experiences. For example, Peña and Quinn (1997) demonstrated that African American and Puerto Rican children performed poorly on a single word labeling vocabulary measure (EOWPVT). Other evidence supports a more positive trend. For example, measures such as the PPVT-III have been demonstrated to be culturally fair (Qi et al., 2006; Washington & Craig, 1999; Williams Smith et al., 2006). Mean standard scores and distributions of scores for African American children do not differ from the normative mean and distribution or from the standard scores and distribution of EA children, indicating that the strides that test developers have been making toward improving the cultural sensitivity of their assessments may be working.

Dialect and Bilingualism

Children from nondominant cultures are referred for special education services at higher rates than expected (Kea et al., 2003). Further, children who are non-native English speakers are more likely to be diagnosed as having a language impairment because the majority of assessments are normed for English-speaking children (Kester & Peña, 2002; Rhodes, Kayser, & Hess, 2000). Assessments that use monolingual standardization samples provide inappropriate estimates of bilingual vocabulary ability. The most common mistake in assessing bilingual children is translating the test to be administered in the examinee's native language. The problem with this is that bilinguals have a different sequence of acquiring words (Tamayo, 1987). In addition, languages differ not only in vocabulary, but also in gender markers, structural rules, dialectical variations, and pragmatic rules (Rhodes et al., 2000).

With respect to receptive vocabulary tasks, it may be difficult for CLD children to link their cultural meaning of a word to a particular picture because a direct translation of that concept may not exist in their native language, or the exemplars of a particular concept in their culture may differ from mainstream exemplars appearing on the assessment. The influence of dialect appears to be very important during the period of emergent and early literacy and dialectical influences diminish as the child gains exposure to the academic environment (Craig & Washington, 2004). It is not yet known if separate norms should be created for children who speak the African American dialet because of variations in dialect. Some researchers suggest that an indicator of dialect (e.g., Diagnostic Evaluation of Language Variation; Seymour, Roeper, & de Villiers, 2003) or acculturation (e.g., African American Acculturation Scale; Landrine & Klonoff, 1994) should accompany the administration of standardized assessments.

Order of Administration for Expressive and Receptive Vocabulary Measures

When administering a battery of assessments, practitioners and researchers must decide on the order in which to administer individual measures. Receptive vocabulary measures require a nonverbal response, such as pointing to a target word, whereas expressive measures require a verbal response. Some of the assessment manuals reviewed in this chapter include recommendations on the order of administration for receptive versus expressive measures. For example, Brownell (2000b, 2000d) recommends that expressive measures be administered before receptive measures. This order may have implications for children who are shy or reticent in providing verbal responses and highlights the importance of establishing rapport with children before assessments are administered.

Interpreting the Results of Assessments of Vocabulary Knowledge

This section provides practical recommendations for how to use the results of vocabulary assessments and answers the question: "Now that I have measured a child's word knowledge, how should I use the information?" Early literacy professionals generally use these measures for four main purposes: (1) screening, (2) identification, (3) progress monitoring, and (4) research.

Vocabulary screenings frequently are administered to determine whether a child's language skills require further evaluation by a speech-language pathologist or an educational specialist. Because screenings are usually quick and informal measures of a child's vocabulary knowledge, early literacy professionals should be cautious when interpreting the results of screenings, and should always seek the advice of a speech-language pathologist when in doubt. Vocabulary assessments also may be used by trained clinical professionals to assist in identifying language impairment in children. Before making a diagnosis, speech-language pathologists will administer a thorough battery of language measures to create a language profile, after which he or she can collaborate with parents, educators and other early literacy professionals to create a plan for intervention or remediation. Another way in which vocabulary assessments can be used is to provide information on the extent to which a child is making gains in his or her abilities over the course of an academic year or in response to an intervention (progress monitoring). Equipped with the results of a progress-monitoring assessment, early literacy professionals can adjust the frequency, intensity, or dosage of children's vocabulary-building exercises as appropriate. Finally, vocabulary assessments can be used for research purposes to describe *how* a child's vocabulary knowledge develops. Continued research on the nature of children's vocabulary knowledge will provide a critical means to equalizing the disparities among students in their later reading achievement.

References

Administration for Children and Families. (2006). Head Start FACES: *Longitudinal Findings on Program Performance, Third Progress Report.* Washington, DC: Child Outcomes Research and Evaluation Branch and the Head Start Bureau, Administration for Children and Families, U.S. Department of Health and Human Services, DHHS. Retrieved May 1, 2006 from: http://www.acf.dhhs.gov/programs/core/pubs_reports/faces/meas_99_intro

Alt, M., Plante, E., & Creusere, M. (2004). Semantic features in fast-mapping: Performance of preschoolers with specific language impairment versus preschoolers with normal language. *Journal of Speech, Language, and Hearing Research, 47,* 407–420.

Baumann, J. F., & Kame'enui, E. J., (1991). Research on vocabulary instruction: Ode to Voltaire. In J. Flood, J. J. D. Lapp, & J. R. Squire (Eds.), *Handbook of research on teaching the English language arts* (pp. 604–632). New York: MacMillan.

Beck, I., & McKeown, M. (1991). Conditions of vocabulary acquisition. In R. Barr, M. L. Kamil, P. B. Mosenthal, & P. D. Pearson (Eds.), *Handbook of reading research* (Vol 2, pp. 789–814). New York: Longman.

Biemiller, A. (2006). Vocabulary development and instruction: A prerequisite for school learning. In D. K. Dickinson & S.B. Neuman (Eds.), *Handbook of early literacy research* (Vol. 2, pp. 41–51). New York: The Guilford Press.

Biemiller, A., & Slonim, N. (2001). Estimating root words vocabulary growth in normative and advantaged populations: Evidence for a common sequence of vocabulary acquisition. *Journal of Educational Psychology, 93*, 498–520.

Brownell, R. (2000a). *Expressive One-Word Picture Vocabulary Test.* Novato, CA: Academic Therapy Publications.

Brownell, R. (2000b). *Expressive One-Word Picture Vocabulary Test manual.* Novato, CA: Academic Therapy Publications.

Brownell, R. (2000c). *Receptive One-Word Picture Vocabulary Test.* Novato, CA: Academic Therapy Publications.

Brownell, R. (2000d). *Receptive One-Word Picture Vocabulary Test manual.* Novato, CA: Academic Therapy Publications.

Carey, S. (1978). The child as a word learner. In M. Halle, J. Bresnan, & G.A. Miller (Eds.), *Linguistic theory and psychological reality* (pp. 264–293). Cambridge, MA: MIT Press.

Carey, S., & Bartlett, E. (1978). Acquiring a single new word. *Papers and Reports on Child Language Development, 15*, 17–29.

Carrow-Woolfolk, E. (1995a). *Oral and Written Language Scales (OWLS).* Circle Pines, MN: American Guidance Service.

Carrow-Woolfolk, E. (1995b). *Oral and Written Language Scales (OWLS) Manual: Listening comprehension and oral expression.* Circle Pines, MN: American Guidance Service.

Chall, J. S. (1996). *Stages of reading development.* Fort Worth, TX: Harcourt Brace College Publishers.

Christian, K., Morrison, F. J., Frazier, J. A., & Massetti, G. (2000). Specificity in the nature and timing of cognitive growth in kindergarten and first grade. *Journal of Cognition and Development, 1*, 429–448.

Condouris, K., Meyer, E., & Tager-Flusberg, H. (2003). The relationship between standardized measures of language and measures of spontaneous speech in children with autism. *American Journal of Speech-Language Pathology, 12*, 349–358.

Craig, H. K., & Washington, J. A. (2000). An assessment battery for identifying language impairments in African American children. *Journal of Speech, Language, and Hearing Research, 43*, 366–379.

Craig, H. K., & Washington, J. A. (2004). Grade-related changes in the production of African American English. *Journal of Speech, Language, and Hearing Research, 47,* 450–463.

Crow, J. T. (1986). Receptive vocabulary acquisition for reading comprehension. *The Modern Language Journal, 70,* 242–250.

Curtis, M. E. (1987). Vocabulary testing and instruction. In M. G. McKeown & M. E. Curtis (Eds.), *The nature of vocabulary acquisition* (pp. 37–51). Hillsdale, NJ: Lawrence Erlbaum.

Dale, E. (1965). Vocabulary measurement: Techniques and major findings. *Elementary English, 42,* 82–88.

Dale, P. S., & Fenson, L. (1996). Lexical development norms for young children. *Behavior Research Methods, Instruments, & Computers, 28,* 125–127.

de Jong, P. F., & van der Leij, A. (2002). Effects of phonological abilities and linguistic comprehension on the development of reading. *Scientific Studies of Reading, 6,* 51–77.

Dunn, L. M., & Dunn, L. M. (1997a). *Peabody Picture Vocabulary Test* (3rd ed.). Circle Pines, MN: American Guidance Service.

Dunn, L. M., & Dunn, L. M. (1997b). *Peabody Picture Vocabulary Test* (3rd ed.). *Examiner's manual.* Circle Pines, MN: American Guidance Service.

Dunn, L. M., & Dunn, D. M. (2007). *Peabody Picture Vocabulary Test* (4th ed.). Bloomington, MN: Pearson Assessments.

Dupuy, H. P. (1974). *The rationale, development, and standardization of a basic word vocabulary test* (DHEW Publication No. [HRA] 74-1334). Washington, DC: U.S. Government Printing Office.

Early Childhood Research Institute on Measuring Growth and Development. (1998). *Theoretical foundations of the Early Childhood Research Institute on Measuring Growth and Development: An early childhood problem-solving model* (Tech. Rep. No. 6). Minneapolis, MN: Center for Early Education and Development, University of Minnesota.

Eyer, J. A., Leonard, L. B., Bedores, L. M., McGregor, K. K., Anderson, B., & Viescas, R. (2002). Fast mapping of verbs by children with specific language impairment. *Clinical Linguistics and Phonetics, 16,* 59–77.

Fenson, L., Dale, P., Reznick, S., Thal, D., Bates, E., Hartung, J., Pethick, S., & Reilly, J. (1993). *MacArthur Communicative Development Inventories: User's guide and technical manual.* Baltimore: Paul H. Brookes.

Fuchs, D., & Fuchs, L. S. (1989). Effects of examiner familiarity on Black, Caucasian, and Hispanic children: A meta-analysis. *Exceptional Children, 55,* 303–308.

Golinkoff, R. M., & Hirsh-Pasek, K. (1999). *How babies talk: The magic and mystery of language in the first three years of life.* New York: Dutton.

Graves, M. F. (1986). Vocabulary learning and instruction. *Review of Research in Education, 13,* 49–89.

Gray, S. (2003). Word-learning by preschoolers with specific language impairment: What predicts success? *Journal of Speech, Language, and Hearing Research, 46,* 56–67.

Gray, S. (2004). Word learning by preschoolers with specific language impairment: Predictors and poor learners. *Journal of Speech, Language, and Hearing Research, 47,* 1117–1132.

Gray, S., Plante, E., Vance, R., & Henrichsen, H. (1999). The diagnostic accuracy of four vocabulary tests administered to preschool-age children. *Language, Speech, and Hearing Services in the Schools, 30,* 196–206.

Hall, D. G., Burns, T. C., & Pawluski, J. L. (2003). Input and word learning: caregivers' sensitivity to lexical category distinctions. *Journal of Child Language, 30,* 711–729.

Hall, W. S., Nagy, W. E., & Linn, R. (1984). *Spoken words: Effects of situation and social group on oral word usage and frequency.* Hillsdale, NJ: Erlbaum.

Hammill, D. D., & Newcomer, P. L. (1997). *Test of Language Development—Primary* (3rd ed.). Austin, TX: Pro-Ed.

Hart, B., & Risley, T. R. (1995). *Meaningful differences in the everyday experience of young American children.* Baltimore: Paul H. Brookes.

Heibeck, T. H., & Markman, E. M. (1987). Word learning in children: An examination of fast mapping. *Child Development, 58,* 1021–1034.

Hirsh-Pasek, K., Kochanoff, A., Newcombe, N. S., & de Villiers, J. (2005). Using scientific knowledge to inform preschool assessment: Making the case for "empirical validity." *Society for Research in Child Development Social Policy Report, 19*(1).

Jackson-Maldonado, D., Bates, E., & Thal, D. J. (2003). *MacArthur Inventario del Desarrollo de Habilidades Comunicativas.* Baltimore: Paul H. Brookes.

Jenkins, J. R., Matlock, B., & Slocum, T. A. (1989). Two approaches to vocabulary instruction: The teaching of individual word meanings and practice in deriving word meaning from context. *Reading Research Quarterly, 24,* 215–235.

Jensen, A. R. (1980). *Bias in mental testing.* New York: The Free Press.

Justice, L. M., Meier, J., & Walpole, S. (2005). Learning new words from storybooks: An efficacy study with at-risk kindergartners. *Language, Speech, and Hearing Services in Schools, 36,* 17–32.

Kay-Raining Bird, E., Chapman, R. S., & Schwartz, S. E. (2004). Fast mapping of words and story recall by individuals with Down syndrome. *Journal of Speech, Language, and Hearing Research, 47,* 1286–1300.

Kea, C. D., Campbell-Whatley, G. D., & Bratton, K. (2003). Culturally responsive assessment for African American students with learning and behavioral challenges. *Assessment for Effective Intervention*, *29*, 27–28.

Kester, E. S., & Peña, E. D. (2002). Language ability assessment of Spanish-English bilinguals: Future directions. *Practical Assessment, Research, & Evaluation*, *8*. Retrieved March 31, 2006 from: http://PAREonline.net/getvn.asp?v=8&n=4

Kim, H., Baydar, N., & Greek, A. (2003). Testing conditions influence the race gap in cognition and achievement estimated by household survey data. *Applied Developmental Psychology*, *23*, 567–582.

Laing, S. P., & Kamhi, A. G. (2003). Alternative assessment of language and literacy in culturally and linguistically diverse populations. *Language, Speech, and Hearing Services in Schools*, *34*, 44–55.

Landrine, H., & Klonoff, E.A. (1994). The African American Acculturation Scale: Development, reliability, and validity. *Journal of Black Psychology*, *20*, 104–127.

Lonigan, C. J., Wagner, R. K., Torgesen, J. K., & Rashotte, C. A. (2006). *Test of Early Preschool Literacy examiner's manual*. Austin, TX: Pro-Ed.

Markman, E.M. (1989). *Categorization and naming in children: Problems of induction*. Cambridge, MA: MIT Press.

McCauley, R., & Swisher, L. (1984). Psychometric review of language and articulation tests for preschool children. *Journal of Speech and Hearing Disorders*, *49*, 34–42.

McConnell, S. R., Priest, J. S., Davis, S. D., & McEvoy, M. A. (2002). Best practices in measuring growth and development in preschool children. In A. Thomas & J. Grimes (Eds.), *Best practices in school psychology* (Vol. 2, 4th ed., pp.1231–1246). Washington, DC: National Association of School Psychologists.

Merriman, W. E., & Bowman, L. (1989). The mutual exclusivity bias in children's early word learning. *Monographs of the Society for Research in Child Development*, *54* (3–4, Serial No. 220).

Missall, K. N., & McConnell, S. R. (2004). Technical Report: *Psychometric characteristics of individual growth and development indicators—Picture naming, rhyming & alliteration*. Minneapolis, MN: Center for Early Education and Development.

Nabors, N. A., Evans, J. D., & Strickland, T. L. (2000). Neuropsychological assessment and intervention with African Americans. In E. Fletcher-Janzen, T. L. Strickland (Eds.), *Handbook of cross-cultural psychology* (pp. 31–42). Dordrecht, The Netherlands: Kluwer Academic Publishers.

Nagy, W. E., & Anderson, R. C. (1984). How many words are there in printed school English? *Reading Research Quarterly*, *19*, 304–330.

Nagy, W. E., & Herman, P. A. (1987). Breadth and depth of vocabulary knowledge: Implications for acquisition and instruction. In M. G.

McKeown & M. E. Curtis (Eds.), *The nature of vocabulary acquisition* (pp. 19–35). Hillsdale, NJ: Lawrence Erlbaum.

Nash, M., & Donaldson, M. L. (2005). Word learning in children with vocabulary deficits. *Journal of Speech, Language, and Hearing Research, 48*, 439–458.

National Reading Panel. (2000). *Teaching children to read: An evidence-based assessment of the scientific research literature on reading and its implications for reading instruction* (NIH Publication No. 00-4754). Washington, DC: National Reading Excellence Initiative.

Newcomer, P., & Hammill, D. (1997). *Test of Language Development— Primary: 3.* Austin, TX: Pro-Ed.

NICHD Early Child Care Research Network. (2005). Pathways to reading: The role of oral language in the transition to reading. *Developmental Psychology, 41*(2), 428–442.

Oetting, J. B., Rice, M. L., & Swank, L. K. (1995). Quick incidental learning (QUIL) of words by school-age children with and without SLI. *Journal of Speech and Hearing Research, 38*, 434–445.

Pearson Assessments. (2006). *PPVT-4: Peabody Picture Vocabulary Test, Fourth Edition.* Retrieved July 14, 2006, from http://ags.pearsonassessments.com/group.asp?nGroupInfoID=a30700

Peña, E., Bedore, L. M., & Rappazza, C. (2003). Comparison of Spanish, English, and Bilingual children's performance across semantic tasks. *Language, Speech, and Hearing Services in Schools, 34*, 5–16.

Peña, E., Iglesias, A., & Lidz, C. S. (2001). Reducing test bias through dynamic assessment of children's word learning ability. *American Journal of Speech-Language Pathology, 10*, 138–154.

Peña, E., & Quinn, R. (1997). Task familiarity: Effects on the test performance of Puerto Rican and African American Children (1997). *Language, Speech, and Hearing Services in Schools, 28*, 323–332.

Puente, A. E., & Ardila, A. (2000). Neuropsychological assessment of Hispanics. In E. Fletcher-Janzen & T. L. Strickland (Eds.), *Handbook of cross-cultural psychology* (pp. 87–104). Dordrecht, The Netherlands: Kluwer Academic Publishers.

Qi, C.H., Kaiser, A. P., Milan, S. E., Yzquierdo, Z., & Hancock, T. B. (2003). The performance of low-income, African American children on the Preschool Language Scale-3. *Journal of Speech, Language, and Hearing Research, 46*, 576–590.

Qi, C. H., Kaiser, A. P., Milan, S. E., & Hancock, T. B. (2006). Language performance of low-income African American and European American Preschool children on the PPVT-III. *Language, Speech, and Hearing Services in Schools, 37*, 5–16.

Read, J. A. S. (2000). *Assessing vocabulary.* Cambridge: Cambridge University Press.

Restrepo, M. A., Schwanenflugel, P. J., Blake, J., Neuharth-Pritchett, S., Cramer, S. E., & Ruston, H. P. (2006). Performance on the PPVT-III and the EVT: Applicability of the measures with African American and European American preschool children.. *Language, Speech, and Hearing Services in Schools, 37*, 17–27.

Rhodes, R. L., Kayser, H., & Hess, R. S. (2000). Neuropsychological differential diagnosis of Spanish speaking preschool children. In E. Fletcher-Janzen, T. L. Strickland, & C. R. Reynolds (Eds.), *Handbook of cross-cultural neuropsychology* (pp. 317–333). New York: Kluwer Academic/Plenum.

Rhyner, P. M., Kelly, D. J., Brantley, A. L., & Krueger, D. M. (1999). Screening low-income African American children using the BLT-2S and the SPELT-P. *American Journal of Speech-Language Pathology, 8*, 44–52.

Rice, M. (1990). Preschooler's QUIL: Quick incidental learning of words. In G. Conti-Ramsden & C. Snow (Eds.), *Children's language* (Vol. 7, pp. 171–196). Hillsdale, NJ: Lawrence Erlbaum Associates.

Rodekohr, R. K., & Haynes, W. O. (2001). Differentiating dialect from disorder: A comparison of two processing tasks and a standardized language test. *Journal of Communication Disorders, 34*, 255–272.

Ryan, R. M., Fauth, R. C., & Brooks-Gunn, J. (2006). Childhood poverty: implications for school readiness and early childhood education. In B. Spodek & O. N. Saracho (Eds.), *Handbook on the education of young children* (2nd ed., pp. 323–346). Mahwah, NJ: Lawrence Erlbaum.

Scarborough, H. (1990). Index of productive syntax. *Applied Psycholinguistics, 11*, 1–22.

Serra, M. C. (1953). How to develop concepts and their verbal representations. *Elementary School Journal, 53*, 275–285.

Seymour, H. N., Roeper, D., & de Villiers, J. (2003). *Diagnostic evaluation of language variation*. San Antonio, TX: The Psychological Corporation.

Shore, W. J., & Durso, F. T. (1990). Partial knowledge in vocabulary acquisition: General constraints and specific detail. *Journal of Educational Psychology, 82*, 315–318.

Smith, M. K. (1941). Measurement of the size of general English vocabulary through the elementary grades and high school. *Genetic Psychology Monographs, 24*, 311–345.

Smith, R.M. (1987). Assessing partial knowledge in vocabulary. *Journal of Educational Measurement, 24*, 217–231.

Snow, C. E., Burns, S., & Griffin, P. (1998). *Preventing reading difficulties in young children*. Washington, DC: National Academy Press.

Stanovich, K. E. (1986). Matthew effects in reading: Some consequences of individual differences in the acquisition of literacy. *Reading Research Quarterly, 21*, 360–407.

Stockman, I. (2000). The new Peabody Picture Vocabulary Test-III: An illusion of unbiased assessment. *Language, Speech, and Hearing Services in Schools, 31*, 340–353.

Tamayo, J. (1987). Frequency of use as a measure of word difficulty in bilingual vocabulary test construction and translation. *Educational and Psychological Measurement, 47*, 893–902.

Teuber, J. F., & Furlong, M. J. (1985). The concurrent validity of the Expressive One-Word Picture Vocabulary Test for Mexican American children. *Psychology in the Schools, 22*, 269–273.

Thal, D. J., O'Hanlon, L., Clemmons, M., & Fralin, L. (1999). Validity of a parent report measure of vocabulary for preschool children with language impairment. *Journal of Speech, Language, and Hearing Research, 42*, 482–496.

Thomas-Tate, S., Washington, J., Craig, H., & Packard, M. (2006). Performance of African American preschool and kindergarten students on the Expressive Vocabulary Test. *Language, Speech, and Hearing Services in Schools, 37*, 143–149.

Torgesen, J. K., Wagner, R. K., Rashotte, C. A., Burgess, S., & Hecht, S. (1997). Contributions of phonological awareness and rapid automatic naming ability to the growth of word-reading skills in second- to fifth-grade children. *Scientific Studies of Reading, 1*, 161–185.

Tzuriel, D. (2001). *Dynamic assessment of young children.* New York: Kluwer Academics/Plenum Press.

Ukrainetz, T. A., Harpell, S., Walsh, C., & Coyle, C. (2000). A preliminary investigation of dynamic assessment with Native American kindergartners. *Language Speech and Hearing Services in Schools, 31*, 142–154.

U.S. Census Bureau. (2004). *More diversity, slower growth.* Retrieved January 28, 2006 from: http://www.census.gov/PressRelease/www/releases/archives/population/001720.html

Vygotsky, L. S. (1962). *Thought and language.* Cambridge, MA: MIT Press.

Vygotsky, L. S. (1978). *Mind in society: The development of higher psychological processes.* Cambridge, MA: Harvard University Press.

Washington, J. A., & Craig, H. K. (1999). Performance of at-risk, African American preschoolers on the Peabody Picture Vocabulary Test-III. *Language, Speech, and Hearing Services in Schools, 30*, 75–82.

Wechsler, D. (1991). *Wechsler Intelligence Scale for Children* (3rd ed.). New York: Psychological Corporation.

Whorf, B. (1956). *Language, thought and reality.* Cambridge, MA: MIT Press.

Wiig, E. H., Secord, W. A., & Semel, E. (2004). *Clinical Evaluation of Language Fundamentals Preschool* (2nd ed.). San Antonio, TX: Harcourt Assessment.

Williams, K. T. (1997). *Expressive Vocabulary Test.* Circle Pines, MN: American Guidance Service.

Williams, K. T. (2007). *Expressive Vocabulary Test.* Bloomington, MN: Pearson Assessments.

Williams Smith, R. S., Bojczyk, K. E., Tannenbaum, K. R., & Torgesen, J. K. (2006, July). *Children's strategy use in selecting foils on the Peabody Picture Vocabulary Test—Third Edition.* Paper presented at the annual meeting of the Society for the Scientific Study of Reading, Vancouver, British Columbia.

Zimmerman, I. L., Steiner, V. G., & Pond, R.E. (2002). *Preschool Language Scale* (4th ed.). San Antonio, TX: The Psychological Corporation.

Chapter 10

Assessing Literacy Motivation and Orientation

Erin M. McTigue
Angela R. Beckman
Joan N. Kaderavek

The Importance of Motivation to Emergent Literacy

A well-known saying is "Success is 1% inspiration, and 99% perspiration." This adage underscores the contribution of motivation and effort in achieving positive outcomes. Common sense suggests that motivation to read potentially plays an important role in reading development. However, the role of motivation in early literacy development has been much less investigated than other variables.

One reason that motivation has been less well investigated is that it is difficult to define. Motivation is multidimensional and dynamic. To tackle the complexity of this construct, researchers attempt to deconstruct it into its components. In the following section, we present multiple approaches to defining motivation for preschool-age children. As will be seen, these models overlap significantly with each other and we strive to highlight similarities. Because Chang and Burns (2005) present a broad, systemic approach to defining motivation, we first present their model of motivation. Next, we present more specific approaches to defining motivation that also can fit within Chang and Burns' systemic model.

Chang and Burn's Systemic Model: Temperament, Motivation, Attention

Drawing from observations of children placed in challenging situations, Chang and Burns (2005) suggest that engagement includes the interrelated components of (a) temperament, (b) motivation, and (c) attention. In their model, a child's personality is a self-organizing system, and a child's temperament (specifically, self-control) and motivation relates to his or her attention skills. For example, when a child seems to have difficulty maintaining attention during a puzzle task, the problem may not be simply a concentration problem. Instead, the child's lack of engagement could be related to the manner in which he or she typically approaches new situations, or, in effect, the child's temperament.

Role of Temperament in Motivation

Several theories emphasize the contribution of a child's temperament or personality to motivation. Multiple researchers (e.g., Lepola, Salonen, & Vauras, 2000; Poskiparta, Niemi, Lepola, Ahtola, & Laine, 2003) draw from the work of Olkinuora, Salonen, and Lehtinen (1984) regarding coping strategies that children use in approaching school-related tasks to focus on. This model has three components: (a) task orientation, (b) ego-defensive orientation, and (c) social dependence orientation. *Task orientation* is similar to intrinsic motivation. Specifically, it describes a child's tendency to explore and master a learning task without an external reward. Students with high task orientation are more likely to persist in a challenging task than students with low task orientation. A high task orientation is beneficial for students' motivation. *Ego-defensive orientation* is a child's ability to reduce negative feelings from a threat of failure. For example, a child with high ego-defensive orientation may avoid a task after failing a similar task or verbally express displeasure at the task. Having low ego-defensive orientation is beneficial for a student's overall motivation. *Social dependence orientation* is a child's propensity to please his or her teacher. Children who frequently seek help and approval from their teacher may have high social dependence. Children with high social dependence are not intrinsically motivated; instead, they are motivated to satisfy their teacher. This type of motivation is not stable over time but rather depends on the type of student-teacher relationship. All three components are interrelated and contribute to the overall observation of a child's motivation.

In a similar approach, Smiley and Dweck (1994) divide temperament into two patterns of reaction when a child is confronted with a challenging task: helpless or mastery. These patterns result from the influences of emotion, cognition, and behavior/performance. A *helpless child* exhibits negative emotions to the task, makes negative attributions of his or her ability, and ultimately decreases on-task performance. In contrast, a *mastery child* exhibits positive emotions to a challenge, makes self-instructing and self-motivating statements, and persists longer in the task by focusing his or her efforts on seeking an effective strategy. Although there have been assumptions that preschool-age children do not follow these patterns of *helpless* and *mastery* because young children are typically more optimistic about their efficacy (even in the face of conflicting information), Smiley and Dweck have found evidence that such patterns of behavior can exist for younger children.

Moving now from the role of temperament in motivation, in the next section, we consider the work of Guthrie and Knowles, to present an how explicit definition of motivation.

Considering Motivation Defined

Guthrie and Knowles (2001) depict motivation as being part intrinsic and part extrinsic. *Intrinsic motivation* comes from a person's desire to be engaged in the task or process without caring about an external reward (Guthrie & Wigfield, 1997). In contrast, *extrinsic motivation* comes from a person's desire to engage in a task for the purpose of gaining an external reward (e.g., teacher approval). They suggest that educators should work to facilitate intrinsic motivation because it is more persistent and is more likely to continue across situations; by contrast extrinsic motivation depends on the situation and may likely disappear with the removal of the reward.

To foster intrinsic motivation, Guthrie and Knowles consider two types of interest—personal interest and situational interest. In the context of reading, *personal interest* stems from a person's attraction to the topic. For example, if a child loves trains, he or she may have a personal interest in reading *The Little Engine That Could*. (Piper, 1976) *Situational interest* exists in the shorter term than personal interest and is a positive emotional state resulting from a particular context. For example, a student who typically does not enjoy the activity of name writing may develop a situational interest if he is writing his name using scented markers rather than a pencil. However, as this interest is situational, the following day, without the availability of scented markers, he may again be resistant to the name-writing task.

Additionally, Guthrie and Knowles (2001) cite *attitude* as contributing to motivation. Their use of the term attitude is similar to other researcher's description of temperament, such as task orientation. According to their definition, reading attitude is a continuum of possible positive and negative feelings. A learner's place on this continuum contributes to whether the learner approaches or avoids a reading situation (Alexander & Filler, 1976).

Contribution of Attention to Motivation and Engagement

Returning to Chang and Burn's systemic perspective of motivation, we also consider the contribution of attention to motivation and engagement. Attention typically is the most observable component of motivation and an important component in learning to read. For example, a child learns phonological awareness by focusing attention away from the meaning of the word and directing attention instead to the letters and sounds of a word (Poskiparta et al., 2003). Weitzman and Greenberg (2002) consider engagement to comprise three components: (a) attention, (b) participation, and (c) interaction. *Attention* focuses on how a child demonstrates interest in an activity and the way in which the child attends to and reacts to the teacher and other members of the class. *Participation* describes how the child participates in the activity, for example, how he or she handles materials. *Interaction* considers the extent to which the child initiates and responds to the teacher and other children. The combination of all three factors contributes to the single concept of engagement. Sipe's work (2002) indicates that literacy engagement includes both expressive and performative types of participation. Clearly, attention is not a binary concept, but rather a complex concept that exists on a continuum.

In summary, motivation is defined as a multidimensional concept with influences from internal sources, such as a child's temperament, as well as external sources, such as the situation. To measure motivation, we can consider indicators such as attention. Next, we consider the importance of exploring and measuring motivation for young children with regard to reading development.

Significance of Motivation for Reading Development

Reading is a socially mediated skill, invented by people and continually inspired by our need to communicate with others. Naturally, the development of such a complex, socially derived skill depends on both cognitive ability and motivation (Lepola et al., 2000).

The Teacher's Perspective

Motivation is a primary concern for many teachers. Teachers report that motivation is a core problem in many students' learning challenges and can result in subsequent behavioral problems when students lose motivation and become frustrated (Edmunds & Bauserman, 2006). Kindergarten teachers report that the most important indication of children's readiness for school is their social-emotional competencies, including aspects of motivation (Rimm-Kaufman, Pianta, & Cox, 2000).

Quality of Learning

Having a personal interest in an academic task affects the quality of learning from the task, with greater personal interest predicting deeper understanding and higher overall quality of learning (Sweet, Guthrie, & Ng, 1998). The presence of motivation frequently predicts when learning will be superficial and temporary, as compared to when learning will be permanent and internalized (Edmunds & Bauserman, 2006). Clearly the goal of school is long-term learning rather than superficial understanding; to reach that goal, motivation may need to be facilitated.

Motivation With Time on Task

Time on task is a powerful contributor to learning. Both personal interest (interest in a subject matter) and situational interest (positive affect from the learning environment) can contribute to increases in reading achievement, primarily due to increased time on the task of reading. Motivated students simply read more and seek out situations involving literacy (Guthrie & Knowles, 2002). Subsequently, motivation can be considered as a mediator of reading development; that is, even if students receive the same quality of literacy instruction, students with higher motivation seemingly benefit more from the instruction than students with lower motivation because of additional self-selected practice (Lepola et al., 2000). Increases in the amount of time that children are engaged in literacy tasks can be viewed as an indicator of instructional efficacy (Russ, Chiang, Rylance, & Bongers, 2001).

Interdependent Development of Reading and Motivation

Longitudinal studies, or studies in which a group of learners is tracked over an extended period of time, provide some of the best indicators of the long-term consequences of motivation on reading development. Longitudinal studies (e.g., Jorm, Share, Matthews, & Maclean, 1986; Whyte, 1993) describe a reciprocal relationship between reading progress and behaviors that are related to motivation (e.g., prosocial behavior). Unfortunately, research also indicates that overall attitudes toward reading decrease as children progress through elementary school (McKenna, Kear, & Ellsworth, 1995).

As mentioned earlier, Guthrie and colleagues (1996) explain the interdependence of motivation and reading with older students through the concept of intrinsic motivation. Increasing students' literacy engagement yields more student reading, which is tied to increases in intrinsic motivation. A recursive cycle involving motivation and amount of reading is created. Evidence indicates that students with higher internal motivation perform better on reading comprehension measures than students with higher external motivation. For example, in a cross-sectional design, Schultz and Switzky (1993) studied the internal motivation and external motivation of elementary and middle-school students with varying levels of academic achievement. When the researchers controlled for students' mental ability (i.e., IQ scores), age, and sex, the students with high internal motivation performed better on measures of reading comprehension than students with high external motivation.

Although the work cited above was conducted with elementary school-age children, Lepola et al. (2000) also found that the interaction of learning skills and motivational tendencies create differing reading careers beginning in preschool. Although the researchers did not observe clear differences in motivation at the preschool level, they did observe how different motivational patterns in preschool could predict levels of success in later reading careers. Specifically children who have high ego-defensiveness (i.e., may avoid difficult tasks) and social dependency (i.e., are reliant on teacher praise) and have lower task orientation (i.e., are motivated to complete a task rather than reach understanding) are likely to have more difficulty learning to read than their peers who do not exhibit these tendencies. In contrast, students with low ego-defensiveness, low social dependency, and high task orientation are likely to have successful reading careers (as measured through the second grade).

Smiley and Dweck (1994) observed similar patterns of interaction between learning skills and motivational tendencies in preschool-age children. They found that performance-oriented children (i.e., those who are motivated to complete a task rather than enjoy the process of learning) may succeed in tasks when they are confident and mirror the performance of learning-oriented children (i.e., those who are motivated to discover new things). However, performance-oriented children struggle when they are not confident in a task, perhaps because they have failed the task before. Learning-oriented children consistently exhibit a mastery pattern, regardless of their task confidence. One crucial implication of these differing approaches to challenges is that, by seeking out challenges, children who are learning-oriented may construct a richer learning environment than performance-oriented children. For example, during center-time, a learning-oriented child may select a challenging three-dimensional puzzle and gain more knowledge about spatial arrangement than the performance-oriented child who may select the same puzzle that he or she completed yesterday. Although Smiley and Dweck did not relate their theory directly to literacy, the pattern can be easily generalized into situations where children select texts to read.

Measures for Assessing
Motivation and Orientation

Measures of motivation and orientation for young children are currently limited in availability. Of the measures that exist, few measure motivation and orientation specific to literacy activities. Although some measures exist for children in elementary through high school (e.g., *Title Recognition Test,* Cunningham & Stanovich, 1991; *Motivation to Read Profile,* Gambrell, Palmer, Cooling, & Mazzoni, 1996; *Reading Activity Inventory,* Guthrie, McGough, & Wigfield, 1994; *Reader Self-Perception Scale,* Henk & Melnick, 1995; *Elementary Reading Attitude Survey,* McKenna & Kear, 1990, as cited in McKenna & Stahl, 2003), few of these are appropriate for children who are kindergarten age or younger. In this chapter, we review measures currently available, including several noncommercial measures that have been designed for young children or may be easily modified for use with young children 3 to 6 years of age. The following three constructs were identified: (1) motivation and orientation to literacy activities, (2) general motivation to learning, and (3) factors contributing to motivation. We describe each of these constructs and tasks to measure these constructs in the subsequent sections of this chapter.

Measuring Motivation and Orientation to Literacy Activities

The first goal in developing this chapter was to identify measures that are specific to children's motivation and orientation to literacy-related tasks. The first two measures discussed here, the Kaderavek and Sulzby Rating of Orientation to Literacy (Kaderavek & Sulzby, 2006) and Sipe's (2002) Expressive Engagement Typology, evaluate children's participation during interactive read-alouds. Both tasks require observation of children by an adult not participating in the read-aloud. The third literacy-related measure, the Pictorial Scale of Perceived Competence and Social Acceptance for Young Children (Harter & Pike, 1983) and a modified version of this measure, the Interest in Literacy Task (Frijiters, Barron, & Brunello, 2000), evaluates children's self-reported feelings about literacy-related activities.

These two measures are presented together, because the only difference between the two are the specific activities children are asked to report.

Kaderavek and Sulzby Rating of Orientation to Book Reading (Kaderavek & Sulzby, 2006)

Introduction. Developed for a research study, the Rating of Orientation to Book Reading (ROB) is designed to monitor levels of children's engagement and attention during book reading interactions with adults. Children's behaviors are rated on a 4-point scale, with scores of 1 and 2 indicating overall low orientation to literacy and scores of 3 and 4 indicating high orientation to literacy. This rating scale is presented in Figure 10–1.

Specific Uses of the Measure. The ROB may be used to identify individual children's level of engagement during read-alouds.

Ways in Which Outcomes of the Measure Are Interpreted and Used for Various Purposes. Information gathered from this rating scale may be used by teachers to identify children who are engaged during read-alouds as well as children who are less engaged or not at all engaged during read-alouds. Children receiving a rating of 1 or 2 on this scale could be identified as needing assistance in participating and engaging during read-alouds. This measure does not provide information regarding how to improve orientation to book reading.

Time to Administer. This rating can be applied to any interactive read-aloud situation. Information needed to complete the rating is obtained in the time it takes to complete the reading of a storybook. However, as it requires active observations throughout the activity, ideally it is administered by a second observer as the reader could not complete both tasks simultaneously. Alternatively, the read-aloud could be video-taped and then rated by the teacher conducting the read-aloud.

Ages for Which the Measure is Appropriate. Kaderavek and Sulzby designed this rating scale for use with children ages 2 to 4 years. It has been used to rate the behaviors of both typically

Rating of Orientation to Book Reading (ROB) Scale

1	2	3	4
(A) Child refuses to participate.	(A) Child demonstrates mild/moderate reluctance to participate and once engaged is only minimally interested during the storybook interaction.	(A) Child is willing to participate in the storybook reading and demonstrates mild/moderate interest in the book.	(A) Child consistently is eager to read the book and is readily engaged in the story.
OR	OR	OR	
(B) Child participates but does not become engaged at any time during bookreading.	(B) Child is only interested in reading a book if it happens to be something he/she is very interested in. Most/many books are not interesting to this child.	(B) Child initially shows some mild resistance but eventually becomes very interested in the storybook.	
	OR	OR	
	(C) Child shows interest but frequently gets up from reading session and the adult has to reengage the child as a participant.	(C) Child generally shows high interest but occasionally gets up from reading session and adult has to reengage the child as a participant.	

Figure 10–1. This figure presents the Rating of Orientation to Book Reading Scale in its entirety. (Copyright by Joan Kaderavek and Elizabeth Sulzby. Reprinted with permission.)

490

developing children and children with specific language impairment (SLI).

How Administered. Use of this rating scale requires careful observation of individual children. Although it could be used during a read-aloud involving several children, it is recommended that only one child be rated at a time. The observer may choose one child at a time to rate during a read-aloud, or may videotape the read-aloud and watch the video once for each child rated, focusing on a specific child during each viewing.

Languages Permitted for Administration. This measure has been used with English-speaking children. This scale could also be used with speakers of other languages if the observer is familiar enough with that language to determine whether or not verbal contributions from children indicate on-task participation. This scale also takes into account nonverbal behaviors, which can be observed in speakers of any language.

Possible Score Types. The observer assigns a single rating on a scale from 1 to 4; 1 indicates refusal to participate or lack of engagement, 2 indicates mild/moderate reluctance or engagement only with high interest books, 3 indicates willingness to participate with occasional reengagement by an adult, and 4 indicates consistent interest and engagement in a story.

Qualifications Required for Administration. No specific training is necessary for administration. The rating scale provides descriptions of children's behaviors during read-alouds that can be used to identify the child's level of orientation. The observer should be familiar with expected language levels of the children to be rated.

Expressive Engagement Typology (Sipe, 2002)

Introduction. Sipe presents an informal rating system measuring expressive engagement during an interactive read-aloud. Sipe defines *expressive engagement* as a type of oral response inspired by a literacy activity. This typology spans a 5-point range, beginning with the lowest level of engagement (defined as *dramatizing*), and moving toward the highest level on the continuum (*taking over*). At the lower ranges of engagement, the text highly shapes the listener's response, such as silently acting out part of the text. At the higher range of engagement, the text becomes a launching point for a child's creative performance/reaction, such as telling one's own story inspired by the text. See Table 10-1 for a summary of Sipe's levels of expressive engagement.

Specific Uses of the Measure. Teachers can use this tool to assess overall engagement of children in a class during read-alouds. Although this scale is qualitative in nature, the teacher can tally the overall mean response levels within each of the five categories. Alternatively, the typology can be used to assess an individual student's engagement with a particular text.

Ways in Which Outcomes of the Measure Are Interpreted and Used for Various Purposes. This typology can serve as an informal measure for teachers working to improve levels of engagement. Teachers can use this as a tool to critique their own style of read-alouds and then adjust their instruction accordingly to encourage different styles/levels of engagement within the class. For this purpose, Sipe (2002) gives specific instructional recommendations to promote each type of engagement. For example, to encourage critiquing, the teacher can ask direct questions which place the child in the story, such as "What would you do in that situation?"

Additionally, this measure can quantify an individual student's response to a text. The teacher could use such information to guide instruction during interactive read-alouds in order to assess a particular student's level of expressed engagement and scaffold the student to reach higher levels of engagement. To find books that are of high interest for reluctant listeners, the teacher could also track students' expressive engagement within a range of text genres and formats.

Time to Administer. This typology can be applied to any interactive read-aloud situation and would not take additional time. However, as it requires active observations throughout the activity, it would need to be administered by a second observer as the

Table 10–1. Descriptions of Sipe's Levels of Expressive Engagement

Typology	Behavioral Description	Example	Instruction to Facilitate This Level of Engagement
1 Dramatizing	Children engage in nonverbal dramatic reenactment.	A child waves her arms to mimic the waves in the story.	Teachers can provide suggestions on how to act out the story.
2 Talking back	Children verbally respond to the story.	A child shouts out, "You better watch out, Red Riding Hood!"	Teachers can model verbal responses and value student responses when they occur
3 Critiquing/ Controlling	Children suggest alternatives in plots, characters, or settings.	Children decide to change Goldilocs's age to their own age.	Teachers can pose questions that encourage the children to take the point-of-view—"What would you say?"
4 Inserting	Children insert themselves (or others) into the story.	After viewing an illustration of Goldilocks with a missing tooth, a child decides that a classmate actually took the tooth.	When reading a book with a pattern, the teacher can reread the book and encourage students to engage in the dialogue.
5 Taking over	Children take over the text and manipulate it for their own purposes.	A child performs an independent song inspired by Chicken Little.	The teacher can encourage high levels of interactions and read texts that facilitate interaction between the author and reader (e.g., Scieszka's *The Stinky Cheese Man*).

Source: Adapted with permission from "Talking Back and Taking Over: Young Children's Expressive Engagement During Storybook Read-Alouds," by L. R. Sipe, 2002, *The Reading Teacher, 55*(5), 476–483. Copyright © 2002 by the International Reading Association.

reader could not complete both tasks simultaneously. Alternatively, the read-aloud could be video-taped and then rated by the teacher.

Ages for Which the Measure Is Appropriate. Sipe and colleagues have used this measure in kindergarten through second-grade classrooms; however, it is also appropriate for preschool classrooms because it measures response to a common preschool practice—the read-aloud. The scale assumes that the listeners of the story are verbally expressive.

Languages Permitted for Administration. This typology measures both nonverbal and verbal participation and is appropriate for speakers of different languages.

Possible Score Types. The scale is not a standardized measure and produces a descriptive score of the student's or class's level of engagement.

Qualifications Required for Administration. No training is available in the administration of the instrument. However, Sipe (2002) provides specific examples for each rating.

Pictorial Scale of Perceived Competence and Social Acceptance for Young Children (Harter & Pike, 1983) and the Interest in Literacy Task (modified version by Frijters, Barron, & Brunello, 2000)

Introduction. The Pictorial Scale of Perceived Competence and Social Acceptance for Young Children (Harter & Pike, 1983, 1984) measures children's self-report of perceived cognitive competence, physical competence, peer acceptance, and maternal acceptance. The cognitive competence subscale contains items related to language and literacy skills.

Frijters et al. (2000) adapted Harter and Pike's scale to create the Interest in Literacy Task. This adaptation contains items specific to children's affective responses to literacy and literacy-related activities. Both the original tool and the adapted version measure children's attitudes about literacy in a picture survey format. Examples of items from each of these measures are presented in Table 10–2.

Specific Uses of the Measure. Teachers may use the Scale of Perceived Competence and Social Acceptance to evaluate children's self-reported perceptions of competence and acceptance by others. Items from the Interest in Literacy Task may be used to evaluate children's self-reported perceptions of competence and acceptance related to specific literacy tasks. Both measures could be used by teachers and clinicians to determine how children perceive their own skills and respond to literacy-related activities or to identify which tasks children do or do not enjoy.

Ways in Which Outcomes of the Measure Are Interpreted and Used for Various Purposes. The Pictorial Scale of Perceived Competence and Social Acceptance for Young Children was designed for research purposes to explore the connections between young children's perceived competence in cognitive and physical domains, as well as perceived acceptance by peers and mothers. The Interest in Literacy Task was also designed for research purposes to explore relationships between ratings on this scale and other literacy-related outcome measures.

Table 10–2. Examples from the Cognitive Competence Subscale of the Pictorial Scale of Perceived Competence and Social Acceptance for Young Children (Harter & Pike, 1983, 1984) and Interest in Literacy Task (Frijters, Baron, & Brunello, 2000)

Measure	*Items*
Cognitive Competence Subscale of the Pictorial Scale of Perceived Competence and Social Acceptance for Young Children (Harter & Pike, 1983, 1984)	• Good at puzzles • Gets stars on paper • Knows names of colors • Good at counting • Knows alphabet • Knows first letter of name
Interest in Literacy Task (Frijters, Barron, & Brunello, 2000)	• Looks at books alone • Gets books for presents • Goes to the library • Reads

Time to Administer. Each of these measures is designed to be administered individually to children. The Pictorial Scale of Perceived Competence and Social Acceptance for Young Children includes 24 items, and takes about 15 to 20 minutes to complete. The Interest in Literacy Task includes just 4 items, and takes approximately 5 minutes per child.

Ages for Which the Measure Is Appropriate. The original measure created by Harter and Pike was designed for preschool and kindergarten children. The modified literacy tasks were designed for use with kindergarten children; however, these items would also be appropriate for preschool children.

How Administered. Administration procedures for both versions of this measure are the same. The assessor presents two pictures of children engaged in the same activity to the child. One picture shows a child with a happy face and the other a child with a sad face (i.e., pictures are identical except for the face). Pictures match the gender of the child participating in the task (i.e., girls are presented with pictures of girls, boys with pictures of boys). The assessor asks a question of the child about the picture. For example, the assessor shows the child a picture of a girl looking at books alone and says: "This girl likes to look at books by herself. This girl does not like to look at books by herself. Which girl is most like you?" After the child points to the face corresponding to her choice, the assessor asks the follow-up question: "Do you like to look at books alone a lot, or just a little?" The child then points to a large circle to indicate "a lot" or a small circle to indicate "a little."

Names of the Subtests. The Cognitive Competence subscale of the Pictorial Scale of Perceived Competence and Social Acceptance for Young Children contains items related to language and literacy. See Table 10–2 for a list of these items. The Interest in Literacy Task consists of four items and contains no subtests.

Languages Permitted for Administration. This task could be administered in any language, as long as the person asking the questions speaks the same language as the child.

Possible Score Types. Scores of 1 to 4 points on each item are determined based on the following criteria:

1: child points to sad face, then large circle

2: child points to sad face, then small circle

3: child points to smiling face, then small circle

4: child points to smiling face, then large circle

Qualifications Required for Administration. No specific training is necessary for administration.

Measuring General Motivation to Learn

Due to the current lack of measures available to evaluate motivation of young children to literacy activities, we include here measures that evaluate young children's general motivation to learn. In this section, we describe five measures that evaluate general persistence, interests, and motivation to learn. The puzzle task (Smiley & Dweck, 1994), provides insight into how children respond to difficult tasks, in this case attempting to complete a puzzle with an incorrect piece. The Children's Behavior Questionnaire (CBQ; Rothbart, 1996) is a parent survey that may be used to obtain behavioral information about children. The remaining three tasks, the Children's Attitudes Toward School (CATS; Henry, Mashburn, & Konold, in press), the Motivation Orientation Questionnaire (Perry, Nordby, & VandeCamp, 2003), and the Structured Student Interview (Perry et al., 2003), involve asking children directly how they feel about various learning tasks.

Puzzle Task (Smiley & Dweck, 1994)

Introduction. Smiley and Dweck (1994) proposed that performance-oriented children are more likely to give up on completing a difficult task than learning-oriented children. Additionally, they hypothesized that confidence in a task can interact with task completion, as children with high task confidence will be more likely to persist on a task. To test this model, they created a puzzle task. Although this task does not directly assess literacy motivation, it may assess intrinsic personality factors that contribute to motivation (including persistence toward difficult literacy tasks).

Specific Uses of the Measure. The puzzle task is an informal measure that teachers can use to better understand situations in which their students would persist or give up on a difficult task. Teachers can use this type of task could be used near the beginning of the year to determine which children may need more coaching to become learning/mastery oriented. To administer this task, students are confronted with impossible tasks, in the form of insolvable puzzles, and the teacher observes how the students cope with the situation. Later, the students self-rate their emotions while working on the insolvable puzzle using an array of five faces, ranging from sad to happy. Finally, the students are given a choice as to which puzzle task they would like to do again. This assesses whether they seek out easier or more challenging tasks.

Ways in Which Outcomes of the Measure Are Interpreted and Used for Various Purposes. This task provides qualitative evidence regarding students' motivation and confidence in various challenging circumstances (e.g., when faced with impossible tasks). Students who are likely to quit a difficult task can be identified. A lack of persistence may affect all areas of their learning.

Time to Administer. The puzzle task requires two sessions. In session 1, children rate their puzzle-solving ability and assemble an age-appropriate puzzle. In session 2, the children complete a series of puzzles: three insolvable puzzles and one solvable puzzle. Then, the students give self-ratings on various dimensions (e.g., their emotions during the puzzle tasks).

Ages for Which the Measure Is Appropriate. This protocol has been used with preschool and kindergarten students.

How Administered. Although Smiley and Dweck (1994) did not indicate how the tasks were administered, to prevent interference by potential competition between students, the tasks should be administered individually. The tasks require considerable materials. To complete the puzzle tasks, the experimenter needs five age-appropriate wooden puzzles: two of which are intact, and three of which are altered to appear solvable but are actually insolvable. To create the insolvable puzzles, the experimenters would replace five or six pieces from a similar looking puzzle (e.g., using two different Cookie Monster© puzzles and mixing up the pieces). For the self-ratings, the experimenter uses a face rating scale with five illustrations representing: (a) very sad; (b) a little sad, (c) in the middle, (d) a little happy, and (e) very happy.

Languages Permitted for Administration. The assessment relies on nonlinguistic observations. However, in order for the students to self-rate their experience, the assessor would need to be able to communicate in the same language as the students.

Possible Score Types. This assessment yields qualitative data.

Qualifications Required for Administration. No training is required to administer this assessment.

Children's Behavior Questionnaire (Rothbart, 1996)

Introduction. The Children's Behavior Questionnaire (CBQ) is a parent survey containing 195 items that provide information about children's behaviors on 15 subscales: Activity Level, Anger/Frustration, Approach, Attentional Focusing, Discomfort, Falling Reactivity and Soothability, Fear, High Intensity Pleasure, Impulsivity, Inhibitory Control, Low Intensity Pleasure, Perceptual Sensitivity, Sadness, Shyness, and Smiling and Laughter. An additional subscale, Attentional Shifting was added more recently. Two subtests, Attentional Focusing and Attentional Shifting, measure constructs related to motivation. An example of selected items from the CBQ appropriate for 4½-year-old children is available from the NICHD Study of Early Child Care and Youth Development Web site at http://secc.rti.org/display.cfm?t=f&i=55A

Specific Uses of the Measure. This measure, designed to assess dimensions of temperament, is appropriate for use at the beginning of a school year for teachers to obtain behavioral information about children from parents or caregivers.

Ways in Which Outcomes of the Measure Are Interpreted and Used for Various Purposes.
This information may help teachers increase their awareness of individual behavioral and learning needs of children in the classroom. Teachers then can use this information to guide instruction.

Time to Administer.
The full CBQ consists of 195 items, and may take approximately 45 minutes to 1 hour to complete. Completion of the two subtests related to motivation requires responding to just 26 items, and would take much less time (approximately 5 to 10 minutes).

Ages for Which the Measure Is Appropriate.
The CBQ was designed to evaluate young children ages 3 to 8 years. Only questions that apply to the child's behavior within the previous 6 months should be answered. Any items that do not apply because of the child's age should be marked N/A.

How Administered.
A parent or caregiver completes the questionnaire, rating each item as it applies to his or her child's behavior within the previous 6 months. For example, one item states: "When picking up toys or other jobs, usually keeps at the task until it's done." The caregiver provides a rating concerning how "true" this statement is in consideration of the child's behaviors during the last 6 months.

Names of the Subtests.
The Attentional Focusing subscale evaluates a child's tendency to maintain focus on a given task. Items describe behaviors demonstrating focus, such as remaining on task until a task is finished, showing strong concentration, and staying on task for a long period of time. Additional items describe behaviors that indicate lack of focus, such as being easily distracted, moving from one task to another without completing a task, or shifting rapidly from one activity to another.

The Attentional Shifting subscale evaluates a child's ability to move from one task to another. Items describe behaviors that demonstrate the ability to move from one task to another, such as easily leaving a project when asked and shifting easily from one activity to another. Additional items describe behaviors that indicate difficulty with shifting attention, such as not seeming to hear instructions when working on a task and having trouble stopping an activity when asked to do something else.

Languages Permitted for Administration. The questionnaire is available only in English; thus, the person completing the questionnaire must read and understand English. Children who speak languages other than English may be evaluated using this scale, as it measures behaviors that are applicable across languages. However, assessors should be aware of cultural differences that may influence children's behaviors.

Possible Score Types. Each item is rated on a scale ranging from 1 to 7, and is assigned one of the following descriptors: 1—extremely untrue, 2—quite untrue, 3—slightly untrue, 4—neither true nor untrue, 5—slightly true, 6—quite true, or 7—extremely true. Assessors may also rate any item not applicable (NA). Some of the items are worded so that 7 is the most positive response (e.g., "When drawing or coloring in a book, shows strong concentration") and other items are worded so that 1 is the most positive response (e.g., "When practicing an activity, has a hard time keeping her/his mind on it"). The purpose of wording items in different ways is to encourage the person completing the survey to consider each item carefully before selecting a response. Items worded so that 1 is the most positive response are marked with an "R" for scoring purposes to alert the scorer that these items need to be reverse scored (i.e., 7 becomes 1, 6 becomes 2, and so forth).

Before summing scores, any item marked with an "R" must be reverse scored. After reverse scoring, the total of each item rating is calculated. The sum is then divided by the total number of items receiving a numerical response (i.e., a rating of 1–7) to obtain a mean scale score.

Qualifications Required for Administration. No specific training is necessary for administration.

Children's Attitudes Toward School (CATS; Henry, Mashburn, & Konold, in press)

Introduction. This measure was developed by Henry et al. (in press; see Table 10-3 and Figure 10-2). These authors identified activities in early childhood classrooms from state curricula, standards of learning, and existing measures of early childhood activities. The measure asks children to report their attitudes toward these activities taking place in their classroom. This measure was tested for reliability and validity on a group of 642 first-grade children. Based on this evaluation, the authors concluded that the CATS "measures children's perceptions of their own attitudes that are independent of children's performance in these skill areas" (p. 29).

Specific Uses of the Measure. Henry et al. (in press) developed this measure with the intent of better understanding young

Table 10–3. List of Items on the Children's Attitudes Toward School

Items on the Children's Attitudes Toward School	
Academics	
Math tests	Homework
Spelling tests	Writing letters and words
Early Literacy	
Writing a story	Reading quietly
Listening to stories	Music activities
Child-Initiated	
Games and doing puzzles	Centers
Playing with building toys	Computers
Recess	

Source: Reprinted with permission. Copyright by Gary T. Henry and Andrew J. Mashburn.

Children's Attitudes Toward School

Instructions

While you've been at school this year, you've done many activities like reading, writing, math, art, and going outside to play. Some of these activities you may really like, some activities you may think are OK, and some activities you may not like at all.

Look at the four faces on this card.

Present the laminated faces by placing the card flat on the table in front of the child

I am going to say an activity that you do in school, and I want you to point to the face that looks like how you feel when you do this activity.

If I say an activity that you don't like, point to this face with a frown.

Point to this face ☹

If I say an activity that you think is OK, point to this face.

Point to this face 😐

If I say an activity that you like, point to this face with the smile.

Point to this face ☺

If I say an activity that you really like, point to this face with the big smile.

Point to this face 😄

This is not a test, and there are no wrong answers. Just point to the face that best describes how you feel when you do this activity in school during this school year.

Notes for Administration:
- Read the instructions that are in **bold**
- Read the items with a neutral tone. Avoid facial expressions or inflections in your voice when reading the items
- Do not offer Don't Know/Not Sure as a response option, but if the child responds in a way that seems the item is not applicable, mark the ? on the score sheet.

Figure 10–2. Complete test instructions for the Children's Attitudes Toward School. (Copyright by Gary T. Henry and Andrew J. Mashburn. Reprinted with permission.)

503

children's attitudes toward school, and learning in general, and how children's attitudes are affected by the pressures of high-stakes testing. Although this measure does not directly address participation in high-stakes testing, it includes items that address skills that might be affected by high-stakes testing.

The CATS could be used early in a school year to identify a baseline level of children's attitudes toward learning. This information could inform teachers about children's relative levels of interest in various learning tasks. Repeated use of this measure would allow teachers to track changes in attitudes over time.

Ways in Which Outcomes of the Measure Are Interpreted and Used for Various Purposes. The CATS measures children's self-reported attitudes toward school in three areas: (1) Academics, (2) Early Literacy, and (3) Child Initiated Activities. Qualitative information obtained from this measure could be used to identify children's preferences for learning activities.

Time to Administer. Minimal time is necessary to administer the 16 items on this measure. Administration of all items may be completed in one session, or divided into two or more sessions for children with shorter attention spans.

Ages for Which the Measure Is Appropriate. This measure is designed for use with preschool through first-grade children.

How Administered. The assessor administers items to individual children. Each item is introduced with the phrase: "How do you feel about . . . ?" The child responds by pointing to one of four faces labeled with words describing that face. Children choose between four possible responses: 1—I don't like it (sad face), 2—It's OK (face with a straight mouth), 3—I like it (smiling face), and 4—I really like it (open mouth smiling face).

Languages Permitted for Administration. This task could be administered in any language, as long as the person asking the questions speaks the same language as the child.

Possible Score Types. The CATS provides qualitative information about children's attitudes toward learning. The items can be interpreted individually or evaluated within the three categories of Academics, Early Literacy, and Child Initiated Activities.

Qualifications Required for Administration. No specific training is necessary for administration.

Motivation Orientation Questionnaire (Perry, Nordby, & VandeKamp, 2003)

Introduction. This questionnaire is designed for teachers to assess their students' motivation orientation toward writing, specifically whether the students have a performance- or mastery-oriented approach to literacy.

Specific Uses of the Measure. This questionnaire (if adapted from writing to literacy tasks in general) would be appropriate to use in the beginning of a school year to gather information on how individual children are motivated. For students who are struggling with literacy tasks, such a questionnaire could yield information as to whether the problem includes a component of motivation. Additionally, a questionnaire could be used to track potential change in motivation throughout the year.

Ways in Which Outcomes of the Measure Are Interpreted and Used for Various Purposes. This questionnaire would provide general information to a teacher as to whether a student has a stronger performance- or mastery-oriented motivation. Such information could be useful to motivate students and set appropriate goals. For example, with students who have an orientation toward performance, teachers could give specific feedback which encourages a more mastery-oriented manner. A teacher may emphasize and track with the student what he or she has learned rather than compliment him or her on the completion of a task.

Time to Administer. This questionnaire is completed for students individually and would require approximately 5 minutes per student.

Ages for Which the Measure Is Appropriate. The questionnaire is designed for first-grade students and emphasizes orientation to writing. However, this scale could be adapted to preschool and kindergarten students by substituting the more general category of "literacy" activities for the specific category of writing.

How Administered. The questionnaire is completed by the teacher for each individual student.

Names of the Subtests. The items are sorted into two scales: Mastery Orientation and Performance Orientation. An example of a *mastery-oriented* item is: "Maintains a positive attitude when faced with difficulty or challenge." In contrast, an example of a *performance-oriented* item is: "Writes only when in a group or when instructed to do so."

Languages Permitted for Administration. This is an observational measure completed by a teacher and could be used to evaluate a child who speaks any language, as long as the teacher understands the child's language.

Possible Score Types. The scores are not standardized and it would be most useful to compare the two scales on a relative basis (mastery vs. performance). Additionally, this scale could be used to track changes in individual students.

Qualifications Required for Administration. No specific training is necessary to complete this questionnaire.

Structured Student Interview (Perry, Nordby, & VanDeKamp, 2003)

Introduction. This student interview includes a combination format of pictorial self-rating (by the children) and open-ended questions. The interview targets motivation for writing activities. Interviews occur in the classroom while students are engaged in writing tasks, so that the questions can refer to the tasks on which the students are currently working.

Specific Uses of the Measure. Similar to the Motivation Orientation Questionnaire, this structured interview procedure would be appropriate to use in the beginning of a school year to gather information on how individual children are motivated. For students who are struggling with literacy tasks, such an interview could yield information as to whether the problem includes a component of motivation. Additionally, this student questionnaire could be used to track potential changes in motivation throughout the year.

Ways in Which Outcomes of the Measure Are Interpreted and Used for Various Purposes. This is an informal measure that yields qualitative information regarding a student's feelings about his or her efficacy as a writer, reactions to teacher critique, and expectations for future success.

Time to Administer. This interview requires a significant amount of time per child. Prior to interviewing the student, the students are taught how to answer using a Likert-type scale (with a range of pictures of happy/sad faces). The interview would occur within the writing/literacy portion of the day.

Ages for Which the Measure Is Appropriate. This interview is designed for first-grade students. However, with appropriate modifications, it could be used with preschool students. For example, instead of using a range of five happy/sad faces, for preschool children, it may be more appropriate to use three faces to provide fewer response options.

How Administered. The interview is administered individually. It cannot be administered by the teacher because it requires the student to be actively engaged in a writing lesson. The interview could be administered by a teacher's aide or classroom volunteer. Perry et al. (2003) describe the procedures and general interview topics (e.g., ask students to identify a good writer in their class, and describe why that student is a good writer).

Names of the Subtests. There are no specific subtests within the interview. The interview requires that the student react to a hypothetical situation regarding a new student's literacy performance in class. Then, students share their general beliefs about writing, self-rate their ability, respond to teacher feedback about their writing, and give their beliefs regarding future success in writing.

Languages Permitted for Administration. The interview format requires that the interviewer and interviewee both speak the same language.

Possible Score Types. The interview yields qualitative information concerning students' feelings about approaches to writing.

Qualifications Required for Administration. No specific training is required for administration.

Factors Contributing to Children's Motivation

The measures presented in the previous sections provide tools that may be used to assess children's motivation to participate in literacy-related tasks as well as their motivation to learn in general. A third area worthy of consideration is the influence of the child's environment on his or her motivation. Pianta (1999) states that "Motivation, or the 'desire' to change, is derived from the *co-action of systems*: both of the child and of context" (p. 38). This claim is supported theoretically by *systems theory*, which describes learning environments as contexts that are dynamic and fluid; that is, children are influenced by the environment, and the environment is influenced by the children. Motivation, as defined by Pianta, is the "propensity to change"; this is an integral part of the classroom system, and is particularly important for learning skills such as reading that are not naturally acquired, but instead are learned through external input from adults.

In this section, we address environmental influences that may contribute to children's motivation to learn and/or participate in activities that promote reading development. Specifically, we consider children's exposure to storybooks and adult-child interactions with storybooks.

Exposure to Storybooks

"Each incidence of reading is predicted to have a small but real effect on attitudes" (McKenna, 2001). Young children who are not yet independent readers depend on the adults in their world to provide them with reading experiences. Thus, it is important to consider the amount and quality of children's exposure to books when evaluating motivation and orientation to literacy. Not only does exposure matter, but parent teaching accounts for variance in children's emergent literacy, and these emergent literacy skills in turn account for variance in reading skills at the end of first grade (Sénéchal & LeFevre, 2002). This is important because attitudes toward reading in the later grades are related to children's reading skills (i.e., poor readers' attitudes toward reading decrease more rapidly than good readers' attitudes) (McKenna, 2001). For these reasons, it is important to consider the types of literacy experiences that children encounter in the home environment as an influence on their motivation to participate in literacy-related activities. Chapter 3 of this book describes several measures of home supports for literacy; we encourage readers to consider one or more of these measures when evaluating factors that may contribute to a child's level of motivation and orientation toward reading.

Adult-Child Interactions Around Storybooks

Another factor that may be related to children's motivation and orientation to storybooks is the interactions that occur with adults around books. Although the direction of this relationship is uncertain, evidence indicates that adults tend to do more to involve children who are already responsive and engaged during activities than children who are not engaged and responsive (Schneider & Hecht, 1995). There is also some evidence that a nurturing environment may contribute to positive changes in children's motivation to achieve (Ames, 1990, cited in Smiley & Dweck, 1994). With consistent reading experiences, children begin to anticipate what interactions around storybooks will be like. A child who has pleasurable past experiences with storybooks will expect more positive experiences; alternatively, a child who has tedious past experiences will expect future negative interactions with storybooks (McKenna, 2001). Features of these interactions and environments are observable, and thus may be measured when considering effects on literacy learning. Chapter 5 of this book describes measures of the quality of shared storybook reading. As there is evidence supporting quality of interactions and environments as a contributing factor to motivation and orientation, we encourage readers to consider using one of these measures in their work with young children.

Special Considerations for Assessing Motivation and Orientation

Previously, we outlined how internal child characteristics influence a child's motivation to read and write. Internal characteristics include temperament, attention, task orientation, ego-defensive orientation, and level of social dependence. Other essential factors also influence a child's learning process and literacy motivation. Learners who face additional challenges potentially impacting literacy motivation include children with learning disabilities, second language learners, children with language impairment (LI), and children reared in disadvantaged homes.

Wells (1985) reported that approximately 11% of children developing typically do not like being read to. Learners who are at risk are likely to experience low reading motivation even more frequently. For example, Kaderavek and Sulzby (1998a) reported that 40% of preschoolers with LI demonstrated low literacy interest during parent-child book reading. The literacy interest of the children with LI was compared to a control group of preschool children developing typically. All of the children developing typically demonstrated high literacy interest, whereas some of the children with LI demonstrated low literacy interest. A comparison parent-child toy-play interaction context also was included. Both children with LI and those who were developing typically demonstrated high engagement during parent-child toy play. Reduced literacy engagement during parent-child book reading also has been documented in preschool children with significant levels of hearing loss (Kaderavek & Pakulski, in press). It has been hypothesized that low interest during parent-child book reading is a factor of (a) the linguistic challenges of book reading (Kaderavek & Justice, 2005) and (b) the fact that book reading is typically adult-directed resulting in more frequent child performance requests (i.e., adult questions, requests to repeat words). Heightened linguistic demands during adult-child interactions often produce reduced child participation and verbal output (Girolametto, Weitzman, van Lieshout, & Duff, 2000). Consequently, children who need more reading exposure may be less willing to participate in reading activities (Lyon, 1999). The findings reported above underscore the importance of assessing literacy motivation in children at risk for reading difficulties.

Assessment of children's motivation should consider children's previous exposure to books and book reading. Morrow (1983), in a comparison of kindergarten children with high and low interest in literature and reading, reported that high-interest children had been read to more frequently and had more books in the home. Kaderavek and Pakulski (in press) reported that assessing a child's literacy interest during a one-time-only book reading was not equivalent to documentation of literacy engagement after repeated exposure. Other researchers also have documented that children's responsiveness to book reading increases with repeated exposure. (Goodsitt, Raitan, & Perlmutter, 1988; Martinez & Roser, 1985; Yaden, 1988).

The *saturation* effect should be considered when monitoring a child's level of engagement during shared book reading. Saturation occurs when additional data do not reveal any new information (Brinton & Fujiki, 2003). At present, it is not known precisely how many book exposures are required for saturation; individual differences in temperament and learning style likely affect saturation levels. But, at a minimum, most children require two to three book exposures before their level of literacy engagement can be reliably gauged.

Motivation assessment protocols should also consider the impact of family perceptions of reading development on children's level of literacy motivation and engagement. Baker and Scher (2002) surveyed 65 families to determine correlations between a family's reported purpose for home reading and children's level of motivation. The first grade children completed the Motivation for Reading scale. Significant negative correlations were found between frequent use of basic skill or ABC-type "workbooks" and child literacy motivation. Specifically, frequent use of basic skill books resulted in reduced levels of children's literacy interest and motivation. This study did not identify the direction of the cause-effect relationship of this finding. It is unclear if parents use skill-type books with less skilled or less motivated early readers, or if the use of basic skill workbooks is less pleasurable to children and results in lower child motivation. In either case, it is important to consider parents' reasons for reading (i.e., do parents read to their child for pleasure and recreation or to "teach the child to read"?) and to investigate the book types most frequently used during home book reading.

Interpreting the Results of Assessments of Motivation and Orientation

It is important to alert early childhood and literacy educators of the potential impact of literacy motivation and orientation on children's reading development. Children's level of literacy engagement can influence the effectiveness of literacy interventions. For example, Justice, Chow, Capellini, Flanigan, and Colton (2003) evaluated literacy orientation pre- and postintervention in 18 4-year-old Head Start preschoolers. Children's orientation to literacy contributed 11.2% of the variance predicting literacy ability following the 12-week intervention. In this study, low orientation appeared to influence the children's responsiveness to the intervention protocol.

A first step to sensitizing oneself to motivation and engagement variables is to carefully observe adults and children during shared book reading. Kaderavek and Sulzby (1998b) outlined an observational protocol that can be used for this purpose. Both adult and child behaviors should be noted during dyadic reading interactions. The observer can note the adult's ability to flexibly adapt the book's text to the child's language level. A highly flexible reader modifies the syntax level and simplifies the vocabulary as needed to enhance children's comprehension and attention. The observer can also note whether the adult asks frequent questions, asks the child to repeat words, and/or attempts to make connections between the book and the child's experiences. Varying levels of scaffolding and the intensity of linguistic demand during the shared book reading provides insight into home variables potentially influencing children's literacy motivation levels.

Observation of adult-child book reading also offers an opportunity to document child behaviors. Relevant child variables include positive and negative aspects of the social interaction and the child's verbal and nonverbal participation. The observer can note whether the child pays attention to illustrations versus the text, demonstrates increased or decreased level of interest and engagement in response to parent questions, and if the child sustains attention throughout the storybook reading. Subtle factors, such as the ones described here, provide insight into modifications in interaction style that could be incorporated to enhance children's literacy motivation. Videotapes of the book reading interactions can be shared with parents and discussed. This process can sensitize parents to subtle variations in their child's performance and literacy interest.

The assessments described in this chapter can assist educators in identifying children who may have decreased motivation and interest in reading. For children who exhibit lowered motivation and interest, teachers should be aware of the linkages between a child's prevailing feelings about reading, the internal emotional states and satisfaction levels derived during literacy interactions, and the likelihood that the child will choose to engage in future literacy interactions. The linkages between feelings about reading, affective response during reading, and feelings stimulated by reading create a dynamic and cyclic motivation model. Mathewson (2004) described this model in detail and outlined several instructional implications, which are presented below in an adapted form.

First, teachers should foster children's sense of exploration and self-direction. This concept should be developed through one-on-one interactions during child-directed activities, shared book reading and writing, and other investigative activities. An "exploration" mindset is a facilitative concept that encourages reading.

Second, children should be exposed to a wide variety of book genres with different content and authors. Teachers should model how different literacy domains (magazines, books, computers) provide opportunities to explore and research interesting topics. An openness to a wide variety of reading and writing activities encourages children to read books, magazines, and newspapers.

Third, classroom settings should encourage reading and writing in many different formats and venues. To the extent possible, children should be encouraged to use personal preferences to direct how and when they interact with books and participate in literacy activities. Keeping literacy opportunities "open" versus "closed" makes it more likely that literacy use will be synchronous with a child's temperament, activity level, and social-emotional style. Young children are more likely to choose to interact with literacy during dramatic play if their environment includes many appealing literacy-related objects (Neuman & Roskos, 1992).

Fourth, teachers should minimize the use of external incentives to motivate children to read. External rewards make it more likely that a child will believe that he should read because the "teacher wants him to" in contrast to reading for him- or herself.

Fifth, teachers and parents should encourage and promote positive feelings during book reading and literacy activities. Children who experience many positive emotions during literacy activities are likely to seek out more literacy activities in the future. An emphasis on "skill activities" can decrease children's enjoyment and propagate a negative cycle of lower motivation and decreased attempts to engage with literacy. Parents should be encouraged to take a "reading for recreation" mindset with young children so that early literacy experiences are associated with positive affect.

In summary, children's level of motivation and interest in literacy is an important domain that should be considered within an emergent literacy assessment protocol. Once assessed, teachers can modify literacy instruction to facilitate the development of motivated and engaged emergent readers.

References

Alexander, J. E., & Filler, R. C. (1976). Attitudes and reading: Reading aids series, *Reading, English, and communication.* Newark, DE: International Reading Association.

Baker, L., & Scher, D. (2002). Beginning readers' motivation for reading in relation to parental beliefs and home reading experiences. *Reading Psychology, 23,* 239-269.

Brinton, B., & Fujiki, M. (2003). Blending quantitative and qualitative methods in language research and intervention. *American Journal of Speech-Language Pathology, 12,* 165-171.

Chang, F., & Burns, B. M. (2005). Attention in preschoolers: Associations with effortful control and motivation. *Child Development, 76,* 247-263.

Cunningham, A. E., & Stanovich, K. E. (1990). Assessing print exposure and orthographic processing skill in children: A quick measure of reading experience. *Journal of Educational Psychology, 82*(4), 733-740.

Edmunds, K. M., & Bauserman, K. L. (2006). What teachers can learn about reading motivation through conversations with children. *The Reading Teacher, 59,* 414-424.

Frijters, J. C., Barron, R. W., & Brunello, M. (2000). Direct and mediated influences of home literacy and literacy interest on prereaders' oral vocabulary and early written language skill. *Journal of Educational Psychology, 92*(3), 466-477.

Gambrell, L. B., Palmer, B. M., Codling, R. M., & Mazzoni, S. A. (1995). Assessing motivation to read. *The Reading Teacher, 49*(7), 518-533.

Girolametto, L., Weitzman, E., van Lieshout, R., & Duff, D. (2000). Directiveness in teachers' language input to toddlers and preschoolers in day care. *Journal of Speech, Language, and Hearing Research, 43,* 1101-1114.

Goodsitt, J., Raitan, J. G., & Perlmutter, M. (1988). Interaction between mothers and preschool children when reading a novel and familiar book. *International Journal of Behavioral Development, 11,* 489-505.

Guthrie, J. T., & Knowles, K. T. (2001). Promoting reading motivation. In L. T. Verhoeven & C. E. Snow (Eds.), *Literacy and motivation: Reading engagement in individuals and groups* (pp. 159-176). Mahwah, NJ: Lawrence Erlbaum Associates.

Guthrie, J., McGough, K., & Wigfield, A. (1994). *Measuring reading activity: An inventory* (Instructional Resource No. 4). Athens, GA: NRRC, Universities of Georgia and Maryland.

Guthrie, J. T., Van Meter, P., McCann, A., Wigfield, A., Bennett, L., Poundstone, C., Rice, M. E., Fabisch, F., Hunt, B., & Mitchell, A. (1996). Growth of literacy engagement: Changes in motivations and strategies during concept-oriented reading instruction. *Reading Research Quarterly, 31,* 306-332.

Guthrie, J. T., & Wigfield, A. (Eds.) (1997). *Reading engagement: Motivating readers through integrated instruction.* Newark: DE: International Reading Association

Harter, S., & Pike, R. (1983). *The Pictorial Scale of Perceived Competence and Social Acceptance for Young Children* (manual). Denver, CO: University of Denver.

Harter, S., & Pike, R. (1984). The Pictorial Scale of Perceived Competence and Social Acceptance for Young Children. *Child Development, 55,* 1969-1982.

Henk, W. A., & Melnick, S. A. (1995). The Reader Self-Perception Scale (RSPS): A new tool for measuring how children feel about themselves as readers. *The Reading Teacher, 48,* 470-482.

Henry, G. T., Mashburn, A. J., & Konold, T. (in press). Developing and evaluating a measure of young children's attitudes towards school and learning. *Journal of Psychoeducational Assessment.*

Jorm, A. F., Share, D. L., Matthews, T., & MacLean, R. (1986). Behavior problems in specific reading retarded and general reading backward children: A longitudinal study. *Journal of Child Psychology and Psychiatry, 27*(1), 33-43.

Justice, L. M., Chow, S., Capellini, C., Flanigan, K. & Colton, S. (2003). Emergent literacy intervention for vulnerable preschoolers: Relative effects of two approaches. *American Journal of Speech-Language Pathology, 12*(3), 320-332.

Kaderavek, J. N., & Justice, L. M. (2005). The effect of book genre in the repeated readings of mothers and their children with language impairment: A pilot investigation. *Child Language Teaching and Therapy*, *21*, 75-92.

Kaderavek, J. N., & Pakulski, L. A. (in press). Mother-child storybook interactions: Literacy orientation of preschoolers with hearing impairment. *Journal of Early Childhood Literacy.*

Kaderavek, J. N., & Sulzby, E. (1998a, November). *Low versus high orientation in children.* Paper presented at the 1998 American-Speech-Language-Hearing Association National Convention, San Antonio, TX.

Kaderavek, J. N., & Sulzby, E. (1998b). Parent-child joint book reading: An observational protocol for young children. *American Journal of Speech-Language Pathology*, *7*, 33-47.

Kaderavek, J. N., & Sulzby, E. (in preparation). *Orientation to book reading: Preschoolers with and without language impairment.* Manuscript in preparation.

Lepola, J., Salonen, P., & Vauras, M. (2000). The development of motivational orientations as a function of divergent reading careers from preschool to second grade. *Learning and Instruction*, *10*, 153-177.

Lyon, G. R. (1999). *The NICHD research program in reading development, reading disorders and reading instruction: A summary of research findings. Keys to Successful Learning: A National Summit on Research in Learning Disabilities.* Washington, DC: National Center for Learning Disabilities.

Martinez, M., & Roser, N. (1985). Read it again: The value of repeated readings during storytime. *The Reading Teacher*, *38*, 782-786.

Mathewson, G. C. (2004). Model of attitude influence upon reading and learning to read. In R. B. Ruddell & N. J. Unrau (Eds.), *Theoretical models and processes of reading* (5th ed., pp. 1431-1461) Newark, DE: International Reading Association.

McKenna, M.C. (2001). Development of reading attitudes. In L. Verhoeven & C. Snow (Eds.), *Literacy and motivation: Reading engagement in individuals and groups* (pp. 135-158). Mahwah, NJ: Lawrence Erlbaum Associates.

McKenna, M. C., & Kear, D. J. (1990). Measuring attitude towards reading: A new tool for teachers. *The Reading Teacher*, *43*(9), 626-639.

McKenna, M. C., Kear, D. J., & Ellsworth, R. A., (1995). Children's attitudes towards reading: A national survey. *Reading Research Quarterly*, *30*(4), 934-956.

McKenna, M. C., & Stahl, S. A. (2003). *Assessment for reading instruction.* New York: The Guilford Press.

Morrow, L. M. (1983). Home and school correlates of early interest in literacy. *Journal of Educational Research*, *76*, 221-230.

NICHD Study of Early Child Care and Youth Development. (n.d.). *Children's behavior questionnaire: 54 months.* Retrieved May 17, 2006, from: http://secc.rti.org/display.cfm?t=f&i=55A

Neuman, S. B., & Roskos, K. (1992). Literacy objects as cultural tools: Effects on children's literacy behaviors in play. *Reading Research Quarterly, 27*(3), 202–225.

Olkinuora, E., Salonen, P., & Lehtinen, E. (1984). *Toward an interactionist theory of cognitive dysfunctions* (Research Monograph No. B10). Turku, Finland: University of Turku, Faculty of Education.

Perry, N. E., Nordby, C. J., & VandeKamp, K. O. (2003). Promoting self-regulated reading and writing at home and school. *Elementary School Journal, 103*(4), 317–338.

Pianta, R. C. (1999). *Enhancing relationships between children and teachers.* Washington, DC: American Psychological Association.

Piper, W. (1976). *The little engine that could.* New York: Platt and Munk.

Poskiparta, E., Niemi, P., Lepola, J., Ahtola, A., & Laine, P. (2003). Motivational-emotional vulnerability and difficulties in learning to read and spell. *British Journal of Educational Psychology, 73,* 187–206.

Rimm-Kaufman, S. E., Pianta, R. C., & Cox, M. J. (2000). Teachers' judgments of problems in the transition to kindergarten. *Early Childhood Research Quarterly, 15*(2), 147–166.

Rothbart, M. K., (1996a). *Children's behavior questionnaire.* Eugene: University of Oregon.

Rothbart, M. K. (1996b). Social development. In M. J. Hanson (Ed.), *Atypical infant development* (pp. 273–309). Austin, TX: Pro-Ed.

Russ, S., Chiang, B., Rylance, B. J., & Bongers, J. (2001). Caseload in special education: An integration of research findings. *Exceptional Children, 67*(2), 161–172.

Schneider, P., & Hecht, B. F. (1995). Interaction between children with developmental delays and their mothers during a book-sharing activity. *International Journal of Disability, Development, and Education, 42*(1), 41–56.

Schultz, G. F., & Switzky, H. N. (1993). The academic achievement of elementary and junior high school students with behavior disorders and their nonhandicapped peers as a function of motivational orientation. *Learning and Individual Differences, 5*(1), 31–42.

Sénéchal, M., & LeFevre, J. (2002). Parental involvement in the development of children's reading skill: A five-year longitudinal study. *Child Development, 73,* 445–460.

Sipe, L. (2002). Talking back and taking over: Young children's expressive engagement during storybook read-alouds. *The Reading Teacher, 55*(5), 476–483.

Smiley, P. A., & Dweck, C. S. (1994). Individual differences in achievement goals among young children. *Child Development, 65*, 1723-1743.

Sweet, A. P., Guthrie, J. T., & Ng, M. M. (1998). Teacher perceptions and student reading motivation. *Journal of Educational Psychology, 90*(2), 210-223.

Weitzman, E., & Greenberg, J. (2002). *Learning language and loving it* (2nd ed.). Toronto, Ontario: The Hanen Centre.

Wells, G. (1985). Preschool literacy-related activities and success in school. In D. Olson, N. Torrance, & A Hildyard (Eds.), *Literacy, language, and learning: The nature and consequences of reading and writing* (pp. 229-255). New York: Cambridge University Press.

Whyte, J. (1993). Longitudinal correlates and outcomes of initial progress for a sample of Belfast boys. *European Journal of Psychology of Education, 8*(3), 325-340.

Yaden, D. B. (1988). Understanding stories through repeated read-alouds: How many does it take? *The Reading Teacher, 41*, 556-566.

Index